16th Workshop on Innovative Use of NLP for Building Educational Applications 2021

Online
20 April 2021

ISBN: 978-1-7138-2957-7

Printed from e-media with permission by:

Curran Associates, Inc.
57 Morehouse Lane
Red Hook, NY 12571

Some format issues inherent in the e-media version may also appear in this print version.

Printed with permission by Curran Associates, Inc. (2021)

For permission requests, please contact the Association for Computational Linguistics at the address below.

Association for Computational Linguistics
209 N. Eighth Street
Stroudsburg, Pennsylvania 18360

Phone: 1-570-476-8006
Fax: 1-570-476-0860

acl@aclweb.org

Additional copies of this publication are available from:

Curran Associates, Inc.
57 Morehouse Lane
Red Hook, NY 12571 USA
Phone: 845-758-0400
Fax: 845-758-2633
Email: curran@proceedings.com
Web: www.proceedings.com

EACL 2021

Innovative Use of NLP for Building Educational Applications

Proceedings of the 16th Workshop

April 20, 2021

Introduction

Welcome to the 16th year of the *Workshop on Innovative Use of NLP for Building Educational Applications* held in conjunction with the 16th Conference of the European Chapter of the Association of Computational Linguistics (EACL 2021). We are fortunate to be able to keep this tradition going – though virtually – with another year of inspiring research! Our 23 papers this year – to be presented as papers and posters – include topics related to education, including automated writing and evaluation, argument and passage detection, grammatical error correction, text simplification, readability and data analytics for text complexity, and NLP and Speech for learning and assessment. The conference will also hold a panel, entitled: *"New Challenges for Educational Technology in the Time of the Pandemic"* intended to shed light on the effect of the pandemic with regard to how we think about educational technology development.

This year we received a total of 44 submissions (excluding one withdrawn submission). We accepted 6 papers as oral presentations and 17 as poster presentations, for an overall acceptance rate of 52 % and 14 % based on only the acceptance of oral presentations. Oral presentations typically represent more mature research. Each paper was reviewed by three members of the Program Committee who were believed to be most appropriate for each paper. We continue to have a strong policy to deal with conflicts of interest. First, we continue to make a concerted effort to resolve conflicts of interest - specifically, we do not assign papers to a reviewer if the paper has an author from their institution. Second, organizing committee members recuse themselves from discussions about papers if there is a conflict of interest.

Papers are accepted on the basis of several factors, including the relevance to a core educational problem space, the novelty of the approach or domain, and the strength of the research. The accepted papers were highly diverse – an indicator of the growing variety of foci in this field. We continue to believe that the workshop framework designed to introduce work in progress and new ideas is important and we hope that the breadth and variety of research accepted for this workshop is represented.

The BEA16 workshop has presentations that apply NLP to topics related to education, as follows: **Automated writing and evaluation**: *Essay Quality Signals as Weak Supervision for Source-based Essay Scoring* (Zhang & Litman), *Automated Classification of Written Proficiency Levels on the CEFR-Scale through Complexity Contours and RNNs* (Kerz et al); **Argument and passage detection**: *Parsing Argumentative Structure in English-as-Foreign-Language Essays* (Putra, Teufel & Tokunaga), *"Sharks are not the threat humans are": Argument Component Segmentation in School Student Essays* (Alhindi & Ghosh), *Training and Domain Adaptation for Supervised Text Segmentation* (Glavaš et al); **Grammatical error correction**: *Synthetic Data Generation for Grammatical Error Correction with Tagged Corruption Models* (Stahlberg & Kumar), *Document-level Grammatical Error Correction* (Yuan & Bryant), *Data Strategies for Low-Resource Grammatical Error Correction* (Flachs et al), and *Assessing Grammatical Correctness in Language Learning* (Katinskaia & Yangarber); **Text simplification, readability and data analytics for text complexity**: *Text Simplification by Tagging* (Omelianchuk et al), *Broad Linguistic Complexity Analysis for Greek Readability Classification* (Chatzipanagiotidis et al), *Towards a Data Analytics Pipeline for the Visualisation of Complexity Metrics in L2 Writings* (Gaillat et al); **NLP and Speech for learning and assessment**: *Employing Distributional Semantics to Organize Task-focused Vocabulary Learning* (Ponnusamy & Meurers), *Detecting Negative Language Transfer Using Models that Represent Language Structure* (Wanderley & Epp), *Teacher's Tools for Estonian as a Second Language in Language Portal* (Sõnaveeb et al), *On the Application of Transformers for Estimating the Difficulty of Multiple-Choice Questions from Text* (Benedetto et al), *Automatically Generating Cause-and-Effect Questions from Passages* (Stasaski et al), **Interventions Recommendation**: *Professionals' Observations Analysis in Special Needs Education* (Muñoz & Bravo-Marquez), *C-Test Collector: A Proficiency Testing Application to Collect Training Data for C-Tests* (Haring et al), *Virtual Pre-Training Teacher Assessment and Feedback via Conversational Agents* (Datta et al), *Using Linguistic Features to Predict the Response Process Complexity Associated with Answering Clinical MCQs* (Yaneva et al), *Character Set Construction for Chinese Language Learning* (Yeung & Lee), and *Negation Scope Resolution for Chinese as a Second Language* (Zhang et al).

We wish to thank everyone who showed interest and submitted a paper, all of the authors for their contributions, the members of the Program Committee for their thoughtful reviews, and everyone who is attending this workshop, virtually!

Finally, our special thanks go to the emergency reviewers who stepped in to provide their expertise and help ensure the highest level of feedback: we acknowledge the help of Beata Beigman Klebanov and Haley Lepp.

Jill Burstein, Educational Testing Service
Andrea Horbach, University of Duisburg-Essen
Ekaterina Kochmar, University of Cambridge
Ronja Laarmann-Quante, University of Duisburg-Essen
Claudia Leacock, Grammarly
Nitin Madnani, Educational Testing Services
Ildikó Pilán, University of Oslo
Helen Yannakoudakis, King's College London
Torsten Zesch, University of Duisburg-Essen

Organizers:

Jill Burstein, Educational Testing Service
Andrea Horbach, University of Duisburg-Essen
Ekaterina Kochmar, University of Cambridge
Ronja Laarmann-Quante, University of Duisburg-Essen
Claudia Leacock, Grammarly
Nitin Madnani, Educational Testing Services
Ildikó Pilán, University of Oslo
Helen Yannakoudakis, King's College London
Torsten Zesch, University of Duisburg-Essen

Program Committee:

Tazin Afrin, University of Pittsburgh
David Alfter, University of Gothenburg
Jason Angel, Instituto Politécnico Nacional
Piper Armstrong, Brigham Young University
Timo Baumann, Universität Hamburg
Lee Becker, Pearson
Kay Berkling, DHBW Cooperative State University Karlsruhe
Chris Bryant, University of Cambridge
Guanliang Chen, Monash University
Mei-Hua Chen, Department of Foreign Languages and Literature
Leshem Choshen, Hebrew University of Jerusalem
Mark Core, University of Southern California
Scott Crossley, Georgia State University
Orphée De Clercq, LT3, Ghent University
Kordula De Kuthy, Tübingen University
Carrie Demmans Epp, University of Alberta
Ann Devitt, Trinity College, Dublin
Mariano Felice, University of Cambridge
Michael Flor, Educational Testing Service
Thomas François, Université Catholique de Louvain
Jennifer-Carmen Frey, Eurac Research
Michael Gamon, Microsoft Research
Cyril Goutte, National Research Council Canada
Masato Hagiwara, Octanove Labs
Jiangang Hao, Educational Testing Service
Marti Hearst, University of California, Berkeley
Trude Heift, Simon Fraser University
Heiko Holz, LEAD Graduate School & Research Network
Chung-Chi Huang, Frostburg State University
Yi-Ting Huang, Academia Sinica
Radu Tudor Ionescu, University of Bucharest
Elma Kerz, RWTH Aachen University
Fazel Keshtkar, St. John's University
Mamoru Komachi, Tokyo Metropolitan University
Ji-Ung Lee, UKP Lab, TU Darmstadt

Diane Litman, University of Pittsburgh
Zitao Liu, TAL Education Group
Peter Ljunglöf, University of Gothenburg; Chalmers University of Technology
Anastassia Loukina, Educational Testing Service
Fabiana MacMillan, Rosetta Stone
Lieve Macken, Ghent University
Montse Maritxalar, University of the Basque Country
James Martin, University of Colorado Boulder
Sandeep Mathias, IIT Bombay
Ditty Mathew, IIT Madras
Stephen Mayhew, Duolingo
Julie Medero, Harvey Mudd College
Detmar Meurers, University of Tübingen
Natawut Monaikul, University of Illinois at Chicago
Farah Nadeem, University of Washington
Diane Napolitano, Associated Press
Hwee Tou Ng, National University of Singapore
Huy Nguyen, LingoChamp
Ulrike Pado, HFT Stuttgart
Long Qin, Singsound Inc
Mengyang Qiu, University at Buffalo
Marti Quixal, University of Tübingen
Taraka Rama, University of North Texas
Lakshmi Ramachandran, A9 (Amazon)
Hanumant Redkar, IIT Bombay
Robert Reynolds, Brigham Young University
Brian Riordan, Educational Testing Service
Alla Rozovskaya, City University of New York
Helmer Strik, Radboud University Nijmegen
Jan Švec, University of West Bohemia
Anaïs Tack, UCLouvain & KU Leuven
Yuen-Hsien Tseng, National Taiwan University
Shalaka Vaidya, Research assistant
Sowmya Vajjala, National Research Council, Canada
Giulia Venturi, Institute for Computational Linguistics
Tatiana Vodolazova, University of Alicante
Elena Volodina, University of Gothenburg, Sweden
Shuting Wang, Facebook
Zarah Weiss, University of Tübingen
Michael White, The Ohio State University; Facebook AI
Alistair Willis, Open University, UK
Victoria Yaneva, NBME; University of Wolverhampton
Seid Muhie Yimam, University of Hamburg
Mingzhi Yu, University of Pittsburgh
Zheng Yuan, University of Cambridge
Klaus Zechner, Educational Testing Service
Fabian Zehner, DIPF, Leibniz Institute for Research and Information in Education

Table of Contents

Conference Program

10:10 - 10:20 Opening remarks
10:20 - 11:00 Session 1
11:00 - 11:30 Coffee Break
11:30 - 12:10 Session 2
12:10 - 13:30 Poster Session 1
13:30 - 15:00 Lunch Break
15:00 - 15:40 Session 3
15:40 - 16:50 Poster Session 2
16:50 - 17:50 Panel
17:50 - 18:00 Closing remarks

Negation Scope Resolution for Chinese as a Second Language

Mengyu Zhang[1], **Weiqi Wang**[2], **Shuqiao Sun**[3] and **Weiwei Sun**[4*]
[1]Wangxuan Institute of Computer Technology, Peking University
[2]School of Chinese as a Second Language, Peking University
[3]Department of Chinese, Bukkyo University
[4]Department of Computer Science and Technology, University of Cambridge
zhang.mengyu@pku.edu.cn; ws390@cam.ac.uk

Abstract

This paper studies Negation Scope Resolution (NSR) for Chinese as a Second Language (CSL), which shows many unique characteristics that distinguish itself from "standard" Chinese. We annotate a new moderate-sized corpus that covers two background L1 languages, viz. English and Japanese[1]. We build a neural NSR system, which achieves a new state-of-the-art accuracy on English benchmark data. We leverage this system to gauge how successful NSR for CSL can be. Different native language backgrounds of language learners result in unequal cross-lingual transfer, which has a significant impact on processing second language data. In particular, manual annotation, empirical evaluation and error analysis indicate two non-obvious facts: 1) L2-Chinese, L1-Japanese data are more difficult to analyze and thus annotate than L2-Chinese, L1-English data; 2) computational models trained on L2-Chinese, L1-Japanese data perform better than models trained on L2-Chinese, L1-English data.

1 Introduction

In an increasingly globalized world, non-native speakers and writers all over the world produce a huge amount of second language (L2) data every day. There is naturally a need to automatically annotate such large-scale *atypical* data with rich lexical, syntactic, semantic and even pragmatic information. High-performance automatic annotation of such data, from an engineering perspective, enables deriving high-quality information by structuring this specific type of data, and from a scientific perspective, enables quantitative studies for Second Language Acquisition (SLA), which is complementary to hands-on experiences in interpreting second language phenomena (Gass, 2013).

It is insufficient to directly apply models designed for first languages to handle the second language data because a second language is a standalone linguistic system (Selinker, 1972) that distinguishes itself from both the source and target languages in linguistic features. We need second language-specific methodologies by taking its characteristics into account. This direction has been recently explored, including syntactic and semantic parsing for English as a Second Language (Nagata and Sakaguchi, 2016; Berzak et al., 2016a; Zhao et al., 2020) and semantic role labeling for Chinese as a Second Language (hereafter L2-Chinese or L2-CHI for short) (Lin et al., 2018).

Negation is a ubiquitous phenomenon in spoken text (27.6 per 1000 words) and in written text (12.8 per 1000 words) (Tottie, 1991). As a type of extra-propositional semantics, negation is relevant to analyze factuality of propositions and thus relevant to accurately understand natural languages which has been proven useful for several NLP applications such as sentiment analysis (Wiegand et al., 2010), machine reading comprehension (Morante and Daelemans, 2012a), automatic question and answer (Councill et al., 2010), etc. In the NLP community, the morpheme or word that expresses negation is called the negation cue, which can be a single word or multiple words. A negation is related to an event, i.e. so-called negation event, which is identified by some keys words, like *need* in (1). If we want to know the complete information conveyed by a negation event such as *what* is not *needed* in (1), we need to identify a **scope** in the sentence, which is a set of words. To be more precise, the negation scope is the maximum part(s) of the sentence that are influenced or negated by negation cue. In (1), the negation scopes are marked with square brackets.

*Work done at Peking University.
[1]Data is available at https://github.com/pkucoli.

Proceedings of the 16th Workshop on Innovative Use of NLP for Building Educational Applications, pages 1–10
April 20, 2021 ©2021 Association for Computational Linguistics

(1) [We needs] actions and not [thoughts].

In this paper, we study Negation Scope Resolution (NSR) for L2-Chinese, the goal of which is to automatically identify the scope of a negation cue. To the best of our knowledge, this is the first study on NSR for a second language. We build a new moderate-sized Chinese corpus that contains manual negation annotations for 8000 sentences written by non-native speakers, as well as their corrections by native speakers. A high inter-annotator agreement is achieved, suggesting the robustness of language comprehension of CSL. All annotated sentences are standard Chinese or L2-Chinese. We consider two typologically distant languages, i.e. English and Japanese, as background native languages of language learners. We use L1-English (L1-ENG for short) and L1-Japanese (L1-JPN for short) to denote them respectively[2]. We also consider the corrected sentences by Chinese native speakers and use "CHI$_{L2\Rightarrow L1}$[3], L1-ENG" and "CHI$_{L2\Rightarrow L1}$, L1-JPN" to denote them. The following are an example of L2-CHI, L1-JPN (2a) as well as its correction (2b).

(2) a. 换 言 说 ， 没有 [宗教 生活 与 日常 生活 差距]。
Change text speak , have-not religion life and ordinary life difference.
'In other words, there is no difference between religious life and ordinary life'

b. 换 言 说 ， [宗教 生活 与 日常 生活 之间] 没有 [距离]。
Change text speak , religion life and ordinary life between have-not difference.
'In other words, there is no difference between religious life and ordinary life'

With the availability of high-quality annotations, we study neural NSR models which have achieved significant advances during the past several years. We build a state-of-the-art system that is based on BERT (Devlin et al., 2018), and study NSR for first and second languages across a wide range of setups. Evaluation gauges how successful NSR for Chinese can be by applying state-of-the-art neural techniques. In particular, we find that the L1 background has a significant impact on the L2 outputs: Models trained on L2-CHI, L1-JPN data achieve better performance than L2-CHI, L1-ENG data. An error analysis indicates that some interesting cross-lingual transfer phenomena resulted from the difference between Chinese and English or Japanese play a significant role. Further linguistically-informed analyses suggest several directions for future study on NLP for second languages.

2 Related Work

2.1 Negation Scope Resolution

There are three corpora annotated with negation cues and negation scopes for English (Morante and Daelemans, 2012b; Konstantinova et al.; Vincze et al., 2008) and one for Chinese (Zou et al., 2015). All of them focus on first languages only. Tab. 1 summarizes the sizes of existing corpora as well as our new creation.

Previous approaches to automatic NSR can be categorized into word-based, syntax-based and semantics-based approaches. Similar to many word-based solutions (Tan et al., 2018; He et al., 2017) to Semantic Role Labeling (Carreras and Màrquez, 2004), NSR can be cast as a sequence labeling problem over word sequence. Each word is assigned a position label, e.g. BEGIN-SCOPE, which indicates if the word s in the scope of a particular cue. Representative sequence labeling models, e.g. linear-chain CRF, semi-Markov CRF and latent variable CRF, have been evaluated (Li and Lu, 2018). Neural models have also been explored in (Fancellu et al., 2016, 2017): for each token the corresponding lemma PoS and cue features are fed into BiLSTM to do binary classification to indicate whether the token is in the negation scopes.

Syntactic parsing provides valuable structural information for semantic analysis. It is a usual case that a negation scope is correlated to a single constituent. Following this property, NSR can be treated as a discriminative ranking problem over constituents returned by a phrase-structure parser. Read et al. (2012) used some hand-written heuristic features derived from constituent syntactic trees to guide a statistical ranker (Read et al., 2012). Dependency-based analysis can also provide effective syntactic analysis. For example, Lapponi et al. (2012) augmented a word-based sequence model with dependency tree based features (Lapponi et al.,

[2] L1 is short for *first language*.

[3] Note that CHI$_{L2\Rightarrow L1}$ is different from L2-Chinese because it is corrected by native speakers and also different from standard L1-Chinese to some extent because the source usage, e.g. lexical selection, has a significant impact.

	Language	#Sentence	#Negation	Source
CD-SCO	English	4,423	1,160	Conan Doyle stories
SFU Review	English	17,263	3,527	Consumer product reviews
BioScope	English	20,924	3,114	Medical & biological texts
CNeSp	Chinese	16,841	4,517	Product, scientific & financial texts
Ours	L2-CHI, L1-ENG	2,098	2,253	
	$\text{CHI}_{\text{L2}\Rightarrow\text{L1}}$, L1-ENG	2,098	2,253	
	L2-CHI, L1-JPN	1,888	2,181	
	$\text{CHI}_{\text{L2}\Rightarrow\text{L1}}$, L1-JPN	1,888	2,181	
	L2/L1-Chinese (Total)	7,972	**8,868**	Learners' essay

Table 1: A comparison of sizes of existing and our corpus. "#Sentence" shows the total numbers of sentences; "#Negation" shows the total numbers of negation expressions (=cues).

2012).

Though the scope of negation is a type of important semantics, it is not included in almost all sentence-level SemBanks, including English Resource Semantics (Flickinger et al.), Groningen Meaning Bank (Bos et al., 2017) and Abstract Meaning Representations (Burns et al., 2016), due to either theoretical or practical considerations. Nevertheless, the output structures provided by a semantic parser have been shown very powerful to assist the discovery of negation scopes (Packard et al., 2014; Basile et al.).

2.2 NLP for Second Languages

Despite the importance of second languages at both the scientific and engineering levels as mentioned earlier, it is little systematically studied in the NLP community. Second language, the language system developed by a learner of a second language, preserves linguistic characteristics from both the native and target languages and thus it is a unique linguistic organization (Selinker, 1972). Therefore, the automatic processing of learner texts is not as simple as directly utilizing the existing machinery designed for native languages (VanPatten and Jegerski, 2010). Before any further exploration, the task should be well formulated based on sound theoretical analysis. There are several attempts to set up annotation schemes for different linguistic layers for learner languages, such as PoS tags and syntactic information (Rosen et al., 2014). Syntactic and semantic parsing for English as a Second Language (Nagata and Sakaguchi, 2016; Berzak et al., 2016b; Zhao et al., 2020) and semantic role labeling for CSL (Lin et al., 2018) have been explored based on annotated corpora.

3 The New Corpus

3.1 The Raw Data

Lang-8 (`https://lang-8.com/`) is a *language-exchange* social networking platform, where second language learners of different languages can put their essays and receive modifications from native speakers. There are about 68,500 Chinese learners registering on this platform, most of whose mother tongues are English (ca. 15,500 users) and Japanese (ca. 25,700 users). Following (Mizumoto et al., 2011; Lin et al., 2018), we build a large-scale parallel Chinese learners' corpus by extracting and cleaning the original sentences (L2) written by Mandarin learners and the corresponding revised version (L1) from native speakers. It consists of 717,241 sentence pairs from writers of 61 different native languages, of which English and Japanese constitute the majority. We carefully select 4,000 sentence pairs and manually annotate them with negative cues and scopes based on parallel linguistic analysis. We notice that learners' native languages can have a great impact on grammatical errors and hence automatic prediction of negative cues and scopes. Therefore, our corpus includes two typologically distinct languages, English and Japanese, each of which has a sub-corpus consisting of 2000 sentences.

3.2 The Annotation Process

Two graduate students are employed to annotate the selected sentences: One annotator has rich experience in computational research on negation, while the other specializes in linguistics. We defined the annotation guideline mainly by combining experiences from the CNeSp Corpus (Zou et al., 2015) and the CD-SCO Corpus (Morante et al., 2011) and adding some modifications based on the unique characteristics of the parallel data. Initially, the two annotators separately annotate the same 800 sentences: 200 sentences are "L2-CHI, L1-ENG" and "CHI$_{L2\Rightarrow L1}$, L1-ENG" pairs, 200 are "L2-CHI, L1-JPN" and "CHI$_{L2\Rightarrow L1}$, L1-JPN" pairs. After this round, annotators compared their annotations and discussed incompatible phenomena to produce the initial annotation guideline. Then the two annotators proceeded to annotate an 800-sentence set independently based on this guideline. It is on this set that we calculate the inter-annotator agreement, as shown in Tab. 2. Based on the disagreement of the second annotation round, we made some minor adjustments to the guideline. Since the agreement is relatively satisfactory, the rest sentences only include single blind annotations. Noted that the annotation was based on the segmentation results produced by the Stanford CoreNLP tool (Manning et al., 2014), and during the annotation process wrong segmentation was corrected.

3.3 Annotation Guidelines

Our annotation guidelines are inspired by the CNeSp Corpus (Zou et al., 2015) and the CD-SCO Corpus (Morante et al., 2011) with exceptions considering characteristics of CSL and Mandarin Chinese. In the following, we will use double underline to mark the negation cue, and square brackets to mark the negation scope.

3.3.1 Annotation of Negation Cues

The words that express negation are negation cues. We do not consider word-internal morphemes that express negation-related meanings. For example, although the negation-like morpheme "无" is included in "无价/*priceless*" and "无话可说/*have nothing to say*", its contribution to the meanings of the word as a whole is non-compositional. Therefore, we do not consider it as a cue. When we meet sentences containing such fixed expressions, we never mark negative cues within a single word. Besides, there are some words that can be mixed up with negative expressions, e.g., "杜绝/*eliminate*", which are not included in our research.

3.3.2 Annotation of Negation Scopes

We try to cover the longest relevant scope in order to capture the exact meaning of a negation. When there are more than one negation cues in one sentence, we will annotate them separately and focus on the most relevant scope of each cue. For example, "没有不必要的东西/*no unnecessary things*", the scope of the second cue is "必要/*necessary*". If the negated verb is the main verb of the sentence, the entire sentence is under the scope. In addition, the scope can be discontinuous, which means that if the subject or the object are elliptical but explicit in another conjunct clause, then we will mark it over clause, as shown in (3). If the sentence contains different clauses and only one of them contains a cue, then we will mark the most relevant part, as shown in (4). But when sub-clauses contain words that are related to the negated fact, such as *save* and *except*, they are included in the negation scope to cover the largest negation scope. In Chinese, the position of some adverbials are very flexible, thereby making it difficult to tell their smallest and specific semantic scopes. Therefore, if the sentence contains different clauses and sentence-level adverbials, we will assign them to their closest clause, as shown in (4). When annotating the negation scope of the negation cue in the second clause, the at the beginning of the sentence is excluded. Conjunctions, e.g., adversative conjunction (虽然/*although*) and cause conjunction (因为/*because*), are excluded from the scope. As for imperative and interrogative sentences, the verb (e.g., 请/*please*) and interrogative pronouns (e.g., 为什么/*why*) are included in the negation scope.

(3) [我] 一直 呆 在 家里 ， 没 [做
I all-along stay at home , not do
坏事 啊]。
troubles A.

'I stayed at home all along and didn't make any troubles.'

(4) 在 日本 ， 年轻人 对 高档 商品
In Japan, young-people for luxuries nearly
没有 兴趣 ， [他们] 没有 [购买 欲]。
not interest , they not buy desire.

'In Japan, young people nearly have no interest in luxuries. They have no desire to buy.'

3.4 Inter-Annotator Agreement

We measured the inter-annotator agreement (IAA) of negation cues and scopes between two independent annotators using two measurements: (1) Kappa (Cohen, 1960) and (2) precision, recall as well as F_1 of one annotator treating the second one as golden standard, which is used as the evaluation metric for evaluating the automatic NSR system (see §5.1). Tab. 2 is a summary of the measurement results, reflecting a high agreement. Note that the length of sentences in our corpus is shorter because of limited language capability of L2 learners. The ratio of disagreement in sentences written by Japanese native speakers is higher than that of sentences written by English native speakers, which may result from the varying complexity of expressions between them.

3.5 Disagreement Analysis

The disagreement between two annotators all occurs in the scope, which mainly appears in the recognition of elliptical subject or object and adverbial adjunct. Ellipsis without any formal markers often occurs in Chinese, especially when there is more than one sub-clauses sharing the same subject, causing the annotators to recognize the subject and object differently. In Ex. (5) from an English native speaker, "很多同事/*many colleagues*" is omitted in the last clause where the scope of "不/*no*" exists.

(5) 很多 同事们 没有 注册， 而且 到
Many colleagues not register, and arrive
中国 晚 了， 不 [会 登录 谷歌 邮箱]。
China late LE, not can sign google email.
'Many colleagues haven't registered and arrived in China late. They couldn't sign in g-mail.'

Another type of disagreement results from the multiple interpretations of sentence meanings. For example, in sentence (6), written by a Japanese native speaker, "有的/*something*", as a pronominal part, refers to some of the "暑假的美好事情/*wonderful memories of summer holidays*", which can also be extended into "有的暑假的美好回忆/*some of the wonderful memories of summer holidays*". This makes annotators have different judgments of the scope.

(6) 暑假 的 美好 的 事情，
Summer-holidays De wonderful De things,
[有的 已经 想] 不 [起来]。
some already remember not QILAI.
'I have not remembered some of the wonderful things in the summer holiday.'

Disagreement can also result from the form regulations, like the Ex. (7). In some southern dialects of China, "有/*have*" can be added before a verb, which is not allowed in Mandarin Chinese. However, in the construction like "有没有/*have or have not + verb*", "有/*have*" cannot be omitted. Two annotators thus interpreted the negation scope differently.

(7) 我 不 知道 [大家 有] 没有 [了解 在
I not know us have not know in
国内 给 外国人 的 实习
domestic give foreigners DE intern
机会]。
opportunities.
'I don't know whether they know opportunities for foreign interns.'

Our corpus contains sentences written by learners who have not reached native-like proficiency, and therefore there are some non-native expressions that are difficult to disambiguate, contributing part of the annotation disagreements. In Ex. (8), written by a Japanese native speaker, both "没有/*do not have*" and "是/*is*" can be treated as the main verb of the sentence. If "没有/*do not have*" is the main verb, then the sentence can be understood as "nothing can be resistant to the antibiotic's effect". In another condition, "抗生素的效果几乎没有/*antibiotic does not affect*" is the adjunct of "大敌/*enemy*".

(8) [这 是 抗生素 的 效果 几乎] 没有 [的
This is antibiotic DE effect nearly no DE
大敌]。
enemy.
'The antibiotic's effect is obvious and it has no enemies.'

4 The Neural NSR Model

In this paper, we focus on the state-of-the-art solution that leverages on neural word-based tagging to solve the problem. The overview of our neural model is shown in Fig. 1. Formally, our task is to predict a sequence y given a word-PoS-cue pair $\langle w, p, c \rangle$ as input. Each $y_i \in y$ is a binary label to show whether the word is inside the negation scope. A sentence may include more than one negation cues. To make sure the neural model is aware of which negation cue is in question, the value of $c_i \in c$ is set to 1 if the current cue is in question, and 0 otherwise. As Fig. 1 shows, we use BERT (Devlin et al., 2018) or ELMo (Peters et al., 2018) or randomly initialized feedforward layers for word embedding of w_i, randomly initialized feedforward layers for PoS embedding of p_i, randomly initialized feedforward layers for cue embedding of c_i. Then we use feed forward layers to compress word embedding vectors of BERT and ELMo to a lower dimension. The concatenation of feature embeddings is fed to an encoder (e.g., BiLSTM). The encoder's outputs then go through feedforward lay-

	C. F_1	S. F_1	T. F_1	C. Kappa	S. Kappa
CD-SCO (Morante and Daelemans, 2012b)	94.88	85.04	91.53	-	-
SFU Review (Konstantinova et al.)	92.79	81.88	-	92.70	87.20
BioScope (Vincze et al., 2008)	98.65	95.91	-	-	-
CNeSp (Zou et al., 2015)	-	-	-	95.00	93.00
L2-CHI, L1-ENG	100.00	92.55	97.12	100.00	96.13
CHI$_{L2\Rightarrow L1}$, L1-ENG	100.00	92.55	97.71	100.00	95.65
L2-CHI, L1-JPN	100.00	90.09	94.62	100.00	92.15
CHI$_{L2\Rightarrow L1}$, L1-JPN	100.00	90.09	94.35	100.00	92.32

Table 2: Inter-annotator agreement with respect to negation cue and scope. Previous negation corpora reported cue-level F_1 (C. F_1) at 91%-95%, scope-level F_1 (S. F_1) at 76%-85%, token-level F_1 (T. F_1) at 88%-92%, and kappa at 87%-91%.

ers for classification. The cross-entropy loss is utilized for training the whole model.

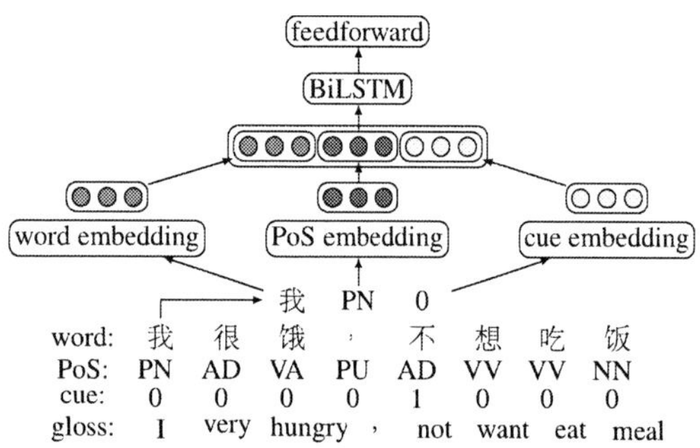

Figure 1: The architecture of our neural NSR model. The meaning of the Chinese sentence is *I'm very hungry but I don't want to have a meal.*

5 Experiments

5.1 Setup

The evaluation metric of the auto NSR system is the same as the *SEM 2012 shared task (Morante and Daelemans, 2012b). We will reproduce the sentence according to the number of negation cues in it and predict each one separately. The system is evaluated with respect to precision, recall, and F1 at both scope-level and token-level. For a scope to be correctly classified, all tokens in a sentence must be correct. Significantly, if an empty negation scope is predicted incorrectly, it counts as precision otherwise, it counts as recall. In our Chinese corpora there are no empty negation scopes, and thus precision is 100%. Therefore, we report the scope recall instead of scope F_1. A sentence may include more than one negation cues. Then we will create as many copies as the number of negation cues.

The word segmentation is manually annotated as provided by our corpus. The PoS tags are produced by the Stanford CoreNLP toolkit (Manning et al., 2014) of which the macro-averaged F_1 over all tree-banks is 90.99% on UPoS. We use BERT as the pre-training models and set max sequence length to 128. BERT is fine-tuned during training the NSR models. We also utilize ELMo and retrain it using the Chinese Gigaword corpus (Huang, 2009). We use 2 feed forward layers to transfer the large output dimension to a lower dimension that is 768-256-50 for BERT and 1024-256-50 for ELMo. The dimension of PoS tag embedding and cue embedding is 50 too. Then the concatenation of word-PoS-cue embedding with dimension of 150 goes through 1 layer BiLSTM with 256 dimensional hidden units, 1 feed forward layer and a softmax layer for predicting the binary output distribution. The dropout of feed forward layers and BiLSTM is 0.2. The neural network is implemented using PyTorch. During training, gradients are updated using Adam (Kingma and Ba, 2014). The learning rate of BERT is 0.00001. The Adam with an initial learning rate of 0.001.

5.2 Main Results on English Data

To evaluate the effectiveness of our model, we conduct experiments on the quite standard English CD-SCO data set (Morante and Daelemans, 2012b). Read et al. (2012), Li and Lu (2018) and we use the TnT tagger (Brants, 2000) and Fancellu et al. (2016) uses the GENIA tagger (Tsuruoka et al., 2005) to produce PoS tags. The results are summarized in Tab. 3. We can clearly see the effectiveness of our architecture.

Model	S-F_1	T-F_1
Read et al. (2012)	72.2	85.3
Fancellu et al. (2016)	77.8	88.7
Packard et al. (2014)	78.7	88.2
Li and Lu (2018)	82.0	88.6
Khandelwal and Sawant (2020)	- -	92.4
Random+BiLSTM	76.8	89.4
ELMo+BiLSTM	82.6	91.6
BERT+BiLSTM	83.7	92.5

Table 3: NSR results on the CD-SCO data. "S-F_1" is the f-score of scope prediction; "T-F_1" is the f-score of token classification.

5.3 Main Results on the Chinese Data

For all experiments on Chinese, we use 5-fold cross-validation. At each fold, as Fig. 2 shows, we build three training scenarios: (1) using all four subsets, (2) $\text{CHI}_{\text{L2}\Rightarrow\text{L1}}$ or L2 subsets, (3) "L2-CHI, L1-ENG" or "$\text{CHI}_{\text{L2}\Rightarrow\text{L1}}$, L1-ENG" or "L2-CHI, L1-JPN" or "$\text{CHI}_{\text{L2}\Rightarrow\text{L1}}$, L1-JPN" subset.

Though another existing negation corpus, i.e. CNeSp (Zou et al., 2015), is available, we do not use it for either training nor test. For a significant number of linguistic phenomena, we have different analyses from CNeSp. Therefore the integration of the two corpora is not straightforward.

We conduct experiments according to the three training scenarios demonstrated by Fig. 2. The BERT-BiLSTM model is utilized. Tab. 4 and 5 show the overall results. As shown in Tab. 4, the token-level F1 score obtained on our corpus is 93.6% which is slightly better than that on the CD-SCO data (92.5%). This may be because that more sentences are available for training (3544 of our corpus, while 982 of the CD-SCO corpus) and shorter sentences are utilized for evaluation (18.0 words of our corpus, while 22.5 words of the CD-SCO corpus). Another important factor is the complexity of second languages. The outputs of second language learners are usually simpler than the ones of native speakers.

We assume that observations from empirical evaluations represent the overall characteristics of second language and native language based on the following facts:

- All sentences in our corpus are randomly selected from the Lang-8 website that contains large-scale sentences and therefore there is no sampling bias in constructing English parallel subset and Japanese parallel subset.
- All the setups and hyper-parameters of each run are the same and therefore there is no modeling bias.
- We use 5-fold cross-validation to prevent train-test split bias.
- We experiment scenarios on several models like BERT-BiLSTM, ELMo-BiLSTM, etc. The same impact is observed on different models.

5.4 An Analysis of Cross-Lingual Influence

Results in Tab. 5 show a distinct and unique phenomenon that models trained on L1-JPN data can predict L1-ENG relatively well, while models trained L1-ENG data perform rather badly on L1-JPN data. This is consistent among all neural models, including BERT-BiLSTM, ELMo-BiLSTM and Random-BiLSTM.

We examine L1-JPN sentences that are wrongly predicted by models trained on L1-ENG data while correctly handled by models trained on L1-JPN data, in order to explain why there is drop on the result in boldface in Tab. 5. Possible reasons for these errors can be a result of the cross-lingual transfer from Japanese to Chinese, which furnishes sentences with characteristics that are not shared by the English language. In the following examples, we use square bracket to mark the golden scope annotation and underline to mark the wrong prediction of trainset-ENG.

(9) 所以 大多数 的 人 觉得 [受] 不
So most DE people believe stand not
[了 日本 的 夏天]。
LE Japan DE summer.
'So most people believe that they cannot stand the summer of Japan.'

(10) [我 还] 没有 [上 小学]
I have not attended elementary-school
的 时候。
DE time.
'When I have not attended elementary school.'

(11) [我们] 不 [应该 恐怕 说错 还有
We not should afraid speak-wrong and
不好意思 的 事]。
embarrassed DE thing.

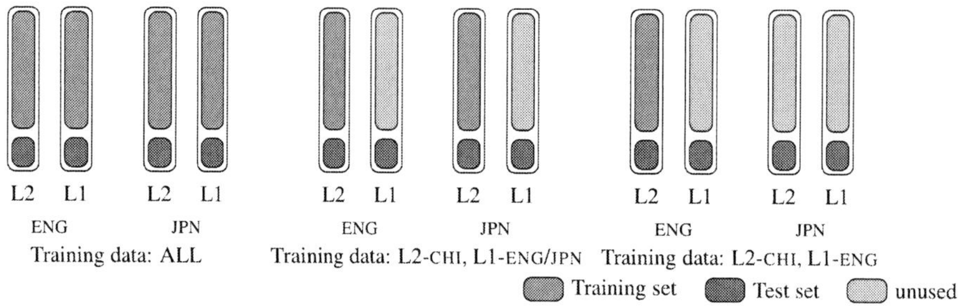

Figure 2: Three different training scenarios.

Train \ Test	L2-CHI, L1-ENG	$\text{CHI}_{L2\Rightarrow L1}$, L1-ENG	L2-CHI, L1-JPN	$\text{CHI}_{L2\Rightarrow L1}$, L1-JPN
ALL	75.8/93.2	76.1/93.4	75.3/93.6	74.7/93.6
L2-CHI, L1-ENG/JPN	75.2/92.9	75.7/93.3	74.8/93.3	74.4/93.6
$\text{CHI}_{L2\Rightarrow L1}$, L1-ENG/JPN	74.8/93.0	75.9/93.4	75.1/93.2	74.5/93.4

Table 4: The scope recall/token F_1 scores obtained by the BERT-BiLSTM.

Train \ Test	L2-CHI, L1-ENG	$\text{CHI}_{L2\Rightarrow L1}$, L1-ENG	L2-CHI, L1-JPN	$\text{CHI}_{L2\Rightarrow L1}$, L1-JPN
L2-CHI, L1-ENG	73.4/67.8/61.3	73.7/69.4/62.9	**71.6/64.9/56.3**	**71.1/64.5/56.9**
$\text{CHI}_{L2\Rightarrow L1}$, L1-ENG	73.4/68.1/61.6	73.8/69.7/62.4	**70.7/65.1/58.2**	**71.0/65.4/57.6**
L2-CHI, L1-JPN	73.2/65.6/57.3	74.7/68.0/60.7	75.2/68.5/62.8	74.2/68.4/61.5
$\text{CHI}_{L2\Rightarrow L1}$, L1-JPN	72.9/65.1/58.0	74.0/68.3/60.8	74.6/68.4/59.8	74.1/68.5/60.7

Table 5: The scope recall scores obtained by the BERT-BiLSTM/ELMo-BiLSTM/Random-BiLSTM.

'We should not be afraid of making oral mistakes or being embarrassment.'

Errors can be categorized into three types: redundant subject, the incorrect judgment of the relative clause, and neglect of parallel components. For example, omitting subjects is common in Japanese while unusual in English, so the system tends to find a subject when testing sentences (see (9)). Besides, the verb phase attributes always come before the core component in Japanese and Chinese, which will be expressed in "DE/的" construction in Chinese and "NO/の" in Japanese, while this phenomenon is replaced by relative clause in English (see (10)). The system that has little experience in this structure thus tends to have difficulties detecting the exact scope. Additionally, the parallel descriptive components connected by coordinating conjunctions in Japanese usually share one core component that is "的事/the thing" which doesn't exist in Chinese and English (see (11)). Therefore, the system may stop when finding the first component that is a complete verb phrase structure.

Based on observations of empirical and error analysis, we give an initial explanation that (1) the cross-lingual transfer occurs unequally to learners with different native backgrounds and on our work there is more cross-linguistic transfer related to negation on Japanese-Chinese than English-Chinese, and (2) the cross-lingual transfer phenomenon on the second languages will directly affect the performance of the computational system which indicates second languages are a stand-along linguistic systems and it distinguishes themselves from both the source and target languages. In summary, when we study computational models for processing second languages it is essential to take the native background into consideration.

6 Conclusion

In this paper, we construct a Chinese negation corpus with sentences written by English, Japanese and Chinese native speakers respectively. Compared to previous negation corpus, our corpus has several highlights: (1) our corpus has the largest scale and higher inter-annotator agreement; (2) our corpus is the first corpus that focuses on second language and contributes parallel sentences. Also, we present a state of the art system for automatic NSR on the English benchmark data. We evaluate our system on our corpus on cross-language training scenarios where a model is trained and tested on different sub-corpora. Results and error analysis show that cross-lingual transfer has a significant impact, but not on all languages equally. The observation that different first language background will have a different impact on the second language acquisition will give inspirations on NLP for second languages.

Acknowledgement

We thank the anonymous reviewers for their useful feedback and suggestions.

References

Valerio Basile, Johan Bos, Kilian Evang, and Noortje. Ugroningen: Negation detection with discourse representation structures. In *SEM 2012: The First Joint Conference on Lexical and Computational Semantics, pages 301–309.

Yevgeni Berzak, Jessica Kenney, Carolyn Spadine, Jing Xian Wang, Lucia Lam, Keiko Sophie Mori, Sebastian Garza, and Boris Katz. 2016a. Universal dependencies for learner english. In Proceedings of the 54th Annual Meeting of the Association for Computational Linguistics (Volume 1), pages 737–746.

Yevgeni Berzak, Jessica Kenney, Carolyn Spadine, Jing Xian Wang, Lucia Lam, Keiko Sophie Mori, Sebastian Garza, and Boris Katz. 2016b. Universal dependencies for learner english. arXiv:1605.04278.

Johan Bos, Valerio Basile, Kilian Evang, Noortje J Venhuizen, and Johannes Bjerva. 2017. The Groningen Meaning Bank. Springer Netherlands.

Thorsten Brants. 2000. Tnt: A statistical part-of-speech tagger. In Proceedings of the Sixth Conference on Applied Natural Language Processing, page 224–231.

Gully A. Burns, Ulf Hermjakob, and José Luis Ambite. 2016. Abstract meaning representations as linked data. In International Semantic Web Conference.

Xavier Carreras and Lluís Màrquez. 2004. Introduction to the CoNLL-2004 shared task: Semantic role labeling. In Proceedings of the Eighth Conference on Computational Natural Language Learning, pages 89–97.

J Cohen. 1960. Kappa: Coefficient of concordance. Educ Psych Measurement, 20:37–46.

Isaac G Councill, Ryan McDonald, and Leonid Velikovich. 2010. What's great and what's not: learning to classify the scope of negation for improved sentiment analysis. In Proceedings of the workshop on negation and speculation in natural language processing, pages 51–59.

Jacob Devlin, Ming-Wei Chang, Kenton Lee, and Kristina Toutanova. 2018. BERT: pre-training of deep bidirectional transformers for language understanding. CoRR, abs/1810.04805.

Federico Fancellu, Adam Lopez, and Bonnie Webber. 2016. Neural networks for negation scope detection. In Proceedings of the 54th Annual Meeting of the Association for Computational Linguistics (Volume 1), pages 495–504.

Federico Fancellu, Adam Lopez, Bonnie Webber, and Hangfeng He. 2017. Detecting negation scope is easy, except when it isn't. In Proceedings of the 15th Conference of the European Chapter of the Association for Computational Linguistics: Volume 2, Short Papers, pages 58–63.

Dan Flickinger, Emily M. Bender, and Woodley Packard. English resource semantics. In Proceedings of the 2016 Conference of the North American Chapter of the Association for Computational Linguistics: Tutorial Abstracts, pages 1–5.

Susan M Gass. 2013. Second language acquisition: An introductory course. Routledge.

Luheng He, Kenton Lee, Mike Lewis, and Luke Zettlemoyer. 2017. Deep semantic role labeling: What works and what's next. In Proceedings of the 55th Annual Meeting of the Association for Computational Linguistics (Volume 1), pages 473–483.

Chu-Ren Huang. 2009. Tagged chinese gigaword corpus 2.0.

Aditya Khandelwal and Suraj Sawant. 2020. NegBERT: A transfer learning approach for negation detection and scope resolution. In Proceedings of the 12th Language Resources and Evaluation Conference, pages 5739–5748, Marseille, France. European Language Resources Association.

Diederik P Kingma and Jimmy Ba. 2014. Adam: A method for stochastic optimization. arXiv:1412.6980.

Natalia Konstantinova, Sheila C.M. de Sousa, Noa P. Cruz, Manuel J. Maña, Maite Taboada, and Ruslan Mitkov. A review corpus annotated for negation, speculation and their scope. In Proceedings of the Eighth International Conference on Language Resources and Evaluation (LREC-2012), pages 3190–3195.

Emanuele Lapponi, Erik Velldal, Lilja Øvrelid, and Jonathon Read. 2012. UiO 2: Sequence-labeling negation using dependency features. In *SEM 2012: The First Joint Conference on Lexical and Computational Semantics (SemEval 2012), pages 319–327.

Hao Li and Wei Lu. 2018. Learning with structured representations for negation scope extraction. In Proceedings of the 56th Annual Meeting of the Association for Computational Linguistics (Volume 2: Short Papers), pages 533–539.

Zi Lin, Yuguang Duan, Yuanyuan Zhao, Weiwei Sun, and Xiaojun Wan. 2018. Semantic role labeling for learner chinese: the importance of syntactic parsing and l2-l1 parallel data. In Proceedings of the 2018 Conference on Empirical Methods in Natural Language Processing, pages 3793–3802.

Christopher D. Manning, Mihai Surdeanu, John Bauer, Jenny Finkel, Steven J. Bethard, and David McClosky. 2014. The Stanford CoreNLP natural language processing toolkit. In Association for Computational Linguistics (ACL) System Demonstrations, pages 55–60.

Tomoya Mizumoto, Mamoru Komachi, Masaaki Nagata, and Yuji Matsumoto. 2011. Mining revision log of language learning sns for automated japanese error correction of second language learners. In Proceedings of 5th International Joint Conference on Natural Language Processing, pages 147–155.

Roser Morante and Walter Daelemans. 2012a. Annotating modality and negation for a machine reading evaluation. In CLEF (Online Working Notes/Labs/Workshop).

Roser Morante and Walter Daelemans. 2012b. Conandoyle-neg: Annotation of negation in conan doyle stories. In Proceedings of the Eighth International Conference on Language Resources and Evaluation, Istanbul.

Roser Morante, Sarah Schrauwen, and Walter Daelemans. 2011. Annotation of negation cues and their scope: Guidelines v1. Computational linguistics and psycholinguistics technical report series.

Ryo Nagata and Keisuke Sakaguchi. 2016. Phrase structure annotation and parsing for learner english. In Proceedings of the 54th Annual Meeting of the Association for Computational Linguistics (Volume 1), volume 1, pages 1837–1847.

Woodley Packard, Emily M. Bender, Jonathon Read, Stephan Oepen, and Rebecca Dridan. 2014. Simple negation scope resolution through deep parsing: A semantic solution to a semantic problem. In Proceedings of the 52nd Annual Meeting of the Association for Computational Linguistics (Volume 1), pages 69–78.

Matthew E. Peters, Mark Neumann, Mohit Iyyer, Matt Gardner, Christopher Clark, Kenton Lee, and Luke Zettlemoyer. 2018. Deep contextualized word representations. CoRR.

Jonathon Read, Erik Velldal, Lilja Øvrelid, and Stephan Oepen. 2012. UiO1: Constituent-based discriminative ranking for negation resolution. In *SEM 2012: The First Joint Conference on Lexical and Computational Semantics (SemEval 2012), pages 310–318.

Alexandr Rosen, Jirka Hana, Barbora Štindlová, and Anna Feldman. 2014. Evaluating and automating the annotation of a learner corpus. Language Resources and Evaluation, 48(1):65–92.

Larry Selinker. 1972. Interlanguage. IRAL-International Review of Applied Linguistics in Language Teaching, 10(1-4):209–232.

Zhixing Tan, Mingxuan Wang, Jun Xie, Yidong Chen, and Xiaodong Shi. 2018. Deep semantic role labeling with self-attention. In Thirty-Second AAAI Conference on Artificial Intelligence.

Gunnel Tottie. 1991. Negation in English speech and writing: A study in variation, volume 4.

Yoshimasa Tsuruoka, Yuka Tateishi, Jin Dong Kim, Tomoko Ohta, and Jun Ichi Tsujii. 2005. Developing a robust part-of-speech tagger for biomedical text. In Advances in Informatics, 10th Panhellenic Conference on Informatics.

Bill VanPatten and Jill Jegerski. 2010. Research in second language processing and parsing, volume 53.

Veronika Vincze, György Szarvas, Richárd Farkas, György Móra, and János Csirik. 2008. The bioscope corpus: biomedical texts annotated for uncertainty, negation and their scopes. BMC Bioinformatics, 9:S9–S9.

Michael Wiegand, Alexandra Balahur, Benjamin Roth, Dietrich Klakow, and Andrés Montoyo. 2010. A survey on the role of negation in sentiment analysis. In Proceedings of the workshop on negation and speculation in natural language processing, pages 60–68.

Yuanyuan Zhao, Weiwei Sun, Junjie Cao, and Xiaojun Wan. 2020. Semantic parsing for English as a second language. In Proceedings of the 58th Annual Meeting of the Association for Computational Linguistics, pages 6783–6794, Online. Association for Computational Linguistics.

Bowei Zou, Qiaoming Zhu, and Guodong Zhou. 2015. Negation and speculation identification in Chinese language. In Proceedings of the 53rd Annual Meeting of the Association for Computational Linguistics and the 7th International Joint Conference on Natural Language Processing (Volume 1), pages 656–665.

Text Simplification by Tagging

Kostiantyn Omelianchuk* **Vipul Raheja*** **Oleksandr Skurzhanskyi***
Grammarly
firstname.lastname@grammarly.com

Abstract

Edit-based approaches have recently shown promising results on multiple monolingual sequence transduction tasks. In contrast to conventional sequence-to-sequence (Seq2Seq) models, which learn to generate text from scratch as they are trained on parallel corpora, these methods have proven to be much more effective since they are able to learn to make fast and accurate transformations while leveraging powerful pre-trained language models. Inspired by these ideas, we present TST, a simple and efficient **T**ext **S**implification system based on sequence **T**agging, leveraging pre-trained Transformer-based encoders. Our system makes simplistic data augmentations and tweaks in training and inference on a pre-existing system, which makes it less reliant on large amounts of parallel training data, provides more control over the outputs and enables faster inference speeds. Our best model achieves near state-of-the-art performance on benchmark test datasets for the task. Since it is fully non-autoregressive, it achieves faster inference speeds by over 11 times than the current state-of-the-art text simplification system.

1 Introduction

Text Simplification is the task of rewriting text into a form that is easier to read and understand while preserving its underlying meaning and information. It has been shown to be valuable in providing assistance in terms of readability and understandability to children (Belder and Moens, 2010; Kajiwara et al., 2013), people with language disabilities like aphasia (Carroll et al., 1998, 1999; Devlin and Unthank, 2006), dyslexia (Rello et al., 2013a,b), or autism (Evans et al., 2014); non-native English speakers (Petersen and Ostendorf, 2007; Paetzold, 2015; Paetzold and Specia, 2016a,b; Pellow and Eskenazi, 2014), and people with low literacy skills or reading ages (Max, 2006; Aluísio et al., 2008; Gasperin et al., 2009; Watanabe et al., 2009). Moreover, it has also been successfully leveraged as a pre-processing step to improve the performance of various NLP tasks such as parsing (Chandrasekar et al., 1996), summarization (Beigman Klebanov et al., 2004; Silveira and Branco, 2012), semantic role labeling (Vickrey and Koller, 2008; Woodsend and Lapata, 2017) and machine translation (Gerber and Hovy, 1998; Štajner and Popovic, 2016; Hasler et al., 2017).

Evolving from the approaches ranging from building hand-crafted rules (Chandrasekar et al., 1996; Siddharthan, 2006) to syntactic and lexical simplification via synonyms and paraphrases (Siddharthan, 2014; Kaji et al., 2002; Horn et al., 2014; Glavaš and Štajner, 2015), the task has gained popularity as a monolingual Machine Translation (MT) problem, where the system learns to "translate" a given complex sentence to its simplified form. Initially, Statistical phrase-based (SMT) and Syntactic-based Machine Translation (SBMT) techniques (Zhu et al., 2010; Specia, 2010; Coster and Kauchak, 2011; Wubben et al., 2012; Narayan and Gardent, 2014; Štajner et al., 2015; Xu et al., 2016a) were successfully applied as a way to learn simplification rewrites implicitly from complex-simple sentence pairs, often in combination with hand-crafted rules or features. More recently, several Neural Machine Translation-based (NMT) systems have been developed with promising results (Sutskever et al., 2014; Cho et al., 2014; Bahdanau et al., 2015), and their successful application to text simplification, either in combination with SMT or other data-driven approaches (Zhang et al., 2017; Zhao et al., 2018b); or strictly as neural models (Wang et al., 2016; Nisioi et al., 2017; Zhang and Lapata, 2017; Štajner and Nisioi, 2018; Guo et al., 2018; Vu et al., 2018; Li et al., 2018; Kriz et al., 2019; Surya et al., 2019; Zhao et al., 2020a), has emerged as the state-of-the-art.

*Authors contributed equally to this work; names are given in alphabetical order.

Proceedings of the 16th Workshop on Innovative Use of NLP for Building Educational Applications, pages 11–25
April 20, 2021 ©2021 Association for Computational Linguistics

Human editors perform several rewriting transformations in order to simplify a sentence, such as lexical paraphrasing, changing the syntactic structure, or removing superfluous information from the sentence (Petersen and Ostendorf, 2007; Aluísio et al., 2008; Mallinson et al., 2020). Therefore, even though NMT-based sequence-to-sequence (Seq2Seq) approaches offer a generic framework for modeling almost any kind of sequence transduction, target texts in these approaches are typically generated from scratch - a process which can be unnecessary for monolingual editing tasks such as text simplification, owing to these aforementioned transformations. Moreover, these approaches have a few shortcomings that make them inconvenient for real-world deployment. First, they give limited insight into the simplification operations and provide little control or adaptability to different aspects of simplification (e.g., lexical vs. syntactical simplification). This inhibits interpretability and explainability, which is crucial for real-world settings. Second, they are not sample-efficient and require a large number of complex-simple aligned sentence pairs for training, which requires considerable human effort to obtain. Third, these models typically employ an autoregressive decoder, i.e., output texts are generated in a sequential, non-parallel fashion, and hence, are generally characterized by slow inference speeds.

Based on the aforementioned observations and issues, text-editing approaches have recently regained significant interest (Gu et al., 2019; Dong et al., 2019; Awasthi et al., 2019; Malmi et al., 2019; Omelianchuk et al., 2020; Mallinson et al., 2020). Typically, the set of edit operations in such tasks is fixed and predefined ahead of time, which on one hand limits the flexibility of the model to reconstruct arbitrary output texts from their inputs, but on the other, leads to higher sample-efficiency as the limited set of allowed operations significantly reduces the search space (Mallinson et al., 2020). This pattern is especially true for monolingual settings where input and output texts have relatively high degrees of overlap. In such cases, a natural approach is to cast the task of conditional text generation into a text-editing task, where the model learns to reconstruct target texts by applying a set of edit operations to the inputs. We leverage this insight in our work, and simplify the task from sequence generation or editing, going a step further, to formulate it as a sequence tagging task. In addition to being sample efficient, thanks to the separation of various edit operations in the form of tags, the system has better interpretability and explainability. Finally, since for sequence tagging we don't need to predict tokens one-by-one as in autoregressive decoders, the inference is naturally parallelizable and therefore runs many times faster.

Following from the success of the aforementioned monolingual edit-tag based systems, we propose to leverage the current state-of-the-art model for Grammatical Error Correction by Omelianchuk et al. (2020) (GECToR) and adapt it to the task of Text Simplification. In summary, we make the following contributions:

- We develop a Text Simplification system by adapting the GECToR model to Text Simplification, leveraging Transformer-based encoders trained on large amounts of human-annotated and synthetic data.[1] Empirical results demonstrate that our system achieves near state-of-the-art performance on benchmark test datasets in terms of readability and simplification metrics.
- We propose crucial data augmentations and tweaks in training and inference and show their significant impact on the task: enabling the model to learn to edit the sentences more effectively, rather than relying heavily on copying the source sentences, leading to a higher quality of simplifications.
- Since our model is a non-autoregressive sequence tagging model, it achieves over 11 times speedup in inference time, compared to the state-of-the-art for Text Simplification.

2 Related Work

Recent text editing works have shown promising results of reformulating multiple monolingual sequence transduction tasks into sequence tagging tasks compared to the conventional Seq2Seq sequence generation formulation. This observation is especially true for tasks where input and output sequences have a large overlap. Generally, these works try to simplify monolingual sequence transduction by explicitly modeling edit operations such as KEEP, ADD/INSERT and DELETE. Alva-Manchego et al. (2017) proposed the first such formulation, employing a BiLSTM to predict edit

[1] Available at `https://github.com/grammarly/gector#text-simplification`

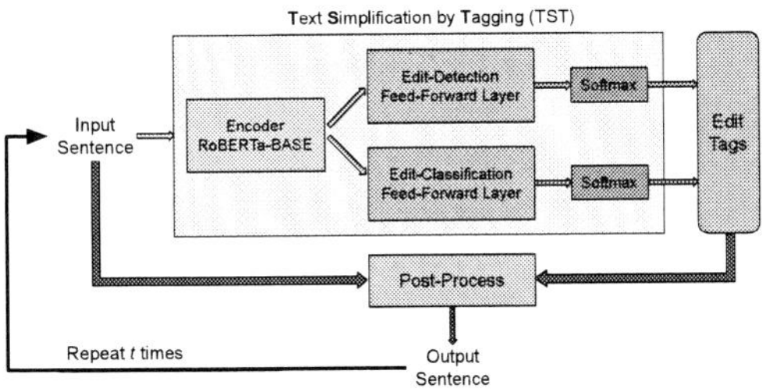

Figure 1: **T**ext **S**implification by **T**agging (TST): A given sentence undergoes multiple iterations of tag-and-edit transformations, where, in each iteration, it is tagged using custom token-level edit-tags, and the sequence of tags is converted back to text by applying those edits, iteratively making simplifying edits.

labels sequentially. Our model for sentence simplification does not rely on external simplification rules nor alignment tools. Ribeiro et al. (2018) proposed an approach applied only to character deletion and insertion and was based on simple patterns. LaserTagger (Malmi et al., 2019) combines a BERT encoder with an autoregressive Transformer decoder to similarly predict the aforementioned three main edit operations for several text editing tasks. In contrast, in our system, the decoder is a softmax layer. Similarly, EditNTS (Dong et al., 2019) and PIE (Awasthi et al., 2019) predict edit labels, developed specifically for text simplification and GEC, respectively. While EditNTS employs an autoregressive encoder-decoder based neural programmer-interpreter model, PIE differs from our work because of our custom edit transformations and incorporation of a pre-trained Transformer encoder for sequence tagging. Levenshtein Transformer (Gu et al., 2019), an autoregressive model that performs text editing by executing a sequence of deletion and insertion actions, is another recent work along similar lines. More recently, Mallinson et al. (2020) proposed Felix - a text-editing-based system for multiple generation tasks, splitting the text-editing task into two subtasks: tagging and insertion. Their tagging model employs a Pointer mechanism, while the insertion model is based on a Masked Language Model.

3 System Description

Following recent works such as Malmi et al. (2019); Awasthi et al. (2019); Omelianchuk et al. (2020), who leveraged similar frameworks for different text editing problems such as GEC, Sentence Fusion, and Abstractive Summarization, we formulate the task of Text Simplification as a tagging problem.

Specifically, our system is based on GECToR (Omelianchuk et al., 2020), an iterative sequence-tagging system that works by predicting token-level edit operations, originally developed for Grammatical Error Correction (GEC). We adapt the GECToR framework for the task of Text Simplification, with minimal modifications to the original architecture. Our system consists of three main parts: (a) defining the custom transformations (token-level edit-tags), (b) performing iterative sequence tagging to convert target sequences to tag sequences, (c) fine-tuning of pre-trained Transformers to predict the tag sequences. Each of these components are described below.

3.1 Edit Transformations

In order to formulate the task as a tagging problem, building on the aforementioned edit-tagging-based approaches, we use custom token-level edit operations (also referred to as **edit-tags** or **transformations**) to perform text simplification. Formally, given a sentence x: $[x_1, x_2, \ldots, x_N]$, and its simplified form y: $[y_1, y_2, \ldots, y_M]$ as the target sentence, we aim to predict an edit tag $t_i \in \tau$ (τ denoting the edit-tag vocabulary) for each token x_i in x, generating a sequence of edit-tags of the same length N as the input sequence x, such that $t_i(x_i)$: applying the edit operation represented by the edit-tag t_i to the input token x_i at each position i, reconstructs the target sequence y, even though $M \leq N$.

We reuse the edit transformations in GECToR, which were developed for GEC. We chose to do so because we found a significantly high overlap of 92.64% in the tag distributions between the GEC and Text Simplification domains. This was done by building the edit-tag vocabularies independently on both (GEC and Text Simplification) datasets and comparing the tag distributions represented by the two vocabularies. This was not surprising since these edit-tags have been obtained from huge amounts of synthetic GEC data, they are expected to have good coverage with many standard monolingual text editing problems. Additionally, using the same edit-tags is a necessary pre-requisite to leverage GEC initialization in the model (Section 4.3), which we later show to be quite impactful for our text simplification system (Section 6.1). Consequently, the edit space τ is of size 5000, out of which 4971 are basic edit-tags and 29 are token-independent GEC-specific edit-tags (such as `$TRANSFORM_VERB_VB_VBZ`, which converts a verb in its base form to its third person singular present tense form). Further, the aforementioned 4971 basic edit-tags are made up of token-independent KEEP and DELETE tags (which simply keep or delete the given word(s) on which they are applied), 1167 token-dependent APPEND tags (such as `$APPEND_just`, which appends the word "just" to the given word) and 3802 token-dependent REPLACE tags (such as `$REPLACE_really`, which replaces the given word with the word "really").

3.2 Iterative Sequence Tagging

As described in Section 3.1, we predict the edit-tags t_i for each input token x_i in the source sequence x. These predicted tag-encoded transformations are then applied to the source sentence to get the simplified sentence. Since some simplification operations in a sentence may depend on others, applying the sequence tagger only once may not be enough to fully generate the simplified form of a given sentence. Accordingly, we use the iterative correction approach from Awasthi et al. (2019) and Omelianchuk et al. (2020), and use the sequence tagger to tag the now modified sequence, and apply the corresponding transformations on the new edit-tags, which changes the sentence further. We repeat this process for a fixed number of iterations, which can be adjusted to trade off qualitative performance for improved speed. In our framework, we experimented between 1-5 iterations.

3.3 Tagging Model

We use the GECToR sequence tagging model with a pre-trained RoBERTa$_{\text{BASE}}$ Transformer (Liu et al., 2019) as the encoder, stacked with two concurrent feed-forward layers, followed by corresponding Softmax layers. Owing to our choice of encoder, we use Byte-Pair Encoding (BPE) (Sennrich et al., 2016) as our tokenization technique.

As shown in Fig. 1, these feed-forward layers are responsible for detecting and classifying edits, respectively. For every position in the input sequence, the edit-detection layer predicts the probability an edit exists, whereas the edit-classification layer predicts the type of edit-tag. The edit-tag sequence generated as the output of the edit-classification layer is gated by the output of the edit-detection layer. i.e. if the output of the edit-detection layer is below the *minimum edit probability* threshold (described in Section 4.6) at any position in the predicted sequence, we do not make any edits.

4 Experimental Setup

4.1 Data Sources

We use **WikiSmall** and **WikiLarge**, two benchmark datasets for the text simplification task[2], for our experiments. These datasets were constructed from automatically-aligned complex-simple sentence pairs from English Wikipedia (EW) and Simple English Wikipedia (SEW). WikiSmall (Zhu et al., 2010) contains one reference simplification per sentence. We use the standardized split of this dataset released by Zhang and Lapata (2017), with $88k$ instances for training, 205 for validation and the same original 100 instances for testing. WikiLarge is a larger set of similarly automatically-aligned complex-simple sentence pairs, compiled from previous extractions of EW-SEW and WikiSmall (Zhu et al., 2010; Woodsend and Lapata, 2011; Kauchak, 2013). Similar to WikiSmall, we use the training set for this dataset provided by Zhang and Lapata (2017) consisting of $296k$ sentence pairs. For simplicity, we refer to this training data (WikiSmall + WikiLarge) as **WikiAll**.

For validation and test sets, we use the Turkcorpus (Xu et al., 2016a) and ASSET (Alva-Manchego et al., 2020) datasets, which were both created from WikiLarge using the same 2000 validation and 359 test source sentences, where each complex sentence consists of multiple crowd-sourced reference simplifications. Specifically, Turkcorpus contains 8 reference simplifications, and ASSET contains 10 references per source sentence.

Table 1 provides other statistics on these datasets.

4.2 Data pre-processing

WikiAll data contains special tokens to represent parentheses (symbolized by `-LRB-` and `-RRB-`) from prior tokenizations. We heuristically decide to remove these tokens (and any tokens between them) from both source and target sentences. Doing this led to consistent improvements in all our experiments, described further in Section 6.2. Additionally, for tokenization, we use the HuggingFace Tokenizers[3] Python library to tokenize the whole

[2]Another widely-used dataset for the task, the Newsela Corpus (Xu et al., 2015), could not be used due to its extremely rigid legal and licensing requirements.

[3]`https://github.com/huggingface/tokenizers`

Split	Dataset		Sentences	Tokens
Train	WikiAll	WikiSmall	88*k*	3.9M
		WikiLarge	296*k*	11.7M
	WikiBT	WikiLarge (En-De)	293*k*	11.2M
		WikiLarge (En-Fr)	293*k*	11.5M
Dev	WikiSmall		205	9.5*k*
	WikiLarge	TurkCorpus	2000	75*k*
		ASSET	2000	72*k*
Test	WikiSmall		100	5*k*
	WikiLarge	TurkCorpus	359	15.8*k*
		ASSET	359	14.1*k*

Table 1: Dataset splits and sizes.

sentence (as opposed to the approach in GECToR which tokenized each word in the sentence separately). This change led faster and more accurate tokenization as the one originally used in RoBERTa.

4.3 Pre-Training

For our experiments, we use two versions of the tagging model described in Section 3.3. The first version is a pre-trained RoBERTa$_{\text{BASE}}$ encoder with randomly initialized feed-forward layers. We refer to this model as **TST-BASE** (**T**ext **S**implification by **T**agging - Baseline). The second version of the model is a TST-BASE model fine-tuned on the Grammatical Error Correction (GEC) task: henceforth denoted as **TST-GEC**.[4]

4.4 Data Augmentation

We hypothesize that our text simplification models can benefit from an increase of the training data, and experimentally confirm this by training and evaluating our models with additional training data. We generate synthetic training data from the source sentences of WikiAll. We used two approaches to do so: back-translation and ensemble distillation, described below.

4.4.1 Back-Translation

We use the Transformer-based NMT models trained by Tiedemann and Thottingal (2020) to generate the back-translated versions of the target side of the parallel WikiAll data. These models were trained on OPUS data[5] using Marian-NMT[6] and released as part of the HuggingFace Transformers Library (Wolf et al., 2019). All models are Transformer encoder-decoders with 6 layers in each component. Specifically, we used the bilingual EN-FR, FR-EN, EN-DE and DE-EN models[7] to translate WikiAll data from (a) English to French, and back to English, and (b) English to German and back to English. Doing so tripled the amount of WikiAll data available for training (Table 1). The backtranslated WikiAll data is henceforth collectively referred to as **WikiBT**.

4.4.2 Ensemble Distillation

We leverage knowledge distillation on ensemble teacher models (Freitag et al., 2017) to augment our training data. We first create an ensemble teacher model by training models on WikiAll and WikiBT data. Specifically, for building the teacher ensemble, we first train the following constituent TST models:

1. TST: Trained on WikiAll
2. TST-GEC: Trained on WikiAll
3. TST: Trained on WikiAll + WikiBT

The predictions of the ensemble are computed by taking the `argmax` of the averaged class-wise probabilities of the constituent models at every token. We get the predictions from this ensemble consisting of the aforementioned three constituent models on WikiAll data. In this way, we produce new references for the training data which can be used by our final model (referred to as the student network) to simulate the teacher network ensemble. We then combine this ensemble-generated training data (hereby referred to as **WikiEns**) together with the original WikiAll data, doubling the amount of training data. Our final model (the student network, denoted henceforth as **TST-FINAL**) is then trained on this combined WikiEns + WikiAll dataset. It is worth noting that the student and the constituent teacher models have exactly the same architecture.

4.5 Training

We train our models with AllenNLP and Transformers. Our baseline (TST-BASE) mostly follows the settings in Omelianchuk et al. (2020). We train the model for 50 epochs, where we freeze the encoder weights during the first two epochs of training. We use Adam optimizer (Kingma and Ba, 2015), where the learning rate starts from 1e-5 and reduces by a factor of 0.1 when the validation loss has stopped

[4] We refer the reader to Omelianchuk et al. (2020) for details on training the model for GEC.

[5] `http://opus.nlpl.eu/`

[6] `https://marian-nmt.github.io/`

[7] `https://huggingface.co/Helsinki-NLP/opus-mt-<L1>-<L2>`

improving for 10 epochs. We perform early stopping after 3 epochs, based on the performance on the validation set. Other training hyper-parameters are listed in Appendix A.

4.6 Inference Tweaks

One of the advantages of edit-tag-based approaches is that they provide greater control over the system output. Building on Omelianchuk et al. (2020), we use *confidence biases* and *minimum edit probability* as additional inference hyper-parameters that we tune to push the model to perform more precise edits.

Specifically, we add confidence biases to the probabilities of KEEP and DELETE edit-tags: responsible for not changing the source token and deleting the source token, respectively. We create these additional hyper-parameters for just these edit-tags because they are the most frequently used edit-tags for the Text Simplification task. Moreover, since they are token-independent, it provides the framework with additional robustness on the task without introducing too many additional hyper-parameters. In this way, we were able to drive the model to keep/delete more tokens if the corresponding confidence bias was positive and to keep/delete fewer tokens if it was negative. We also add a sentence-level minimum edit probability threshold (ϵ) for the output of the edit detection layer. This hyper-parameter enabled the model to predict only the most confident edits. Thus, we were able to increase precision by trading off the recall and achieve better performance.

These hyper-parameters were tuned using a combination of random search and Bayesian search (Nogueira, 2014) on the respective validation sets. Section 6 further describes the impact of the aforementioned tweaks on the system. Final values of these hyper-parameters are listed in Appendix A.

4.7 Evaluation Metrics

We report the results using two widely used metrics in Text Simplification literature: **FKGL** (Kincaid et al., 1975), and **SARI** (Xu et al., 2016b). Prior work has also used **BLEU** (Papineni et al., 2002) as a metric, but recent work has found that it is not a suitable metric for evaluating text simplification, because it was found to be negatively correlated with simplicity, essentially penalizing simpler sentences (Sulem et al., 2018).

FKGL (**F**lesch-**K**incaid **G**rade **L**evel) is used to measure the readability of the generated sentence, where a lower score indicates simpler output. FKGL doesn't use source sentences or references for computing the score. It is a linear combination of the number of words per sentence (system output) and the number of syllables per word. On the other hand, SARI (**S**ystem output **A**gainst **R**eferences and against the **I**nput sentence) evaluates the quality of the output by comparing the generated sentence to a set of reference sentences in terms of correctly inserted, kept and deleted n-grams ($n \in 1, 2, 3, 4$). We report the overall SARI metric, and scores on the three rewrite operations used in SARI: the F1-scores of add (ADD), delete (DELETE) and keep (KEEP) operations. FKGL and SARI are both measured at corpus-level. We computed all the evaluation metrics using the EASSE[8] Python package (Alva-Manchego et al., 2019).

5 Results

5.1 Text Simplification and Readability

Table 2 summarizes the results of our evaluations on TurkCorpus, ASSET and WikiSmall test sets. To ensure robustness of results, we report average scores of 4 runs with different random seeds. We compare the results of our baseline model (TST-BASE) and our final model (TST-FINAL) against recent state-of-the-art Neural Text Simplification models. Additionally, we compare against a reference baseline similar to Martin et al. (2020b), where we compute the scores in a leave-one-out scenario where each reference is evaluated against all the others and then scores are averaged over all references. TST-FINAL consists of all the enhancements mentioned in Section 4 added on top of TST-BASE: data pre-processing, GEC-initialization, data augmentation, and inference tweaks. In terms of the FKGL score, our system achieves better results than the reference baselines on TurkCorpus, and comes within 0.5 points on ASSET and WikiSmall. Compared to the state-of-the-art (Martin et al., 2020b), it improves by 0.23 FKGL points on average, indicating that the simplifying edits made by TST are easier to understand.

In terms of SARI metrics, TST-BASE achieves a competitive score of 39.17 on TurkCorpus, and a state-of-the-art SARI score of 43.11 on WikiSmall, outperforming the previous state-of-the-art result by a huge margin of 6.19 SARI points. This shows that simply using our baseline architecture to train a Text Simplification model on WikiAll can achieve

[8] https://github.com/feralvam/easse

	SARI↑	ADD↑	DELETE↑	KEEP↑	FKGL↓
Recent Works					
Xu et al. (2016b)	39.96	5.96	41.42	72.52	7.29
Nisioi et al. (2017)	35.66	2.99	28.96	**75.02**	8.42
Zhang and Lapata (2017)	37.27	-	-	-	6.62
Alva-Manchego et al. (2017)‡	37.08	2.94	43.20	65.10	**5.35**
Vu et al. (2018)	36.88	-	-	-	-
Zhao et al. (2018a)	40.42	5.72	42.23	73.41	7.79
Guo et al. (2018)	37.45	-	-	-	7.41
Qiang (2018)	37.21	-	-	-	6.56
Surya et al. (2019)	34.96	-	-	-	-
Dong et al. (2019)	38.22	3.36	39.15	72.13	7.3
Zhao et al. (2020b)	37.25	2.87	40.06	68.82	-
Mallinson et al. (2020)	38.13	3.55	40.45	70.39	8.98
Martin et al. (2020a)	41.38	-	-	-	7.29
Martin et al. (2020b)	**42.53**$_{\pm 0.36}$	-	-	-	7.60$_{\pm 1.06}$
Reference Baseline	40.02$_{\pm 0.72}$	6.21$_{\pm 0.60}$	**70.15**$_{\pm 1.35}$	43.69$_{\pm 1.46}$	8.77$_{\pm 0.19}$
Our System					
TST-BASE	39.17$_{\pm 0.77}$	3.62$_{\pm 0.41}$	41.61$_{\pm 3.14}$	72.29$_{\pm 1.45}$	8.08$_{\pm 0.31}$
TST-FINAL	41.46$_{\pm 0.32}$	**6.96**$_{\pm 0.44}$	47.87$_{\pm 0.75}$	69.56$_{\pm 1.19}$	7.87$_{\pm 0.19}$

‡ Quoted from the re-implementation by Dong et al. (2019).

(a) TurkCorpus

	SARI↑	ADD↑	DELETE↑	KEEP↑	FKGL↓
Recent Works					
Martin et al. (2020a)	40.13	-	-	-	7.29
Martin et al. (2020b)	44.15$_{\pm 0.6}$	-	-	-	7.60$_{\pm 1.06}$
Reference Baseline	**44.89**$_{\pm 0.90}$	**10.17**$_{\pm 1.20}$	58.76$_{\pm 2.24}$	**65.73**$_{\pm 2.03}$	**6.49**$_{\pm 0.42}$
Our System					
TST-BASE	37.4$_{\pm 1.62}$	3.62$_{\pm 0.59}$	47.22$_{\pm 4.5}$	61.37$_{\pm 0.52}$	8.08$_{\pm 0.31}$
TST-FINAL	43.21$_{\pm 0.3}$	8.04$_{\pm 0.29}$	**64.25**$_{\pm 1.22}$	57.35$_{\pm 1.68}$	6.87$_{\pm 0.27}$

(b) ASSET

	SARI↑	ADD↑	DELETE↑	KEEP↑	FKGL↓
Recent Works					
Zhang and Lapata (2017)	27.24	-	-	-	7.55
Alva-Manchego et al. (2017)‡	30.50	2.72	76.31	12.46	9.38
Vu et al. (2018)	29.75	-	-	-	-
Guo et al. (2018)	28.24	-	-	-	6.93
Qiang (2018)	26.49	-	-	-	10.75
Dong et al. (2019)	32.35	2.24	**81.30**	13.54	**5.47**
Zhao et al. (2020b)	36.92	2.04	72.79	35.93	-
Reference Baseline	-	-	-	-	8.74
Our System					
TST-BASE	43.11$_{\pm 1.87}$	4.66$_{\pm 1.31}$	61.13$_{\pm 4.73}$	**63.54**$_{\pm 2.75}$	8.41$_{\pm 1.01}$
TST-FINAL	**44.67**$_{\pm 1.26}$	**8.12**$_{\pm 0.92}$	64.87$_{\pm 2.09}$	61.01$_{\pm 1.76}$	9.29$_{\pm 0.9}$

‡ Quoted from the re-implementation by Dong et al. (2019).

(c) WikiSmall

Table 2: Comparison of our system against recent state-of-the-art Neural Text Simplification models on TurkCorpus, ASSET and WikiSmall test sets.

competitive performance on the task. On the other hand, the TST-FINAL makes significant improvements over TST-BASE. On TurkCorpus and ASSET, it comes within 1 SARI point of the current state-of-the-art (Martin et al., 2020b), outperforming all other prior text simplification models in literature. On WikiSmall, it further improves its state-of-the-art performance from TST-BASE to achieve a SARI score of 44.67.

It can be seen that compared to prior works, the most significant improvements in both the TST models come from ADD and DELETE operations. It is noteworthy that TST-FINAL is able to achieve the highest F1 scores on ADD (6.96) and DELETE (47.87) SARI operations reported in literature on TurkCorpus. On the ASSET dataset, the F1 scores on ADD and DELETE operations improve further to 8.04 and 64.25 respectively, improving by large margins over TST-BASE. Similarly, it outperforms the state-of-the-art on ADD operations on WikiSmall. This shows that models proposed in prior works learned a safe, but inefficient strategy of simplification - leaning heavily on copying the sources sentences directly, owing to their high KEEP scores. By contrast, our model learns to edit the sentences better, as shown by the lower rates of keeping the source sentences unchanged. This is further verified by the fact that outputs of prior works[9] have much longer output sentence lengths (avg. 19.26 words) compared to ours (avg. 16.7 words), leading to more effective simplifications.

5.2 Inference Time

We also compare our system's inference times against the current state-of-the-art text simplification systems. Specifically, we compare against ACCESS (trained on WikiLarge data) (Martin et al., 2020a) and BART+ACCESS (Martin et al., 2020b) (trained on WikiLarge + MINED data) systems. We used the publicly available model checkpoint for ACCESS to compare against Martin et al. (2020a). Direct comparison against BART+ACCESS was not possible because of the lack of publicly available code. Therefore, we used BART (Lewis et al., 2020) for text summarization as a proxy for Martin et al. (2020b). We ran all systems with batch size 128 on the TurkCorpus test set 100 times, using NVIDIA Tesla V100. Within a single run, the results were averaged across all batches. We took into account only the actual inference time and omitted any initialization times.

The results in Table 3 show that the inference speeds[10] of TST are at least 6 times faster than ACCESS and 11.75 times faster than pure BART which is the crucial component of the current state-of-the-art (Martin et al., 2020b). The impact of a non-autoregressive model architecture can be clearly seen here since TST is a sequence tagging system and does not need to predict edits one-by-one as done by auto-regressive transformer decoders (like the one used in ACCESS). There-

[9]Measured on TurkCorpus. This information was not available for ASSET and WikiSmall

[10]We compared ACCESS and BART with beam size 8 and TST with 2 iterations, as reported on TurkCorpus

System	Inference time (sec)
BART, beam size = 8	2.82
BART, beam size = 2	1.95
ACCESS, beam size = 8	1.43
ACCESS, beam size = 1	1.14
TST, 5 iterations	0.43
TST, 4 iterations	0.39
TST, 3 iterations	0.33
TST, 2 iterations	0.24
TST, 1 iteration	0.13

Table 3: Average inference time per batch. In the context of TST, iterations refers to the number of iterations mentioned in Section 3.2

fore, the inference is naturally parallelizable and therefore runs many times faster.

6 Ablation Study

In this section, we present ablation experiments for each of the enhancements described in Section 4, and applied to TST-BASE to obtain TST-FINAL. The results of these experiments (Table 4) are reported on SARI and FKGL scores, averaged between ASSET and TurkCorpus test datasets. Each result is reported using an average of 4 runs for each experiment. Overall, the enhancements improve the SARI score by 4.0 points and FKGL by 0.21 points, while reducing variance in both cases.

6.1 GEC Initialization

We improve our strong baseline model TST-BASE by pre-training it on the GEC task.[11] Even though we find that using TST-GEC leads to modest immediate improvements (+0.1 SARI point) compared to TST-BASE, we found that adding other enhancements without the GEC-pre-training were not as effective, with the final model (TST-BASE + Filtering + WikiEns + InfTweaks) achieving an average SARI score of 40.01 - significantly lower than the one with GEC-pre-training (42.3).

These results show that pre-training TST-BASE on GEC is an effective way to initialize the model for Text Simplification, since it equips the model to make additions and deletions, which are then further improved during training on the text simplification data. This was also not unexpected because the edit-tags were obtained from huge amounts of GEC data, and are expected to have good coverage with regards to many standard monolingual text editing problems - as also observed by a high overlap in the tag distributions between the GEC and Text Simplification domains (Section 3.1).

[11] We refer the reader to Omelianchuk et al. (2020) for details on training the model for GEC.

System	SARI ↑	FKGL ↓
TST	38.3 ± 1.36	8.08 ± 0.31
+ GEC	38.4 ± 0.83	8.32 ± 0.26
+ Filtering	39.1 ± 0.48	7.66 ± 0.25
+ WikiBT	39.5 ± 0.01	7.5 ± 0.06
+ WikiEns (- WikiBT)	40.3 ± 0.15	**7.48 ± 0.2**
+ InfTweaks	**42.3 ± 0.25**	7.87 ± 0.19

Table 4: Average SARI and FKGL scores (ASSET and TurkCorpus test sets)

6.2 Data Pre-processing

As mentioned in Section 4.2, we removed special tokens found in Wikipedia data such as `-LRB-` and `-RRB-`, along with the text enclosed by these tokens, in both source and target sentences. We find that using GEC initialization together with filtering brackets was beneficial to the system (+0.8 SARI points), and also decreased the variance in the results. The benefit of this step is towards improving text simplification quality is also seconded by a significantly reduced FKGL score (-0.66 points).

6.3 Data Augmentation

We explored two strategies of data augmentation: enriching training data with (i) back-translated data (WikiBT), (ii) ensemble-generated data (WikiEns). Augmenting the training data using WikiEns leads to a bigger boost compared to just adding WikiBT (+1.2 vs +0.4). We also experimented with adding both synthetic datasets (WikiEnd + WikiBT) to the WikiAll training data, but the performance was worse compared to using only WikiEns.

6.4 Inference Tweaks

Finally, we describe the effect of tuning the inference hyper-parameters for our model obtained so far. Using these tweaks (Section 4.6) is one of the most crucial components of our system. Overall, it is not just able to affect the sequence generation, but also gives us the biggest boost (+2.0 points). Our final model with inference tweaks comfortably outperforms its predecessor on all datasets, demonstrating their effectiveness on the task.

7 Conclusion

This paper introduces TST, a novel approach to text simplification, by reformulating the task into a much simpler one of sequence tagging. We build TST by adapting the GECToR framework for GEC. We show that most of its performance gains are owed to simplistic data augmentations and tweaks in training and inference. These modifications allow us to derive maximal benefit from the already existing pre-trained Transformer-based encoders on large amounts of human-annotated and synthetic data, making TST a simple, powerful, easily reusable method for monolingual editing tasks. Since TST is able to progressively make simplifying edits via explicit edit-tag operations, the transformations resulting from TST are better explainable and interpretable than any other NMT-based Seq2Seq approaches. Finally, TST is fully non-autoregressive, enabling it to perform faster inference than any other state-of-the-art text simplification methods. Our empirical results demonstrate that it achieves near state-of-the-art performance on benchmark test datasets for text simplification.

A major motivation in this work was to minimize changes to the original model to keep the system simple, fast, and reproducible. Hence, we restricted our system to only use WikiAll data and its derivatives (vs. any external data like the state-of-the-art system by Martin et al. (2020b)). While we did not fully beat the state-of-the-art on the task, we believe that using larger models (eg. RoBERTa$_{\text{LARGE}}$), ensembles, or external data will likely lead to better SARI scores at the cost of speed and system complexity: ideas we plan to explore in future work.

References

Sandra M. Aluísio, Lucia Specia, T. A. S. Pardo, E. Maziero, Helena de Medeiros Caseli, and R. P. M. Fortes. 2008. A corpus analysis of simple account texts and the proposal of simplification strategies: first steps towards text simplification systems. In *SIGDOC '08*.

Sandra M. Aluísio, Lucia Specia, Thiago A. S. Pardo, Erick G. Maziero, Helena M. Caseli, and Renata P. M. Fortes. 2008. A corpus analysis of simple account texts and the proposal of simplification strategies: First steps towards text simplification systems. In *Proceedings of the 26th Annual ACM International Conference on Design of Communication*, SIGDOC '08, page 15–22, New York, NY, USA. Association for Computing Machinery.

Fernando Alva-Manchego, Joachim Bingel, Gustavo Paetzold, Carolina Scarton, and Lucia Specia. 2017. Learning how to simplify from explicit labeling of complex-simplified text pairs. In *Proceedings of the Eighth International Joint Conference on Natural Language Processing (Volume 1: Long Papers)*, pages 295–305, Taipei, Taiwan. Asian Federation of Natural Language Processing.

Fernando Alva-Manchego, Louis Martin, Antoine Bordes, Carolina Scarton, Benoît Sagot, and Lucia Specia. 2020. ASSET: A dataset for tuning and evaluation of sentence simplification models with multiple rewriting transformations. In *Proceedings of the 58th Annual Meeting of the Association for Computational Linguistics*, pages 4668–4679, Online. Association for Computational Linguistics.

Fernando Alva-Manchego, Louis Martin, Carolina Scarton, and Lucia Specia. 2019. Easse: Easier automatic sentence simplification evaluation. *arXiv preprint arXiv:1908.04567*.

Abhijeet Awasthi, Sunita Sarawagi, Rasna Goyal, Sabyasachi Ghosh, and Vihari Piratla. 2019. Parallel iterative edit models for local sequence transduction. In *Proceedings of the 2019 Conference on Empirical Methods in Natural Language Processing and the 9th International Joint Conference on Natural Language Processing (EMNLP-IJCNLP)*, pages 4260–4270, Hong Kong, China. Association for Computational Linguistics.

Dzmitry Bahdanau, Kyunghyun Cho, and Yoshua Bengio. 2015. Neural machine translation by jointly learning to align and translate. In *3rd International Conference on Learning Representations, ICLR 2015, San Diego, CA, USA, May 7-9, 2015, Conference Track Proceedings*.

Beata Beigman Klebanov, Kevin Knight, and Daniel Marcu. 2004. Text simplification for information-seeking applications. In *On the Move to Meaningful Internet Systems 2004: CoopIS, DOA, and ODBASE*, pages 735–747, Berlin, Heidelberg. Springer Berlin Heidelberg.

J. D. Belder and Marie-Francine Moens. 2010. Text simplification for children. In *SIGIR 2010*.

John Carroll, Guido Minnen, Yvonne Canning, Siobhan Devlin, and John Tait. 1998. Practical simplification of english newspaper text to assist aphasic readers. In *Proceedings of the AAAI-98 Workshop on Integrating Artificial Intelligence and Assistive Technology*, pages 7–10.

John Carroll, Guido Minnen, Darren Pearce, Yvonne Canning, Siobhan Devlin, and John Tait. 1999. Simplifying text for language-impaired readers. In *Ninth Conference of the European Chapter of the Association for Computational Linguistics*, Bergen, Norway. Association for Computational Linguistics.

R. Chandrasekar, Christine Doran, and B. Srinivas. 1996. Motivations and methods for text simplification. In *COLING 1996 Volume 2: The 16th International Conference on Computational Linguistics*.

Kyunghyun Cho, Bart van Merriënboer, Caglar Gulcehre, Dzmitry Bahdanau, Fethi Bougares, Holger Schwenk, and Yoshua Bengio. 2014. Learning phrase representations using RNN encoder–decoder for statistical machine translation. In *Proceedings of the 2014 Conference on Empirical Methods in Natural Language Processing (EMNLP)*, pages 1724–1734, Doha, Qatar. Association for Computational Linguistics.

Will Coster and David Kauchak. 2011. Learning to simplify sentences using Wikipedia. In *Proceedings of the Workshop on Monolingual Text-To-Text Generation*, pages 1–9, Portland, Oregon. Association for Computational Linguistics.

Siobhan Devlin and Gary Unthank. 2006. Helping aphasic people process online information. In *Proceedings of the 8th International ACM SIGACCESS Conference on Computers and Accessibility*, Assets '06, page 225–226, New York, NY, USA. Association for Computing Machinery.

Yue Dong, Zichao Li, Mehdi Rezagholizadeh, and Jackie Chi Kit Cheung. 2019. EditNTS: An neural programmer-interpreter model for sentence simplification through explicit editing. In *Proceedings of the 57th Annual Meeting of the Association for Computational Linguistics*, pages 3393–3402, Florence, Italy. Association for Computational Linguistics.

Richard Evans, Constantin Orăsan, and Iustin Dornescu. 2014. An evaluation of syntactic simplification rules for people with autism. In *Proceedings of the 3rd Workshop on Predicting and Improving Text Readability for Target Reader Populations (PITR)*, pages 131–140, Gothenburg, Sweden. Association for Computational Linguistics.

Markus Freitag, Yaser Al-Onaizan, and B. Sankaran. 2017. Ensemble distillation for neural machine translation. *ArXiv*, abs/1702.01802.

Caroline Gasperin, Erick Galani Maziero, Lucia Specia, Thiago A. S. Pardo, and Sandra M. Aluísio. 2009. Natural language processing for social inclusion : a text simplification architecture for different literacy levels.

Laurie Gerber and Eduard Hovy. 1998. Improving translation quality by manipulating sentence length. In *Machine Translation and the Information Soup*, pages 448–460, Berlin, Heidelberg. Springer Berlin Heidelberg.

Goran Glavaš and Sanja Štajner. 2015. Simplifying lexical simplification: Do we need simplified corpora? In *Proceedings of the 53rd Annual Meeting of the Association for Computational Linguistics and the 7th International Joint Conference on Natural Language Processing (Volume 2: Short Papers)*, pages 63–68, Beijing, China. Association for Computational Linguistics.

Jiatao Gu, Changhan Wang, and Junbo Zhao. 2019. Levenshtein transformer. In *Advances in Neural Information Processing Systems 32*, pages 11181–11191. Curran Associates, Inc.

Han Guo, Ramakanth Pasunuru, and Mohit Bansal. 2018. Dynamic multi-level multi-task learning for sentence simplification. In *Proceedings of the 27th International Conference on Computational Linguistics*, pages 462–476, Santa Fe, New Mexico, USA. Association for Computational Linguistics.

Eva Hasler, Adrià de Gispert, Felix Stahlberg, Aurelien Waite, and Bill Byrne. 2017. Source sentence simplification for statistical machine translation. *Computer Speech & Language*, 45:221 – 235.

Colby Horn, Cathryn Manduca, and David Kauchak. 2014. Learning a lexical simplifier using Wikipedia. In *Proceedings of the 52nd Annual Meeting of the Association for Computational Linguistics (Volume 2: Short Papers)*, pages 458–463, Baltimore, Maryland. Association for Computational Linguistics.

Nobuhiro Kaji, Daisuke Kawahara, Sadao Kurohashi, and Satoshi Sato. 2002. Verb paraphrase based on case frame alignment. In *Proceedings of the 40th Annual Meeting of the Association for Computational Linguistics*, pages 215–222, Philadelphia, Pennsylvania, USA. Association for Computational Linguistics.

Tomoyuki Kajiwara, Hiroshi Matsumoto, and Kazuhide Yamamoto. 2013. Selecting proper lexical paraphrase for children. In *Proceedings of the 25th Conference on Computational Linguistics and Speech Processing (ROCLING 2013)*, pages 59–73, Kaohsiung, Taiwan. The Association for Computational Linguistics and Chinese Language Processing (ACLCLP).

David Kauchak. 2013. Improving text simplification language modeling using unsimplified text data. In *Proceedings of the 51st Annual Meeting of the Association for Computational Linguistics (Volume 1: Long Papers)*, pages 1537–1546, Sofia, Bulgaria. Association for Computational Linguistics.

J Peter Kincaid, Robert P Fishburne Jr, Richard L Rogers, and Brad S Chissom. 1975. Derivation of new readability formulas (automated readability index, fog count and flesch reading ease formula) for navy enlisted personnel.

Diederik P. Kingma and Jimmy Ba. 2015. Adam: A method for stochastic optimization. In *3rd International Conference on Learning Representations, ICLR 2015, San Diego, CA, USA, May 7-9, 2015, Conference Track Proceedings*.

Reno Kriz, João Sedoc, Marianna Apidianaki, Carolina Zheng, Gaurav Kumar, Eleni Miltsakaki, and Chris Callison-Burch. 2019. Complexity-weighted loss and diverse reranking for sentence simplification. In *Proceedings of the 2019 Conference of the North American Chapter of the Association for Computational Linguistics: Human Language Technologies, Volume 1 (Long and Short Papers)*, pages 3137–3147, Minneapolis, Minnesota. Association for Computational Linguistics.

Mike Lewis, Yinhan Liu, Naman Goyal, Marjan Ghazvininejad, Abdelrahman Mohamed, Omer Levy, Veselin Stoyanov, and Luke Zettlemoyer. 2020. BART: Denoising sequence-to-sequence pretraining for natural language generation, translation, and comprehension. In *Proceedings of the 58th Annual Meeting of the Association for Computational Linguistics*, pages 7871–7880, Online. Association for Computational Linguistics.

Tianyu Li, Yun Li, Jipeng Qiang, and Yun-Hao Yuan. 2018. Text simplification with self-attention-based pointer-generator networks. In *Neural Information Processing*, pages 537–545, Cham. Springer International Publishing.

Yinhan Liu, Myle Ott, Naman Goyal, Jingfei Du, Mandar Joshi, Danqi Chen, Omer Levy, Mike Lewis, Luke Zettlemoyer, and Veselin Stoyanov. 2019. Roberta: A robustly optimized BERT pretraining approach. *CoRR*, abs/1907.11692.

Jonathan Mallinson, Aliaksei Severyn, Eric Malmi, and Guillermo Garrido. 2020. Felix: Flexible text editing through tagging and insertion. *arXiv preprint arXiv:2003.10687*.

Eric Malmi, Sebastian Krause, Sascha Rothe, Daniil Mirylenka, and Aliaksei Severyn. 2019. Encode, tag, realize: High-precision text editing. In *Proceedings of the 2019 Conference on Empirical Methods in Natural Language Processing and the 9th International Joint Conference on Natural Language Processing (EMNLP-IJCNLP)*, pages 5054–5065, Hong Kong, China. Association for Computational Linguistics.

Louis Martin, Éric de la Clergerie, Benoît Sagot, and Antoine Bordes. 2020a. Controllable sentence simplification. In *Proceedings of The 12th Language Resources and Evaluation Conference*, pages 4689–4698, Marseille, France. European Language Resources Association.

Louis Martin, Angela Fan, Éric de la Clergerie, Antoine Bordes, and Benoît Sagot. 2020b. Multilingual unsupervised sentence simplification. *arXiv preprint arXiv:2005.00352*.

Aurélien Max. 2006. Writing for language-impaired readers. In *Computational Linguistics and Intelligent Text Processing*, pages 567–570, Berlin, Heidelberg. Springer Berlin Heidelberg.

Shashi Narayan and Claire Gardent. 2014. Hybrid simplification using deep semantics and machine translation. In *Proceedings of the 52nd Annual Meeting of the Association for Computational Linguistics (Volume 1: Long Papers)*, pages 435–445, Baltimore, Maryland. Association for Computational Linguistics.

Sergiu Nisioi, Sanja Štajner, Simone Paolo Ponzetto, and Liviu P. Dinu. 2017. Exploring neural text simplification models. In *Proceedings of the 55th Annual Meeting of the Association for Computational Linguistics (Volume 2: Short Papers)*, pages 85–91, Vancouver, Canada. Association for Computational Linguistics.

Fernando Nogueira. 2014. Bayesian Optimization: Open source constrained global optimization tool for Python.

Kostiantyn Omelianchuk, Vitaliy Atrasevych, Artem Chernodub, and Oleksandr Skurzhanskyi. 2020. GECToR – grammatical error correction: Tag, not rewrite. In *Proceedings of the Fifteenth Workshop on Innovative Use of NLP for Building Educational Applications*, pages 163–170, Seattle, WA, USA â†' Online. Association for Computational Linguistics.

Gustavo Paetzold. 2015. Reliable lexical simplification for non-native speakers. In *Proceedings of the 2015 Conference of the North American Chapter of the Association for Computational Linguistics: Student Research Workshop*, pages 9–16, Denver, Colorado. Association for Computational Linguistics.

Gustavo Paetzold and Lucia Specia. 2016a. Understanding the lexical simplification needs of non-native speakers of English. In *Proceedings of COLING 2016, the 26th International Conference on Computational Linguistics: Technical Papers*, pages 717–727, Osaka, Japan. The COLING 2016 Organizing Committee.

Gustavo H. Paetzold and Lucia Specia. 2016b. Unsupervised lexical simplification for non-native speakers. In *Proceedings of the Thirtieth AAAI Conference on Artificial Intelligence*, AAAI'16, page 3761–3767. AAAI Press.

Kishore Papineni, Salim Roukos, Todd Ward, and Wei-Jing Zhu. 2002. Bleu: a method for automatic evaluation of machine translation. In *Proceedings of the 40th Annual Meeting of the Association for Computational Linguistics*, pages 311–318, Philadelphia, Pennsylvania, USA. Association for Computational Linguistics.

David Pellow and Maxine Eskenazi. 2014. An open corpus of everyday documents for simplification tasks. In *Proceedings of the 3rd Workshop on Predicting and Improving Text Readability for Target Reader Populations (PITR)*, pages 84–93, Gothenburg, Sweden. Association for Computational Linguistics.

Sarah E. Petersen and Mari Ostendorf. 2007. Text simplification for language learners: A corpus analysis. In *In Proceedings of Workshop on Speech and Language Technology for Education*.

Jipeng Qiang. 2018. Improving neural text simplification model with simplified corpora. *arXiv preprint arXiv:1810.04428*.

Luz Rello, Ricardo Baeza-Yates, Stefan Bott, and Horacio Saggion. 2013a. Simplify or help? text simplification strategies for people with dyslexia. In *Proceedings of the 10th International Cross-Disciplinary Conference on Web Accessibility*, W4A '13, New York, NY, USA. Association for Computing Machinery.

Luz Rello, Ricardo Baeza-Yates, and Horacio Saggion. 2013b. The impact of lexical simplification by verbal paraphrases for people with and without dyslexia. In *Computational Linguistics and Intelligent Text Processing*, pages 501–512, Berlin, Heidelberg. Springer Berlin Heidelberg.

Joana Ribeiro, Shashi Narayan, Shay B. Cohen, and Xavier Carreras. 2018. Local string transduction as sequence labeling. In *Proceedings of the 27th International Conference on Computational Linguistics*, pages 1360–1371, Santa Fe, New Mexico, USA. Association for Computational Linguistics.

Rico Sennrich, Barry Haddow, and Alexandra Birch. 2016. Neural machine translation of rare words with subword units. In *Proceedings of the 54th Annual Meeting of the Association for Computational Linguistics (Volume 1: Long Papers)*, pages 1715–1725, Berlin, Germany. Association for Computational Linguistics.

Advaith Siddharthan. 2006. Syntactic Simplification and Text Cohesion. *Research on Language and Computation*, 4(1):77–109.

Advaith Siddharthan. 2014. A survey of research on text simplification. *International Journal of Applied Linguistics*, 165(2):259–298.

Sara Botelho Silveira and António Branco. 2012. Enhancing multi-document summaries with sentence simplification. In *In ICAI 2012: International Conference on Artificial Intelligence, Las Vegas*.

Lucia Specia. 2010. Translating from complex to simplified sentences. In *Proceedings of the 9th International Conference on Computational Processing of the Portuguese Language*, PROPOR'10, page 30–39, Berlin, Heidelberg. Springer-Verlag.

Sanja Štajner, Hannah Béchara, and Horacio Saggion. 2015. A deeper exploration of the standard PB-SMT approach to text simplification and its evaluation. In *Proceedings of the 53rd Annual Meeting of the Association for Computational Linguistics and the 7th International Joint Conference on Natural Language Processing (Volume 2: Short Papers)*, pages 823–828, Beijing, China. Association for Computational Linguistics.

Sanja Štajner and Sergiu Nisioi. 2018. A detailed evaluation of neural sequence-to-sequence models for in-domain and cross-domain text simplification. In *Proceedings of the Eleventh International Conference on Language Resources and Evaluation (LREC-2018)*, Miyazaki, Japan. European Languages Resources Association (ELRA).

Sanja Štajner and Maja Popovic. 2016. Can text simplification help machine translation? In *Proceedings of the 19th Annual Conference of the European Association for Machine Translation*, pages 230–242.

Elior Sulem, Omri Abend, and Ari Rappoport. 2018. BLEU is not suitable for the evaluation of text simplification. In *Proceedings of the 2018 Conference on Empirical Methods in Natural Language Processing*, pages 738–744, Brussels, Belgium. Association for Computational Linguistics.

Sai Surya, Abhijit Mishra, Anirban Laha, Parag Jain, and Karthik Sankaranarayanan. 2019. Unsupervised neural text simplification. In *Proceedings of the 57th Annual Meeting of the Association for Computational Linguistics*, pages 2058–2068, Florence, Italy. Association for Computational Linguistics.

Ilya Sutskever, Oriol Vinyals, and Quoc V Le. 2014. Sequence to sequence learning with neural networks. In Z. Ghahramani, M. Welling, C. Cortes, N. D. Lawrence, and K. Q. Weinberger, editors, *Advances in Neural Information Processing Systems 27*, pages 3104–3112. Curran Associates, Inc.

Jörg Tiedemann and Santhosh Thottingal. 2020. OPUS-MT — Building open translation services for the World. In *Proceedings of the 22nd Annual Conferenec of the European Association for Machine Translation (EAMT)*, Lisbon, Portugal.

David Vickrey and Daphne Koller. 2008. Sentence simplification for semantic role labeling. In *Proceedings of ACL-08: HLT*, pages 344–352, Columbus, Ohio. Association for Computational Linguistics.

Tu Vu, Baotian Hu, Tsendsuren Munkhdalai, and Hong Yu. 2018. Sentence simplification with memory-augmented neural networks. In *Proceedings of the 2018 Conference of the North American Chapter of the Association for Computational Linguistics: Human Language Technologies, Volume 2 (Short Papers)*, pages 79–85, New Orleans, Louisiana. Association for Computational Linguistics.

Tong Wang, Ping Chen, John Rochford, and Jipeng Qiang. 2016. Text simplification using neural machine translation.

Willian Massami Watanabe, Arnaldo Candido Junior, Vinícius Rodriguez Uzêda, Renata Pontin de Mattos Fortes, Thiago Alexandre Salgueiro Pardo, and Sandra Maria Aluísio. 2009. Facilita: Reading assistance for low-literacy readers. In *Proceedings of the 27th ACM International Conference on Design of Communication*, SIGDOC '09, page 29–36, New York, NY, USA. Association for Computing Machinery.

Thomas Wolf, Lysandre Debut, Victor Sanh, Julien Chaumond, Clement Delangue, Anthony Moi, Pierric Cistac, Tim Rault, Rémi Louf, Morgan Funtowicz, Joe Davison, Sam Shleifer, Patrick von Platen, Clara Ma, Yacine Jernite, Julien Plu, Canwen Xu,

Teven Le Scao, Sylvain Gugger, Mariama Drame, Quentin Lhoest, and Alexander M. Rush. 2019. Huggingface's transformers: State-of-the-art natural language processing. *ArXiv*, abs/1910.03771.

Kristian Woodsend and Mirella Lapata. 2011. Learning to simplify sentences with quasi-synchronous grammar and integer programming. In *Proceedings of the 2011 Conference on Empirical Methods in Natural Language Processing*, pages 409–420, Edinburgh, Scotland, UK. Association for Computational Linguistics.

Kristian Woodsend and Mirella Lapata. 2017. Text rewriting improves semantic role labeling. In *Proceedings of the 26th International Joint Conference on Artificial Intelligence*, IJCAI'17, page 5095–5099. AAAI Press.

Sander Wubben, Antal van den Bosch, and Emiel Krahmer. 2012. Sentence simplification by monolingual machine translation. In *Proceedings of the 50th Annual Meeting of the Association for Computational Linguistics (Volume 1: Long Papers)*, pages 1015–1024, Jeju Island, Korea. Association for Computational Linguistics.

Wei Xu, Chris Callison-Burch, and Courtney Napoles. 2015. Problems in current text simplification research: New data can help. *Transactions of the Association for Computational Linguistics*, 3:283–297.

Wei Xu, Courtney Napoles, Ellie Pavlick, Quanze Chen, and Chris Callison-Burch. 2016a. Optimizing statistical machine translation for text simplification. *Transactions of the Association for Computational Linguistics*, 4:401–415.

Wei Xu, Courtney Napoles, Ellie Pavlick, Quanze Chen, and Chris Callison-Burch. 2016b. Optimizing statistical machine translation for text simplification. *Transactions of the Association for Computational Linguistics*, 4:401–415.

Xingxing Zhang and Mirella Lapata. 2017. Sentence simplification with deep reinforcement learning. In *Proceedings of the 2017 Conference on Empirical Methods in Natural Language Processing*, pages 584–594, Copenhagen, Denmark. Association for Computational Linguistics.

Yaoyuan Zhang, Zhenxu Ye, Yansong Feng, Dongyan Zhao, and Rui Yan. 2017. A constrained sequence-to-sequence neural model for sentence simplification. *ArXiv*, abs/1704.02312.

Sanqiang Zhao, Rui Meng, Daqing He, Saptono Andi, and Parmanto Bambang. 2018a. Integrating transformer and paraphrase rules for sentence simplification. *arXiv preprint arXiv:1810.11193*.

Sanqiang Zhao, Rui Meng, Daqing He, Andi Saptono, and Bambang Parmanto. 2018b. Integrating transformer and paraphrase rules for sentence simplification. In *Proceedings of the 2018 Conference on Empirical Methods in Natural Language Processing*, pages 3164–3173, Brussels, Belgium. Association for Computational Linguistics.

Yanbin Zhao, Lu Chen, Zhi Chen, and Kai Yu. 2020a. Semi-supervised text simplification with back translation and asymmetric denoising autoencoders. In *The Thirty-Fourth AAAI Conference on Artificial Intelligence, AAAI 2020, The Thirty-Second Innovative Applications of Artificial Intelligence Conference, IAAI 2020, The Tenth AAAI Symposium on Educational Advances in Artificial Intelligence, EAAI 2020, New York, NY, USA, February 7-12, 2020*, pages 9668–9675. AAAI Press.

Yanbin Zhao, Lu Chen, Zhi Chen, and Kai Yu. 2020b. Semi-supervised text simplification with back-translation and asymmetric denoising autoencoders. In *AAAI*, pages 9668–9675.

Zhemin Zhu, Delphine Bernhard, and Iryna Gurevych. 2010. A monolingual tree-based translation model for sentence simplification. In *Proceedings of the 23rd International Conference on Computational Linguistics (Coling 2010)*, pages 1353–1361, Beijing, China. Coling 2010 Organizing Committee.

A Model Configurations

Table 5 describes the list of hyper-parameters used for TST-FINAL model. In Table 6, we list the inference tweaks hyper-parameters found by Bayesian Search on TurkCorpus and ASSET datasets.

Hyperparameter name	Value
learning_rate	1e-5
transformer_model	roberta-base
accumulation_size	2
batch_size	128
cold_steps_count	2
n_epoch	50
patience	3
vocab_size	5000
max_len	50
min_len	3
pieces_per_token	5
filter_brackets	0/1
seed	1/2/3/11
normalize	1

Table 5: The list of hyper-parameters used during training

B Simplification Examples

Various examples from our system are shown in Table 7. Examining the simplifications, we see reduced sentence length, sentence splitting of a complex sentence into multiple shorter sentences, and the use of simpler vocabulary. Manual comparison between TST-BASE and TST-FINAL shows that the first system tends to delete some complex words from the text. For example, "theoretically possible" gets shortened to just "possible," and "administrative district" to "district". TST-FINAL model tends to be more creative and changes phrases to simpler versions like "is theoretically possible" to "might be" or "an administrative district" to "a part of." However, this aggressive and creative strategy sometimes also generates ungrammatical output like in the last example in Table 7. While it rarely happens, but the model might also change the meaning of the original sentence. For example, replacing "the five" to "the three." It is worth noticing that the same problem of meaning change is present in the reference sentences as well: where "the five" got replaced with "one of four".

Model description	Tuned dataset	Seed	Del conf	Keep conf	Iterations	Min error probability
TST w/o InfTweaks	-	-	0	0	5	0
TST with InfTweaks	Turk	1	-0.84	-0.66	2	0.04
TST with InfTweaks	Turk	2	-0.93	-0.51	3	0.02
TST with InfTweaks	Turk	3	-0.86	-0.68	2	0.03
TST with InfTweaks	Turk	11	-0.88	-0.61	2	0.03
TST with InfTweaks	ASSET	1	-0.66	-0.9	3	0.02
TST with InfTweaks	ASSET	2	-0.72	-0.88	3	0.02
TST with InfTweaks	ASSET	3	-0.52	-0.89	3	0.04
TST with InfTweaks	ASSET	11	-0.72	-0.91	3	0.02

Table 6: Inference hyper-parameters found by the Bayesian Search on TurkCorpus and ASSET development sets

Original	he also **completed two collections** of short stories **entitled** the ribbajack & other curious yarns and seven strange and ghostly tales .
Reference	he also **wrote two books** of short stories **called ,** the ribbajack & other curious yarns and seven strange and ghostly tales .
TST-BASE	he also **wrote** two collections of short stories **called** the ribbajack & other curious yarns and seven strange and ghostly tales .
TST-FINAL	he also **wrote a series** of short stories **called** the ribbajack & other curious yarns and seven strange and ghostly tales .
Original	it **is theoretically possible** that the other editors who may have **reported** you , and the administrator who blocked you , are part of a conspiracy against someone half a world away they 've never met in person .
Reference	it is theoretically possible that the other editors who may **have written about** you, and the **officer** who blocked you, are part of **a bad plan** against someone **miles** away, they 've never met **face to face** .
TST-BASE	it is possible that the other editors who may have reported you , and the administrator who blocked you , are part of a conspiracy against someone half a world away they ' ve never met in person .
TST-FINAL	it **might be** that the other editors who may have **sent** you , and the administrator who blocked you , are part of a conspiracy against someone half a world away where they 've never met in person .
Original	as a result , although many mosques will not enforce violations , both men and women when attending a mosque must **adhere to these guidelines** .
Reference	as a result , both men and women must follow this rule when they attend a mosque , even though many mosques do not enforce these rules
TST-BASE	both men and women when **going** a mosque must **follow these rules** .
TST-FINAL	both men **,** and women **that attend** mosque **,** must **follow the law** .
Original	hinterrhein is **an administrative district in** the canton of graubünden , switzerland .
Reference	hinterrhein is a district **of** the canton of graubünden , switzerland .
TST-BASE	hinterrhein is a district **of** the canton of graubünden , switzerland .
TST-FINAL	hinterrhein is **a part of** the canton of graubünden in the switzerland .
Original	a majority of south indians speak one of the five dravidian languages — kannada , malayalam , tamil , telugu and tulu .
Reference	**many** of the south indians **are dravidians and they speak one of four** dravidian languages — kannada , malayalam , tamil **or** telugu .
TST-BASE	**most** of south indians speak one of the five dravidian languages — kannada , malayalam , tamil , telugu and tulu .
TST-FINAL	**most of the people** speak **speakers from the three** dravidian languages **spoken are ,** kannada , malayalam , tamil , telugu **,** and tulu .

Table 7: Examples of simplifications by TST

Employing distributional semantics to organize task-focused vocabulary learning

Haemanth Santhi Ponnusamy **Detmar Meurers**

University of Tübingen, Germany

{hsp,dm}@sfs.uni-tuebingen.de

Abstract

How can a learner systematically prepare for reading a book they are interested in? In this paper, we explore how computational linguistic methods such as distributional semantics, morphological clustering, and exercise generation can be combined with graph-based learner models to answer this question both conceptually and in practice. Based on highly structured learner models and concepts from network analysis, the learner is guided to efficiently explore the targeted lexical space. They practice using multi-gap learning activities generated from the book. In sum, the approach combines computational linguistic methods with concepts from network analysis and tutoring systems to support learners in pursuing their individual reading task goals.

1 Introduction

Learning vocabulary is a major component of foreign language learning. In the school context, initially, vocabulary learning is typically organized around the words introduced by the textbook. In addition to the incrementally growing vocabulary lists, some textbooks also provide thematically organized word banks. When other texts are read, the publisher or the teacher often provides annotations for new vocabulary items that appear in the text. A range of tools has been developed to support vocabulary learning, from digital versions of file cards to digital text editions offering annotations.

While such applications serve the needs of the formal learning setting in the initial foreign language learning phase, where the texts that are read are primarily chosen to systematically introduce the language, later the selection of texts to be read can in principle follow the individual interests of the student or adult, which boosts the motivation to engage with the book. Linking language learning to a functional goal that someone actually wants to achieve using language is in line with the idea of Task-Based Language Teaching (TBLT), a prominent strand in language teaching (Ellis, 2009).

Naturally, not all authentic texts are accessible to every learner, but linguistically-aware search engines, such as FLAIR (Chinkina and Meurers, 2016), make it possible to identify authentic texts that are at the right reading level and are rich in the language constructions next on the curriculum. Where the unknown vocabulary that the reader encounters in such a setting goes beyond around 2% of unknown words in a text that can be present without substantial loss of comprehension (Schmitt et al., 2011), many digital reading environments provide the option to look up a word in a dictionary. Yet, frequently looking up words in such a context is cumbersome and distracts the reader from the world of the book they are trying to engage with. Relatedly, one of the key criteria of TBLT is that learners should rely on their own resources to complete a task (Ellis, 2009). But this naturally can require pre-task activities preparing the learner to be able to successfully tackle the task (Willis and Willis, 2013). But how can a learner systematically prepare for reading a text or book they are interested in reading?

In this paper, we explore how computational linguistic methods such as distributional semantics, morphological clustering, and exercise generation can be combined with graph-based learner models to answer this question both conceptually and in practice. On the practical side, we developed an application that supports vocabulary learning as a pre-task activity for reading a self-selected book. The conceptual goal is to automatically organize the lexical-semantic space of any given English book in the form of a graph that makes it possible to sequence the vocabulary learning in a way efficiently exploring the space and to visualize this graph for the users as an open learner model (Bull

Proceedings of the 16th Workshop on Innovative Use of NLP for Building Educational Applications, pages 26–36
April 20, 2021 ©2021 Association for Computational Linguistics

and Kay, 2010) showing their growing mastery of the book's lexical space. Lexical learning is fostered and monitored through automatically generated multi-gap activities (Zesch and Melamud, 2014) that support learning and revision of words in the contexts in which they occur in the book.

In section 2 we discuss how a book or other text chosen by the learner is turned in to a graph encoding the lexical space that the learner needs to engage with to read the book, and how words that are morphologically related as word families (Bauer and Nation, 1993) are automatically identified and compactly represented in the graph (2.1.1). In section 3 we then turn to the use of the graph representation of the lexical semantic space of the book to determine the reader's learning path and represent their growing lexical knowledge as spreading activation in the graph. In section 4, the conceptual ideas are realized in an application. We discuss how the new learner cold-start problem is avoided using a very quick word recognition task we implemented, before discussing the content selection and activity generation for practice and testing activities. Section 6 then provides a conceptual evaluation of the approach and compares it with related work, before concluding in section 7.

2 Constructing a structured domain model for the lexical space of a book

Going beyond the benefits of interactivity and adaptivity of individualized digital learning tools, supporting learner autonomy is known to be important for boosting motivation and self-regulation skills (Godwin-Jones, 2019). This includes the choice of reading material a learner wants to engage with, where the texts prepared by a teacher or publisher cannot reflect the interests of individual students, the topics and genres they want to explore in the foreign language. The freedom of choosing a text that the learner wants to engage with also identifying a clear functional goal for learning vocabulary – learning new words to enable us to read a text of interest, so that the interest in the content coincides with the interest in further developing the language skills. In that sense learning vocabulary becomes a pre-task activity in the spirit of task-based language learning. Organizing vocabulary learning in this way also helps turn the otherwise open-ended challenge of learning the lexical space of a new language to the clearly delineated task of mastering a sub-space. This functionally guided approach contrasts with the approach of other vocabulary learning tools selecting random infrequent lexical items from the language to be learned, which given their rare and often highly specialized nature are likely to only be useful for impressing friends when playing foreign language scrabble.

To make text-driven vocabulary learning work, we need to map the text selected by the learner into a structured domain to support systematic and efficient learning of the lexical space as used in the book. We distinguish the process of structuring the vocabulary used in the book, independent of the learner's background, from the representation of the individual learner's knowledge. The former is tackled in this section and can be regarded as our domain model, while the latter is a learner model that essentially is an overlay over the domain model, and will be discussed in section 3.

Since vocabulary learning is about establishing form-meaning connections, in principle the basic unit best suited for this would be word senses. At the same time, full automatic word sense disambiguation is complex, error prone, and often domain-specific – and in the context of a given book, a given word will often occur with the same meaning. We, therefore, limit ourselves to only disambiguating homographs in terms of their part-of-speech (POS), following Wilks and Stevenson (1998). Throughout our approach, we therefore use <word, POS> pairs as basic units. To POS annotate the book selected by the user, we use the Spacy NLP tools (http://spacy.io). Given our focus on learning the characteristic vocabulary of the book, we eliminate stop words as well as word-POS pairs appearing less than five times in the given book.

2.1 Semantic and thematic relations

To structure the lexical space in terms of meaning, there are two related options. Words can be semantically related, e.g., *tiger*, *elephant*, and *crocodile* all have the property of being wild animals; from the perspective of a WordNet, they are hyponyms of *wild animal*. On the other hand, words can also be thematically related, such as *blackboard*, *teacher*, and *chalk* all belonging to a school theme. Gholami and Khezrlou (2014) highlights the benefits of the semantic approach over the thematic approach from the perspective of a tutor. As we are building a system that acts as a tutor tracking and fostering the learner's vocabulary knowledge, we decided to focus on semantic relatedness.

2.1.1 Word families

Complementing the lexical semantic relationships, words are also related to each other through derivational and inflectional morphology. Many of these morphological processes are semantically transparent. Bauer and Nation (1993) proposed the idea of grouping words into so-called *word families* stating that "once the base word or even a derived word is known, the recognition of other members of the family requires little or no extra effort". The creation of word families is based on criteria involving frequency, regularity, productivity, and predictability of all the English affixes. Bauer and Nation (1993) arranged the inflectional affixes and common derivational affixes into the graded levels, as exemplified on the left-hand side of Figure 1.

2	develop develops developed developing	wood wood's woods wooded	bright brighter brightest
3	developable undevelopable developers(s) undeveloped	woody woodiest woodier woodiness	brightly brightish brightness
4	development(s) developmental developmentally		
5	developmentwise semideveloped antidevelopment	wooden	brighten
6	redeveloped predevelopment	anti-wooden	

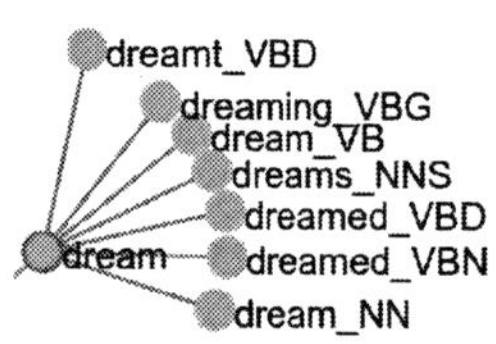

Figure 1: A word family example (Bauer and Nation, 1993) and an expanded family node in our graph

We adopt the idea of word families to compactly represent morphologically related words. The graph on the right side of Figure 1 exemplifies the word family that becomes visible when selecting the lemma *dream* in our graph representation (where word families normally are shown in collapsed form and represented by their underlying lemma). We currently put words up to level three, which generally will be transparently related, into one family – though in the future one could make this a parameter, which could also depend on the level of the learner.

2.2 Generating a lexical graph of word families and their semantic relations

To structure the lexical space of the user selected book in terms of a semantically related word graph, we start with a distributional semantic vector representation of each word, which we obtain from the pre-trained model of GloVe (Pennington et al., 2014) based on the co-occurrence statistics of the words form a large Common Crawl data-set (http://commoncrawl.org). Such word embeddings capture the distributional semantic properties of words (Goldberg and Levy, 2014).

On this basis, the relationship score between the families is computed to be the maximum pair-wise cosine similarity score of all its members. Let F_1 be a family with m members and F_2 be a family with n members. The relationship score between two families F_1 and F_2 is the maximum of cosine similarity score of all $m \times n$ pairs.

$$w_{12} = \max_{i \in F_1; j \in F_2} \frac{V_i * V_j}{\|V_i\| \|V_j\|}$$

where, w_{12} is the cosine similarity between the families F_1 and F_2

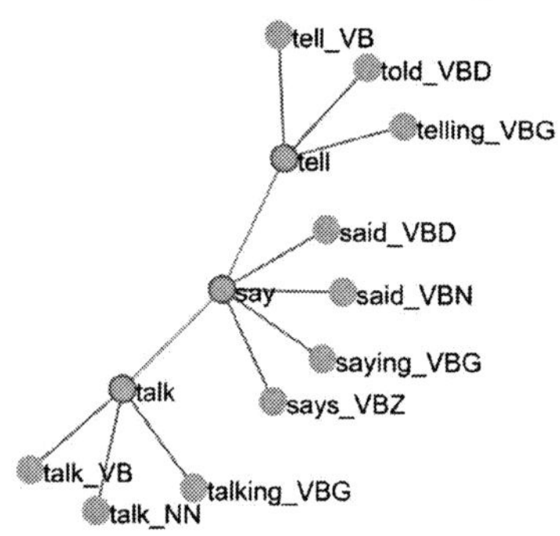

Figure 2: Formula for computing relationship between families and an example illustrating the result

The result is a network of word families, where families with members closer in the semantic vector space are connected with higher weights.

Following D'Angelo and West (1997), the number of edges in the graph can be computed as $e = \frac{n \times (n-1)}{2}$, where e is the total number of edges and n is the number of nodes (families) in the graph. The number of edges in the graph thus grows exponentially as the number of nodes increases.

When inspecting graphs derived for sample texts, we observe the majority of the connections are weak. To obtain a graph of semantic relationships that meaningfully structure the vocabulary used in a book, we focus on the stronger relationship and eliminate edges with weights less than 0.3.

We also observed that the node families of very frequently occurring verbs tend to be very densely connected, and this impact of frequency on distributional semantic measures has been discussed in the literature (Patel et al., 1998; Weeds et al., 2004). In order to control for this kind of over-sensitivity of distributional semantic measures for highly frequent words, we restrict the node degree to a maximum threshold. Based on experiments with sample data, only the five edges with the highest weight are retained for each node.

As a result of the method described in this section, we obtain a lexical graph for the user-provided text that structures and compactly represents the lexical space of the text in a graph-based domain model. This is the lexical space that the user wants to explore and master enough to be able to read the book. In terms of computational linguistic methods, on the one hand, distributional semantics creates the overall structure of a *meaning*-connected lexical space, on the other hand, word families organize and collapse *forms* that are related by morphological processes in the linguistic system.

2.3 Example generation of graphs for books

To test the graph construction, we chose three books as a sample to study the characteristics of the vocabulary space created by our application: (a) Twenty Thousand Leagues Under the Sea by Jules Verne, (b) Harry Potter and the Sorcerer's Stone by J. K. Rowling and (c) A Game of Thrones: A Song of Ice and Fire by George R. R. Martin.

	Unique words	Learning targets	Graph nodes	Graph edges
a)	10k	1.7k	1.3k	3.3k
b)	6.5k	1.2k	1k	2.4k
c)	14k	3.7k	2.5k	5.6k

Table 1: Example graphs derived for three books

Table 1 shows the size of the text and the graph created for each book. Selecting the <word, POS> pairs occurring at least five times in the entire text, we find that 15–25% of the words from the text qualifies as lexical learning targets. These targets are grouped into families as discussed in 2.1.1, with each family being represented as a node in the graph. The resulting set of graph nodes representing word families is 20-30% smaller than the initial set of learning targets. The families then are linked as explained in section 2.2. The average number of links a family has with other families is around 2.5.

Some example word family clusters formed for these books at a threshold of similarity scores greater than 0.7 are shown in Figure 3. Only the root nodes of each family are shown. The examples illustrate that the semantically close families form meaningfully interpretable clusters.

3 Representing the lexical knowledge of a learner: an open learner model

With a structured domain model established for the vocabulary space to be explored by the user, we want to make use of it to efficiently guide the learner to cover the space and track learning in a learner model. The learner model is an overlay on the domain model that helps us track the learner's vocabulary knowledge in terms of a mastery score associated with each word family. On the basis of the learner model, we then can propose the next set of words to be practiced in a way that reduces the number of interactions required to cover the vocabulary space. It also serves as an open learner model (Bull and Kay, 2010) by allowing the user to view and explore the lexical space of the book as a graph, with each node being colored according to the current mastery score. In this section, we discuss how this is achieved.

3.1 Central node selection for efficient exploration of the vocabulary graph

Identifying the nodes that are more central than others is one of the vital tasks in network analysis (Freeman, 1978; Bonacich, 1987; Borgatti, 2005; Borgatti and Everett, 2006). Freeman (1978) formulated three major centrality measures for a node in a network: (a) *degree centrality:* a measure of strength of ties of each nodes in the network, (b) *closeness centrality:* a measure of closeness of a node to all other nodes in the network, and (c) *betweenness centrality*: a measure of the number of elements of a set S, the set of shortest paths of other node pairs in the network passing through a node.

The degree centrality measure is a greedy approach looking only at the immediate neighbours to decide the central node, whereas the closeness centrality measure accounts for the bigger picture of the entire network. So closeness centrality seems best suited for our goal of efficient coverage of the network, in our case: the graph representing the vocabulary of the given book. While the basic

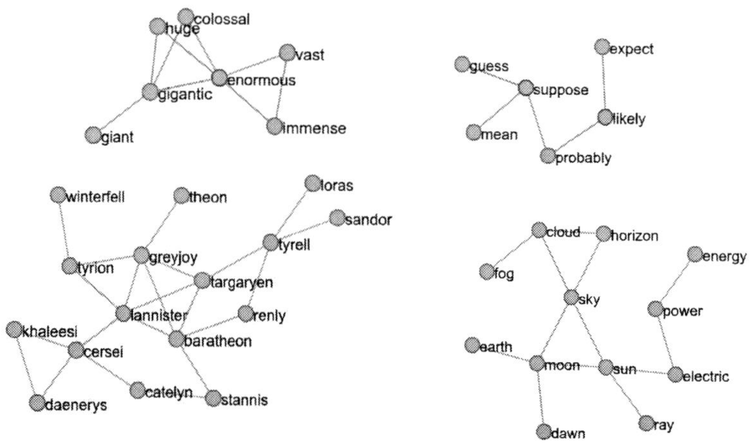

Figure 3: Example family clusters from the graphs resulting for the sample books

closeness centrality notion is only defined for fully connected networks, Wasserman et al. (1994) successfully extends it to apply to any graph. Based on this metric, we choose the top 20 (word family) nodes for a learning session and chose a word from each of those 20 families.[1]

Selecting the next words to be learned based on closeness centrality brings up the problem that neighbors that are tightly bound to the central node are likely to have a similar closeness centrality score. So when selecting the words to be practiced only based on closeness centrality, we would risk practicing closely related lexical items rather than systematically introducing the learner to the broader lexical space. In order to avoid this issue, we exclude the immediate neighbours of a word that was selected from that learning session. This supports a more distributed selection of words.

3.2 Mastery scores and updating them in the graph to capture learning

Each node in the graph is associated with a mastery score ranging from 0 to 1, with 1 indicating that the learner masters the word. We initialize the master score of each node with 0.5 and interpret this as a middle ground, where the model is uncertain about the learner's knowledge about that word.

The mastery score is updated based on the learner responses in the learning activities. To address the bottleneck that the system is tied to such a thin stream of evidence about the learner's lexical knowledge, we make use of the fact that the learner model is based on a network of semantically related word families. We use this to spread some activation from a word for which the learner has shown mastery to semantically closely related words to indicate that this word is more likely to also be known.

Let r be the learner response for a learning activity involving a word from the family F_i. Then the update to its mastery m_i is updated using $\Delta m_i = m_i * \alpha * r$. The update to the mastery score of its immediate neighbours is weighted based on the similarity score between the families $\Delta m_j = m_j * (\beta * r * w_{ij})$ where m_j is the mastery score of F_j, a neighbouring family of F_i attached with a edge weight of w_{ij}. α and β are tune-able parameters for the magnitude of an update.[2] $r \in \{-1, +1\}$ indicate the polarity of the learner's response, $+1$ for the learner responding correctly and -1 an incorrect response.

Figure 4 provides a close-up view of the graph with enlarged nodes highlighting the nodes selected for a learning activities. The figure also illustrates the color representation of the mastery level and the spreading activation to neighboring nodes. Initially, all nodes are grey, corresponding to a mastery level of 0.5. The closer the level gets to 1, the greener the node appears, and the closer to 0, the redder. A node the user has practiced with mixed success can result in a 0.5 level again, which then is shown in yellow to distinguish nodes that have already been practiced from the untouched grey ones.

[1] Currently, the word is randomly chosen from the words in the word family. One could consider selecting forms of particular relevance (e.g., irregular ones) or taking language use characteristics into account.

[2] We set both α and β to 0.3, which requires the least connected nodes to receive a minimum of two positive responses for them to count as mastered.

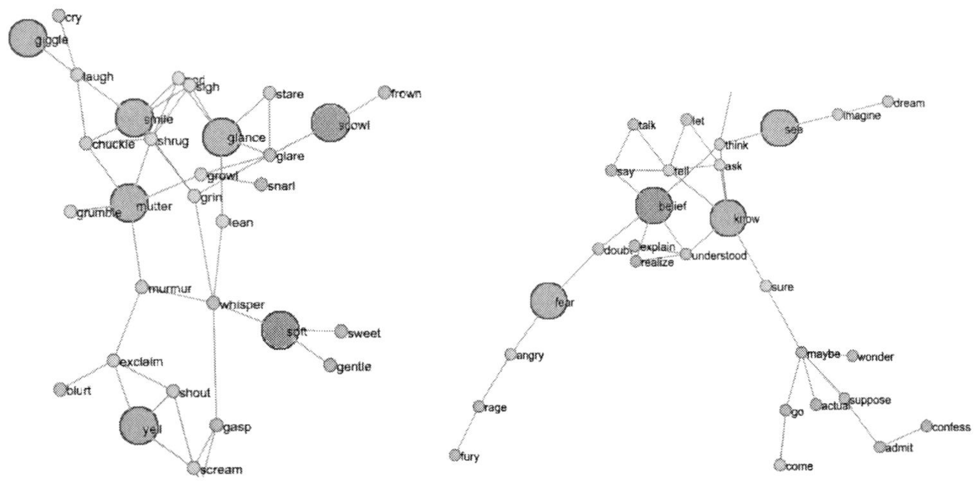

Figure 4: A close-up view of a learner model showing nodes selected for practice

While the colored visualization of the lexical space serves as an open learner model allowing learners to inspect the current state of their knowledge in relation to the lexical demands of the book, the mastery level also plays a role in selecting the next words to be practiced, with words over 0.8 no longer being selected. In the future, we plan to add a component that takes into account memory decay and the so-called spacing effect (Sense et al., 2016) to optimize when a word is selected again.

4 Putting it all together in an application

4.1 A warm start for the learner model

Given that we are targeting learners beyond the beginner stage, it is important to determine their vocabulary knowledge to avoid a cold start of the learner model. Starting from a blank slate would require many interactions with the system until the learner model reflects the learner's lexical competence – a time during which the system cannot optimally select the words to be learned next.

To avoid this cold start problem, we implemented a short web-based vocabulary Yes/No test, a format long used for vocabulary estimation (Sims, 1929; Tilley, 1936; Goulden et al., 1990). The participants see a checklist of words and select whether they know the word or not. While there is a rich literature on the test and adjustments have been proposed to counter its weaknesses as a competence diagnostic (Meara and Buxton, 1987; Beeckmans et al., 2001; Huibregtse et al., 2002; Mochida and Harrington, 2006), it readily enables learners to quickly initialize their learner model.

The words included in the test are selected from the graph using the same central node selection approach introduced in section 3.1, and the mechanism spreading activation to related nodes discussed in section 3.2 allows the system to make additional use of the information from the test.

4.2 Activity generation: practicing and testing in the target context

Content creation for vocabulary learning activities typically is a task requiring human effort so that adapting the material to individual learners' language competence and interests is beyond the reach of traditional methods. To overcome this limitation, we generate activities based on the target text for which the user wants to acquire the vocabulary. While there are multiple activity types one could consider, we implemented multi-gap activities (Zesch and Melamud, 2014), given that they make it possible for the learner to engage with a word using several sentence contexts drawn from the targeted book. Given the frequency threshold used in constructing the domain model graph, there are at least five sentences for each word in the book. We rank sentences to determine which sentences are best out of context. Fortunately, this issue has been addressed in lexicography, where authentic sentences are used in dictionaries to illustrate word usage. Kilgarriff et al. (2008) developed GDEX, a method to identify sentences that are well-suited to illustrate word meaning within a single sentence context. GDEX considers factors such as the sentence length, use of rare words and anaphora, target word occurrence in main clauses, sentence completeness, and target word collocations towards the end of sentences. Sentence length and rare word usage are the highly weighted features. We adapted GDEX for our purpose of ranking sentences for vocabulary activities and customized the rare word feature to reflect the individual learner's vocabulary knowledge as recorded in the learner model.

Learning and testing in the system are conducted in sessions. Each session consists of the top 20 central nodes from the learner model that are below the mastery score threshold. Multi-gap activities consisting of three to four sentences in which the target word chosen from the central node word family occurs are used for both learning and testing. The sentences are initially shown with the occurrences replaced by a blank. For each activity, four lexical options are provided: the target word and three distractors chosen from the book, as discussed below. Figure 5 shows an activity targeting the word family *scowl* in a learning session for the book "A Game of Thrones: A Song of Ice and Fire", after the correct word was selected by the learner.

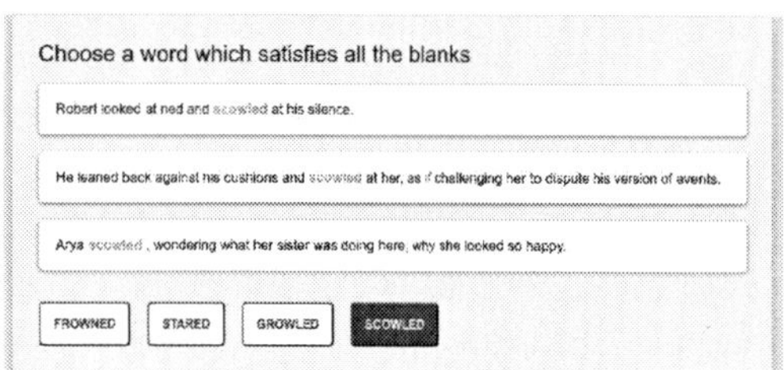

Figure 5: An example activity

In the learning mode, the learners are provided with learning aid such as dictionary lookup, translations, and word usage examples from within and outside the targeted book. The mastery scores in the learner model are not updated during training mode. In the testing mode, no such support is provided and the score for the target family and its neighbors is updated based on the user responses.

Distractor generation is a critical part of multi-gap learning activities. We are interested in distractors that require some cognitive effort to discriminate, actively engaging the learner with the choices in the different sentence contexts. Thus in the step of choosing distractors, morpho-syntactically appropriate forms are used to focus the choice on the meaning rather than grammatical surface cues. To identify challenging distractors, we select the appropriate forms from neighboring graph nodes. We empirically established that edge weights between 0.5 to 0.8 seems to be a suitably challenging distractor. This avoids synonyms that are too closely related to be distinguishable from the target, but also semantically unrelated words that are too easy to rule out. The edge weight for nodes that are not immediate neighbors is computed as the product of the edge weights connecting the nodes. Often the best distractors turn out to be two hops away. We are considering combining such a distractor generation based on the domain model with other strategies discussed by Zesch and Melamud (2014).

5 Evaluation

To empirically evaluate the approach, we first want to establish that it works as described. There are a number of components and parameters involved in generating the graph, selecting the nodes to be practiced, and updating the learner model. So we ran experiments with simulated users who performed the activities at different levels of accuracy. In addition to a a cold-start setting, where the system initially knows nothing about the learner, we also performed warm-start simulations for users at different proficiency levels. As a second step, we envisage conducting studies with language learners in authentic learning contexts. Testing educational tools in real-life contexts is crucial for establishing that an approach is effective in the complex authentic education contexts with the rich set of cognitive, motivational, and social variables at stake there. While in Meurers et al. (2019) we illustrate the feasibility of conducting such randomized controlled field studies, this clearly is an endeavor of its own, beyond the scope of this paper.

In the first set of experiments, we cold start the system with the learner model set to the default .5 chance level for every word family, and we simulated learners with performance levels of 60%, 70%, 80%, 90%, and 100%. As baseline approach for comparison, we include a traditional flashcard setup tackling words in a linear fashion, one by one, where each word is independent of the other words. Throughout, we assume that mastery is achieved when a word has reached .8 or more.

Table 2 shows the number of learning sessions, each consisting of 20 words, that the user would need to complete to fully master all learning targets in the given books in our and the baseline setup. We see that under the 100% accuracy condition, where the learner successfully completes each activity they work on, the baseline approach requires

Learning targets		Setup	# of sessions given accuracy rate of 100%	90%	80%	70%	60%
a)	1.7k	our	85	100	120	195	1280
		baseline	170	235	340	650	3150
b)	1.2k	our	65	75	90	140	735
		baseline	120	165	245	475	2490
c)	3.7k	our	165	190	240	395	2850
		baseline	370	505	745	1390	7230

Table 2: Number of interactions required to master the vocabulary for simulated learners at given accuracy rate

exactly twice the number of learning targets when compared to our graph based approach spreading the activation to semantically related words and taking semantically transparent word families into account. The difference becomes even more pronounced when the accuracy for completing the activities is set to more realistic levels between 60 and 90%. Note the steep increase in the number of sessions needed by learners performing exercises with only 60% accuracy. This showcases that the ability to interpret lexical material in context, based on an understanding of the domain of the book from which the exercises are drawn, is important for determining which book one can successfully prepare for. Overall, while the simulation experiments clearly are based on a very simple model of learning, the observations reported should carry over to more sophisticated learning models in which initial learning gains are higher than later ones and also modeling forgetting of what has been learned.

In the second set of experiments, we assume an accuracy of 90% and instead consider the effect of proficiency differences as indicated by the learner's CEFR level. Instead of simulating the web-based book-specific vocabulary test we implemented as discussed in section 4.1, we base are simulation experiments on Meara and Milton's estimation of the knowledge of the most frequent 5000 lemmatized English words for learners at different CEFR levels as reported in Milton and Alexiou (2009). Simplifying their estimates for the number of known words distributed over the frequency bands to the upper bound given for the number of words learned in the first four proficiency levels (A1: 1500, A2: 2500, B1: 3250, B2: 3750), we started the simulation by setting the mastery score of those nodes to 0.75 for which the head word of the family occurs frequently enough (as determined by reference to SUBTLEX-US; Brysbaert and New, 2009) to be included in the set for the given proficiency level. The learner model thus encodes that the learner is likely to know the word, but the positive bias alone is not sufficient to cross the 0.8 level indicating mastery so that additional evidence is required to mark them as known. Table 3 sums up the results of the second set of experiments.

Learning targets		Setup	# of sessions at given proficiency A1	A2	B1	B2
a)	1.7k	our	80	75	69	68
		baseline	175	147	139	123
b)	1.2k	our	54	47	43	42
		baseline	92	77	72	70
c)	3.7k	our	169	157	149	142
		baseline	421	380	376	357

Table 3: Number of interactions required to master the vocabulary for simulated learners with 90% accuracy when starting out at the specified proficiency level

For example, an A2 learner only needs 47 sessions to master the learning targets for book b) assuming an accuracy of 90% in completing the exercises, whereas in the cold start condition we saw in Table 2, one would need 75 sessions. The number of sessions estimated for this warm-start condition seems realistic for using the approach in practice, especially considering that one naturally does not need to learn all of the words to be able to read a book (Schmitt et al., 2011).

6 Related work

While the experimental evaluation provides some insights into the practical viability of the approach, given the conceptual nature of our proposal, we here also contextualize and compare the approach with related work to discuss where it conceptually advances the state of the art. Our approach can be characterized by the following aspects: First, the user can select what they want to learn the vocabulary for; they pick the text of the book they want to be able to read, i.e., the functional task goal. Second, the system automatically creates a domain model graph representing the lexical semantic space to be learned. Third, a learner model is created as an overlay of the domain model graph and records the mastery of the concepts by the learner, with updates to the learner model spreading activation through the graph to indirectly activate related concepts as a way to avoid explicit interaction for every word. Fourth, it determines in which order the words can be learned in such a way that the lexical space is efficiently explored, prioritizing the words that are central nodes. Fifth, the system compactly represents word families to allow the visualization and open learner model to be concise and usable with minimal number of interactions. Sixth, the system supports learning of the words using multi-gap activities using sentences drawn from the actual book to be read.

Putting this approach into context of the related work on vocabulary learning, there is a large number of applications designed to support vocabulary learning – though, as we will see, the above characteristics clearly seem to set our approach apart from what is offered in this domain.

Foreign language textbooks systematically provide a list of vocabulary items per chapter and there are many specialized or general file card applications for memorizing these sentences including *Phase-6.de*, *Quizlet.com*, or *Ankiweb.net*. Other tools offer more language-related functionality.

Lextutor (https://lextutor.ca) is a website offering a collection of tools to learn vocabulary using lexical resources such as frequency-based vocabulary lists and corpus data. *List learn* supports learners in choosing words from frequency-based word lists and working with corpus concordances. *Grouplex* lets the learner select from a 2k crowd-sourced word list and practice them in fill-in-the-blank activities, with hints based on dictionary definition and POS tags. *Flash* employs cards showing words on one side and lexical support on the other. Apart from word meaning and usage, *MorphoLex* supports learning regular inflectional and derivational affixes based on the word family levels of Bauer and Nation (1993). Other lextutor tools target reading texts with support from concordances and dictionaries. *Resource assisted reading* lets the user choose a pre-processed book, but *Hyper text* allows the learner to upload their text. While Lextutor offers a variety of tools and corpus resources, none of them offer personalized learning, performance tracking, or structured vocabulary spaces.

Memrise.com is a commercial flashcard-based vocabulary learning application focused on beginners, with learning units grouped by theme with little freedom for the learner to choose contents of interest. *Duolingo.com* is a strictly guided application supporting the users to learn a foreign language using various learning activities offering some gamification elements but no personalized vocabulary learning for texts or domains of personal interest. *Vocabulary.com* is a gamified free vocabulary list learning application that lets learners choose from collections and the literature to practice the words in multiple-choice questions activities to choose the correct meaning phrase for the given word usage. The literature only is a source of vocabulary though, it is not used as testing context or learning goal, and the vocabulary domain is not semantically structured or to construct a structured learner model. *Cabuu.app* supports learning of vocabulary lists scanned from books by associating each item with gestures.

Overall, while there is a rich landscape of applications supporting vocabulary learning, the six characteristics of the method presented in this paper set our approach apart – especially the use of distributional semantic methods to create a graph representation for any book or text the user wants to read, to efficiently organize and individually support and track the learning in this lexical space.

7 Conclusion

In this paper, we discussed the methodological basis and realization of a tool allowing the learner to systematically learn the lexical material needed to be able to read a book they are interested in. Automatically structuring the lexical space and sequencing the learning is achieved through distributional semantic methods, the automatic identification of word families, and concepts from network analysis. The graph-based domain model that is automatically derived from the given book serves as the foundation of a learner model supporting the selection of an efficient learning path through the lexical space to be acquired. Multi-gap activities are automatically generated from the targeted book and used for practice and testing activities.

In addition to self-guided learning for people interested in reading specific books, which may be particularly useful in the context of so-called intensive reading programs, the approach is particularly well-suited for the English for Specific Purposes context, where both the language and the particular content domain are of direct importance. Given this kind of integration of language and content learning, a similar affinity exists to so-called Content and Language Integrated Learning (Coyle et al., 2010).

Acknowledgements

We would like to thank Himanshu Bansal for his contribution to the initial stages of this project, and we are grateful to the reviewers for the helpful suggestions and pointers they provided.

References

Laurie Bauer and Paul Nation. 1993. Word families. *International Journal of Lexicography*, 6(4):253–279.

Renaud Beeckmans, June Eyckmans, Vera Janssens, Michel Dufranne, and Hans Van de Velde. 2001. Examining the yes/no vocabulary test: Some methodological issues in theory and practice. *Language Testing*, 18(3):235–274.

Phillip Bonacich. 1987. Power and centrality: A family of measures. *American Journal of Sociology*, 92(5):1170–1182.

Stephen P. Borgatti. 2005. Centrality and network flow. *Social Networks*, 27(1):55–71.

Stephen P. Borgatti and Martin G. Everett. 2006. A graph-theoretic perspective on centrality. *Social Networks*, 28(4):466–484.

Marc Brysbaert and Boris New. 2009. Moving beyond Kučera and Francis: A critical evaluation of current word frequency norms and the introduction of a new and improved word frequency measure for American English. *Behavior Research Methods*, 41(4):977–990.

Susan Bull and Judy Kay. 2010. Open learner models. In R. Nkambou, J. Bourdeau, and R. Mizoguchi, editors, *Advances in intelligent tutoring systems*, pages 301–322. Springer.

Maria Chinkina and Detmar Meurers. 2016. Linguistically-aware information retrieval: Providing input enrichment for second language learners. In *Proceedings of the 11th Workshop on Innovative Use of NLP for Building Educational Applications (BEA)*, pages 188–198, San Diego, CA. ACL.

Do Coyle, Philip Hood, and David Marsh. 2010. *Content and language integrated learning*. Ernst Klett Sprachen.

John P. D'Angelo and Douglas B. West. 1997. Mathematical thinking. *Problem Solving and Proofs*.

Rod Ellis. 2009. Task-based language teaching: Sorting out the misunderstandings. *International Journal of Applied Linguistics*, 19(3):221–246.

Linton C. Freeman. 1978. Centrality in social networks conceptual clarification. *Social Networks*, 1(3):215–239.

Javad Gholami and Sima Khezrlou. 2014. Semantic and thematic list learning of second language vocabulary. *CATESOL Journal*, 25(1):151–162.

Robert Godwin-Jones. 2019. Riding the digital wilds: Learner autonomy and informal language learning. *Language Learning & Technology*, 23(1):8–25.

Yoav Goldberg and Omer Levy. 2014. word2vec explained: Deriving Mikolov et al.'s negative-sampling word-embedding method. *arXiv preprint arXiv:1402.3722*.

Robin Goulden, Paul Nation, and John Read. 1990. How large can a receptive vocabulary be? *Applied Linguistics*, 11(4):341–363.

Ineke Huibregtse, Wilfried Admiraal, and Paul Meara. 2002. Scores on a yes-no vocabulary test: Correction for guessing and response style. *Language Testing*, 19(3):227–245.

Adam Kilgarriff, Milos Husák, Katy McAdam, Michael Rundell, and Pavel Rychlý. 2008. Gdex: Automatically finding good dictionary examples in a corpus. In *Proceedings of the XIII EURALEX international congress*, pages 425–432. Universitat Pompeu Fabra Barcelona, Spain.

Paul Meara and Barbara Buxton. 1987. An alternative to multiple choice vocabulary tests. *Language Testing*, 4(2):142–154.

Detmar Meurers, Kordula De Kuthy, Florian Nuxoll, Björn Rudzewitz, and Ramon Ziai. 2019. Scaling up intervention studies to investigate real-life foreign language learning in school. *Annual Review of Applied Linguistics*, 39:161–188.

James Milton and Thomaï Alexiou. 2009. Vocabulary size and the Common European Framework of Reference for languages. In *Vocabulary studies in first and second language acquisition*, pages 194–211. Springer.

Kira Mochida and Michael Harrington. 2006. The yes/no test as a measure of receptive vocabulary knowledge. *Language Testing*, 23(1):73–98.

Malti Patel, John A Bullinaria, and Joseph P Levy. 1998. Extracting semantic representations from large text corpora. In *4th Neural Computation and Psychology Workshop, London, 9–11 April 1997*, pages 199–212. Springer.

Jeffrey Pennington, Richard Socher, and Christopher D. Manning. 2014. Glove: Global vectors for word representation. In *Proceedings of the 2014 Conference on Empirical Methods in Natural Language Processing (EMNLP)*, pages 1532–1543.

Norbert Schmitt, Xiangying Jiang, and William Grabe. 2011. The percentage of words known in a text and reading comprehension. *The Modern Language Journal*, 95(1):26–43.

Florian Sense, Friederike Behrens, Rob R. Meijer, and Hedderik van Rijn. 2016. An individual's rate of forgetting is stable over time but differs across materials. *Topics in Cognitive Science*, 8(1):305–321.

Verner Martin Sims. 1929. The reliability and validity of four types of vocabulary tests. *The Journal of Educational Research*, 20(2):91–96.

Harvey C. Tilley. 1936. A technique for determining the relative difficulty of word meanings among elementary school children. *The Journal of Experimental Education*, 5(1):61–64.

Stanley Wasserman, Katherine Faust, et al. 1994. *Social network analysis: Methods and applications*. Cambridge University Press.

Julie Weeds, David Weir, and Diana McCarthy. 2004. Characterising measures of lexical distributional similarity. In *Proceedings of the 20th International Conference on Computational Linguistics (COLING)*, pages 1015–1021.

Yorick Wilks and Mark Stevenson. 1998. The grammar of sense: Using part-of-speech tags as a first step in semantic disambiguation. *Natural Language Engineering*, 4(2):135–143.

Jane Willis and David Willis. 2013. *Doing task-based teaching*. Oxford University Press.

Torsten Zesch and Oren Melamud. 2014. Automatic generation of challenging distractors using context-sensitive inference rules. In *Proceedings of the Ninth Workshop on Innovative Use of NLP for Building Educational Applications (BEA)*, pages 143–148, Baltimore, Maryland. Association for Computational Linguistics.

Synthetic Data Generation for Grammatical Error Correction with Tagged Corruption Models

Felix Stahlberg and Shankar Kumar
Google Research
{fstahlberg, shankarkumar}@google.com

Abstract

Synthetic data generation is widely known to boost the accuracy of neural grammatical error correction (GEC) systems, but existing methods often lack diversity or are too simplistic to generate the broad range of grammatical errors made by human writers. In this work, we use error type tags from automatic annotation tools such as ERRANT to guide synthetic data generation. We compare several models that can produce an ungrammatical sentence given a clean sentence and an error type tag. We use these models to build a new, large synthetic pre-training data set with error tag frequency distributions matching a given development set. Our synthetic data set yields large and consistent gains, improving the state-of-the-art on the BEA-19 and CoNLL-14 test sets. We also show that our approach is particularly effective in adapting a GEC system, trained on mixed native and non-native English, to a native English test set, even surpassing real training data consisting of high-quality sentence pairs.

1 Introduction

Grammatical error correction (GEC) systems aim to automatically correct grammatical and other types of writing errors in text. It is common to view this problem as a sequence-to-sequence task (i.e. ungrammatical sentence → grammatical sentence) and borrow models that were originally developed for neural machine translation (NMT) (Chollampatt and Ng, 2018; Junczys-Dowmunt et al., 2018; Ge et al., 2018b). Back-translation (Sennrich et al., 2016) is a synthetic data generation technique for NMT that employs a translation system trained in the reverse direction to synthesize source sentences from sentences in the target language, and is still one of the most effective strategies to use monolingual data in NMT training. Similarly, synthetic training data generation for GEC has also been widely studied in the literature (Brockett et al., 2006; Foster and Andersen, 2009; Rozovskaya and Roth, 2010; Felice et al., 2014; Rei et al., 2017; Kasewa et al., 2018; Xie et al., 2018; Ge et al., 2018a,b; Kiyono et al., 2019; Lichtarge et al., 2019; Stahlberg and Byrne, 2019; Zhao et al., 2019; Xu et al., 2019; Grundkiewicz et al., 2019; Choe et al., 2019; Takahashi et al., 2020). This work is inspired by previous efforts to use ideas from back-translation for GEC (Kasewa et al., 2018; Xie et al., 2018; Kiyono et al., 2019). In contrast to prior work, we use error type tags such as `SPELL` (spelling error) or `SVA` (subject-verb agreement error) to control the output of our corruption models and generate more realistic as well as diverse grammatical errors. Our tagged corruption models are trained to output the corrupted sentence given a clean sentence and an error tag, e.g.:

> "`NOUN:INFL` There were a lot of sheep."
> → "There were a lot of sheeps."

The tags mitigate the tendency of untagged corruption models to produce simplistic corruptions since many error type tags require more complex rewrites. In general, there is a one-to-many mapping from a clean sentence to a noisy sentence. Using a regular corruption model, many of these synthetic errors tend to be simplistic,[1] but adding tag information allows the model to generate specific patterns of errors that can be found in actual GEC corpora. The benefit of covering a wide range of error types when generating pseudo data for GEC has also been demonstrated by Takahashi et al. (2020); Wan et al. (2020). Moreover, the tag distribution in the synthetic data can be made to match the distribution of a specific target domain. We use this distribution matching technique to adapt a GEC system to better correct errors by native speakers.

[1]Example outputs from untagged and tagged corruption models can be found in Appendix B.

Proceedings of the 16th Workshop on Innovative Use of NLP for Building Educational Applications, pages 37–47
April 20, 2021 ©2021 Association for Computational Linguistics

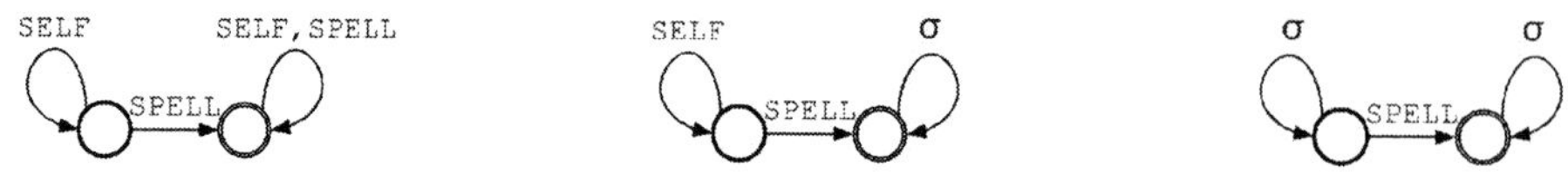

(a) NoSigma (b) PostSigma (c) PrePostSigma

Figure 1: Constraining FSTs for the SPELL tag. The σ-self loops can match any tag. SELF is used by Seq2Edits to mark source spans that are not modified.

As an alternative to adding the tag directly to the input sequence, we add inference-time constraints to the recently proposed Seq2Edits model (Stahlberg and Kumar, 2020) to force the generation of a particular tag. We implement such constraints using Finite State Transducers (FSTs). We then use these corruption models to generate synthetic training data that follows a desired tag distribution, for example the tag distribution on the development set. Using our new synthetic pretraining sets[2] we report state-of-the-art results on two popular GEC test sets (BEA-test: 74.9 $F_{0.5}$, CoNLL-14: 68.3 $F_{0.5}$). In our experiments on GEC for native English, a model fine-tuned on synthetic data that follows a native English error-tag distribution can even surpass a model fine-tuned on high-quality, real (i.e. non-synthetic) data.

2 Tagged Corruption Models

At the core of our approach is a model that generates an ungrammatical sentence from a clean sentence given an error tag $t \in \mathcal{T}$ that describes the desired type of error. $\mathcal{T}$ is the set of 25 error type tags supported by the automatic annotation toolkit ERRANT (Felice et al., 2016; Bryant et al., 2017).

A straightforward way to train such a tagged corruption model is to annotate a parallel corpus with ERRANT, prepend the ERRANT tag to the clean sentence, and train a model such as a standard Transformer (Vaswani et al., 2017) to generate the ungrammatical sentence.[3] This idea is similar to the multi-lingual NMT system of Johnson et al. (2017) that adds the target language ID tag to the source sentence.

Alternatively, the recently proposed Seq2Edits[4] (Stahlberg and Kumar, 2020) model is able to directly predict error tags along with the edits, and does not need to be provided error tags in the input sequence. Instead, during beam search we constrain the tag output tape of Seq2Edits with an FST that forces the generation of a certain tag. Fig. 1 illustrates three types of constraint FSTs with the example tag, SPELL. All FSTs require at least one occurrence of the SPELL tag. NoSigma (Fig. 1a) is the most restrictive constraint as it only allows SPELL and SELF (used by Seq2Edits for unmodified source spans). PostSigma (Fig. 1b) allows other tags after SPELL, but constrains the hypothesis to start with either SELF or SPELL to prevent beam search from committing to a corruption that

Tag	Log-prob.	Corruption model output
ADJ	-3.06	There were a lot of many sheep.
ADJ:FORM	-2.49	There were a more better of sheep.
ADV	-2.63	There were a lot of sheep there.
CONJ	-1.39	And there were a lot of sheep.
CONTR	-0.90	There're a lot of sheep.
DET	-1.06	There were lot of sheep.
K	-1.45	There were a lot of.
MORPH	-0.67	There were a lot of sheeps.
NOUN	-3.31	There were a lot of seep.
NOUN:INFL	-0.61	There were a lot of sheeps.
NOUN:NUM	-1.33	There were a lots of sheep.
NOUN:POSS	-0.92	There were a lot of sheep's.
ORTH	-0.79	There were alot of sheep.
OTHER	-2.60	There were many sheep.
PART	-1.22	There were a lot off sheep.
PREP	-1.08	There were a lot sheep.
PRON	-1.55	It was a lot of sheep.
PUNCT	-1.00	There were a lot of sheep
SPELL	-2.79	There were a lot of sheeps.
VERB	-2.58	There had a lot of sheep.
VERB:FORM	-2.34	There being a lot of sheep.
VERB:INFL	-1.09	There were a lot of sheeps.
VERB:SVA	-0.44	There was a lot of sheep.
VERB:TENSE	-0.57	There are a lot of sheep.
WO	-1.87	There were a lot sheep of.

Table 1: Outputs of a tagged Seq2Edits corruption model for the example input sentence "There were a lot of sheep.". The ERRANT error type tags are described in Bryant et al. (2017).

[2]The data set will be made publicly available.

[3]If a sentence pair has multiple tags we duplicate it in the training set for each unique tag. This potentially enables the corruption model to learn co-occurrences of error categories since multiple errors may be labelled with a single tag.

[4]A short description of the Seq2Edits model is provided in Appendix A for convenience.

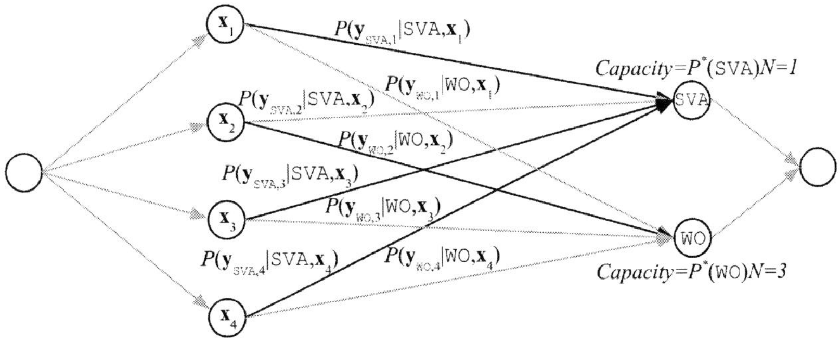

Figure 2: The minimum-cost flow graph of the *Offline-Optimal* method for a training set of $N = 4$ sentences, two error type tags (SVA: subject-verb agreement, and WO: word order) and the desired tag distribution $P^*(\texttt{SVA}) = 0.25$ and $P^*(\texttt{WO}) = 0.75$. Each sentence is represented by a node on the left side with a flow capacity of one. Each tag is represented by a node on the right side with a capacity equal to the absolute number of sentences for each tag $P^*(t)N$. Arcs connecting sentences and tags are weighted by the corruption model score $P(\mathbf{y}_{t,n}|t, \mathbf{x}_n)$. A possible flow through the graph is highlighted in orange, this assigns the WO tag to the sentences $\mathbf{x}_1$, $\mathbf{x}_3$, $\mathbf{x}_4$ and the SVA tag to the sentence $\mathbf{x}_2$.

is incompatible with SPELL.[5] PREPOSTSIGMA (Fig. 1c) allows other tags both before and after SPELL.

Table 1 lists example outputs of a tagged Seq2Edits corruption model for all 25 ERRANT tags and demonstrates the model's capability to generate a broad variety of realistic errors.

3 Synthetic Data Generation with Tagged Corruption Models

For a grammatical input sentence $\mathbf{x}_n$ ($n \in [1, N]$ where N is the training set size), we denote the corrupted sentence according to the tag $t \in \mathcal{T}$ as $\mathbf{y}_{t,n}$. Our goal is to assign a single tag t_n^* to each training sentence such that the overall distribution follows a certain desired tag distribution $P^*(t)$:

$$\forall t \in \mathcal{T} : P^*(t) \approx \frac{|\{t_n^* = t | n \in [1, N]\}|}{N} \quad (1)$$

We compare three different methods: *Offline-Optimal*, *Offline-Probabilistic*, and *Online*.

Offline-Optimal The *Offline-Optimal* method frames this task as a constrained optimization problem:

$$\max_{\mathbf{t}^*} \sum_{n=1}^{N} \log P(\mathbf{y}_{t_n^*,n} | t_n^*, \mathbf{x}_n) \quad (2)$$

under the constraint that the observed distribution of tags matches the desired distribution, i.e. Eq. 1 is satisfied. Fig. 2 illustrates that this is an instance of a well-studied problem called maximum weighted bipartite matching (Schrijver, 2003) and can be solved efficiently with a standard minimum-cost flow solver.

Offline-Probabilistic The intuition behind the *Offline-Probabilistic* method is to first draw a tag according to the desired tag distribution $P^*(t)$ and then sample sentences which are most likely to contain this tag, i.e. draw N sentences from the distribution $P((\mathbf{x}, \mathbf{y})|t)$.

$$P((\mathbf{x}, \mathbf{y})|t) = \frac{P(\mathbf{x}, \mathbf{y})P(t|\mathbf{x}, \mathbf{y})}{\sum_{n=1}^{N} P(\mathbf{x}_n, \mathbf{y}_n)P(t|\mathbf{x}_n, \mathbf{y}_n)} = \frac{P(t|\mathbf{x}, \mathbf{y})}{\sum_{n=1}^{N} P(t|\mathbf{x}_n, \mathbf{y}_n)},$$

where we assume each sentence-pair has the same probability $P(\mathbf{x}, \mathbf{y}) = \frac{1}{N}$.

$$P(t|(\mathbf{x}, \mathbf{y})) = \frac{P(t, \mathbf{x}, \mathbf{y})}{P(\mathbf{x}, \mathbf{y})} = \frac{P(\mathbf{x})P(t|\mathbf{x})P(\mathbf{y}|t, \mathbf{x})}{P(\mathbf{x}, \mathbf{y})} \approx \frac{\frac{1}{N}\frac{1}{|\mathcal{T}|}P(\mathbf{y}|t, \mathbf{x})}{\frac{1}{N}} = \frac{1}{|\mathcal{T}|}P(\mathbf{y}|t, \mathbf{x}),$$

where we assume that a) each sample has equal probability i.e. $P(\mathbf{x}) \approx P(\mathbf{x}, \mathbf{y}) = \frac{1}{N}$, b) each tag is equally likely given the source sentence, $P(t|\mathbf{x}) = \frac{1}{|\mathcal{T}|}$, where $|\mathcal{T}|$ is the size of the tag

[5] An example of this garden-path problem would be a subject-verb-agreement (SVA) constraint, but all active hypotheses in the beam already contain an adjective error and the correct subject and verb (e.g.: "SVA He owns a large bike with tiny wheels" → "He owns a wide bike with...").

Data set	Synthetic	Number of sentences	Used for
WikiEdits (Lichtarge et al., 2019)	No	170M	Pre-training
RoundTripGerman (Lichtarge et al., 2019)	Yes	176M	Pre-training
Lang-8 (Mizumoto et al., 2011)	No	1.9M	Stage 1 fine-tuning
FCE-train (Yannakoudakis et al., 2011)	No	26K	Stage 2 fine-tuning
BEA-train (Bryant et al., 2019)	No	34K	Stage 2 fine-tuning
This work: $C4_{200M}$	Yes	200M	Pre-training

Table 2: Training data sets used in this work.

vocabulary. $P(\mathbf{y}|t,\mathbf{x})$ is the probability assigned by the corruption model to the target sequence $\mathbf{y}$ given the source $\mathbf{x}$ and tag t.

Unlike the *Offline-Optimal* approach, this method does not guarantee that each sentence from the original training set will be included in the sample. However, this may not matter in practice when drawing from a large pool of examples.

Online A major limitation that prevents the *Offline-Optimal* and *Offline-Probabilistic* methods from scaling up efficiently is that we need to run the corruption model for every combination of tag and source sentence ($\Omega(N|\mathcal{T}|)$ runtime).[6] The *Online* method avoids this computational complexity by drawing the tag t_n^* for each example from the desired tag distribution $P^*(\cdot)$, and then generating the target $\mathbf{y}_n$ given the source $\mathbf{x}_n$ and tag t_n^*.

$$\forall n \in [1, N] : t_n^* \sim P^*. \quad (3)$$

Thus, it does not rely on the corruption model probabilities. The *Online* method assigns tags on-the-fly to each sentence independently and hence runs in $\Theta(N)$.

4 Results

For comparability to related work, we report span-based ERRANT $F_{0.5}$-scores on the development and test sets (BEA-dev and BEA-test) of the BEA-2019 shared task (Bryant et al., 2019). We use the M2 scorer (Dahlmeier and Ng, 2012) to compute $F_{0.5}$-scores on the CoNLL-13 (Ng et al., 2013) and CoNLL-14 (Ng et al., 2013) sets, and the GLEU metric (Napoles et al., 2015) on JFLEG-dev and JFLEG-test (Napoles et al., 2017).

4.1 Training Setup

All our grammar *correction* models are standard Seq2Seq (*not* Seq2Edits) Transformers (Vaswani et al., 2017) trained with Adafactor (Shazeer and Stern, 2018) using the Tensor2Tensor (Vaswani et al., 2018) TensorFlow (Abadi et al., 2015) library. Our *corruption* models are either standard Transformers or Seq2Edits models (Stahlberg and Kumar, 2020).[7] We use a Tensor2Tensor joint 32K subword vocabulary and the 'Big' hyper-parameter set for all our models. For our tagged corruption models we extend the subword vocabulary by the 25 ERRANT error tags.

We use both existing and new data sets to train our models (Table 2). WikiEdits and RoundTripGerman are large but noisy pre-training sets described by Lichtarge et al. (2019). In this work we introduce a new synthetic pre-training corpus – $C4_{200M}$ – that we generated by applying our corruption methods to 200M sentences sampled randomly from the Colossal Clean Crawled Corpus (Raffel et al., 2020, C4).[8] Our final *correction* models are trained using the two stage fine-tuning recipe of Lichtarge et al. (2020): after pre-training we first fine-tune on Lang-8 (Mizumoto et al., 2011) and then on BEA+FCE which is the combination of the FCE corpus (Yannakoudakis et al., 2011) and the training split of the Cambridge English Write & Improve corpus used in the BEA-2019 shared task (Bryant et al., 2019). Our *corruption* models are trained using a similar setup but do not use $C4_{200M}$ in pre-training. In our ablation experiments, however, we modify specific stages of this training pipeline to gain more insight into our methods.

4.2 Synthetic vs. Real Parallel Data

In initial experiments (Tables 3 to 5) we explore how well our synthetic data generation methods can replace real parallel data. The corruption models used in this section are fine-tuned on Lang-8 but not on BEA+FCE. The seed correction model is pre-trained on WikiEdits and RoundTripGerman and fine-tuned on Lang-8. We discard the source sentences in BEA+FCE, replace them with synthetic

[6]We ignore the runtime of beam search when describing the asymptotic time complexity for simplification.

[7]The focus of our work was to examine techniques for synthetic data correction while keeping the *correction* model fixed. Hence, we do not use Seq2Edits models for *correction*.

[8]We filtered C4 with language ID and removed sentences longer than 250 words before selecting the 200M sentences.

Corruption model	Constraint	Tagged input?	Offline-Optimal P	Offline-Optimal R	Offline-Optimal $F_{0.5}$	Offline-Probabilistic P	Offline-Probabilistic R	Offline-Probabilistic $F_{0.5}$	Online P	Online R	Online $F_{0.5}$
a Full sequence	-	✓	54.5	16.7	37.5	51.0	20.7	39.4	53.5	18.5	38.8
b Seq2Edits	NoSigma		57.2	21.8	43.2	57.1	25.6	45.8	57.5	26.4	46.6
c Seq2Edits	PostSigma		56.5	21.6	42.7	56.6	25.7	45.6	59.4	27.2	48.0
d Seq2Edits	PrePostSigma		56.3	22.4	43.3	55.7	25.5	45.0	53.0	30.6	46.2
e Seq2Edits	-	✓	55.3	26.7	45.5	55.6	25.9	45.2	54.4	29.0	46.3

Table 3: *Tagged* synthetic data generation where tags are chosen according to the BEA-dev tag distribution. The GEC seed model (Table 4a) is fine-tuned on BEA+FCE with synthetic source sentences and evaluated on the BEA-dev set. Rows **a** and **e** prepend the desired tag to the input sequence while rows **b-d** use FST constraints.

	GEC data (2. fine-tuning) Source	Target	BEA-dev P	R	$F_{0.5}$
a	N/A (Seed model)		57.0	12.8	33.7
b	Real data	BEA+FCE	56.5	35.2	50.4
c	Synthetic (Full seq.)	BEA+FCE	57.6	20.6	42.4
d	Synthetic (Seq2Edits)	BEA+FCE	53.4	20.6	40.5

Table 4: *Untagged* synthetic data generation. The seed GEC model (row **a**) is fine-tuned on BEA+FCE target sentences that are either paired with the real source sentences (row **b**) or with back-translated source sentences using either a full sequence Transformer (row **c**) or a Seq2Edits (row **d**) corruption model.

System	Test set ($F_{0.5}$) A2	B2	C2	N2
Baselines				
a Seed model	37.6	34.1	31.4	22.2
b FT on real data	**50.3**	**51.5**	**44.1**	42.1
Synthetic data using target tag distributions $P^*(t)$				
c CEFR-A (A1)	47.4	46.2	39.0	39.0
d CEFR-B (B1)	47.1	46.0	40.9	38.0
e CEFR-C (C1)	47.1	46.2	37.1	39.1
f Native (N1)	47.8	49.2	42.8	**42.9**

Table 5: Adapting GEC to non-native or native English. In rows **c-f** the GEC seed model (row **a**) is fine-tuned on BEA+FCE with source sentences synthesized by a tagged Seq2Edits corruption model by following proficiency-dependent tag distributions (A1, B1, C1, or N1). FT denotes fine-tuning.

corruptions of the target sentences, and fine-tune the seed correction model on this synthetic data, i.e. all models in Tables 3 to 5 are trained by fine-tuning the same seed model (Table 4a and 5a) on the same set of target sentences but different sets of source sentences.

Data generation without tags Fine-tuning the seed model on the real parallel data improves the $F_{0.5}$-score on BEA-dev by 16.7 points (33.7 → 50.4 in rows **a** and **b** of Table 4). Our goal is to close the gap relative to the $F_{0.5}$ of 50.4 using synthetic source sentences. The corruption models in rows **c** and **d** of Table 4 do not use any error tags, which is similar to previous attempts to apply back-translation to GEC (Kasewa et al., 2018).

Data generation with tags Table 3 reports results from the tag-based corruption methods introduced in this work. Seq2Edits (rows **b-e**) is more amenable to tag-based corruption than a standard full sequence Transformer model (row **a**) because tag prediction is a component of the Seq2Edits model. Interestingly, the *Offline-Optimal* method tends to perform worse than *Offline-Probabilistic* and *Online* in the constrained Seq2Edits experiments (rows **b-e**). We hypothesize that *Offline-Optimal* might generate duller and more systematic errors because the corruption model score is used to pair tags with sentences. Increasing the diversity of synthetic errors by selecting non-optimal tag-sentence pairs ultimately improves the usefulness of the synthetic data.[9]

Comparing Table 4 with Table 3 we observe that controlling the tag distribution of the synthetic data from a Seq2Edits model outperforms traditional back-translation without tags. Our best model (*Online* column in Table 3c) achieves an $F_{0.5}$-score of 48.0 which is much better than our best system without tags (42.4 $F_{0.5}$ in Table 4c) and remarkably close to the oracle score of 50.4 $F_{0.5}$ (Table 4b) obtained using a model trained on real parallel data.

For all experiments in the remainder of this paper we used the unconstrained tagged Seq2Edits corruption models (Table 3e) because it yields reasonable gains across all methods (*Offline-Optimal*, *Offline-Probabilistic*, and *Online*) and is easiest and most practical to run on a large scale.[10] Furthermore, we will only use the *Online* method to avoid the computational overhead of *Offline-Optimal* and *Offline-Probabilistic*.

[9]The same intuition motivates our experiments in Sec. 4.3 that replace beam search with sampling.

[10]We noticed that constrained decoding (Table 3b-d) often fails in large-scale experiments if the selected tag and source sentence are incompatible.

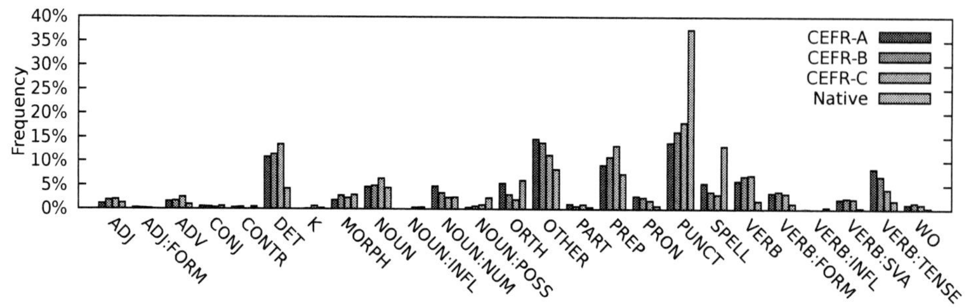

Figure 3: ERRANT error tag distributions on BEA-dev for non-native (CEFR levels A, B, C) and native English.

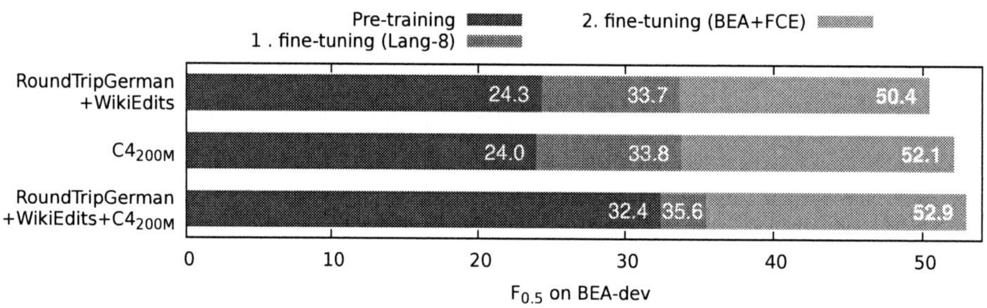

Figure 4: Using $C4_{200M}$ (tagged Seq2Edits corruption model, BEA-dev tag distribution) in pre-training. The 2-stage fine-tuning setup is described in Sec. 4.1.

Adapting GEC to English proficiency levels A potential use case for tagged corruption models is to adapt a GEC model to the proficiency level of the user by changing the target tag distribution $P^*(t)$ of the synthetic fine-tuning set. Each sentence in the BEA-dev development set is annotated with English proficiency labels (CEFR-levels A, B, C, and 'N' for native English). We split BEA-dev using these labels, and then split each set again into two parts (development/test), resulting in eight disjoint subsets A1, A2, B1, B2, C1, C2, N1, N2 with about 500 sentences each. We use A1, B1, C1, and N1 to estimate proficiency-dependent target tag distributions. As before we fine-tune the seed model on the BEA-train target sentences with synthetic source sentences that follow one of these tag distributions, but evaluate the fine-tuned models on the A2, B2, C2, and N2 splits. Table 5 shows that the tag distributions from A1, B1, and C1 yield similar performance (rows **c-e** in Table 5) across most test sets. This suggests that our method is not effective at discriminating between the different CEFR-levels of non-native English. However, using the tag distribution from native speakers (N1 in Table 5f) does yield substantial gains on the native English test set (42.9 $F_{0.5}$ on N2), even surpassing the real parallel data (42.1 $F_{0.5}$ Table 5b). This demonstrates the potential of tag-based corruption for improving GEC of native English.

Fig. 3 shows that the error tag distribution for native English differs significantly from the non-native distributions. Native speakers (orange bar) tend to make more punctuation (`PUNCT`), and spelling (`SPELL`) mistakes whereas the determiner errors (`DET`) are more common in non-native text.

4.3 The $C4_{200M}$ Synthetic Data Set

We showed in the previous section that using an unconstrained tagged Seq2Edits corruption model that follows the BEA-dev tag distribution works well in a controlled setup (corrupting ~60K clean target sentences from BEA+FCE). We now apply the same corruption model to a much larger, clean data set ($C4_{200M}$) consisting of 200M sentences and use the resulting synthetic data set as an additional pre-training set for our GEC models. Fig. 4 reports performance from three different GEC models with different pre-training sets, each using the 2-stage fine-tuning pipeline described in Sec. 4.1. The RoundTripGerman+WikiEdits model resembles the baseline of Lichtarge et al. (2020). Using $C4_{200M}$ instead of RoundTripGerman+WikiEdits

Tag distribution	Decoding	BEA-dev			CoNLL-13			JFLEG-dev
$P^*(t)$		P	R	$F_{0.5}$	P	R	$F_{0.5}$	GLEU
a None (no tags)	Beam search	58.1	36.5	51.9	58.5	29.0	48.6	57.2
b BEA-dev	Beam search	58.0	39.3	52.9	58.5	33.0	50.7	57.9
c CoNLL-13	Beam search	58.8	39.6	53.6	58.9	33.3	51.0	57.9
d JFLEG-dev	Beam search	58.3	39.1	53.1	58.9	31.6	50.2	57.6
e Uniform	Beam search	59.1	39.6	53.8	58.3	33.4	50.7	57.7
f None (no tags)	Sampling	57.5	36.0	51.4	56.9	29.4	47.9	57.1
g BEA-dev	Sampling	59.5	**41.3**	**54.7**	**59.2**	**34.7**	**51.9**	**58.5**
h CoNLL-13	Sampling	58.6	40.7	53.9	58.5	33.3	50.8	58.1
i JFLEG-dev	Sampling	59.0	39.7	53.8	58.2	34.0	51.0	58.4
j Uniform	Sampling	**59.6**	40.6	54.5	58.3	34.3	51.1	58.3

Table 6: Using different target tag distributions to corrupt $C4_{200M}$ with a tagged Seq2Edits corruption model, either using beam search or sampling. We report the best of five training runs after two-stage fine-tuning according to the performance on the development set.

GEC data (pre-training)		BEA-dev		
Synthetic source	Target	P	R	$F_{0.5}$
a Untagged corruption	WikiEdits	40.8	4.0	14.3
b RoundTripGerman	WikiEdits	33.6	11.6	24.3
c Tagged corruption	WikiEdits	39.7	20.2	33.3

Table 7: Data generation on WikiEdits for pre-training. Models are pre-trained on a mix of the original WikiEdits data set and a synthetic data set that consists of WikiEdits target sentences corrupted with either (1) an untagged Seq2Edits corruption model (row **a**), (2) round-trip translation via German (row **b**, or row 1 in Fig. 4), or (3) a tagged Seq2Edits corruption model (row **c**) following the BEA-dev tag distribution.

improves the final $F_{0.5}$-score to 52.1. Combining all three pre-training sets leads to a large jump in $F_{0.5}$ to 32.4 after pre-training. The gains are reduced after fine-tuning, but our best model still uses all three pre-training sets (52.9 $F_{0.5}$ after the second fine-tuning stage). The gains in Fig. 4 from using $C4_{200M}$ can be attributed to a) the tagged corruption method, or b) the use of C4 rather than Wikipedia which covers a broader range of text types. In the ablation experiment in Table 7, rather than using $C4_{200M}$, we corrupted the WikiRevision target sentences with various corruption methods. Tagged corruption (row **c**) outperforms both untagged corruption (row **a**) and round-trip translation (row **b**) when the target sentences are kept constant.

A crucial practical question is whether our approach is sensitive to the particular target tag distribution $P^*(t)$, and if the synthetic $C4_{200M}$ training data can help generalization to other development sets. Rows **b-e** in Table 6 show the performance after fine-tuning for four different tag distributions: BEA-dev, CoNLL-13, JFLEG-dev, and Uniform. Each row reports the performance of a model pre-trained using RoundTripGerman+WikiEdits and $C4_{200M}$ corrupted using the desired tag distribution followed by the 2-stage fine-tuning, i.e. row **b** corresponds to row 3 in Fig. 4. All tagged corruption models improve upon the untagged models (rows **a** and **f**).[11] In contrast to our adaptation experiments in Table 5, the variations between different tag distributions are small. This indicates that even though choosing the *correct* tag distribution is crucial for adapting GEC to native English, at the pre-training stage the ability of tagged corruption models to generate diverse errors is more important than matching a particular distribution.

Previous work on back-translation has found that it can be beneficial to use sampling instead of beam search for synthetic data generation (Edunov et al., 2018; Kiyono et al., 2019). We confirm these findings for our tagged corruption models: Sampling (Table 6g-j) outperforms beam search (Table 6b-e) for all tag distributions except CoNLL-13. Using sampling and the BEA-dev tag distribution (Table 6g) yields good performance across all development sets. The BEA-dev tag distribution reflects a wide range of grammatical errors across various proficiency levels compared to other corpora such as CoNLL-14 (mostly beginner) or FCE (School) (Bryant et al., 2019). Table 8 situates this single model and an ensemble of five analogously trained models in the context of related work. For our final models in Table 8 we follow Lichtarge et al. (2019, 2020); Stahlberg and Kumar (2020) and multiply the model score of the identity mapping with a factor (tuned on the development set) to balance precision and recall.[12] Our single model outperforms other single models on CoNLL-14 and JFLEG-

[11] For more insight into the difference between untagged and tagged corruptions see Appendix B.

[12] This factor is around 1.0 for BEA-dev and CoNLL-13 (i.e. no impact) but it helps to re-balance precision and recall on JFLEG (around 2.0).

System	BEA-test			CoNLL-14			JFLEG-test
	P	R	$F_{0.5}$	P	R	$F_{0.5}$	GLEU
Single systems							
Kiyono et al. (2019)	65.5	59.4	64.2	67.9	44.1	61.3	59.7
Omelianchuk et al. (2020)	**79.2**	53.9	**72.4**	**77.5**	40.1	65.3	-
Lichtarge et al. (2020)	67.6	62.5	66.5	69.4	43.9	62.1	63.8
Kaneko et al. (2020)	67.1	60.1	65.6	69.2	45.6	62.6	61.3
Wan et al. (2020)	66.9	60.6	65.5	69.5	47.3	63.5	-
This work	72.1	**64.4**	70.4	72.8	**49.5**	**66.6**	**64.7**
Ensembles							
Grundkiewicz et al. (2019)	72.3	60.1	69.5	-	-	64.2	61.2
Kiyono et al. (2019)	74.7	56.7	70.2	72.4	46.1	65.0	61.4
Omelianchuk et al. (2020)	**79.4**	57.2	73.7	**78.2**	41.5	66.5	-
Lichtarge et al. (2020)	75.4	64.7	73.0	74.7	46.9	66.8	**64.9**
Kaneko et al. (2020)	72.3	61.4	69.8	72.6	46.4	65.2	62.0
Wan et al. (2020)	72.6	61.3	70.0	72.3	48.8	65.9	-
This work	77.7	**65.4**	**74.9**	75.6	**49.3**	**68.3**	64.7

Table 8: Comparison of our final system with related work.

test. Our ensemble establishes new state-of-the-art scores on BEA-test (74.9 $F_{0.5}$) and CoNLL-14 (68.3 $F_{0.5}$). We would like to emphasize that these gains are achieved without modifying the GEC model architecture – our GEC models are vanilla Transformers that were pre-trained using our new synthetic $C4_{200M}$ data set. We will make our data set publicly available to make it easy for other researchers to benefit from our work. Appendix C contains example outputs from our system trained with $C4_{200M}$ that demonstrate improved fluency and better handling of long-range reorderings.

5 Related Work

The body of literature on synthetic data generation for GEC is large. Various heuristics have been proposed to inject synthetic noise into grammatical sentences such as random word- or character-level insertion, substitution, deletion, or shuffling operations (Lichtarge et al., 2019; Zhao et al., 2019; Xu et al., 2019), using spell checkers (Grundkiewicz et al., 2019), or randomly applying word edits extracted from the training data (Choe et al., 2019). Kasewa et al. (2018); Stahlberg and Byrne (2019) applied back-translation (Sennrich et al., 2016) to GEC and reported substantial gains. Similar to MT (Edunov et al., 2018), back-translation for GEC can be further improved by adding noise to the decoding process (Xie et al., 2018) or by using sampling instead of beam search (Kiyono et al., 2019). Fluency-boost learning (Ge et al., 2018a,b) can also be used to generate additional sentence pairs during training. Lichtarge et al. (2019) proposed to generate noisy counterparts of grammatical English sentences by translating them to another language (e.g. German) and back ("round-trip translation"), a technique we also use in this work. The use of tags for back-translation in MT has been explored by Caswell et al. (2019). Our tagged corruption models are inspired by Wan et al. (2020) who generated synthetic sentences from latent representations that are perturbed using explicit error type tags. Our approach of adding the tags to the input sequence is simpler as it requires no modifications to the model architecture or training procedure.

6 Conclusion

We have introduced a synthetic data generation method for grammatical error correction that is able to produce a wide range of realistic grammatical errors. Our method is based on grammar corruption models that corrupt a clean sentence given an error type tag. Conditioning on the error type tag enables us to control synthetic data generation much more precisely than alternative methods such as round-trip translations or tag-independent back-translation. We explored different ways of using these tagged corruption models to generate synthetic data that follows a certain error tag distribution. We found that fine-tuning a model on synthetic data that follows a native English error tag distribution can even outperform fine-tuning on genuine parallel data from a mixture of proficiency levels. Along with this paper we publish a new 200M sentence data set for GEC – $C4_{200M}$. Using $C4_{200M}$ in pre-training of vanilla Transformer GEC models yields state-of-the-art performance on two standard GEC test sets (BEA-test and CoNLL-14). We expect this corpus to further stimulate the development of new data-driven approaches in GEC.

References

Martín Abadi, Ashish Agarwal, Paul Barham, Eugene Brevdo, Zhifeng Chen, Craig Citro, Greg S. Corrado, Andy Davis, Jeffrey Dean, Matthieu Devin, Sanjay Ghemawat, Ian Goodfellow, Andrew Harp, Geoffrey Irving, Michael Isard, Yangqing Jia, Rafal Jozefowicz, Lukasz Kaiser, Manjunath Kudlur, Josh Levenberg, Dandelion Mané, Rajat Monga, Sherry Moore, Derek Murray, Chris Olah, Mike Schuster, Jonathon Shlens, Benoit Steiner, Ilya Sutskever, Kunal Talwar, Paul Tucker, Vincent Vanhoucke, Vijay Vasudevan, Fernanda Viégas, Oriol Vinyals, Pete Warden, Martin Wattenberg, Martin Wicke, Yuan Yu, and Xiaoqiang Zheng. 2015. TensorFlow: Large-scale machine learning on heterogeneous systems. Software available from tensorflow.org.

Chris Brockett, William B. Dolan, and Michael Gamon. 2006. Correcting ESL errors using phrasal SMT techniques. In *Proceedings of the 21st International Conference on Computational Linguistics and 44th Annual Meeting of the Association for Computational Linguistics*, pages 249–256, Sydney, Australia. Association for Computational Linguistics.

Christopher Bryant, Mariano Felice, Øistein E. Andersen, and Ted Briscoe. 2019. The BEA-2019 shared task on grammatical error correction. In *Proceedings of the Fourteenth Workshop on Innovative Use of NLP for Building Educational Applications*, pages 52–75, Florence, Italy. Association for Computational Linguistics.

Christopher Bryant, Mariano Felice, and Ted Briscoe. 2017. Automatic annotation and evaluation of error types for grammatical error correction. In *Proceedings of the 55th Annual Meeting of the Association for Computational Linguistics (Volume 1: Long Papers)*, pages 793–805, Vancouver, Canada. Association for Computational Linguistics.

Isaac Caswell, Ciprian Chelba, and David Grangier. 2019. Tagged back-translation. In *Proceedings of the Fourth Conference on Machine Translation (Volume 1: Research Papers)*, pages 53–63, Florence, Italy. Association for Computational Linguistics.

Yo Joong Choe, Jiyeon Ham, Kyubyong Park, and Yeoil Yoon. 2019. A neural grammatical error correction system built on better pre-training and sequential transfer learning. In *Proceedings of the Fourteenth Workshop on Innovative Use of NLP for Building Educational Applications*, pages 213–227, Florence, Italy. Association for Computational Linguistics.

Shamil Chollampatt and Hwee Tou Ng. 2018. A multilayer convolutional encoder-decoder neural network for grammatical error correction. In *Proceedings of the Thirty-Second AAAI Conference on Artificial Intelligence*.

Daniel Dahlmeier and Hwee Tou Ng. 2012. Better evaluation for grammatical error correction. In *Proceedings of the 2012 Conference of the North American Chapter of the Association for Computational Linguistics: Human Language Technologies*, pages 568–572, Montréal, Canada. Association for Computational Linguistics.

Sergey Edunov, Myle Ott, Michael Auli, and David Grangier. 2018. Understanding back-translation at scale. In *Proceedings of the 2018 Conference on Empirical Methods in Natural Language Processing*, pages 489–500, Brussels, Belgium. Association for Computational Linguistics.

Mariano Felice, Christopher Bryant, and Ted Briscoe. 2016. Automatic extraction of learner errors in ESL sentences using linguistically enhanced alignments. In *Proceedings of COLING 2016, the 26th International Conference on Computational Linguistics: Technical Papers*, pages 825–835, Osaka, Japan. The COLING 2016 Organizing Committee.

Mariano Felice, Zheng Yuan, Øistein E. Andersen, Helen Yannakoudakis, and Ekaterina Kochmar. 2014. Grammatical error correction using hybrid systems and type filtering. In *Proceedings of the Eighteenth Conference on Computational Natural Language Learning: Shared Task*, pages 15–24, Baltimore, Maryland. Association for Computational Linguistics.

Jennifer Foster and Øistein E. Andersen. 2009. Generrate: Generating errors for use in grammatical error detection. In *Proceedings of the Fourth Workshop on Innovative Use of NLP for Building Educational Applications*, EdAppsNLP '09, pages 82–90, Stroudsburg, PA, USA. Association for Computational Linguistics.

Tao Ge, Furu Wei, and Ming Zhou. 2018a. Fluency boost learning and inference for neural grammatical error correction. In *Proceedings of the 56th Annual Meeting of the Association for Computational Linguistics (Volume 1: Long Papers)*, pages 1055–1065, Melbourne, Australia. Association for Computational Linguistics.

Tao Ge, Furu Wei, and Ming Zhou. 2018b. Reaching human-level performance in automatic grammatical error correction: An empirical study. *arXiv preprint arXiv:1807.01270*.

Roman Grundkiewicz, Marcin Junczys-Dowmunt, and Kenneth Heafield. 2019. Neural grammatical error correction systems with unsupervised pre-training on synthetic data. In *Proceedings of the Fourteenth Workshop on Innovative Use of NLP for Building Educational Applications*, pages 252–263, Florence, Italy. Association for Computational Linguistics.

Melvin Johnson, Mike Schuster, Quoc V. Le, Maxim Krikun, Yonghui Wu, Zhifeng Chen, Nikhil Thorat, Fernanda Viégas, Martin Wattenberg, Greg Corrado, Macduff Hughes, and Jeffrey Dean. 2017. Google's multilingual neural machine translation system: Enabling zero-shot translation. *Transactions of the Association for Computational Linguistics*, 5:339–351.

Marcin Junczys-Dowmunt, Roman Grundkiewicz, Shubha Guha, and Kenneth Heafield. 2018. Approaching neural grammatical error correction as a low-resource machine translation task. In *Proceedings of the 2018 Conference of the North American Chapter of the Association for Computational Linguistics: Human Language Technologies, Volume 1 (Long Papers)*, pages 595–606, New Orleans, Louisiana. Association for Computational Linguistics.

Masahiro Kaneko, Masato Mita, Shun Kiyono, Jun Suzuki, and Kentaro Inui. 2020. Encoder-decoder models can benefit from pre-trained masked language models in grammatical error correction. In *Proceedings of the 58th Annual Meeting of the Association for Computational Linguistics*, pages 4248–4254, Online. Association for Computational Linguistics.

Sudhanshu Kasewa, Pontus Stenetorp, and Sebastian Riedel. 2018. Wronging a right: Generating better errors to improve grammatical error detection. In *Proceedings of the 2018 Conference on Empirical Methods in Natural Language Processing*, pages 4977–4983, Brussels, Belgium. Association for Computational Linguistics.

Shun Kiyono, Jun Suzuki, Masato Mita, Tomoya Mizumoto, and Kentaro Inui. 2019. An empirical study of incorporating pseudo data into grammatical error correction. In *Proceedings of the 2019 Conference on Empirical Methods in Natural Language Processing and the 9th International Joint Conference on Natural Language Processing (EMNLP-IJCNLP)*, pages 1236–1242, Hong Kong, China. Association for Computational Linguistics.

Jared Lichtarge, Chris Alberti, and Shankar Kumar. 2020. Data weighted training strategies for grammatical error correction. *Transactions of the Association for Computational Linguistics*, 8:634–646.

Jared Lichtarge, Chris Alberti, Shankar Kumar, Noam Shazeer, Niki Parmar, and Simon Tong. 2019. Corpora generation for grammatical error correction. In *Proceedings of the 2019 Conference of the North American Chapter of the Association for Computational Linguistics: Human Language Technologies, Volume 1 (Long and Short Papers)*, pages 3291–3301, Minneapolis, Minnesota. Association for Computational Linguistics.

Tomoya Mizumoto, Mamoru Komachi, Masaaki Nagata, and Yuji Matsumoto. 2011. Mining revision log of language learning SNS for automated Japanese error correction of second language learners. In *Proceedings of 5th International Joint Conference on Natural Language Processing*, pages 147–155, Chiang Mai, Thailand. Asian Federation of Natural Language Processing.

Courtney Napoles, Keisuke Sakaguchi, Matt Post, and Joel Tetreault. 2015. Ground truth for grammatical error correction metrics. In *Proceedings of the 53rd Annual Meeting of the Association for Computational Linguistics and the 7th International Joint Conference on Natural Language Processing (Volume 2: Short Papers)*, pages 588–593, Beijing, China. Association for Computational Linguistics.

Courtney Napoles, Keisuke Sakaguchi, and Joel Tetreault. 2017. JFLEG: A fluency corpus and benchmark for grammatical error correction. In *Proceedings of the 15th Conference of the European Chapter of the Association for Computational Linguistics: Volume 2, Short Papers*, pages 229–234, Valencia, Spain. Association for Computational Linguistics.

Hwee Tou Ng, Siew Mei Wu, Yuanbin Wu, Christian Hadiwinoto, and Joel Tetreault. 2013. The CoNLL-2013 shared task on grammatical error correction. In *Proceedings of the Seventeenth Conference on Computational Natural Language Learning: Shared Task*, pages 1–12, Sofia, Bulgaria. Association for Computational Linguistics.

Kostiantyn Omelianchuk, Vitaliy Atrasevych, Artem Chernodub, and Oleksandr Skurzhanskyi. 2020. GECToR – grammatical error correction: Tag, not rewrite. In *Proceedings of the Fifteenth Workshop on Innovative Use of NLP for Building Educational Applications*, pages 163–170, Seattle, WA, USA Online. Association for Computational Linguistics.

Colin Raffel, Noam Shazeer, Adam Roberts, Katherine Lee, Sharan Narang, Michael Matena, Yanqi Zhou, Wei Li, and Peter J. Liu. 2020. Exploring the limits of transfer learning with a unified text-to-text transformer. *Journal of Machine Learning Research*, 21(140):1–67.

Marek Rei, Mariano Felice, Zheng Yuan, and Ted Briscoe. 2017. Artificial error generation with machine translation and syntactic patterns. In *Proceedings of the 12th Workshop on Innovative Use of NLP for Building Educational Applications*, pages 287–292, Copenhagen, Denmark. Association for Computational Linguistics.

Alla Rozovskaya and Dan Roth. 2010. Generating confusion sets for context-sensitive error correction. In *Proceedings of the 2010 Conference on Empirical Methods in Natural Language Processing*, pages 961–970, Cambridge, MA. Association for Computational Linguistics.

A. Schrijver. 2003. *Combinatorial Optimization - Polyhedra and Efficiency*. Springer.

Rico Sennrich, Barry Haddow, and Alexandra Birch. 2016. Improving neural machine translation models with monolingual data. In *Proceedings of the 54th Annual Meeting of the Association for Computational Linguistics (Volume 1: Long Papers)*, pages 86–96, Berlin, Germany. Association for Computational Linguistics.

Noam Shazeer and Mitchell Stern. 2018. Adafactor: Adaptive learning rates with sublinear memory cost. *arXiv preprint arXiv:1804.04235*.

Felix Stahlberg and Bill Byrne. 2019. The CUED's grammatical error correction systems for BEA-2019. In *Proceedings of the Fourteenth Workshop on Innovative Use of NLP for Building Educational Applications*, pages 168–175, Florence, Italy. Association for Computational Linguistics.

Felix Stahlberg and Shankar Kumar. 2020. Seq2Edits: Sequence transduction using span-level edit operations. In *Proceedings of the 2020 Conference on Empirical Methods in Natural Language Processing (EMNLP)*, pages 5147–5159, Online. Association for Computational Linguistics.

Yujin Takahashi, Satoru Katsumata, and Mamoru Komachi. 2020. Grammatical error correction using pseudo learner corpus considering learner's error tendency. In *Proceedings of the 58th Annual Meeting of the Association for Computational Linguistics: Student Research Workshop*, pages 27–32, Online. Association for Computational Linguistics.

Ashish Vaswani, Samy Bengio, Eugene Brevdo, Francois Chollet, Aidan Gomez, Stephan Gouws, Llion Jones, Łukasz Kaiser, Nal Kalchbrenner, Niki Parmar, Ryan Sepassi, Noam Shazeer, and Jakob Uszkoreit. 2018. Tensor2Tensor for neural machine translation. In *Proceedings of the 13th Conference of the Association for Machine Translation in the Americas (Volume 1: Research Papers)*, pages 193–199, Boston, MA. Association for Machine Translation in the Americas.

Ashish Vaswani, Noam Shazeer, Niki Parmar, Jakob Uszkoreit, Llion Jones, Aidan N Gomez, Ł ukasz Kaiser, and Illia Polosukhin. 2017. Attention is all you need. In I. Guyon, U. V. Luxburg, S. Bengio, H. Wallach, R. Fergus, S. Vishwanathan, and R. Garnett, editors, *Advances in Neural Information Processing Systems 30*, pages 5998–6008. Curran Associates, Inc.

Zhaohong Wan, Xiaojun Wan, and Wenguang Wang. 2020. Improving grammatical error correction with data augmentation by editing latent representation. In *Proceedings of the 28th International Conference on Computational Linguistics*, pages 2202–2212, Barcelona, Spain (Online). International Committee on Computational Linguistics.

Ziang Xie, Guillaume Genthial, Stanley Xie, Andrew Ng, and Dan Jurafsky. 2018. Noising and denoising natural language: Diverse backtranslation for grammar correction. In *Proceedings of the 2018 Conference of the North American Chapter of the Association for Computational Linguistics: Human Language Technologies, Volume 1 (Long Papers)*, pages 619–628, New Orleans, Louisiana. Association for Computational Linguistics.

Shuyao Xu, Jiehao Zhang, Jin Chen, and Long Qin. 2019. Erroneous data generation for grammatical error correction. In *Proceedings of the Fourteenth Workshop on Innovative Use of NLP for Building Educational Applications*, pages 149–158, Florence, Italy. Association for Computational Linguistics.

Helen Yannakoudakis, Ted Briscoe, and Ben Medlock. 2011. A new dataset and method for automatically grading ESOL texts. In *Proceedings of the 49th Annual Meeting of the Association for Computational Linguistics: Human Language Technologies*, pages 180–189, Portland, Oregon, USA. Association for Computational Linguistics.

Wei Zhao, Liang Wang, Kewei Shen, Ruoyu Jia, and Jingming Liu. 2019. Improving grammatical error correction via pre-training a copy-augmented architecture with unlabeled data. In *Proceedings of the 2019 Conference of the North American Chapter of the Association for Computational Linguistics: Human Language Technologies, Volume 1 (Long and Short Papers)*, pages 156–165, Minneapolis, Minnesota. Association for Computational Linguistics.

Broad Linguistic Complexity Analysis for Greek Readability Classification

Savvas Chatzipanagiotidis
Universität Tübingen, Germany
sv.chtz@gmail.com

Maria Giagkou
Institute for Language & Speech Processing, Greece
mgiagkou@ilsp.gr

Detmar Meurers
Universität Tübingen, Germany
detmar.meurers@uni-tuebingen.de

Abstract

This paper explores the linguistic complexity of Greek textbooks as a readability classification task. We analyze textbook corpora for different school subjects and textbooks for Greek as a Second Language, covering a very wide spectrum of school age groups and proficiency levels. A broad range of quantifiable linguistic complexity features (lexical, morphological and syntactic) are extracted and calculated.

Conducting experiments with different feature subsets, we show that the different linguistic dimensions contribute orthogonal information, each contributing towards the highest result achieved using all linguistic feature subsets. A readability classifier trained on this basis reaches a classification accuracy of 88.16% for the Greek as a Second Language corpus.

To investigate the generalizability of the classification models, we also perform cross-corpus evaluations. We show that the model trained on the most varied text collection (for Greek as a school subject) generalizes best.

In addition to advancing the state of the art for Greek readability analysis, the paper also contributes insights on the role of different feature sets and training setups for generalizable readability classification.

1 Introduction

Automatic readability classification systems are intended to assess whether a text is appropriate for a given group of readers. The groups of readers differ in terms of their level of education in their first language (L1), their second language proficiency (L2), or in terms of their special needs (e.g., due to cognitive disabilities). Textbooks play a major role in fostering language development in school, and educational policy documents such as the US Common Core State Standards (CCSSO, 2010) make explicit that the texts should offer a "staircase of increasing complexity so that all students are ready for the demands of college- and career-level reading no later than the end of high school."[1] Correspondingly, in the US context there are a number of research and commercial approaches to measuring text difficulty for English (Nelson et al., 2012). Research continues in this domain, e.g., investigating features from second language acquisition (Vajjala and Meurers, 2012) or psycholinguistic research (Howcroft and Demberg, 2017), training neural networks (Azpiazu and Pera, 2019), broadening the corpus basis (Vajjala and Lučić, 2018), and externally grounding the ratings (Redmiles et al., 2019).

For second language learners, texts at an appropriate level of proficiency are of particular importance, with a substantial strand of computational linguistic research focusing on this target group, e.g., (François and Fairon, 2012; Pilán et al., 2014; Xia et al., 2016), and parallel automated proficiency evaluation approaches analyzing L2 writing, e.g., (Lu, 2010; Giagkou et al., 2015; Weiss and Meurers, 2019b). While much of the initial computational linguistic research on readability focused on English, research targeting other languages is also increasingly emerging, e.g., (Hancke et al., 2012; Falkenjack et al., 2013; Dell'Orletta et al., 2014; Giagkou et al., 2017). Some recent approaches employ neural networks and deep learning for classification-related tasks (Martinc et al., 2019; Conneau et al., 2017). For instance, Martinc et al. (2019) employed neural classifiers on English and Slovenian corpora using unsupervised and supervised techniques to assess readability, outperforming some previous state-of-the-art approaches.

In this paper, we focus on the Greek language and investigate readability classification using a

[1]http://purl.org/ccss/ela-keyshifts

Proceedings of the 16th Workshop on Innovative Use of NLP for Building Educational Applications, pages 48–58
April 20, 2021 ©2021 Association for Computational Linguistics

broad range of linguistic complexity features on a comprehensive collection of five textbook corpora covering various subjects, and Greek as a second language. We first explore which feature groups and combinations thereof best predict the school grade or proficiency level assigned by the publisher. Going beyond the typical within-corpus setup, we then conduct cross-corpus tests to study how well the models trained on different feature sets and corpora generalize across data sets.

The paper is organized as follows: Section 2 presents the textbook corpora and section 3 the linguistic complexity feature sets used in the readability classification experiments. Section 4 then spells out the experimental setup and the results, before concluding in section 5.

2 Data

Our data consists of five corpora of Greek texts used as educational material for different school subjects and educational contexts. We use four corpora from previous work on Greek (Giagkou, 2009; Georgatou, 2016), in addition to a Greek as a Second Language (GSL) textbooks corpus compiled for the needs of the research at hand. Table 1 provides an overview of the corpora, their number of texts and average text lengths.

Corpus	Texts	Total Tokens	Avg. Tokens
Greek	520	181.267	348
History	835	344.202	412
Science	782	199.471	255
E.DIA.M.ME.	432	106.990	248
GSL	600	164.367	273
Total Number	**3.169**	**996.297**	

Table 1: Descriptive statistics of the data set used

The *Greek* corpus (Giagkou, 2009) comprises authentic texts from the official coursebooks used in Greek schools for teaching the subject Greek from the second grade of primary school to the second grade of upper secondary school. The texts cover a wide range of domains and text types, from descriptive to argumentative texts and literature. The *History* corpus (Georgatou, 2016) consists of texts from the official history textbooks used in the Greek educational system, and the *Science* corpus (Georgatou, 2016) combines the textbooks for the *Geology, Biology and Chemistry* subjects.

For each of the three curriculum subjects, the corpora delineate textbooks at three different levels: *primary school*, *lower secondary school*, and *upper secondary school*, which correspond to ISCED 1, 2, and 3 in the International Standard Classification of Education (ISCED).

The *E.DIA.M.ME.* corpus (Georgatou, 2016) includes coursebooks for Greek as a heritage language. The texts are divided into five levels, which, in turn, correspond to grades of the greek educational system. The *E.DIA.M.ME.* project[2] aims to promote the Greek language to Greek migrants living abroad and non-native Greeks who want to learn the Greek language. As mentioned by Damanakis (2011), the learning material for *E.DIA.M.ME.* project has been designed and composed according to the CERF guidelines, allowing a partial matching between these five levels and the six CERF-proficiency levels. In particular, the fourth E.DIA.M.ME level corresponds both to the B2 and C1 CERF level. For our three-level CERF classification, we assigned the fourth E.DIA.M.ME level to the higher level (C). Finally, we compiled a Greek as a Second Language (GSL) corpus by collecting and digitizing reading material from seven coursebooks of Greek L2 and from past certification tests in Greek, for which the respective Common European Framework of Reference for Languages (CEFR) level (Council of Europe, 2001) was indicated by the publisher.[3]

For the *E.DIA.M.ME.* Greek as a heritage language corpus and the Greek as a Second Language (GSL) corpus, the CEFR framework provide a three level classification into Basic (A), Independent (B), and Proficient (C) users of Greek.

The distribution of texts per level is noted in the confusion matrices shown in Tables 3, 4, 5, 7, and 8 in the following sections.

3 Linguistic complexity analysis

We used a state-of-the-art Greek dependency parser (Prokopidis and Papageorgiou, 2017) of the Institute for Language and Speech Processing (ILSP) to annotate the corpora. The CoNLL-format files produced by the parser were used as input to our

[2] *E.DIA.M.ME.* project: `http://www.ediamme.edc.uoc.gr/diasporanew/index.php?lang=en`

[3] Since the C2 level was underrepresented, we supplemented it with texts crawled from native Greek websites, with minimal external validation of the level through `http://www.greek-language.gr/certification/readability`

code performing the complexity features extraction, returning a vector of feature values for each text.

Greek is an inflected language with rich morphology, allowing relative flexible word order in sentence construction. We computed a broad set of linguistic complexity features capturing lexical, morphological, and syntactic characteristics. We combined measures from Greek readability research (Giagkou, 2009; Giagkou et al., 2017; Georgatou, 2016) with features originally introduced for German (Hancke et al., 2012) and added cognitively-motivated features from psycholinguistic research on English (Liu, 2008; Gibson, 2000; Shain et al., 2016) used in research on L2 and academic language development (Weiss and Meurers, 2019a,b). Together with some traditional readability formulas, for each text we computed an overall set of 215 features[4]:

- Lexical (67 features): Lexical variation measures, including POS-specific ones, e.g., type-token ratios, noun verb ratio, verb variation, modifier token ratio; token-length lexical sophistication
- Morphological (77 features): Aspects of inflections, derivation, adjective degrees, common noun ratio, passive verb ratio; Mean size of paradigm (MSP) and Morphological feature entropy (MFE) (Çöltekin and Rama, 2018)
- Syntactic (68 fetures): Parse-tree derived measures, e.g., avg. parse tree height, dependent clause ratio; features based on POS or grammatical functions per sentence, e.g., subject-verb ratio; 16 features are cognitively-motivated based on Dependency Locality Theory (DLT) (Gibson, 2000; Shain et al., 2016) and Mean Dependency Distance (Liu, 2008)
- Readability formulas (3): FOG, SMOG and a version of Flesch Reading Ease Score for the Greek Language (Tzimokas and Matthaioudaki, 2014)

4 Classification experiments

The classification experiments were conducted using *WEKA* (Hall et al., 2009). We initially compared several machine learning algorithms, including Logistic Regression, Multilayer Perceptron and Sequential Minimal Optimization (SMO). The SMO classifier systematically outperformed other options, so we here focus on the results discussion of the SMO classifier[5]. For all our experiments, we report accuracy using 10-fold cross validation and the F-score.

To study the impact of the groups of complexity features (lexical, morphological, syntactic), we ran machine learning experiments with each individual linguistic feature subset, then with binary combinations thereof (lexical & morphological, lexical & syntactic, morphological & syntactic), with all 212 linguistic features, and finally with all 215 features.

To investigate the informativity of individual features, we ranked features using Weka's *Info Gain (IG) Attribute Evaluation* (Gnanambal et al., 2018) and ran experiments with the Top 30 features as well as with all features with an IG > 0.1.

4.1 Results for ISCED classification

Figure 1[6] sums up the performance of the three-level ISCED classifiers for the different feature groups for the three school subjects Greek, Science, and History.

The results indicate a strikingly similar pattern in History and Science corpora. For each of the three linguistic feature groups (lexical, morphological, syntactic), the classifier reaches around 75% accuracy (74.97%–76.88%), which, compared to the 33% random baseline, clearly demonstrates that the History and Science texts in different school levels systematically differ in each of these linguistic dimensions.

Interestingly, the accuracy increases about 5% when combining any two linguistic feature groups (78.68%–81.58%). This means that the features from the different linguistic domains do not encode the same information, but contribute distinct complexity differences. This is confirmed by the additional rise in accuracy to around 84%, when all three linguistic domains are combined (83.83%/84.78%).

The performance of the classifier on the Greek corpus is substantially poorer and more varied. This corpus comprises texts from the Greek Language subject, that is designed to provide both

[4] The full list of features and their computation is available at `https://osf.io/2qdzw/?view_only=1dfd5710735a449db14d2d84022c4adb`

[5] The comparison of different algorithms was conducted as part of Chatzipanagiotidis (2020)

[6] We here use line graphs in order to visually represent the results for the different feature groups of the different corpora in a compact way, also supporting transparent within- and cross-corpus comparison.

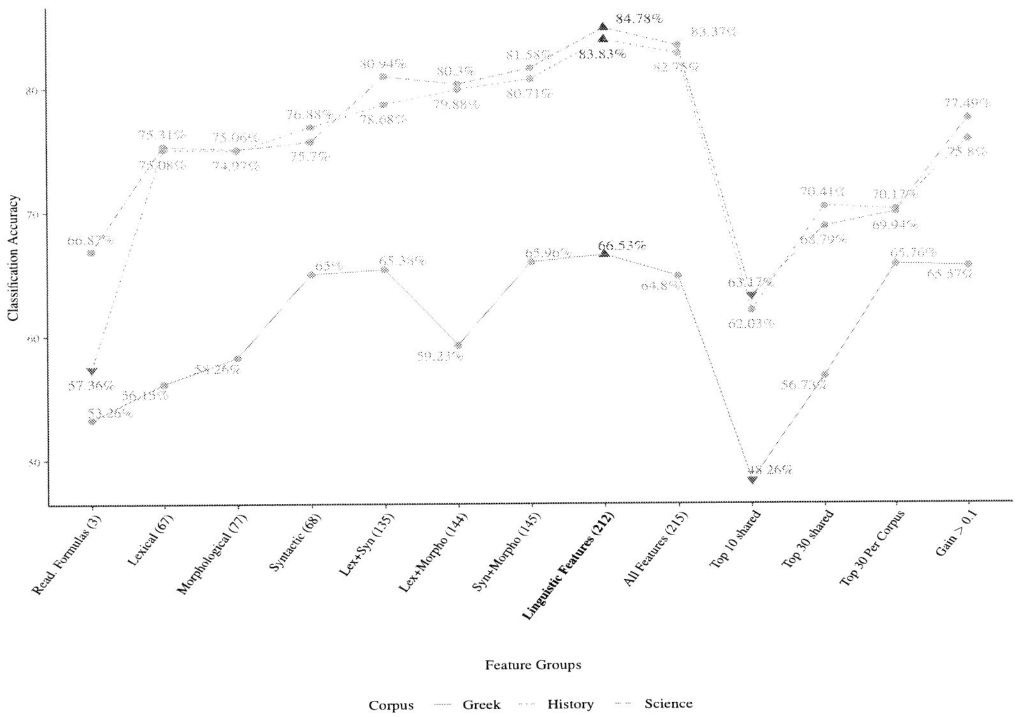

Figure 1: Ten-fold cross validation results for three-level ISCED classification

an understanding of grammar and critical reading skills, using different text types by a range of important authors. The heterogeneity of the texts could explain the low classification accuracy for the lexical features (56.15%), and the grammar component of the curriculum the slightly higher results for morphology (58.26%) and syntax (65%). While the History and Science texts seem to be systematically and coherently written in a way reflecting the incremental complexification of language in all its dimensions, that goal seems to have played much less of a role in the selection of texts for the Greek Language subject.

The classifier trained on the most informative features per corpus (*Info Gain > 0.1*) supports classification with good accuracy, though it is outperformed by any combination of two or more linguistic feature groups. When training classifiers on smaller feature groups, such as the 10 or 30 features ranked highest for the three corpora combined or the top 30 features for each corpus, we can see that the performance is systematically reduced. High classification accuracy thus is not driven by a few highly informative features, but linked to informing the classifier broadly about different dimensions of linguistic modeling. Simply adding more features is not what matters here; this is illustrated by the traditional readability formulae, which actually lower the overall results when included in the set.

Table 2 summarises the best results from the experiments discussed above. For all three corpora, the best performing classifiers are those trained on all 212 linguistic features.

Corpus	Accuracy	Weighted Avg. F-score
Greek	**66.53%**	0.660
History	**83.83%**	0.838
Science	**84.78%**	0.842

Table 2: Best results for Greek school subject corpora

Tables 3, 4, and 5 provide the confusion matrices for the three educational levels. We see that erroneous classifications mostly occur in adjacent levels, with the ISCED-2 level being the most challenging in the Greek and Science corpora.

ISCED	1 (predicted)	2 (predicted)	3 (predicted)	All	F-score
1	**313**	11	21	345	0.892
2	26	**68**	32	126	0.630
3	18	11	**282**	311	0.873

Table 5: Confusion matrix for Science corpus

ISCED	1	2	3	All	F-score
	predicted				
1	**147**	33	9	189	0.762
2	41	**82**	50	173	0.512
3	9	32	**117**	158	0.701

Table 3: Confusion matrix for Greek corpus

ISCED	1	2	3	All	F-score
	predicted				
1	**199**	10	11	220	0.907
2	15	**214**	45	274	0.782
3	5	49	**287**	341	0.839

Table 4: Confusion matrix for History corpus

4.2 Results for CEFR classification

Figure 2 shows the results of the three-level CEFR classification for the Greek as a Second Language corpus (GSL) and the Greek as a heritage language corpus (E.DIA.M.ME.) for each feature group.

The classifiers trained on the GSL corpus, with lexical, syntactic, and morphological features, as individual sets or combined, exhibit higher accuracy when compared to the ISCED classification results. Again, the combination of the 212 linguistic features resulted in the highest score (88.16%).

For the E.DIA.M.ME. corpus, we also obtain high accuracies, but a different pattern. Here the combination of lexical and syntactic features resulted in the best performing classifier (81.25%). Morphological features alone resulted in less reliable classification, and they additionally did not contribute to the classifier's performance when added to the feature set. These results indicate that for native Greeks living abroad, the focus of the material is on vocabulary and syntax, whereas morphology is less systematically introduced and complexified across levels.

The models based on a selection of the most informative features on the one hand confirm the pattern seen before, with larger feature sets performing better. But again the performance of the set of features with Info Gain > 0.1 is higher than in the previous experiments, and it reaches a noteworthy accuracy score in the E.DIA.M.ME. corpus. This finding confirms that not all dimensions of linguistic modeling are systematically complexified across CEFR classes in this corpus.

Table 6 summarises the best results for the heritage language and the second language corpora.

The confusion matrix in Table 7 illustrates where

Corpus	Accuracy	Weighted Avg. F-score	Best Performing Feature Group
GSL	**88.16%**	0.861	All Linguistic Features
E.DIA.M.ME.	**81.25%**	0.803	Lexical & Syntactic Features

Table 6: Summary of highest accuracy results for Greek heritage and second language corpora

the few texts are incorrectly classified for the GSL corpus, with all but one placed in an adjacent class.

CEFR	A	B	C	All	F-score
	predicted				
A	**181**	19	0	200	0.905
B	18	**157**	25	200	0.793
C	1	20	**179**	200	0.886

Table 7: Confusion matrix for Greek as a Second Language (GSL) corpus

For the E.DIA.M.ME corpus, Table 8 shows that texts from the intermediate level B were frequently misassigned, most often to the higher level (C).

CEFR	A	B	C	All	F-score
	predicted				
A	**158**	3	6	167	0.898
B	16	**39**	28	83	0.549
C	11	17	**154**	182	0.832

Table 8: Confusion matrix for Greek as a heritage language (E.DIA.M.ME) corpus

This result may be due to the fact that the E.DIA.M.ME level alignment to CEFR B2 and C1 levels is known to be unclear (Damanakis, 2011), but also due to the smaller size of the E.DIA.M.ME level B training set in our data. The finding is also in line with previous research on the linguistic features discriminating CEFR levels in the E.DIA.M.ME corpus (Giagkou et al., 2017), according to which the linguistic features investigated capture a significant shift in Greek reading skills during the transition from C1 to C2 CEFR level, but the transition from level A to B was not as clearly reflected.

Putting the results into the context of previous research on Greek readability classification, the classifiers substantially outperform previous work. While Giagkou (2009) reported an overall accuracy of 80.59%, this was for a two-level classification task, making the results not directly comparable. A more direct comparison is possible with Georga-

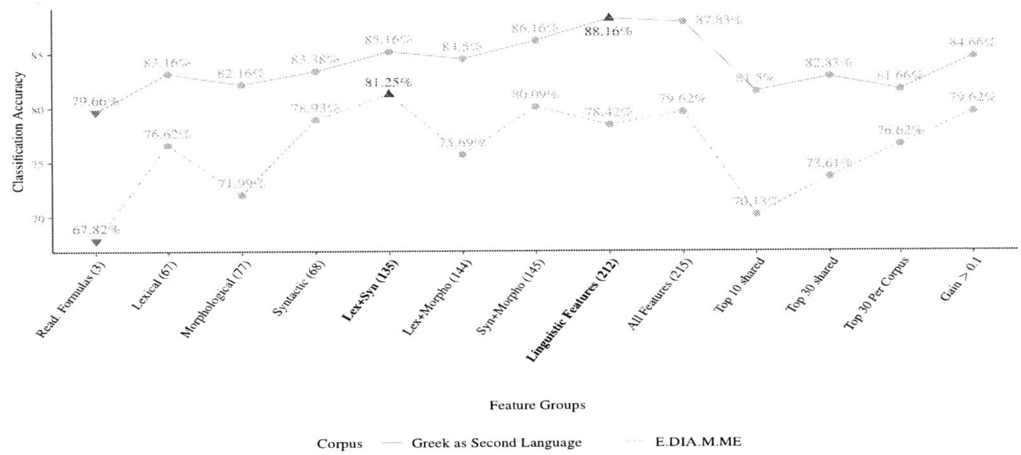

Figure 2: Ten-fold cross validation results for three-level CEFR classification

tou (2016) three-level ISCED classification results. Table 9 summarizes the accuracy of her classifiers compared to our best results in the respective corpora. For her experiments, Georgatou (2016) created a set of 153 complexity features which served as input variables to train the SMO classifier.

Corpus	Georgatou (2016)	This paper	Improv.
Greek	59.61%	66.53%	6.92
History	78.92%	83.83%	4.91
Science	76.47%	84.78%	8.31

Table 9: Comparison of results to Georgatou (2016)

Complementing this quantitative improvement of 5-8%, the empirical breadth provided by our combined and extended corpus base arguably contributes as much to advancing the state of the art – making it possible to conduct detailed cross-corpus analyses, as discussed in Section 4.4.

4.3 Analyzing the contributions of the different feature groups across corpora

It is already apparent from the findings reported so far that different feature groups and their combinations result in different classification results per corpus. To further investigate the influence of the feature groups on the classification models, we investigated the distribution of the most informative features per corpus. Figure 3 provides an overview of the number of features from the different feature groups with an Info Gain > 0.1 for the three level classification for the different corpora.

The first apparent aspect in Figure 3 is the total number of informative features (Info Gain>0.1) in the five corpora. For the E.DIA.M.ME. and GSL corpora, a substantially higher number of features is informative than for the school subjects corpora (Greek, History and Science). For instance, in the GSL corpus, more than half of all features (152 out of 215) are informative. This means that the linguistic features capture and model the complexity of the Greek heritage and second language material more effectively than that of the texts written for the different subjects taught in Greek schools. This may be due to the fact that the adoption of the CEFR guidelines in the development of Greek heritage and second language learning materials highlights the need to incrementally complexify the linguistic properties of the materials as the language proficiency develops; teaching the language here is the undisputed focus. In the development of the textbooks for the different school subjects in Greece, the subject to be taught will be the main concern so that the increased complexification of language to foster mastery of complex, academic language receives less of a central role. Also for the school subject Greek, the textbooks comprise authentic texts (writings of well-known writers among them) rather than being selected or written to foster academic language development. In the absence of a respective framework and descriptors for the development of academic language, the developers of school textbooks in Greece seem to focus more on the coverage of the curriculum topics, without equally catering for the linguistic properties of the texts that would correspond to the students' academic language development. Nevertheless, remember that the classifiers for the History and Sci-

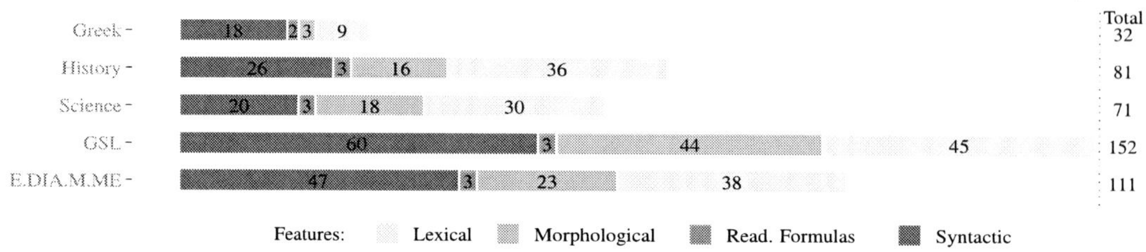

Figure 3: Feature evaluation: Features with Info Gain > 0.1 per corpus

ence corpora achieved accuracies of around 84% when considering a broad set of linguistic features. So incremental complexification of the language does already receive attention in the state-organized school books in Greece – which contrasts positively with the general lack of systematic language complexification in Geography textbooks published by commercial school book publishers in Germany as reported by Berendes et al. (2018).

A closer investigation of the History and Science corpora reveals a comparable distribution of the top informative features; lexical features proved to be more predictive with the syntactic ones following in the second place. On the other hand, only 32 features in total proved to be informative for the Greek corpus. More than half of the features are syntactic ones. These results, in addition to the classification accuracy scores in the three school subject corpora, highlight another characteristic: the domain-specific corpora (History and Science) make use of multiple dimensions of linguistic complexification. In contrast, the classification for the Greek corpus is more challenging, since only a small number of features, mainly the syntactic ones, show a significant distinctive variation throughout the school stages.

Moving to Greek as heritage or second language, the top features have a similar distribution in both corpora. A significant number of lexical, morphological and syntactic features are strong predictors, with the latter feature group being the most prominent. The prominence of syntactic features is in line with Giagkou et al. (2017), where the width and height of syntactic trees, the use of the genitive case and of adjectives, among others, were identified as successful discriminators of CEFR levels in the E.DIA.M.ME. corpus.

While the performance of readability formulae as a feature group was poor, they are among the informative features across corpora. This confirms that formulas based on simple measures of sentence and word length are an easy way to approximate complexity, though our experiments showed that they become irrelevant or even counterproductive when deeper linguistic complexity analyses are available.

4.4 Cross-corpus evaluation

To investigate the generalizability of the trained models, we conducted cross-corpus analyses, by systematically testing the models trained on one corpus on the other corpora. Table 10 summarises the results for classifiers trained on the different feature subsets. To facilitate comparison, the Table also includes the 10-fold cross-validation within-corpus results discussed in the previous sections.

Compared to the within-corpus analyses, the accuracies for cross-corpus evaluation are substantially reduced, though all still perform considerably above the random baseline of 33%. The classifiers trained on the heritage (E.DIA.ME.E.) or second language corpora (GSL) still exhibit acceptable accuracies of over 60%, when either is tested against the other. For the three school subject corpora (Greek, History, Science), the cross-corpus results drop below 60% (with the History classifier trained with Lexical and Syntactic features faring slightly better when evaluated on the Science corpus). Accuracy is higher when training and testing happens across the domain-specific curriculum subjects (History and Science). For interpreting the results, note that these two corpora share the same text genre, with both consisting of informational texts. Together with the lower performance for the Greek corpus, which belongs to a different genre, consisting mostly of literary texts, our investigation confirms the importance of genre effects in readability estimation (Sheehan et al., 2008). The classifiers generalize well across corpora of the same genre (informational texts on History and Science), but the Greek corpus classifier trained mostly on literary texts fails to generalize to informational texts.

Corpus		**Feature set**								
Models from:	Evaluated at:	Lex	Morpho	Syn	Lex & Syn	Lex& Morpho	Syn& Morpho	Ling. Feat	All Feat	Info Gain > 0.1
Greek	10-Fold	56.15	58.26	65.00	65.38	59.23	65.96	**66.53**	64.80	65.57
	History	56.52	51.97	55.44	**58.56**	51.73	52.93	55.20	55.80	56.64
	Science	38.10	**51.40**	40.15	36.18	47.44	40.28	40.28	40.66	36.82
History	10-Fold	75.08	74.97	76.88	78.68	79.88	80.71	**83.83**	82.75	75.80
	Greek	45.96	48.46	**54.03**	49.42	49.42	51.15	51.53	50.96	50.96
	Science	60.99	43.35	**61.89**	58.05	49.48	43.73	41.04	41.30	49.61
Science	10-Fold	75.31	75.06	75.70	80.94	80.30	81.58	**84.78**	83.37	77.49
	Greek	45.57	46.92	42.88	43.84	44.42	46.73	46.69	**48.07**	45.76
	History	54.85	42.63	**57.96**	55.32	54.37	46.22	51.61	51.73	50.17
GSL	10-Fold	83.16	82.16	83.38	85.16	84.5	86.16	**88.16**	87.83	84.66
	E.DIA.M.ME.	**64.12**	59.49	59.02	61.11	58.10	59.25	61.11	59.72	59.02
E.DIA.M.ME.	10-Fold	76.62	71.99	78.93	**81.25**	75.69	80.09	78.42	79.62	79.62
	GSL	**63.50**	56.66	60.16	61.00	57.33	59.83	59.99	59.00	60.83

Table 10: Cross-corpus analysis

The lower performance of the models based on the Greek corpus may be due to the smaller corpus size compared to the History and Science corpora.

Interestingly, while the full set of 212 linguistic features outperformed all other feature combinations in almost all of the within-corpus experiments, this is not the case in the cross-corpus experiments. In most cross-corpus tests the classifiers trained with single feature groups achieved the best results. This is consistent with our exploration of the most informative features per corpus (Section 4.3), where we found that different numbers of features from different linguistic sets were found to be informative in a given corpus.

Comparing the best accuracy scores achieved in within-corpus testing with the respective scores from the cross-corpus evaluation, an interesting pattern emerges: the Greek classifier, which was the lowest performer in within-corpus evaluation (66.53%) – presumably because it is trained on the most heterogeneous collection of texts, not originally written as teaching material – shows the lowest performance drop when applied to other corpora. So the classifier in cross-corpus testing seems to benefit from the wider domain and range of text types in its training material that make the within-corpus evaluation a harder task. There is thus a trade-off: A less specialized classifier, trained on a general corpus instead of a domain-specific one, is preferable in exhibiting a more stable behaviour when generalizing to other domains. At the same time, a generic readability modeling solution, pertinent to various text types and domains, then cannot be as finely attuned to domain- and text type-specific readability assessment.

5 Conclusions

In this paper, we addressed the issue of Greek readability classification based on a broad range of textbooks, from History and Science via Greek as a school subject to Greek as a heritage language and as a second language. We analyzed these textbook corpora covering all levels of school or language proficiency in terms of a set of complexity features covering three domains of linguistic modeling. Given that Greek is a highly inflected language with relatively free word order, particular emphasis was placed on the coverage of morphological and syntactic characteristics. While we designed the feature set to advance the state of the art for Greek readability research, we hope that it also encourages the development of such rich linguistic complexity feature sets for the broadening set of languages being investigated under related research perspectives.

In a series of three-class classification experiments, our feature set supported accuracy scores of up to 88%, outperforming the previous results for Greek readability classification. The lower accuracy obtained for the Greek as school subject corpus can be explained by its more heterogeneous nature as a collection of original texts and its smaller size. It probably also indicates that complexification of Greek as a school and academic language so far lacks a systematic framework and descriptors. In comparison, the adoption of the CEFR guidelines in the development of Greek as a Second Language learning materials arguably contributed to the very high accuracies achieved by our approach for the GSL corpus.

When comparing the classifiers trained on single feature groups to classifiers trained on combinations of feature sets, we observed that combinations of different linguistic feature domains systematically improved the results. In almost all within-corpus experiments, the results indicate that the richer the linguistic information, the better the classification performance.

The cross-corpus evaluation testing the generalizability of the classification models reduced classification accuracy. While the linguistic complexity features are capable of capturing complexification of language in general, the weighting of the evidence for readability classification in a strict sense thus is domain specific. Interestingly, the most successful model in terms of generalizability was the one with the lowest performance in the within-corpus validation results, namely the classifier trained on the heterogeneous Greek as a school subject corpus. While models trained on data covering a wide range of text types and domains generalize better, their top performance is lower than that of domain-specific models.

To foster further research on Greek readability classification, the four non-commercial textbook corpora we used for the reported research will become freely accessible through CLARIN.EL.

6 Acknowledgments

The authors would like to thank the Institute for Language and Speech Processing (ILSP) for its support and for providing access to the ILSP NLP pipeline for Greek. Special thanks to Spyridoula Georgatou for sharing three corpora for the purpose of this study. We thank the anonymous reviewers for their insightful comments and suggestions.

References

Ion Madrazo Azpiazu and Maria Soledad Pera. 2019. Multiattentive recurrent neural network architecture for multilingual readability assessment. *Transactions of the Association for Computational Linguistics*, 7:421–436.

Karin Berendes, Sowmya Vajjala, Detmar Meurers, Doreen Bryant, Wolfgang Wagner, Maria Chinkina, and Ulrich Trautwein. 2018. Reading demands in secondary school: Does the linguistic complexity of textbooks increase with grade level and the academic orientation of the school track? *Journal of Educational Psychology*, 110(4):518–543.

CCSSO. 2010. Common core state standards for English language arts & literacy in history/social studies, science, and technical subjects. Technical report, National Governors Association Center for Best Practices, Council of Chief State School Officers, Washington D.C. `http://www.corestandards.org/assets/CCSSI_ELA%20Standards.pdf`.

Savvas Chatzipanagiotidis. 2020. Combining machine learning techniques with broad linguistic analysis of readability in Greek. Master's thesis, international studies in computational linguistics, Eberhard Karls Universität Tübingen.

Çağrı Çöltekin and Taraka Rama. 2018. Exploiting universal dependencies treebanks for measuring morphosyntactic complexity. In *Proceedings of First Workshop on Measuring Language Complexity*, pages 1–7.

Alexis Conneau, Holger Schwenk, Loïc Barrault, and Yann Lecun. 2017. Very deep convolutional networks for text classification. In *Proceedings of the 15th Conference of the European Chapter of the Association for Computational Linguistics: Volume 1, Long Papers*, pages 1107–1116, Valencia, Spain. Association for Computational Linguistics.

Council of Europe. 2001. *Common European Framework of Reference for Languages: learning, teaching, assessment*. Cambridge University Press. Council for Cultural Co-operation. Education Committee. Modern Languages Division.

Michail Damanakis. 2011. Assessment of Greek-language education abroad by 2010 and its prospects [in Greek]. `http://ediamme.edc.uoc.gr/diaspora/index.php?id=248:apotimisi-tis-mexri-to-2010`.

Felice Dell'Orletta, Simonetta Montemagni, and Giulia Venturi. 2014. Assessing document and sentence readability in less resourced languages and across textual genres. *Recent Advances in Automatic Readability Assessment and Text Simplification. Special issue of the International Journal of Applied Linguistics*, 165(2):163–193.

Johan Falkenjack, Katarina Heimann Mühlenbock, and Arne Jönsson. 2013. Features indicating readability in Swedish text. In *Proceedings of the 19th Nordic Conference of Computational Linguistics (NODALIDA 2013)*, pages 27–40.

Thomas François and Cédrick Fairon. 2012. An "AI readability" formula for French as a foreign language. In *Proceedings of the 2012 Joint Conference on Empirical Methods in Natural Language Processing and Computational Natural Language Learning*, pages 466–477.

Spyridoula Georgatou. 2016. Approaching readability features in Greek school books. Master's thesis, international studies in computational linguistics, Eberhard Karls Universität Tübingen.

Maria Giagkou. 2009. *Corpora and language education: exploitation potentials in teaching Greek and construction of pedagogically relevant corpora* [in Greek]. Ph.d thesis, National and Kapodistrian University of Athens, Department of Philosophy, Athens.

Maria Giagkou, Giorgos Fragkakis, Dimitrios Pappas, and Harris Papageorgiou. 2017. Feature extraction and analysis in Greek L2 texts in view of automatic labeling for proficiency levels. In *Proceedings of the ICGL12*, volume 1, pages 357–368. Romiosini/CeMoG, Freie Universitat Berlin.

Maria Giagkou, Vicky Kantzou, Spyridoula Stamouli, and Maria Tzevelekou. 2015. Discriminating CEFR levels in Greek L2: a corpus-based study of young learners' written narratives. *Bergen Language and Linguistics Studies*, 6.

Edward Gibson. 2000. The dependency locality theory: A distance-based theory of linguistic complexity. In Alec Marantz, Yasushi Miyashita, and Wayne O'Neil, editors, *Image, language, brain: papers from the First Mind Articulation Project Symposium*, pages 95–126. MIT.

S Gnanambal, M Thangaraj, VT Meenatchi, and V Gayathri. 2018. Classification algorithms with attribute selection: an evaluation study using weka. *International Journal of Advanced Networking and Applications*, 9(6):3640–3644.

Mark Hall, Eibe Frank, Geoffrey Holmes, Bernhard Pfahringer, Peter Reutemann, and Ian H Witten. 2009. The WEKA data mining software: an update. *ACM SIGKDD explorations newsletter*, 11(1):10–18.

Julia Hancke, Sowmya Vajjala, and Detmar Meurers. 2012. Readability classification for German using lexical, syntactic, and morphological features. In *Proceedings of COLING 2012*, pages 1063–1080.

David M Howcroft and Vera Demberg. 2017. Psycholinguistic models of sentence processing improve sentence readability ranking. In *Proceedings of the 15th Conference of the European Chapter of the Association for Computational Linguistics: Volume 1, Long Papers*, pages 958–968.

Haitao Liu. 2008. Dependency distance as a metric of language comprehension difficulty. *Journal of Cognitive Science*, 9(2):159–191.

Xiaofei Lu. 2010. Automatic analysis of syntactic complexity in second language writing. *International journal of corpus linguistics*, 15(4):474–496.

Matej Martinc, Senja Pollak, and Marko Robnik-Šikonja. 2019. Supervised and unsupervised neural approaches to text readability. *arXiv preprint arXiv:1907.11779*.

J. Nelson, C. Perfetti, D. Liben, and M. Liben. 2012. Measures of text difficulty: Testing their predictive value for grade levels and student performance. Technical report, The Council of Chief State School Officers.

Ildikó Pilán, Elena Volodina, and Richard Johansson. 2014. Rule-based and machine learning approaches for second language sentence-level readability. In *Proceedings of the ninth workshop on innovative use of NLP for building educational applications*, pages 174–184.

Prokopis Prokopidis and Haris Papageorgiou. 2017. Universal Dependencies for Greek. In *Proceedings of the NoDaLiDa 2017 Workshop on Universal Dependencies (UDW 2017)*, pages 102–106, Gothenburg, Sweden. Association for Computational Linguistics.

Elissa Redmiles, Lisa Maszkiewicz, Emily Hwang, Dhruv Kuchhal, Everest Liu, Miraida Morales, Denis Peskov, Sudha Rao, Rock Stevens, Kristina Gligorić, et al. 2019. Comparing and developing tools to measure the readability of domain-specific texts. In *Proceedings of the 2019 Conference on Empirical Methods in Natural Language Processing and the 9th International Joint Conference on Natural Language Processing (EMNLP-IJCNLP)*, pages 4833–4844.

Cory Shain, Marten Van Schijndel, Richard Futrell, Edward Gibson, and William Schuler. 2016. Memory access during incremental sentence processing causes reading time latency. In *Proceedings of the workshop on computational linguistics for linguistic complexity (CL4LC)*, pages 49–58.

Kathleen M Sheehan, Irene Kostin, and Yoko Futagi. 2008. When do standard approaches for measuring vocabulary difficulty, syntactic complexity and referential cohesion yield biased estimates of text difficulty. In *Proceedings of the 30th Annual Conference of the Cognitive Science Society, Washington DC*. Citeseer.

Dimitrios Tzimokas and Marina Matthaioudaki. 2014. Deiktes anagnosimotitas: zitimata efarmogis kai axiopistias [in Greek]. In *Major Trends in Theoretical and Applied Linguistics 3*, pages 367–384. De Gruyter Open Poland.

Sowmya Vajjala and Ivana Lučić. 2018. OneStopEnglish corpus: A new corpus for automatic readability assessment and text simplification. In *Proceedings of the thirteenth workshop on innovative use of NLP for building educational applications*, pages 297–304. Association for Computational Linguistics.

Sowmya Vajjala and Detmar Meurers. 2012. On improving the accuracy of readability classification using insights from second language acquisition. In *Proceedings of the seventh workshop on building educational applications using NLP*, pages 163–173. Association for Computational Linguistics.

Zarah Weiss and Detmar Meurers. 2019a. Analyzing linguistic complexity and accuracy in academic language development of German across elementary and secondary school. In *Proceedings of the Fourteenth Workshop on Innovative Use of NLP for Building Educational Applications*, pages 380–393, Florence, Italy. Association for Computational Linguistics.

Zarah Weiss and Detmar Meurers. 2019b. Broad linguistic modeling is beneficial for German L2 proficiency assessment. In *Widening the Scope of Learner Corpus Research. Selected Papers from the Fourth Learner Corpus Research Conference*, Louvain-La-Neuve. Presses Universitaires de Louvain.

Menglin Xia, Ekaterina Kochmar, and Ted Briscoe. 2016. Text readability assessment for second language learners. In *Proceedings of the 11th Workshop on Innovative Use of NLP for Building Educational Applications*, pages 12–22, San Diego, CA. Association for Computational Linguistics.

Character Set Construction for Chinese Language Learning

Chak Yan Yeung, John Lee
Department of Linguistics and Translation
City University of Hong Kong
Hong Kong SAR, China
cyyeung91@gmail.com, jsylee@cityu.edu.hk

Abstract

To promote efficient learning of Chinese characters, pedagogical materials may present not only a single character, but a set of characters that are related in meaning and in written form. This paper investigates automatic construction of these character sets. The proposed model represents a character as averaged word vectors of common words containing the character. It then identifies sets of characters with high semantic similarity through clustering. Human evaluation shows that this representation outperforms direct use of character embeddings, and that the resulting character sets capture distinct semantic ranges.

1 Introduction

To promote efficient vocabulary acquisition, pedagogical materials may present the learner with a set of related words, rather than a single word. The set often consists of words belonging to the same "family"; for English, family members may share the same root, such as the words *special, specialize, specialty, especially*, etc. These families can be constructed in a straightforward manner from morphological databases and analyzers.[1]

An analogous strategy for teaching Chinese is the "character family", i.e. a set of characters that are similar in meaning and written form. A natural criterion for family membership is the semantic component, or semantic radical, of the character. The family based on the component 'sun', for example, includes the characters for 'sunny', 'sunshine' and 'dawn' as members (Table 1).

In comparison to word families in English, character families tend to exhibit less semantic regularity. Some family members may have unrelated meaning, or have obscured semantic relation in modern Chinese. For example, the character *cuò* 'wrong' belongs to the 'metal' family, and the character *zuó* 'past' belongs to the 'sun' family (Table 1). When preparing character sets for use in computer-assisted language learning (CALL) applications, manual selection is often necessary to ensure that the sets illustrate semantic regularity.

This paper investigates automatic construction of character sets. The proposed method can be expected to expedite the generation of these sets for more components and for a larger variety of semantic categories, with the goal of enhancing the coverage and effectiveness of CALL applications for learning Chinese.

2 Research Questions

For each semantic component, we define its "character family" to consist of all characters that contain the component. As shown in Table 1, not all family members have sufficiently related meaning to serve as good examples in pedagogical materials. Given a family, the *character set construction* task is to identify a subset of its characters that are semantically close. In designing an algorithm for this task, we address two research topics:

Character representation (Q1) The character representation should reflect the "overall" meaning of the character in a variety of contexts. We compare the use of character and word embeddings in constructing character sets (Section 4).

Subfamilies (Q2) All family members are traditionally viewed as capturing the general meaning of its semantic component. We investigate whether some families can be clustered into subfamilies to produce character sets with more tightly related meaning (Section 5).

[1] Examples include CELEX (Baayen et al., 1995) and Morfessor (Creutz and Lagus, 2006).

Proceedings of the 16th Workshop on Innovative Use of NLP for Building Educational Applications, pages 59–63
April 20, 2021 ©2021 Association for Computational Linguistics

Semantic component	Character family	
	Example character sets	Other characters
日 *rì* 'sun'	晴 *qíng* 'sunny', 暉 *huī* 'sunshine', 曉 *xiǎo* 'dawn'	昨 *zuó* 'past'
金 *jīn* 'metal'	銅 *tóng* 'copper', 鐵 *tiě* 'iron', 銀 *yín* 'silver'	錯 *cuò* 'wrong'
頁 *yè* 'page'	頭 *tóu* 'head', 額 *é* 'forehead', 頸 *jǐng* 'neck'	類 *lèi* 'type'
女 *nǚ* 'female'	Subfamily #1: 嫁 *jià* 'marry', 娶 *qǔ* 'marry', 婚 *hūn* 'marriage' Subfamily #2: 姨 *yí* 'aunt', 姐 *jiě* 'older sister', 妹 *mèi* 'younger sister'	始 *shǐ* 'begin'

Table 1: Each character family is associated with a semantic component and its members consist of all characters that contain the component. Semantic similarity can be strong for some family members ("Character sets" column) but less apparent for others ("Other characters" column).

3 Background

Chinese words are composed of characters. According to Li and Kang (1993), 81% of the characters are "semantic-phonetic compounds", which can be decomposed into two components. The phonetic component gives pronunciation clues. The semantic component, often used for organizing characters into families (Table 1), indicates the semantic range of the character.

The rest of this section summarizes research on Chinese subword structures in CALL (Section 3.1) and in natural language processing (Section 3.2).

3.1 CALL for Chinese characters

There are considerable pedagogical benefits in highlighting the semantic regularity in character families (Tse et al., 2007; Leong et al., 2011). Many CALL applications for Chinese have therefore featured these families, including web-based tutorials (Chen et al., 2011) and Scrabble-like character formation games (Lam et al., 2001; Lee and Yeung, 2020).

It is however well known that not all members in a character family have related meaning in modern Chinese. A character is called *transparent* if its meaning is similar or directly related to that of its semantic component. For example, in the 'metal' family, the characters *tóng* 'copper' and *tiě* 'iron' are transparent, while the character *cuò* 'wrong' is not (Table 1). According to an analysis of primary school material (Chung and Leung, 2008), only 64% to 82% of the characters have meaning that is related or somewhat related to its semantic component. A direct consequence is that semantic components are not uniformly useful in aiding comprehension (Liow et al., 1999). Character sets therefore often require manual curation, which constrains their use in interactive CALL applications.

3.2 Subword representation in Chinese

Various algorithms have been proposed to train embeddings for Chinese at the subword level. Contextual embeddings such as BERT (Devlin et al., 2019) are designed to derive character embeddings in a specific sentential context. In contrast, identifying the general or overall meaning of a character is the main objective in the character set construction task. Our evaluation will focus on the use of context-free embeddings.

Context-free embeddings at the word-, character- and component levels (Lu et al., 2016; Yu et al., 2017; Cao et al., 2018; Devlin et al., 2019) have been applied to many downstream tasks in Chinese NLP, but there has not been any quantitative evaluation on their use in creating character sets for CALL. Besides direct use of character embeddings, a possible approach is to measure similarity between character and component embeddings, as suggested by a qualitative study on the 'illness' component (Yu et al., 2017). An alternative is to exploit embeddings of words formed by the character, although the character's semantic contribution to different words may vary (Xu et al., 2016). Our study evaluates character sets produced by a number of these approaches.

4 Character representation

We address Q1 by evaluating two character representations for the character set construction task: given a family F, identify a subset of N characters, say $S = \{c_1, ..., c_N\} \subseteq F$, that have the most similar or related meaning.

4.1 Approach

A simple approach would be to retrieve characters with the closest meaning to the semantic component associated with F. This method can be problematic, however, since the dominant meaning of a component may differ from those of the family members. For example, members of the family associated with the component *yè* are semantically related to "head", but as a standalone character *yè* means 'page' in modern Chinese (Table 1).

We instead measure semantic similarity between characters. Using a set of 7.6 million sentences from Chinese Wikipedia, we trained context-free embeddings $\vec{c}$ and $\vec{w}$ for each character c and word w with the joint learning model proposed by Yu et al. (2017). We compare two methods for generating the representation $v(c)$ for a character c:

Character vector The baseline directly uses the character embeddings, i.e., $v(c) = \vec{c}$.

Averaged word vectors The meaning of some characters may be more clearly expressed within words. From the Wikipedia dataset, we retrieve the k most frequent words $w_1, \ldots, w_k$ that contain the character c. We then average the word vectors of these k words, i.e. defining $v(c) = \frac{1}{k} \sum_{i=1,\ldots,k} \vec{w_i}$.

We assign a score to each candidate character set S by summing the cosine similarity for all its character pairs c_i, c_j:

$$score(S) = \sum_{i,j \leq N, i \neq j} cos(v(c_i), v(c_j)) \quad (1)$$

We then choose the character set that maximizes this score.

4.2 Set-up

We extracted all characters that can be decomposed into two components from the open-source dataset HanziJS.[2] Each character was then assigned to the two character families associated with its two components.[3] We included only characters listed in the *Hanyu Shuiping Kaoshi* (HSK) (Hanban, 2014), the most popular scheme for learning Chinese as a foreign language.

[2]https://github.com/nieldlr/hanzi

[3]Manual inspection would be needed to distinguish between phonetic and semantic components. For a fully automatic algorithm, we relied on the model to learn the distinction rather than manually filtering out phonetic components.

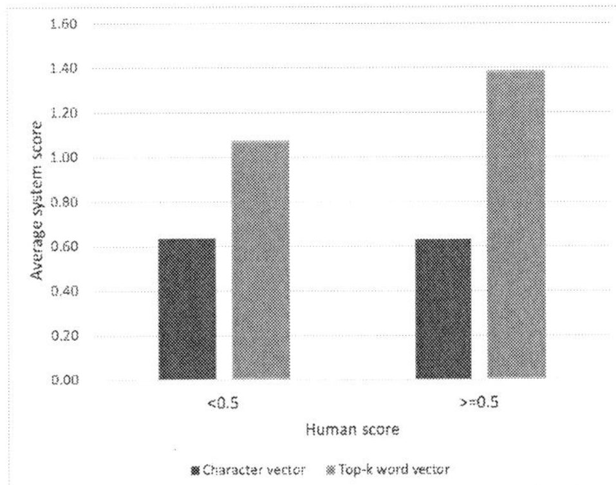

Figure 1: The "Averaged word vectors" method (top-k word vectors) assigns higher scores to similar character pairs (rated 0.5 or over) than dissimilar pairs (rated below 0.5); in contrast, the "Character vector" method does not clearly distinguish the similar and dissimilar pairs.

There were 2,285 characters distributed in 600 character families. We randomly selected ten character families for evaluation. For each family, we constructed two character sets of size $N = 3$ using the two methods for generating $v(c)$ (Section 4.1), with the settings $k = \{5, 10, 15\}$.

4.3 Evaluation

We presented two human judges with all character pairs within the 20 character sets. Both native speakers of Chinese, the judges rated each pair according to the annotation scheme of the SemEval-2012 shared task on Chinese word similarity (Jin and Wu, 2012). The similarity score ranged from 0 (not at all related) to 5 (identical).

We computed the correlation between the averaged human scores and the cosine similarity $cos(v(c_i), v(c_j))$ as generated by the two methods described in Section 4.1. The "Character vector" method attained a Pearson correlation coefficient of only 0.09.[4] The "Averaged word vectors" method achieved a coefficient of 0.80[5], outperforming the "Character vector" method. This coefficient was obtained at $k = 5$, i.e., averaging the 5 most frequent words. Performance degraded at higher values of k, likely because of increased sensitivity to the corpus domain.

To visualize the correlation, we compared the cosine similarity $cos(v(c_i), v(c_j))$ of the similar char-

[4]Correlation with human scores was not significant, at $p > 0.05$

[5]Correlation with human scores was significant, at $p < 0.006$

acter pairs (defined as those with human ratings of 0.5 and above) and the dissimilar pairs. As shown in Figure 1, the "Averaged word vectors" method produces substantially higher similarity scores for the similar pairs than the dissimilar pairs, while the "Character vector" method does not clearly distinguish the similar and dissimilar pairs.

These results suggest that averaged word vectors are more effective for character set construction than direct use of character embeddings. The most frequent words likely play significant roles in shaping the "general" meaning of a character as perceived by native speakers.

5 Subfamilies

We next address Q2 by dividing a family into subfamilies, and evaluating the quality of character sets generated from the subfamilies.

5.1 Approach

We used K-means clustering to produce subfamilies F_i from a character family F. The number of clusters for each family was determined by the silhouette value, which measures the distance between each point in a cluster to the points in its neighboring clusters.[6]

We extracted a character set of size $N = 3$ from each subfamily using the "Averaged word vectors" method at $k = 5$, which obtained the best results (Section 4.3). We identified the two subfamilies F_1 and F_2 with the highest-scoring character sets in terms of $score(S)$, as defined in Section 4.1. For evaluation, we compare the following sets:

Subfamily #1 The character set produced by F_1.

Subfamily #2 The character set produced by F_2.

Mixed Subfamilies The character set produced by randomly swapping one character between Subfamily #1 and Subfamily #2.

Random The character set produced by random selection among characters in F.

5.2 Set-up

Among the 600 character families (Section 4.2), K-means clustering discovered two clusters in 14 character families, and three clusters in 5 character families. Table 1 shows two clusters, or subfamilies, identified in the character family of the component *nǚ* 'female', semantically associated with matrimony and relatives, respectively. We randomly selected eight of these families for evaluation.

Character set	Average score
Subfamily #1	1.67
Subfamily #2	1.32
Mixed Subfamilies	0.75
Random	0.53

Table 2: Human scores on character sets constructed from two subfamilies and two baselines (Section 5.1)

5.3 Evaluation

Similar to the previous experiment, the two human judges rated the similarity of all character pairs in the generated character sets.

As shown in Table 2, the character sets Subfamily #1 (1.67) and Subfamily #2 (1.32) achieved the highest average similarity scores. Both outperformed[7] the Random set, which attained an average of 0.53 only. This result indicates that our proposed method is able to identify characters within a family that are more semantically related than other family members.

Further, Subfamily #1 (1.67) outperformed[8] Mixed Subfamilies (0.75), suggesting that the judges perceived semantic differences between the two subfamilies. Subfamily #2 (1.32) also scored higher than Mixed Subfamilies, although the difference was not significant[9], likely due to the lower degree of similarity between its members compared to their Subfamily #1 counterparts.

6 Conclusion

We have presented the first quantitative study on automatic construction of Chinese character sets to facilitate language learning. We have evaluated a number of methods for character representation and family clustering. Experimental results showed that averaged word vectors achieved statistically significant improvement over direct use of character vectors. Further, K-means clustering produced subfamilies that yielded character sets with distinctive meaning. It is hoped that these methods will help expand the variety and coverage of character

[6]We used the implementation in scikit-learn (Pedregosa et al., 2011). We allowed a maximum of 10 clusters per family, and rejected clusters with less than 5 characters.

[7]Statistically significant at $p < 0.025$ by t-test

[8]Statistically significant at $p < 0.002$ by t-test

[9]At $p = 0.27$

sets for use in CALL applications for Chinese.

Acknowledgements

We gratefully acknowledge support from an Applied Research Grant (project #9667175) at City University of Hong Kong, and a grant from the Hong Kong Institute for Data Science (project #9360163) at City University of Hong Kong.

References

Harald Baayen, Richard Piepenbrock, and Léon Gulikers. 1995. *The CELEX lexical database (CD-ROM)*.

Shaosheng Cao, Wei Lu, Jun Zhou, and Xiaolong Li. 2018. cw2vec: Learning Chinese Word Embeddings with Stroke n-gram Information. In *Proc. 32nd AAAI Conference on Artificial Intelligence*.

Hsueh-Chih Chen, Li-Yun Chang, Kuo-En Chang, Yu-Shiou Chiou, and Yao-Ting Sung. 2011. Chinese Orthography Database and Its Application in Teaching Chinese Characters (in Chinese). *Bulletin of Educational Psychology (Special Issue on Reading)*, 43:269–290.

Flora Hoi Ki Chung and Man Tak Leung. 2008. Data analysis of Chinese characters in primary school corpora of Hong Kong and mainland China: preliminary theoretical interpretations. *Clinical Linguistics and Phonetics*, 22(4-5):379–389.

Mathias Creutz and Krista Lagus. 2006. Morfessor in the Morpho Challenge. In *Proc. PASCAL Challenge Workshop on Unsupervised Segmentation of Words into Morphemes*.

Jacob Devlin, Ming-Wei Chang, Kenton Lee, and Kristina Toutanova. 2019. BERT: Pretraining of Deep Bidirectional Transformers for Language Understanding. In *Proc. NAACL-HLT*.

Hanban. 2014. *International Curriculum for Chinese Language and Education*. Beijing Language and Culture University Press, Beijing, China.

Peng Jin and Yunfang Wu. 2012. SemEval-2012 Task 4: Evaluating Chinese Word Similarity. In *Proc. First Joint Conference on Lexical and Computational Semantics (*SEM)*, pages 374–377.

H. C. Lam, W. W. Ki, N. Law, A. L. S. Chung, P. Y. Ko, A. H. S. Ho, and S. W. Pun. 2001. Designing CALL for Learning Chinese Characters. *Journal of Computer Assisted Learning*, 17:115–128.

John Lee and Chak Yan Yeung. 2020. Computer-assisted learning for chinese based on character families. In *Information Management and Big Data*, pages 299–305, Cham. Springer International Publishing.

Che Kan Leong, Shek Kam Tse, Ka Yee Loh, and Wing Wah Ki. 2011. Orthographic Knowledge Important in Comprehending Elementary Chinese Text by Users of Alphasyllabaries. *Reading Psychology*, 32(3):237–271.

Y. Li and J. S. Kang. 1993. Analysis of Phonetics of the Ideophonetic Characters in Modern Chinese. In *Information Analysis of Usage of Characters in Modern Chinese (in Chinese)*, pages 84–98, Shanghai. Shanghai Education Publisher.

Susan J. Rickard Liow, Siok Keng Tng, and Cher Leng Lee. 1999. Chinese Characters: Semantic and Phonetic Regularity Norms for China, Singapore, and Taiwan. *Behavior Research Methods, Instruments, and Computers*, 31(1):155–177.

Yanan Lu, Yue Zhang, and Donghong Ji. 2016. Multi-prototype Chinese Character Embedding. In *Proc. 10th International Conference on Language Resources and Evaluation (LREC)*, page 855–859.

Fabian Pedregosa, Gaël Varoquaux, Alexandre Gramfort, Vincent Michel, Bertrand Thirion, Olivier Grisel, Mathieu Blondel, Peter Prettenhofer, Ron Weiss, Vincent Dubourg, et al. 2011. Scikit-learn: Machine learning in python. *Journal of machine learning research*, 12(Oct):2825–2830.

Shek Kam Tse, Ference Marton, Wing Wah Ki, and Elizabeth Ka Yee Loh. 2007. An Integrative Perceptual Approach to Teaching Chinese Characters. *Instructional Science*, 35:375–406.

Jian Xu, Jiawei Liu, Liangang Zhang, Zhengyu Li, and Huanhuan Chen. 2016. Improve Chinese Word Embeddings by Exploiting Internal Structure. In *Proc. NAACL-HLT*, page 1041–1050.

Jinxing Yu, Xun Jian, Hao Xin, and Yangqiu Song. 2017. Joint Embeddings of Chinese Words, Characters, and Fine-grained Subcharacter Components. In *Proc. Conference on Empirical Methods in Natural Language Processing (EMNLP)*, page 286–291.

Identifying negative language transfer in learner errors using POS information

Leticia Farias Wanderley
EdTeKLA Research Group
Department of Computing Science
University of Alberta
fariaswa@ualberta.ca

Carrie Demmans Epp
EdTeKLA Research Group
Department of Computing Science
University of Alberta
cdemmansepp@ualberta.ca

Abstract

A common mistake made by language learners is the misguided usage of first language rules when communicating in another language. In this paper, n-gram and recurrent neural network language models are used to represent language structures and detect when Chinese native speakers incorrectly transfer rules from their first language (i.e., Chinese) into their English writing. These models make it possible to inform corrective error feedback with error causes, such as negative language transfer. We report the results of our negative language detection experiments with n-gram and recurrent neural network models that were trained using part-of-speech tags. The best performing model achieves an F1-score of 0.51 when tasked with recognizing negative language transfer in English learner data.

1 Introduction

Advances in grammatical error correction (GEC) research allow writing editors to provide real-time corrective feedback to language learners. GEC systems are trained on parallel erroneous and corrected learner data to detect and suggest corrections for user errors. State-of-the-art GEC systems apply neural machine translation to learn how to correct grammatical errors in English learner data (Bryant et al., 2019). These systems also use metadata, such as the learners' native languages and their proficiency levels in the target language, to support the GEC task (Nadejde and Tetreault, 2019).

The direct corrective feedback derived from GEC systems' predictions helps learners improve their writing and increase their language understanding. However, direct corrective feedback is not the only type of information that can aid language learning (Bacquet, 2019). Learners also benefit from metalinguistic feedback. This feedback type can support learners' reflections on their language usage and, consequently, increase their grammatical awareness (Karim and Nassaji, 2020).

One metalinguistic phenomenon that often causes confusion and errors in learner writing is the occurrence of language transfer. The language transfer phenomenon is characterized by learners reusing rules from their first languages (L1s) when communicating in a second one[1] (L2) (Lado, 1957). When the L1 and L2 grammars diverge, learners who apply L1 rules make mistakes. This particular version of language transfer is called negative language transfer, and it is a significant source of errors in second language learner speaking and writing.

This paper explores the application of language models to represent language structures and detect negative language transfer in learner essays written by Chinese native speakers. The proposed methods aim to identify incorrect learner utterances that have structural patterns that are more similar to the learners' L1 (Chinese) than to their L2 (English). In this paper, we demonstrate that a recurrent neural network trained to identify a part-of-speech (POS) tag sequence's source language outperformed POS n-gram models in negative language transfer detection. The RNN model achieved an F1-score of 0.51 on the negative language transfer detection task analysing POS tag sequences extracted from learner errors. The output of this language model can be used to inform metalinguistic feedback, tying the incorrect utterances to differences between the L1 and English rules. By enabling negative language transfer detection in learner writing, language learners will have access to interpretable information about their errors' potential causes along with direct corrective feedback for those errors.

[1] By second language, we mean any additional language beyond the learner's mother tongue.

Proceedings of the 16th Workshop on Innovative Use of NLP for Building Educational Applications, pages 64–74
April 20, 2021 ©2021 Association for Computational Linguistics

2 Related work

When writing in another language, writers are prone to leave behind certain traces of their native languages. This fact is the foundation for the native language identification task. This task makes use of computational models to determine the L1 of a text's author (Tetreault et al., 2013; Malmasi et al., 2017). Native language identification models aim to uncover usage patterns that distinguish native speakers of a certain language when writing in English. Rabinovich et al. (2018) explored the usage of cognates in non-native English writing to cluster the authors' text according to their native languages' families. Cognates are words from distinct languages that are similar in meaning and form. As demonstrated by Rabinovich et al. (2018), non-native English writers show a preference for using English words that have cognates in their L1. Furthermore, Flanagan et al. (2015) have shown that it is possible to employ the authors' error patterns to discriminate between L1s, as English learners' writing errors are highly correlated to their native languages.

Learner writing errors are useful in yet another computational task. The aforementioned grammatical error correction task aims to detect and correct errors in learner data (Ng et al., 2013, 2014; Bryant et al., 2019). State-of-the-art GEC systems model the task as a neural machine translation procedure in which the erroneous learner data is the source language, and its corrected version is the target language (Bryant et al., 2019). Throughout the years, researchers have explored the impact of using L1-specific learner data to train GEC systems: see Rozovskaya and Roth (2011), Chollampatt et al. (2016), and Nadejde and Tetreault (2019) for examples. These researchers have found that whether GEC models are exclusively trained with L1-specific data or whether this data is only used to fine-tune the model, GEC benefits from information about learners' L1s. In addition to that, Nadejde and Tetreault (2019) explored fine-tuning GEC systems to learners' English proficiency levels and L1s. They found that information about both learner aspects improves GEC performance.

English non-native speakers transfer patterns and rules from their L1s into English writing. This phenomenon has been explored by native language identification and grammatical error correction systems. Moreover, the phenomenon has been demonstrated in experimental investigations of the contrastive analysis hypothesis (Lado, 1957), as reported in papers by Wong and Dras (2009) and Berzak et al. (2015). Berzak et al. (2015) found a correlation between structural error distribution in English as a second language learners' writing and typological differences between the learners' L1s and English. Their work used the L1's structural properties to predict challenging grammatical areas in English as a second language writing.

One of the challenges for language learners is that they are often unaware that they reuse structures from their L1s (Wanderley and Demmans Epp, 2020). One way to alleviate this difficulty is to provide error feedback that contains information about possible error sources (Bacquet, 2019). Linguists and education researchers have long debated what is the best way to provide feedback in a second language setting. Some argue that no feedback should be given, while others posit that learners should have access to a different range of error feedback types, such as direct, indirect, comprehensive, and focused (Bitchener et al., 2005). More recent research has found that providing metalinguistic feedback can increase language learners' writing accuracy (Bacquet, 2019; Karim and Nassaji, 2020). Unlike direct corrective feedback, which simply highlights and corrects learner errors, metalinguistic feedback can help learners understand their errors by calling attention to the errors and describing possible causes (Lyster and Ranta, 1997). To understand whether students value metalinguistic feedback about negative language transfer, Watts (2019) examined Japanese students' familiarity with the phenomenon. These learners highlighted how being aware of language transfer effects helped improve their English writing.

While natural language processing (NLP) tasks and language learners benefit from information about negative language transfer, we are not aware of previous research that automatically detects this phenomenon. Recently, Monaikul and Di Eugenio (2020) applied traditional and neural natural language processing methods to detect preposition omission errors with the aim of informing negative language transfer feedback. Preposition errors are one of the most common types of negative language transfer errors in second language learning. In their paper, the authors proposed applying the preposition error detection output to generate metalinguistic contrastive feedback for language learners and teachers (Monaikul and Di Eugenio, 2020).

Dataset	Number of sentences
Global Voices	138 582
WMT19	11 960
Combined	150 542

Table 1: Training datasets sizes

Error type	Count
Structural negative language transfer	1457
Structural not negative language transfer	914
Total	2371

Table 2: Structural negative language transfer error counts from the test dataset

We envision a similar application of our results. However, our focus is on detecting additional negative language transfer errors. We want to detect all those that come from learners inappropriately applying structural patterns from their L1s when writing in English.

3 Data

3.1 Training data

In this paper, we explore the application of shallow syntactic language models in negative language transfer detection. We use the part-of-speech sequences within a language to create what we call a shallow syntactic language model, thus representing language structures. Instead of representing the probability of word sequences in a language, these models compute the likelihood of POS tag sequences. As we wanted to model L1 and English structures with these models, we needed textual data in both languages. To ensure that the shallow syntactic language models in the L1 and in English were equivalent in number of training samples and context, parallel data in those languages were used for training.

Two parallel datasets were used to train the Chinese and English models. These datasets are available online and are aligned at the sentence level (Tiedemann, 2012). The first data source is the Global Voices dataset (Prokopidis et al., 2016). It contains multilingual parallel media stories from the Global Voices website[2]. The second dataset is the news test set from the ACL 2019 Fourth Conference on Machine Translation (WMT19)[3] (Barrault et al., 2019). Table 1 presents the number of parallel sentences in each dataset. These datasets were chosen because they contain text that observes simple yet grammatical language structures, patterns that language learners are familiar with and encouraged to use.

[2]https://globalvoices.org/

[3]http://statmt.org/wmt19/translation-task.html

3.2 Test data

Our test data consists of error annotated English learner data. This data was extracted from the First Certificate in English (FCE) dataset (Yannakoudakis et al., 2011). The FCE exam is an upper-intermediate English language certification. The 1244 essays in the FCE dataset were written by English as a second language learners who took the exam between 2000 and 2001. These essays were manually error annotated. During the annotation process, the FCE annotators applied the error coding system described in Nicholls (2003) to highlight writing errors and correct them.

The FCE dataset is suitable to our task because each essay is annotated with the native language of its writer (Yannakoudakis et al., 2011). In addition to the original FCE data, the highlighted errors were annotated with information regarding their relation to negative language transfer. Each error in the dataset is accompanied by a flag indicating whether its grammatical structure resembles the learner's L1. The negative language transfer annotation process was performed by a native speaker of English and Mandarin Chinese who teaches Chinese as a foreign language. The annotation results can be accessed through our research laboratory's website[4]. In total, there are 3092 errors in essays written by Chinese native speakers. Out of these, 1776 (57.4%) are negative language transfer related (Wanderley et al., 2021). The negative language transfer annotation allows the evaluation of our proposed detection methods. It is our gold-standard.

Since we aim to detect structural negative language transfer, we filtered the errors on the test set to only contain structural errors. We borrow some of the definition of structural errors from Berzak et al. (2015), filtering out spelling and word replacement errors from the test dataset. The resulting dataset contains 2371 structural error instances. Among those, 61.45% are related to negative language transfer and 38.55% are not (see Table 2).

[4]https://github.com/EdTeKLA/LanguageTransfer

Language	Min	Q1	Median	Q3	Max
English	1	12	19	29	258
Chinese	1	6	10	16	230

Table 3: Length statistics of part-of-speech tagged training sequences

	Training split	Evaluation split
Chinese	120 433	30 109
English	120 433	30 109

Table 4: Number of sequences belonging to the training and evaluation splits that were used in hyperparameter tuning

3.3 Data preprocessing

As previously mentioned, we used Chinese and English parallel data to build shallow syntactic language models. These models were trained with POS tag sequences extracted from the parallel training sentences. The data was POS tagged using the Python library spaCy[5].

SpaCy is an NLP library that has pre-trained Chinese and English POS taggers. SpaCy's pre-trained taggers allowed the sentences from the training data to be POS tagged according to their languages. They were tagged either by a POS tagger trained on Chinese text or by one trained on English text. Table 3 summarizes the training sequences' lengths. While the training sentences were tagged by one of two POS taggers (i.e., English or Chinese), the FCE dataset sentences were only tagged with spaCy's English POS tagger.

The Universal Dependencies[6] POS tagset was used. This treebank defines syntactic annotations that are common among a variety of languages, including English and Chinese (Nivre et al., 2016). It fits our experiments as it allows us to model language structures using a shared POS tagset, and consequently, consistently compare a single POS tag sequence across languages.

4 Methods

4.1 N-gram baseline

N-gram language models are a statistical NLP approach to language modelling that represents a language as its token sequence distribution. These models output the likelihood of a sequence belonging to the language they represent (Jurafsky and Martin, 2009). N-gram shallow syntactic language models represent a language's structure as the distribution of POS tag sequences in the language. These models function in a straightforward way. During training they derive a probability distribution over all possible POS tag sequences in the training data. Then, when provided a test sequence, they compute its likelihood based on the training probability distribution.

N-gram shallow syntactic language models were used to assign probabilities to POS tag sequences extracted from learner errors. As one n-gram model is only able to represent one language. We trained one model on POS tag sequences extracted from the English sentences and another model on POS tag sequences extracted from the Chinese text. After the models were trained, each erroneous sequence in the FCE dataset was evaluated by both n-gram models separately, and the probability values output by the n-gram models were compared. If the Chinese model's output for a POS tag sequence was higher than the English model's output, the error which generated that POS tag sequence was classified as negative language transfer.

The n-gram shallow syntactic language models used in our experiments were trained using the Python interface for KenLM[7]. KenLM is a language model package that applies several performance improvement techniques to its n-gram modelling implementation. For example, KenLM applies modified Kneser-Ney smoothing to the n-gram distribution (Heafield et al., 2013). Moreover, this language model implementation improves querying time by using trie data structures and linear probing to store and retrieve n-gram probabilities (Heafield, 2011).

The best parameter setting for the n-gram models was selected through a systematic search over the parameter space. In this process, 20% of each monolingual training dataset was kept as an evaluation set. The remaining 80% was used to train n-gram shallow syntactic language models with varying n-gram lengths (2 to 6). See Table 4 for the number of training and evaluation sequences used in this tuning process. The n-gram models that achieved the best accuracy (96.94%) in identifying the language of POS tag sequences extracted from evaluation sentences had n = 5. That is, they analysed one sequence of five POS tags at a time.

[5]https://spacy.io/

[6]https://universaldependencies.org/

[7]https://kheafield.com/code/kenlm/

4.2 Recurrent neural network approach

Recurrent neural networks (RNNs) are artificial neural networks known to effectively model sequential data, such as natural language (Dyer et al., 2016). Mikolov et al. (2010) have shown that RNN architectures outperform other statistical methods in language modelling tasks. In RNN architectures, each unit's output is based not only on its respective input but also on the output of preceding units. Hence, these networks are able to take previous context into account when processing current information. This recurrent aspect of RNN architectures is particularly relevant to language modelling tasks, in which tokens are often related to remote neighbours.

One advantage of RNNs over n-gram models in detecting negative language transfer is that a single network is able to learn how to differentiate between languages. As opposed to the n-gram baseline that needed one model for English and one for Chinese, a single RNN model can be trained to identify a POS tag sequence's originating language based on its structure. During training, the RNN model learned how to predict language from POS tag sequences extracted from English and Chinese text. Then, for each erroneous POS tag sequence in the FCE dataset, the trained RNN would predict English or Chinese, according to which language structure the POS tag sequence most resembled. If the network returned "Chinese", the error which generated that POS tag sequence was flagged as negative language transfer.

The RNN implementation from the Python library PyTorch[8] was used in our experiments. The model was trained for ten epochs with Adam optimization (Kingma and Ba, 2015). Each of the 17 POS tags in the Universal Dependencies tagset was converted into a one-hot-encoding vector of length 17, i.e., each distinct tag in the tagset was represented by one position in the vector. Using these vector representations, the POS tag sequences in the training and test datasets were converted to POS tag vector arrays, preserving the original POS tag sequences' orders.

Similarly to the n-gram baseline, the RNN hyperparameters were selected from a set of options in the parameter space. The evaluation of the hyperparameter settings was made on 20% of the training data (the evaluation split), while the network was trained on the remaining 80% of the training data. Table 4 provides the number of POS tag sequences included in each split. In total, four parameters were tuned - the number of hidden units (8, 16, 32, 64, 128, 256, or 512 units); the learning rate (0.01, 0.001, 0.0001, 0.00001, or 0.000001); the batch size (1, 2, 4, 8, 16, or 32 samples per mini batch); and the loss function (negative log likelihood[9] or binary cross entropy with logits[10]). The RNN models analysed in the hyperparameter tuning procedure were trained for 10 epochs. The best performing model, which achieved 95.16% accuracy on the evaluation set, had 16 hidden units, learning rate = 0.0001, mini batch size = 1, and negative log likelihood as its loss function.

Note that the best evaluation accuracy achieved in the RNN hyperparameter tuning was not as high as the one achieved in the n-gram models' tuning procedure. These results are a reflection of the type of data being modelled in this task. The POS tag sequences extracted from sentences in Chinese and English are from high-quality (i.e., grammatical and manually translated) data that is characterized by a high degree of regularity which is well-represented by n-gram models. Each n-gram model trained on one of the parallel datasets can accurately classify POS tag sequences as belonging to a language or not. The n-gram model for one language cannot, however, infer whether the POS tag sequences belong to the language represented by the other model. In this aspect, RNN-based models are more fitted to the task. They are able to specifically differentiate between Chinese and English structures and decide to which language a POS tag sequence belongs.

4.3 Test sequences

Among other aspects, structural errors in the FCE dataset vary with regards to length and dependency. For example, a wrong word order error consists of several words incorrectly arranged. The number of incorrect words in wrong word order errors is always greater than one, while an unnecessary adverb error, for instance, consists of one single incorrect word. As for the dependency aspect, the incorrect words from an error usually are in conflict with another word in the sentence. The positions of the word involved differ according to error type. For

[8] `https://pytorch.org/`

[9] `https://pytorch.org/docs/stable/generated/torch.nn.NLLLoss.html`

[10] `https://pytorch.org/docs/stable/generated/torch.nn.BCEWithLogitsLoss.html`

Incorrect sentence	**Error subtype**	**Padded error span**	**Error + unigram span**	**Error + bigram span**
Moreover, the stars and artists were *only from* six countries.	Wrong word order	were *only from* six AUX ADV ADP NUM	*only from* six ADV ADP NUM	*only from* six countries ADV ADP NUM NOUN
They flew out of the window and hit *directly* the headmaster's head.	Unnecessary adverb	hit *directly* the VERB ADV DET	*directly* the ADV DET	*directly* the headmaster ADV DET NOUN
This are only my immature views.	Pronoun agreement	*This* are DET AUX	*This* are DET AUX	*This* are only DET AUX ADV
This *remind* me of what I experienced.	Verb agreement	This *remind* me DET VERB PRON	*remind* me VERB PRON	*remind* me of VERB PRON ADP

Table 5: Learner errors and test windows examples

example, a pronoun agreement error is often caused by disagreement with the subsequent word. However, a verb agreement error usually comes from an incongruence with its preceding word. Table 5 presents learner error examples along with their distinct lengths and dependencies. These distinctive aspects prompted the design of experiments that evaluated different spans of erroneous POS tag sequences.

The negative language transfer detection models received POS tag sequences extracted from learner errors as test input. To attempt to capture error dependencies in these sequences, we defined and tested three different POS tag sequence spans. Regardless of the span selected, all of the error's POS tags were included in the test sequences. The spans only defined how much of the error's surrounding context was included in the test POS tag sequences. They defined whether the POS tags preceding and following the errors would be part of the sequence evaluated by the shallow syntactic language models.

The first input span considered was the padded error sequence. These test sequences contained the POS tag that precedes the erroneous tags, the tags extracted from the error, and the subsequent POS tag, which is the one that comes immediately after the erroneous tags. The preceding and subsequent tags were only included if there were words before and after the error, e.g., when the error occurred on the first word of a sentence, the preceding tag was not included in the input test sequence as it did not exist. The second and third spans that were tested took into account the POS tags extracted from the error followed by POS tags from words that followed the error. One of them considers the tag from the word that immediately follows the error, while the other considers the tags from the error's two subsequent words. They are referred to as "error + unigram" and "error + bigram" spans. Table 5 illustrates the POS tag spans used in the experiments.

There is one type of error that required an adjustment to the span definitions. Omission errors, such as missing noun errors, happen when the learner has not included a word that was necessary. If represented by the error + unigram span following its general definition, these errors would consist of an isolated tag, but this representation could not convey much of the error's context. For this reason, omission errors were represented by slightly modified versions of the error + unigram and error + bigram spans. When representing missing word errors, the error + unigram span consisted of the POS tags extracted from the two words that followed the error. Similarly, the error + bigram span consisted of the POS tags extracted from the three words after the error when an omission error occurred. This adjustment was envisioned to maintain the amount of information represented by each error span consistent throughout the experiments.

Compared to the POS tag sequences used for training the n-gram and RNN models, the test POS tag sequences extracted from learner errors are short. Table 6 presents a summary of the test sequences' lengths. The median values for these sequence lengths indicate that most learner errors involved a single incorrect word.

Span	Min	Q1	Median	Q3	Max
Padded error	1	3	3	3	14
Error + unigram	1	2	2	3	13
Error + bigram	1	3	3	4	14

Table 6: Part-of-speech tagged test sequence lengths

		P	R	F1
N-gram				
	Padded error	0.68	0.32	0.43
	Error + unigram	0.64	0.34	0.45
	Error + bigram	0.66	0.27	0.38
RNN				
	Padded error	0.69	0.34	0.46
	Error + unigram	0.67	**0.41**	**0.51**
	Error + bigram	**0.70**	0.35	0.46

Table 7: Negative language transfer detection results

The decision to analyse manually annotated learner errors implies a setting that may be hard to reproduce, as in reality learner error information is not always available or correctly identified. The POS tag sequences analysed by the shallow syntactic language models were extracted from sentences in which the exact location and type of the errors was known. Although grammatical error correction research has achieved impressive results, it is not a solved task. In applying negative language transfer detection techniques to GEC system outputs it would be necessary to keep in mind and design around possible misclassifications.

5 Results

Table 7 presents the precision, recall, and F1-score results for the structural negative language transfer detection task. The error spans being equal, the RNN approach results outperformed the n-gram baseline in all metrics. Both approaches yielded the highest recall and F1-scores when analysing errors represented by the error + unigram span. However, the precision scores achieved in these experimental settings were the lowest ones within each approach.

The n-gram baseline paired with the padded error representation was more precise in classifying negative language transfer than the RNN when it analysed errors represented with the error + unigram span. However, the recall scores yielded by these two experimental combinations show that the RNN approach was able to retrieve more negative language transfer errors than the n-gram baseline. Although both n-gram and RNN approaches achieved analogous precision results, especially when analysing padded errors, the n-gram baseline was consistently outperformed on recall. These results indicate that comparable precision came with a lower recall cost for the baseline.

The high precision compared to low recall rates achieved by the n-gram baseline can be attributed to the fact that these models compute their output values from independent probability distributions derived from the training data. This may indicate that these models excel in classifying negative language transfer when there is a clear distinction in usage of the error structure between the languages. For example, if a learner applied a language structure that is frequent in Chinese but extremely rare in English, the Chinese n-gram model would assign a much higher probability than the English n-gram model, and the error would be correctly classified as negative language transfer. However, these very prominent usage differences are scarce in our data. As the FCE test-takers are learning English, they may not fully apply Chinese rules but instead combine rules from the two languages. This interlingual process makes the error structures ambiguous to our independent n-gram models.

The results in Table 7 suggest that the RNN's capability of distinguishing between languages might make it more suitable for the negative language transfer detection task. The RNN model that used the error + unigram test span achieved the highest recall and F1-score results in correctly classifying errors as negative language transfer. Moreover, the RNN model with the error + bigram span yielded the highest precision results across all experiments.

6 Discussion

The error coding used by the FCE annotators is useful to our error analysis as it allows the learner errors to be grouped by error subtype (Nicholls, 2003). Analysing which error subtypes cause the shallow syntactic language models to misclassify negative language transfer errors provides insights as to how our methods could be revised to better support the task.

Our models performed poorly when detecting negative language transfer in replacement errors. Replacement errors commonly occur when the learner uses the correct part-of-speech, but incorrect word in a sentence. For example, the word "many" in the sentence "how many you charge?" was flagged as a quantifier replacement error in the FCE dataset. Both n-gram and RNN shallow syntactic language models performed poorly in identifying whether replacement errors were related to negative language transfer. This may have occurred due to the POS tag representation of these errors not conveying a lot of information about the error's source. The erroneous and correct POS tag sequences follow the same pattern, a pattern that is acceptable in English.

The POS tag representation of errors also hindered negative language transfer detection for errors involving verb tenses, forms, and agreement. The Universal Dependencies tagset annotates verbs with one of two tags, "VERB" or "AUX". None of these tags contains information about verb features, such as tense, form, or person. These features would be useful in detecting verb usage patterns that are more common in Chinese than English and could be related to negative language transfer. These error subtype results indicate that the models would benefit from a more detailed POS tagset. A tagset that encapsulates more word features in their tags, such as the Penn Treebank tagset (Marcus et al., 1993). The challenge in using a more detailed tagset is that it needs to be common between English and the learners' L1 (in our case, Chinese). The Universal Dependencies tagset is the only tagset we are aware of that fits this commonality requirement.

Chinese speakers who are learning English as a second language usually have trouble with punctuation marks, as these symbols are employed differently in Chinese (Liu, 2011). For example, in Chinese, commas are used to mark the end of a complete thought (Xue and Yang, 2011). In our experiments, the POS tag span selection was fundamental to the detection of negative language transfer in missing punctuation errors. Both the n-gram and RNN approaches achieved the highest F1-scores when detecting negative language transfer in missing punctuation errors when using the padded error span. When evaluating the padded error span for missing punctuation errors, the RNN model achieved an F1-score of 0.48. The error + unigram and error + bigram spans yielded F1-scores of 0.43 and 0.41, respectively. A few possible explanations for this disparity in scores are that the errors' previous contexts helped the models correlate the errors to the Chinese language, or the lack of punctuation in between the spans' POS tags is divergent from English grammar rules.

Another common mistake for Chinese speakers who are learning English is determiner omission. As determiners do not exist in the Chinese language, learners tend to neglect their application in English (Robertson, 2000). Contrary to our initial assumption, missing determiner errors were better classified by the RNN model when using the error + unigram span. The previous context from the padded error span did not help the classification. One hypothesis for this behaviour is that it is common for determiners, as opposed to other parts-of-speech that usually follow determiners, to appear at the beginning of sentences in English. As there are no determiner equivalents in Chinese, whenever the RNN analysed a POS tag sequence that should begin with a determiner in English, but would not in Chinese, the sequence was classified as negative language transfer. In these cases, the padded error span contained another POS tag preceding the position where the determiner should have been. The RNN model might have been confused by this preceding POS tag, as there are mid-sentence situations in English in which determiners are not necessary.

The hypothesis that the RNN expected determiners to be at the beginning of English sequences as opposed to Chinese ones is corroborated by the error + bigram span also yielding a higher F1-score than the padded error span in this setting. The error + bigram span is analogous to the error + unigram span as it begins with the POS tag extracted from the word that should be preceded by a determiner.

To further investigate errors in model classification of negative language transfer, we charted the overall task performance and F1-scores for some specific subtypes of learner transfer (Figure 1). This figure shows that although the error + unigram representation yielded the highest overall F1-score in the n-gram baseline setting, certain predefined sub-types of negative language transfer were better represented by the padded error span. This difference was seen when the learner had not used punctuation or determiners even though they were needed. In the missing punctuation case, the n-gram models with the padded error span outperformed all of the RNN results. This indicates that the padded error span and n-gram models were more capable of representing the distinction between Chinese and English punctuation usage. In

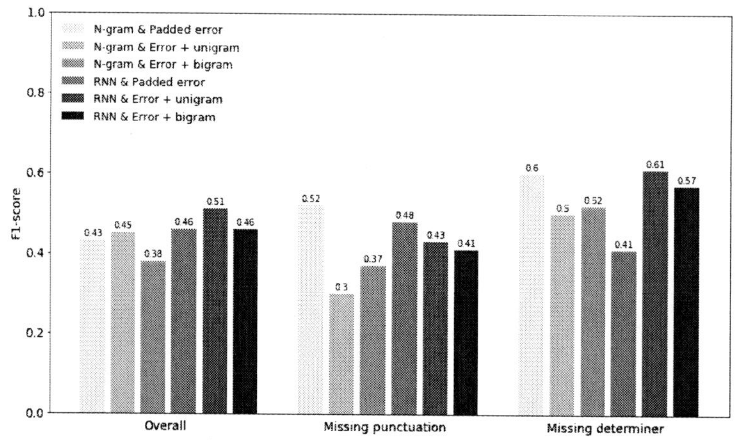

Figure 1: F1-scores for shallow syntactic language models and error spans combinations

this experimental setting, the n-gram models were able to detect when a POS tag sequence was meant to contain a punctuation mark in English but that punctuation mark was not necessary in Chinese.

As for the missing determiner errors, the padded error span also outperformed the other error spans in the n-gram shallow syntactic language models setting. Unlike the RNN, n-gram models do not have such a defined concept of sentence beginning. This distinction may help explain the padded error span's performance in the n-gram setting. The n-gram models' computation is based on how common a POS tag sequence is. In that case, the padded error span POS tags were able to indicate that while a determiner would follow and precede certain tags in English, it would not in Chinese. The n-gram models correctly identified a Chinese structural pattern in missing determiner errors' POS tag sequences because their POS tags were not followed or preceded by determiners.

Overall, the language modelling techniques used in our experiments were able to model the distinction between English and Chinese structures when analysing POS tag sequences extracted from sentences in those languages. When applied to the edits extracted from Chinese native speakers' English writing errors, the models achieved good precision in identifying errors related to negative language transfer. However, they were unable to detect a large portion of the negative language transfer related errors, i.e., low recall scores were observed.

As a future step, it would be interesting to attempt to detect negative language transfer with more powerful language modelling techniques, such as transformer models. Unlike RNN-based language models, transformer-based approaches do not rely solely on recurrent features to represent language structures (Vaswani et al., 2017). The self-attention mechanisms employed by these models could be beneficial in detecting language patterns in learner text that are more similar to the learners' L1s than to English.

7 Conclusion

Our experiments show that shallow syntactic language models can identify some negative language transfer related errors in English learner writing. While improvements can be made regarding the level of detail of the structural representation, our experiments indicate that it is possible to detect aspects of transferred language structures.

Negative language transfer detection methods, such as the ones we described, can support the generation of error feedback that connects learners' mistakes to their first languages. This type of information can help language learners become more aware of rule divergences between English and their L1s, and as a result increase their writing accuracy. In the future, we hope to apply the methods described above to other first languages and learner datasets, such as the Lang-8 Corpus of Learner English (Mizumoto et al., 2011).

Acknowledgements

We acknowledge the financial support of the Natural Sciences and Engineering Research Council of Canada [RGPIN-2018-03834].

References

Gaston Bacquet. 2019. Is corrective feedback in the ESL classroom really effective? A background study. *International Journal of Applied Linguistics and English Literature*, 8:147–154.

Loïc Barrault, Ondřej Bojar, Marta R. Costa-jussà, Christian Federmann, Mark Fishel, Yvette Graham, Barry Haddow, Matthias Huck, Philipp Koehn, Shervin Malmasi, Christof Monz, Mathias Müller, Santanu Pal, Matt Post, and Marcos Zampieri. 2019. Findings of the 2019 conference on machine translation (WMT19). In *Proceedings of the Fourth Conference on Machine Translation (Volume 2: Shared Task Papers, Day 1)*, pages 1–61, Florence, Italy. Association for Computational Linguistics.

Yevgeni Berzak, Roi Reichart, and Boris Katz. 2015. Contrastive analysis with predictive power: Typology driven estimation of grammatical error distributions in ESL. In *Proceedings of the Nineteenth Conference on Computational Natural Language Learning*, pages 94–102, Beijing, China. Association for Computational Linguistics.

John Bitchener, Stuart Young, and Denise Cameron. 2005. The effect of different types of corrective feedback on ESL student writing. *Journal of Second Language Writing*, 14(3):191 – 205.

Christopher Bryant, Mariano Felice, Øistein E. Andersen, and Ted Briscoe. 2019. The BEA-2019 shared task on grammatical error correction. In *Proceedings of the Fourteenth Workshop on Innovative Use of NLP for Building Educational Applications*, pages 52–75, Florence, Italy. Association for Computational Linguistics.

Shamil Chollampatt, Duc Tam Hoang, and Hwee Tou Ng. 2016. Adapting grammatical error correction based on the native language of writers with neural network joint models. In *Proceedings of the 2016 Conference on Empirical Methods in Natural Language Processing*, pages 1901–1911, Austin, Texas. Association for Computational Linguistics.

Chris Dyer, Adhiguna Kuncoro, Miguel Ballesteros, and Noah A. Smith. 2016. Recurrent neural network grammars. In *Proceedings of the 2016 Conference of the North American Chapter of the Association for Computational Linguistics: Human Language Technologies*, pages 199–209, San Diego, California. Association for Computational Linguistics.

Brendan Flanagan, Chengjiu Yin, Takahiko Suzuki, and Sachio Hirokawa. 2015. Prediction of learner native language by writing error pattern. In *Learning and Collaboration Technologies*, pages 87–96, Cham. Springer International Publishing.

Kenneth Heafield. 2011. KenLM: Faster and smaller language model queries. In *Proceedings of the Sixth Workshop on Statistical Machine Translation*, pages 187–197, Edinburgh, Scotland. Association for Computational Linguistics.

Kenneth Heafield, Ivan Pouzyrevsky, Jonathan H. Clark, and Philipp Koehn. 2013. Scalable modified Kneser-Ney language model estimation. In *Proceedings of the 51st Annual Meeting of the Association for Computational Linguistics (Volume 2: Short Papers)*, pages 690–696, Sofia, Bulgaria. Association for Computational Linguistics.

Daniel Jurafsky and James H. Martin. 2009. *Speech and Language Processing (2nd Edition)*. Prentice-Hall, Inc., USA.

Khaled Karim and Hossein Nassaji. 2020. The revision and transfer effects of direct and indirect comprehensive corrective feedback on ESL students' writing. *Language Teaching Research*, 24(4):519–539.

Diederik P. Kingma and Jimmy Ba. 2015. Adam: A method for stochastic optimization. In *3rd International Conference on Learning Representations, ICLR 2015, San Diego, CA, USA, May 7-9, 2015, Conference Track Proceedings*.

Robert Lado. 1957. *Linguistics Across Cultures: Applied Linguistics for Language Teachers*. University of Michigan Press.

Xing Liu. 2011. The not–so–humble "Chinese comma": Improving English CFL students' understanding of multi–clause sentences. In *Proceedings of the 9th New York International Conference on Teaching Chinese*.

Roy Lyster and Leila Ranta. 1997. Corrective feedback and learner uptake: Negotiation of form in communicative classrooms. *Studies in Second Language Acquisition*, 19(1):37–66.

Shervin Malmasi, Keelan Evanini, Aoife Cahill, Joel Tetreault, Robert Pugh, Christopher Hamill, Diane Napolitano, and Yao Qian. 2017. A report on the 2017 native language identification shared task. In *Proceedings of the 12th Workshop on Innovative Use of NLP for Building Educational Applications*, pages 62–75, Copenhagen, Denmark. Association for Computational Linguistics.

Mitchell P. Marcus, Beatrice Santorini, and Mary Ann Marcinkiewicz. 1993. Building a large annotated corpus of English: The Penn Treebank. *Computational Linguistics*, 19(2):313–330.

Tomas Mikolov, Martin Karafiát, Lukas Burget, Jan Cernocký, and Sanjeev Khudanpur. 2010. Recurrent neural network based language model. In *Proceedings of the 11th Annual Conference of the International Speech Communication Association, INTERSPEECH 2010*, volume 2, pages 1045–1048.

Tomoya Mizumoto, Mamoru Komachi, Masaaki Nagata, and Yuji Matsumoto. 2011. Mining revision log of language learning SNS for automated Japanese error correction of second language learners. In *Proceedings of 5th International Joint Conference on Natural Language Processing*, pages 147–155, Chiang Mai, Thailand. Asian Federation of Natural Language Processing.

Natawut Monaikul and Barbara Di Eugenio. 2020. Detecting preposition errors to target interlingual errors in second language writing. In *FLAIRS Conference*, pages 290–293.

Maria Nadejde and Joel Tetreault. 2019. Personalizing grammatical error correction: Adaptation to proficiency level and L1. In *Proceedings of the 5th Workshop on Noisy User-generated Text (W-NUT 2019)*, pages 27–33, Hong Kong, China. Association for Computational Linguistics.

Hwee Tou Ng, Siew Mei Wu, Ted Briscoe, Christian Hadiwinoto, Raymond Hendy Susanto, and Christopher Bryant. 2014. The CoNLL-2014 shared task on grammatical error correction. In *Proceedings of the Eighteenth Conference on Computational Natural Language Learning: Shared Task*, pages 1–14, Baltimore, Maryland. Association for Computational Linguistics.

Hwee Tou Ng, Siew Mei Wu, Yuanbin Wu, Christian Hadiwinoto, and Joel Tetreault. 2013. The CoNLL-2013 shared task on grammatical error correction. In *Proceedings of the Seventeenth Conference on Computational Natural Language Learning: Shared Task*, pages 1–12, Sofia, Bulgaria. Association for Computational Linguistics.

Diane Nicholls. 2003. The Cambridge Learner Corpus: Error coding and analysis for lexicography and ELT. In *Proceedings of the Corpus Linguistics 2003 conference*, volume 16, pages 572–581.

Joakim Nivre, Marie-Catherine de Marneffe, Filip Ginter, Yoav Goldberg, Jan Hajič, Christopher D. Manning, Ryan McDonald, Slav Petrov, Sampo Pyysalo, Natalia Silveira, Reut Tsarfaty, and Daniel Zeman. 2016. Universal Dependencies v1: A multilingual treebank collection. In *Proceedings of the Tenth International Conference on Language Resources and Evaluation (LREC'16)*, pages 1659–1666, Portorož, Slovenia. European Language Resources Association (ELRA).

Prokopis Prokopidis, Vassilis Papavassiliou, and Stelios Piperidis. 2016. Parallel global voices: a collection of multilingual corpora with citizen media stories. In *Proceedings of the Tenth International Conference on Language Resources and Evaluation (LREC'16)*, pages 900–905.

Ella Rabinovich, Yulia Tsvetkov, and Shuly Wintner. 2018. Native language cognate effects on second language lexical choice. *Transactions of the Association for Computational Linguistics*, 6:329–342.

Daniel Robertson. 2000. Variability in the use of the English article system by Chinese learners of English. *Second Language Research*, 16(2):135–172.

Alla Rozovskaya and Dan Roth. 2011. Algorithm selection and model adaptation for ESL correction tasks. In *Proceedings of the 49th Annual Meeting of the Association for Computational Linguistics: Human Language Technologies*, pages 924–933, Portland, Oregon, USA. Association for Computational Linguistics.

Joel Tetreault, Daniel Blanchard, and Aoife Cahill. 2013. A report on the first native language identification shared task. In *Proceedings of the Eighth Workshop on Innovative Use of NLP for Building Educational Applications*, pages 48–57, Atlanta, Georgia. Association for Computational Linguistics.

Jörg Tiedemann. 2012. Parallel data, tools and interfaces in OPUS. In *Proceedings of the Eighth International Conference on Language Resources and Evaluation (LREC'12)*, pages 2214–2218, Istanbul, Turkey. European Language Resources Association (ELRA).

Ashish Vaswani, Noam Shazeer, Niki Parmar, Jakob Uszkoreit, Llion Jones, Aidan N Gomez, Ł ukasz Kaiser, and Illia Polosukhin. 2017. Attention is all you need. In *Advances in Neural Information Processing Systems*, volume 30. Curran Associates, Inc.

Leticia Farias Wanderley and Carrie Demmans Epp. 2020. Identifying negative language transfer in writing to increase English as a Second Language learners' metalinguistic awareness. In *Companion Proceedings 10th International Conference on Learning Analytics & Knowledge (LAK20)*.

Leticia Farias Wanderley, Nicole Zhao, and Carrie Demmans Epp. 2021. Negative language transfer in learner English: A new dataset. In *Proceedings of the 2021 Conference of the North American Chapter of the Association for Computational Linguistics: Human Language Technologies*. In press.

David Alistair Watts. 2019. RAISING AWARENESS OF LANGUAGE TRANSFER WITH ACADEMIC ENGLISH WRITING STUDENTS AT A JAPANESE UNIVERSITY. *Frontier of Foreign Language Education*, 2:191–200.

Sze-Meng Jojo Wong and Mark Dras. 2009. Contrastive analysis and native language identification. In *Proceedings of the Australasian Language Technology Association Workshop 2009*, pages 53–61, Sydney, Australia.

Nianwen Xue and Yaqin Yang. 2011. Chinese sentence segmentation as comma classification. In *Proceedings of the 49th Annual Meeting of the Association for Computational Linguistics: Human Language Technologies*, pages 631–635.

Helen Yannakoudakis, Ted Briscoe, and Ben Medlock. 2011. A new dataset and method for automatically grading ESOL texts. In *Proceedings of the 49th Annual Meeting of the Association for Computational Linguistics: Human Language Technologies*, pages 180–189, Portland, Oregon, USA. Association for Computational Linguistics.

Document-level grammatical error correction

Zheng Yuan and **Christopher Bryant**
ALTA Institute, University of Cambridge, United Kingdom
Department of Computer Science and Technology, University of Cambridge, United Kingdom
{zheng.yuan, christopher.bryant}@cl.cam.ac.uk

Abstract

Document-level context can provide valuable information in grammatical error correction (GEC), which is crucial for correcting certain errors and resolving inconsistencies. In this paper, we investigate context-aware approaches and propose document-level GEC systems. Additionally, we employ a three-step training strategy to benefit from both sentence-level and document-level data. Our system outperforms previous document-level and all other NMT-based single-model systems, achieving state of the art on a common test set.

1 Introduction

Grammatical error correction (GEC) attempts to automatically detect and correct grammatical errors in text. With recent advances in sequence-to-sequence modelling, neural machine translation (NMT) has been widely applied to GEC (Yuan and Briscoe, 2016; Ji et al., 2017; Junczys-Dowmunt et al., 2018; Yuan et al., 2019) and state-of-the-art results have been reported (Kaneko et al., 2020; Lichtarge et al., 2020). Cross-sentence context has proven useful for language modelling (Wang and Cho, 2016), dialogue systems (Serban et al., 2016) and machine translation (Wang et al., 2017; Voita et al., 2018). In error correction, we observe that certain errors can only be detected and/or corrected using wider context, which may fall outside the current sentence. However, existing GEC systems typically process each sentence independently, ignoring document-level context. These sentence-level systems may fail to correct document-level errors (e.g. verb tense errors, pronoun errors, run-on sentences) or propose inconsistent corrections throughout a document:

(a) In the chat room, she created a close relationship with eight people. She talks (**talked**) to them every night, trust (**trusted / ~~trusts~~**) them and share (**shared / ~~shares~~**) her life with them. Then eventually, she discovered that the eight people were one as the other person was using eight different identities to chat with her all the time.

(b) I would like to recommend walking. Because there are a lot of beautiful trees. → I would like to recommend walking **because** there are a lot of beautiful trees.

For example, all the errors (red) in Example (a) could feasibly be corrected (bold) using either the present or past tense if we only consider the target sentence in isolation, but the wider context reveals the correction using the present tense is ungrammatical (strikethrough). Similarly, a sentence-level system is also unable to handle cases where sentences should be merged such as in Example (b).

To date, GEC evaluation has always been carried out at the sentence level. As a result, successful corrections of these document-level errors would not be given any credit (or even be unfairly penalised) and systems proposing inconsistent modifications would not be penalised. On the one hand, GEC should look beyond the current sentence and use more context to build context-aware GEC systems; on the other hand, systems should be better evaluated at the document rather than sentence level.

This paper makes the following contributions. First, we compare different architectures to capture wider context for NMT-based GEC and show that simple document-level approaches can be applied to improve GEC performance. Second, we present a three-step training strategy to effectively use both sentence-level and document-level parallel data for GEC. Third, we report state of the art on a publicly available test set. Finally, we perform the first document-level GEC evaluation and release

Proceedings of the 16th Workshop on Innovative Use of NLP for Building Educational Applications, pages 75–84
April 20, 2021 ©2021 Association for Computational Linguistics

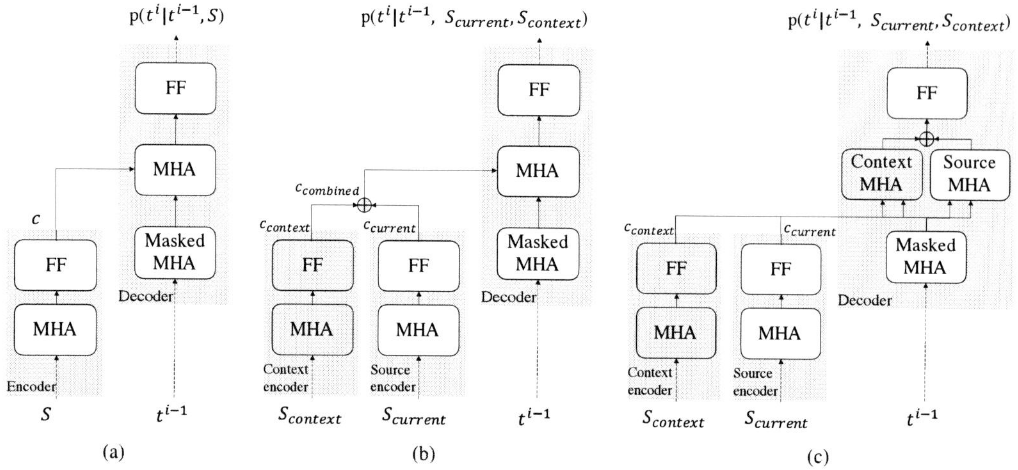

Figure 1: (a) The original Transformer, (b) the multi-encoder model with encoder side integration (**MultiEnc-enc**), and (c) the multi-encoder model with decoder side integration (**MultiEnc-dec**). The newly introduced components are highlighted in yellow. FF: Feed Forward, MHA: Multi-Head Attention.

our document-level evaluation scripts to facilitate research in the area.[1]

2 Document-level GEC

NMT was originally developed to work sentence by sentence (Sutskever et al., 2014). Recent work has explored context-aware extensions. A simple strategy of concatenating preceding sentences was investigated by Tiedemann and Scherrer (2017). Multi-encoder approaches have been proposed, including using different encoder architectures (Bawden et al., 2018; Chollampatt et al., 2019; Stojanovski and Fraser, 2018), and applying multiple integration strategies (Wang et al., 2017; Voita et al., 2018; Bawden et al., 2018).

Various adaptations of NMT for GEC have been investigated and recent progress has been driven by the use of artificial data (Kaneko et al., 2020; Lichtarge et al., 2020). However most systems focus on sentence-level correction, where each sentence is processed in isolation. The only previous work that has considered a wider context for GEC that we are aware of is by Chollampatt et al. (2019), who extended a convolutional neural encoder-decoder model with an auxiliary encoder and attention gating. They only used document-level data in their training however, and still performed evaluation at the sentence level, which is therefore unable to ascertain the real improvements of document-level systems.

[1] https://github.com/chrisjbryant/doc-gec

In this work, we use the Transformer sequence-to-sequence model (Vaswani et al., 2017) as our baseline system and investigate three context-aware extensions for GEC.

2.1 Baseline encoder-decoder framework

The Transformer follows an encoder-decoder architecture (Figure 1a). Each layer of the encoder contains a multi-head self-attention mechanism and a feed-forward network. The decoder inserts a third sub-layer, which performs multi-head attention over the output of the encoder stack.

2.2 Single-encoder models

Similar to Tiedemann and Scherrer (2017), the single-encoder GEC model uses the standard Transformer encoder to process the current source sentence and its context together, treating them as a long input sequence. The model architecture remains unchanged. We instead modify the input by concatenating preceding sentences to the current one, separated by a special token.

2.3 Multi-encoder models

Multi-encoder models encode the source sentence and its context separately. The original encoder in the Transformer reads and encodes the source sentence. Additionally, a new context encoder is introduced to process the context in a parallel fashion to the source encoder. The resulting context representation is integrated into the model architecture on the encoder or decoder side:

Encoder side integration As shown in Figure 1b, the original source encoder reads the current source sentence $S_{current}$ and produces a vector representation $c_{current}$. The context encoder encodes the auxiliary context input $S_{context}$ and computes a context representation $c_{context}$. The outputs from both encoders are combined via a gated sum:

$$c_{combined} = \lambda c_{current} + (1 - \lambda) c_{context} \quad (1)$$

where the gating weight λ is given by:

$$\lambda = \sigma(W\,[c_{current}; c_{context}] + b) \quad (2)$$

where σ is the logistic sigmoid function, and W and b are learnable parameters.

The combined representation $c_{combined}$ is then used as a single input to the decoder which stays intact.

Decoder side integration Two encoder representations $c_{current}$ and $c_{context}$ are used as separate inputs to the decoder (Figure 1c). We modify the Transformer decoder, so that the multi-head attention sub-layer contains two components: one performs multi-head attention over the output of the encoder stack for the current sentence $c_{current}$ using the masked multi-head self-attention output, and the other attends directly to the context encoder representation $c_{context}$. These two attention operations are performed in parallel and combined with a gating mechanism.

3 Experiments

3.1 Datasets

To train document-level GEC models, we select document-level corpora: the Cambridge English Write & Improve (W&I) corpus (Bryant et al., 2019), the First Certificate in English (FCE) dataset (Yannakoudakis et al., 2011), the National University of Singapore Corpus of Learner English (NUCLE) (Dahlmeier et al., 2013) and the Cambridge Learner Corpus (CLC) (Nicholls, 2003).[2] All the datasets were annotated by expert annotators at the document level and typically consist of learner essays. We use FCE-dev as our development set and report results on FCE-test, BEA-dev (Granger, 1998; Bryant et al., 2019) and the CoNLL-2014 test set (Ng et al., 2014).[3] More information about these datasets is provided in Appendix A, Table A.1.

3.2 Document-level GEC evaluation

To better understand the performance of document-level systems, we perform the first document-level GEC evaluation. We do this using the ERRANT Scorer (Bryant et al., 2017), the official scorer of the BEA-2019 shared task (Bryant et al., 2019). Since reference files are normally only available at the sentence level, we reprocess the raw untokenised data to produce new reference files at the document level.[4] This is necessary because edits that cross sentence boundaries are normally deleted in sentence-level GEC (see Example (b) in Section 1). It is also worth noting that for datasets with multiple references (i.e. CoNLL-2014), scores are computed against all the document-level edits of a single annotator simultaneously rather than mixed-and-matched from different annotators for each sentence. In other words, while sentence-level evaluation chooses the best reference amongst all annotators *for each sentence*, document-level evaluation chooses the best reference amongst all annotators *for each document*. This means document-level evaluation is more restricted than sentence-level evaluation and hence explains why the document-level scores in our experiments on CoNLL-2014 are much lower than the sentence-level scores.

3.3 Training

The implementation is done using Fairseq, an open-source sequence modelling toolkit (Ott et al., 2019).[5] We use the Transformer model as the basic model architecture and follow the hyper-parameter settings in 'Transformer (big)' in Vaswani et al. (2017). We apply byte pair encoding (Sennrich et al., 2016) with 8k merge operations learned from the target side of the training data. Source word embeddings are shared between the source and context encoders.[6] In our experiments, one preceding source sentence is given as the context. Each model is trained on one machine with four NVIDIA Tesla P100 GPUs.

Since large-scale document-level GEC corpora are limited and existing methods for artificial error generation work at the sentence level (Felice and

[2] All public data is available at: `https://www.cl.cam.ac.uk/research/nl/bea2019st/#data`

[3] We do not use BEA-test or JFLEG (Napoles et al., 2017) because document-level context for these datasets is not available.

[4] This preprocessing was done using a modified version of the `json_to_m2.py` script released with the BEA-2019 shared task data.

[5] `https://github.com/pytorch/fairseq`

[6] Detailed hyper-parameters are listed in Appendix B.

Model	BEA-dev			FCE-test			CoNLL-2014		
	P	R	$F_{0.5}$	P	R	$F_{0.5}$	P	R	$F_{0.5}$
Baseline	58.49	38.29	52.91	63.65	42.27	57.80	59.96	27.08	48.25
SingleEnc	56.94	**43.16**	53.52	61.63	**44.95**	57.37	59.78	27.27	48.27
MultiEnc-enc	62.06	41.71	56.54	**65.55**	42.68	59.20	63.23	27.96	50.49
MultiEnc-dec	**62.64**	40.72	**56.55**	65.36	44.17	**59.64**	**64.57**	**28.65**	**51.62**

Table 1: Document-level evaluation results of our proposed document-level GEC models. The highest scores are marked in bold. P: precision, R: recall.

Stage	Data	P	R	$F_{0.5}$
Pre-training	sent.	57.52	32.65	49.91
Training	doc.	58.49	38.29	52.91
Fine-tuning	doc.	62.64	40.72	56.55
No pre-training	-	59.62	40.52	54.48
No fine-tuning	-	58.49	38.29	52.91

Table 2: Performance of **MultiEnc-dec** on BEA-dev after each training stage and ablation tests. sent.: sentence-level data, doc.: document-level data.

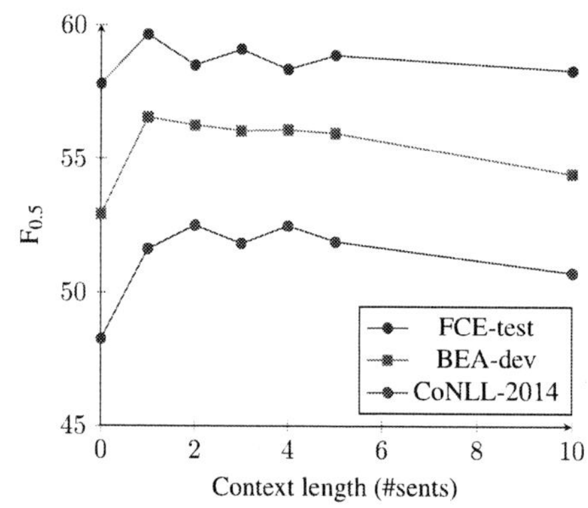

Figure 2: The effect of context length.

Yuan, 2014; Rei et al., 2017; Kiyono et al., 2019), we extract both sentence-level and document-level parallel training examples from the document-level GEC corpora. To train **MultiEnc-enc** and **MultiEnc-dec**, we employ a three-step training strategy: 1) pre-training on all sentence-level parallel data from *CLC* + *FCE-train* + *W&I-train* + *NUCLE* to learn sentence-level model parameters (the newly introduced components are therefore inactivated - see Figure 1b and 1c); 2) continue training with *CLC* document-level parallel data to update all model parameters; and 3) fine-tuning on a combination of small, in-domain document-level data from *FCE-train* + *W&I-train* + *NUCLE*. Both **Baseline** and **SingleEnc**, which follow the standard Transformer, are similarly first trained using *CLC*, then fine-tuned with in-domain *FCE-train* + *W&I-train* + *NUCLE* data, but without mixing both sentence-level and document-level examples.

3.4 Results

In Table 1, we can see that simply concatenating preceding sentences (**SingleEnc**) does not yield a consistent improvement in $F_{0.5}$ (recall improves at the cost of precision). Since longer inputs make the encoder-decoder attention harder to optimise, more training data may be needed. Both our document-level models outperform the sentence-level **Baseline**.[7] **MultiEnc-dec** gives the decoder more flexibility to access context directly, and produces better results on FCE-test and CoNLL-2014 than **MultiEnc-enc**, but makes no difference on BEA-dev. We also find that document-level context seems more useful in some datasets than others, which improves the **Baseline** by up to 3.64 $F_{0.5}$ on BEA-dev, 3.37 on CoNLL-2014, but just 1.84 on FCE-test.

Multi-stage training Results in Table 2 demonstrate the effectiveness of the three-step training strategy and the benefits of using both sentence-level and document-level data. The ablation study, in which we remove one training step at a time, also suggests that it is crucial to have both pre-training and fine-tuning stages as performance drops when removing either of them.

Context length Figure 2 shows how the performance changes in relation to an increasing number of context sentences. The best performance is achieved when including only one preceding sentence for FCE-test and BEA-dev, but two for CoNLL-2014. This could possibly be explained by the difference in document length in each dataset: CoNLL-2014 documents contain twice as many sentences on average than FCE-test and BEA-dev

[7]We perform two-tailed paired T-tests, where $p < 0.001$.

Example (a)		
	Context	Then we went to Taxco.
	Source	We stay in a very luxurious hotel.
	Reference	We **stayed** in a very luxurious hotel.
	Baseline	We stay in a very luxurious hotel.
	Our model	We **stayed** in a very luxurious hotel.
Example (b)		
	Context	The motorcycle is the most dangerous transport ...
	Source	... some riders still keep breaking the rule.
	Reference	... some riders still keep breaking the rule.
	Baseline	... some cyclists still keep breaking the rule.
	Our model	... some riders still keep breaking the rule.

Table 3: Example outputs from **MultiEnc-dec**. More system output examples are given in Appendix D.

System	FCE-test			CoNLL-2014		
	P	R	$F_{0.5}$	P	R	$F_{0.5}$
MultiEnc-dec	**69.9**	44.2	**62.6**	**74.3**	39.0	**62.9**
Chollampatt et al. (2019)	52.2	28.3	44.6	65.6	30.1	53.1
Kaneko et al. (2020)	65.0	49.6	61.2†	69.2	45.6	62.6
Lichtarge et al. (2020)	-	-	-	69.4	43.9	62.1

Table 4: Comparison of NMT-based single-model GEC systems. †current state of the art

documents. But we also notice that very long context is not often helpful in resolving many different kinds of grammatical errors, suggesting that long-distance context has limited impact on GEC.

3.5 Error analysis

Our error analysis shows that the biggest gains are observed for subject-verb agreement, preposition, noun number, determiner and pronoun errors.[8] This confirms our hypothesis that correction of errors involving agreement, coreference or tense is more likely to rely on information outside the current sentence (e.g. `VERB:SVA` +10.40 $F_{0.5}$, `PRON` +8.32, and `VERB:TENSE` +5.95 - see Example (a) in Table 3). It is not surprising that our system is good at handling errors that cross sentence boundaries (e.g. `CONJ` +6.40 and `PUNCT` +3.75). Manual inspection reveals that improvements also come from topic-aware lexical choice (e.g. 'riders' vs. 'cyclists' for 'motorcycle' - see Example (b) in Table 3).

4 Comparison with NMT-based GEC systems

We perform sentence-level evaluation on the FCE-test and CoNLL-2014 test sets using the M^2 Scorer (Dahlmeier and Ng, 2012). A comparison of NMT-based single model systems is made in Table 4. Our **MultiEnc-dec** system outperforms previous document-level GEC systems from Chollampatt et al. (2019) on both test sets by large margins. Our single-model system outperforms all NMT-based single-model systems and achieves state of the art on FCE-test without exploiting any artificial data. Our GEC system also yields much higher precision, which is a desirable property of a practical system. As the performance of our document-level system is underestimated by sentence-level evaluation, we expect further performance gains over other sentence-level systems.

[8]The full error type-specific performance is presented in Appendix C.

5 Conclusion

We have investigated document-level approaches to NMT-based GEC and presented a three-step training strategy to use both sentence-level and document-level data. We have shown that context is useful in GEC but very long context is not necessary for improved performance. Experiments on three test sets demonstrated the effectiveness of our document-level GEC models. Our best system outperforms all NMT-based single-model GEC systems and achieves state of the art on FCE-test. By drawing attention to this understudied area in GEC, we hope to motivate future efforts to build better context-aware GEC systems. We have also performed the first document-level GEC evaluation and make our document-level evaluation scripts available to facilitate research in this area.

Acknowledgments

We would like to thank Cambridge Assessment for supporting this research, and the anonymous reviewers for their useful feedback. We would also like to thank Shiva Taslimipoor, Christopher Davis, Andrew Caines, and Ted Briscoe for feedback on early drafts of this paper. This work was performed using resources provided by the Cambridge Service for Data Driven Discovery operated by the University of Cambridge Research Computing Service, provided by Dell EMC and Intel using Tier-2 funding from the Engineering and Physical Sciences Research Council (capital grant EP/P020259/1), and DiRAC funding from the Science and Technology Facilities Council. We acknowledge NVIDIA for an Academic Hardware Grant.

References

Rachel Bawden, Rico Sennrich, Alexandra Birch, and Barry Haddow. 2018. Evaluating discourse phenomena in neural machine translation. In *Proceedings of the 2018 Conference of the North American Chapter of the Association for Computational Linguistics: Human Language Technologies, Volume 1 (Long Papers)*, pages 1304–1313, New Orleans, Louisiana. Association for Computational Linguistics.

Christopher Bryant, Mariano Felice, Øistein E. Andersen, and Ted Briscoe. 2019. The BEA-2019 shared task on grammatical error correction. In *Proceedings of the Fourteenth Workshop on Innovative Use of NLP for Building Educational Applications*, pages 52–75, Florence, Italy. Association for Computational Linguistics.

Christopher Bryant, Mariano Felice, and Ted Briscoe. 2017. Automatic annotation and evaluation of error types for grammatical error correction. In *Proceedings of the 55th Annual Meeting of the Association for Computational Linguistics (Volume 1: Long Papers)*, pages 793–805, Vancouver, Canada. Association for Computational Linguistics.

Shamil Chollampatt, Weiqi Wang, and Hwee Tou Ng. 2019. Cross-sentence grammatical error correction. In *Proceedings of the 57th Annual Meeting of the Association for Computational Linguistics*, pages 435–445, Florence, Italy. Association for Computational Linguistics.

Daniel Dahlmeier and Hwee Tou Ng. 2012. Better evaluation for grammatical error correction. In *Proceedings of the 2012 Conference of the North American Chapter of the Association for Computational Linguistics: Human Language Technologies*, pages 568–572, Montréal, Canada. Association for Computational Linguistics.

Daniel Dahlmeier, Hwee Tou Ng, and Siew Mei Wu. 2013. Building a large annotated corpus of learner English: The NUS corpus of learner English. In *Proceedings of the Eighth Workshop on Innovative Use of NLP for Building Educational Applications*, pages 22–31, Atlanta, Georgia. Association for Computational Linguistics.

Mariano Felice and Zheng Yuan. 2014. Generating artificial errors for grammatical error correction. In *Proceedings of the Student Research Workshop at the 14th Conference of the European Chapter of the Association for Computational Linguistics*, pages 116–126, Gothenburg, Sweden. Association for Computational Linguistics.

Sylviane Granger. 1998. The computer learner corpus: A versatile new source of data for SLA research. In Sylviane Granger, editor, *Learner English on Computer*, pages 3–18. Addison Wesley Longman, London and New York.

Jianshu Ji, Qinlong Wang, Kristina Toutanova, Yongen Gong, Steven Truong, and Jianfeng Gao. 2017. A nested attention neural hybrid model for grammatical error correction. In *Proceedings of the 55th Annual Meeting of the Association for Computational Linguistics (Volume 1: Long Papers)*, pages 753–762, Vancouver, Canada. Association for Computational Linguistics.

Marcin Junczys-Dowmunt, Roman Grundkiewicz, Shubha Guha, and Kenneth Heafield. 2018. Approaching neural grammatical error correction as a low-resource machine translation task. In *Proceedings of the 2018 Conference of the North American Chapter of the Association for Computational Linguistics: Human Language Technologies, Volume 1 (Long Papers)*, pages 595–606, New Orleans, Louisiana. Association for Computational Linguistics.

Masahiro Kaneko, Masato Mita, Shun Kiyono, Jun Suzuki, and Kentaro Inui. 2020. Encoder-decoder models can benefit from pre-trained masked language models in grammatical error correction. In *Proceedings of the 58th Annual Meeting of the Association for Computational Linguistics*, pages 4248–4254, Online. Association for Computational Linguistics.

Shun Kiyono, Jun Suzuki, Masato Mita, Tomoya Mizumoto, and Kentaro Inui. 2019. An empirical study of incorporating pseudo data into grammatical error correction. In *Proceedings of the 2019 Conference on Empirical Methods in Natural Language Processing and the 9th International Joint Conference on Natural Language Processing (EMNLP-IJCNLP)*, pages 1236–1242, Hong Kong, China. Association for Computational Linguistics.

Jared Lichtarge, Chris Alberti, and Shankar Kumar. 2020. Data weighted training strategies for grammatical error correction. *Transactions of the Association for Computational Linguistics*, 8:634–646.

Courtney Napoles, Keisuke Sakaguchi, and Joel Tetreault. 2017. JFLEG: A fluency corpus and benchmark for grammatical error correction. In *Proceedings of the 15th Conference of the European Chapter of the Association for Computational Linguistics: Volume 2, Short Papers*, pages 229–234, Valencia, Spain. Association for Computational Linguistics.

Hwee Tou Ng, Siew Mei Wu, Ted Briscoe, Christian Hadiwinoto, Raymond Hendy Susanto, and Christopher Bryant. 2014. The CoNLL-2014 shared task on grammatical error correction. In *Proceedings of the Eighteenth Conference on Computational Natural Language Learning: Shared Task*, pages 1–14, Baltimore, Maryland. Association for Computational Linguistics.

Diane Nicholls. 2003. The Cambridge Learner Corpus - error coding and analysis for lexicography and ELT. In *Proceedings of the Corpus Linguistics 2003 Conference*, pages 572–581.

Myle Ott, Sergey Edunov, Alexei Baevski, Angela Fan, Sam Gross, Nathan Ng, David Grangier, and Michael Auli. 2019. fairseq: A fast, extensible toolkit for sequence modeling. In *Proceedings of the 2019 Conference of the North American Chapter of the Association for Computational Linguistics (Demonstrations)*, pages 48–53, Minneapolis, Minnesota. Association for Computational Linguistics.

Marek Rei, Mariano Felice, Zheng Yuan, and Ted Briscoe. 2017. Artificial error generation with machine translation and syntactic patterns. In *Proceedings of the 12th Workshop on Innovative Use of NLP for Building Educational Applications*, pages 287–292, Copenhagen, Denmark. Association for Computational Linguistics.

Rico Sennrich, Barry Haddow, and Alexandra Birch. 2016. Neural machine translation of rare words with subword units. In *Proceedings of the 54th Annual Meeting of the Association for Computational Linguistics (Volume 1: Long Papers)*, pages 1715–1725, Berlin, Germany. Association for Computational Linguistics.

Iulian Vlad Serban, Alessandro Sordoni, Yoshua Bengio, Aaron Courville, and Joelle Pineau. 2016. Building End-To-End Dialogue Systems Using Generative Hierarchical Neural Network Models. In *Proceedings of the Thirty-Second AAAI Conference on Artificial Intelligence (AAAI-16)*, Phoenix, Arizona, USA. Association for the Advancement of Artificial Intelligence.

Dario Stojanovski and Alexander Fraser. 2018. Coreference and coherence in neural machine translation: A study using oracle experiments. In *Proceedings of the Third Conference on Machine Translation: Research Papers*, pages 49–60, Brussels, Belgium. Association for Computational Linguistics.

Ilya Sutskever, Oriol Vinyals, and Quoc V Le. 2014. Sequence to Sequence Learning with Neural Networks. In Z. Ghahramani, M. Welling, C. Cortes, N. D. Lawrence, and K. Q. Weinberger, editors, *Advances in Neural Information Processing Systems 27*, pages 3104–3112. Curran Associates, Inc.

Jörg Tiedemann and Yves Scherrer. 2017. Neural machine translation with extended context. In *Proceedings of the Third Workshop on Discourse in Machine Translation*, pages 82–92, Copenhagen, Denmark. Association for Computational Linguistics.

Ashish Vaswani, Noam Shazeer, Niki Parmar, Jakob Uszkoreit, Llion Jones, Aidan N Gomez, Ł ukasz Kaiser, and Illia Polosukhin. 2017. Attention is All you Need. In I. Guyon, U. V. Luxburg, S. Bengio, H. Wallach, R. Fergus, S. Vishwanathan, and R. Garnett, editors, *Advances in Neural Information Processing Systems 30*, pages 5998–6008. Curran Associates, Inc.

Elena Voita, Pavel Serdyukov, Rico Sennrich, and Ivan Titov. 2018. Context-aware neural machine translation learns anaphora resolution. In *Proceedings of the 56th Annual Meeting of the Association for Computational Linguistics (Volume 1: Long Papers)*, pages 1264–1274, Melbourne, Australia. Association for Computational Linguistics.

Longyue Wang, Zhaopeng Tu, Andy Way, and Qun Liu. 2017. Exploiting cross-sentence context for neural machine translation. In *Proceedings of the 2017 Conference on Empirical Methods in Natural Language Processing*, pages 2826–2831, Copenhagen, Denmark. Association for Computational Linguistics.

Tian Wang and Kyunghyun Cho. 2016. Larger-context language modelling with recurrent neural network. In *Proceedings of the 54th Annual Meeting of the Association for Computational Linguistics (Volume 1: Long Papers)*, pages 1319–1329, Berlin, Germany. Association for Computational Linguistics.

Helen Yannakoudakis, Ted Briscoe, and Ben Medlock. 2011. A new dataset and method for automatically grading ESOL texts. In *Proceedings of the 49th Annual Meeting of the Association for Computational Linguistics: Human Language Technologies*, pages 180–189, Portland, Oregon, USA. Association for Computational Linguistics.

Zheng Yuan and Ted Briscoe. 2016. Grammatical error correction using neural machine translation. In *Proceedings of the 2016 Conference of the North American Chapter of the Association for Computational Linguistics: Human Language Technologies*, pages 380–386, San Diego, California. Association for Computational Linguistics.

Zheng Yuan, Felix Stahlberg, Marek Rei, Bill Byrne, and Helen Yannakoudakis. 2019. Neural and FST-based approaches to grammatical error correction. In *Proceedings of the Fourteenth Workshop on Innovative Use of NLP for Building Educational Applications*, pages 228–239, Florence, Italy. Association for Computational Linguistics.

A Corpus statistics

Split	Dataset	#tokens	#sents	#docs	Doc. length (avg. #sents)
Train	FCE-train	454,736	28,350	2,116	13
	W&I-train	628,720	34,308	3,000	11
	NUCLE	1,161,567	57,151	1,397	41
	CLC	28,988,729	1,961,065	206,418	10
Dev	FCE-dev	34,748	2,191	159	14
Test	FCE-test	41,932	2,695	194	14
	BEA-dev	86,973	4,384	350	13
	CoNLL-2014	30,144	1,312	50	26

Table A.1: Summary of datasets used in our experiments. All datasets were preprocessed using spaCy.[9]

B Hyper-parameter settings

Model architecture	Transformer (big)
Max tokens	3,584
Optimiser	Adam
	$(\beta_1 = 0.9, \beta_2 = 0.98, \epsilon = 1 \times 10^{-8})$
Learning rate schedule	Same as in Vaswani et al. (2017)
Loss function	Label smoothed cross entropy
	$(\epsilon_{ls} = 0.1)$
Dropout	0.3
Gradient clipping	1.0
Beam size	12

[9]https://spacy.io

C Error analysis

In order to better understand the performance of our document-level GEC systems, we perform a detailed error analysis on BEA-dev using the ERRANT Scorer (Table C.1). The largest improvements in $F_{0.5}$ over the sentence-level baseline are observed for VERB:SVA (+10.40), followed by PREP (+10.00), NOUN:NUM (+8.65), DET (+8.57), PRON (+8.32), CONJ (+6.40), VERB:TENSE (+5.95), VERB:FORM (+5.58) and PUNCT (+3.75). Results for NOUN:INFL (+31.25), VERB:INFL (+26.92), WO (+7.9) and ADJ:FORM (+6.94) are not highlighted because they are rare and only account for a small fraction of the data (0.05%, 0.08%, 1.16%, and 0.16% respectively).

Error type	**Sentence-level baseline**			**Document-level system**			**Diff. $F_{0.5}$**
	P	**R**	**$F_{0.5}$**	**P**	**R**	**$F_{0.5}$**	
ADJ	42.55	15.62	31.65	44.44	15.62	32.47	+0.82
ADJ:FORM	66.67	33.33	55.56	100.00	25.00	62.50	+6.94
ADV	48.21	20.15	37.71	42.11	17.91	33.15	-4.56
CONJ	35.71	11.90	25.51	46.15	14.29	31.91	+6.40
CONTR	88.24	51.72	77.32	85.00	58.62	77.98	+0.66
DET	55.52	42.19	52.22	63.72	51.33	60.79	+8.57
MORPH	62.96	34.87	54.23	70.65	33.33	57.73	+3.50
NOUN	35.90	11.60	25.30	38.10	13.26	27.71	+2.41
NOUN:INFL	60.00	75.00	62.50	100.00	75.00	93.75	+31.25
NOUN:NUM	60.39	50.40	58.09	74.21	47.58	66.74	+8.65
NOUN:POSS	65.00	46.43	60.19	63.04	51.79	60.42	+0.23
ORTH	75.53	55.59	70.47	71.22	59.94	68.63	-1.84
OTHER	40.92	18.95	33.21	38.14	22.49	33.48	+0.27
PART	56.52	44.07	53.50	58.54	40.68	53.81	+0.31
PREP	53.77	34.40	48.33	64.67	41.90	58.33	+10.00
PRON	48.39	33.15	44.31	55.71	43.09	52.63	+8.32
PUNCT	63.53	49.60	60.15	70.07	47.26	63.90	+3.75
SPELL	82.09	58.41	75.94	86.15	53.85	76.92	+0.98
VERB	48.11	20.23	37.71	44.81	21.59	36.88	-0.83
VERB:FORM	64.35	59.15	63.24	71.14	60.85	68.82	+5.58
VERB:INFL	50.00	50.00	50.00	80.00	66.67	76.92	+26.92
VERB:SVA	61.01	68.79	62.42	72.41	74.47	72.82	+10.40
VERB:TENSE	58.10	38.28	52.65	63.50	44.77	58.60	+5.95
WO	51.47	39.77	48.61	64.71	37.50	56.51	+7.9
Total	58.49	38.29	52.91	62.64	40.72	56.55	+3.64

Table C.1: Error type-specific performance of the sentence-level **Baseline** and the document-level **MultiEnc-dec** on BEA-dev. The last column shows the difference in $F_{0.5}$ between document-level and sentence-level systems.

D GEC system output examples

Context	In the chat room, she created a close relationship with eight people.
Source	She talks to them every night, trust them and share her life with them.
Reference	She **talked** to them every night, **trusted** them and **shared** her life with them.
Baseline	She talks to them every night, trusts them and shares her life with them.
Our model	She **talked** to them every night, **trusted** them and **shared** her life with them.

Context	Solar heaters have been introduced in houses instead of water heaters.
Source	Rain water storage system to increase water level.
Reference	**and rain** water storage **systems** to increase water **levels**.
Baseline	Rain water storage system to increase water level.
Our model	**and rain** water storage **systems** to increase water **levels**.

Context	My favourite sport is volleyball. When I am on the beach I like playing with my sister in the sand and then we go in the sea.
Source	It is very funny.
Reference	It is **great fun**.
Baseline	It is very funny.
Our model	It is **great fun**.

Context	It was the first time for me to play basketball.
Source	I think I were very good.
Reference	I think I **was** very good.
Baseline	I think I am very good.
Our model	I think I **was** very good.

Essay Quality Signals as Weak Supervision for Source-based Essay Scoring

Haoran Zhang
Department of Computer Science
University of Pittsburgh
Pittsburgh, PA 15260
colinzhang@cs.pitt.edu

Diane Litman
Department of Computer Science & LRDC
University of Pittsburgh
Pittsburgh, PA 15260
dlitman@pitt.edu

Abstract

Human essay grading is a laborious task that can consume much time and effort. Automated Essay Scoring (AES) has thus been proposed as a fast and effective solution to the problem of grading student writing at scale. However, because AES typically uses supervised machine learning, a human-graded essay corpus is still required to train the AES model. Unfortunately, such a graded corpus often does not exist, so creating a corpus for machine learning can also be a laborious task. This paper presents an investigation of replacing the use of human-labeled essay grades when training an AES system with two automatically available but weaker signals of essay quality: word count and topic distribution similarity. Experiments using two source-based essay scoring (evidence score) corpora show that while weak supervision does not yield a competitive result when training a neural source-based AES model, it can be used to successfully extract Topical Components (TCs) from a source text, which are required by a supervised feature-based AES model. In particular, results show that feature-based AES performance is comparable with either automatically or manually constructed TCs.

1 Introduction

Essay grading is a laborious task that can consume much teacher time and effort, especially for classes with a large number of students. While human essay grading has high reliability and validity, human grading can also be biased and inconsistent over time. Under such conditions, Automatic Essay Scoring (AES) has been proposed as a fast and effective solution to the problem of grading student writing at scale, minimizing effort and assuring consistency. Many AES systems have been developed to evaluate the content, structure, and quality of written essays via natural language processing (NLP) and machine-learning techniques.

Over the more than 50 year history of AES research, the majority of work has used feature-based models (Louis and Higgins, 2010; Persing et al., 2010; Yannakoudakis and Briscoe, 2012; Persing and Ng, 2015; Farra et al., 2015; McNamara et al., 2015; Cummins et al., 2016; Ghosh et al., 2016; Nguyen and Litman, 2018; Amorim et al., 2018; Cozma et al., 2018). However, these models require carefully designed hand-crafted features to represent essays. Recently, neural network models have drawn increasing attention (Alikaniotis et al., 2016; Taghipour and Ng, 2016; Dong and Zhang, 2016; Dong et al., 2017; Farag et al., 2018; Jin et al., 2018; Li et al., 2018; Tay et al., 2018; Nadeem et al., 2019; Mayfield and Black, 2020) due to their powerful ability to generate essay representations automatically and to generate reliable essay score predictions.

No matter whether a feature-based or neural network model is used, state-of-the-art AES systems are all supervised, which means that the model needs to be trained on a large number of human-graded essays. Unfortunately, such a human-graded corpus often does not exist, and grading a corpus of essays is a laborious task. To address this problem, we investigate using a weakly supervised AES approach, where automatically available essay quality signals replace the use of human-labeled scores when training a state-of-the-art neural network model for source-based essay scoring. We define ***essay quality signals*** in this work as scores that reflect the quality of essays. The human-labeled holistic score is the most common essay quality signal, and is typically used for supervised machine learning. We instead explore the use of two automated essay quality signals, namely word count and topic distribution similarity between student essays and a source article, in a weakly supervised machine learning AES approach.

Our work focuses on the response-to-text assess-

Proceedings of the 16th Workshop on Innovative Use of NLP for Building Educational Applications, pages 85–96
April 20, 2021

ment (RTA) (Correnti et al., 2013), a particular source-based essay writing task. In source-based writing, students read a source article before writing an essay that responds to a prompt related to the source article. In order to guide students on revising an RTA essay after receiving feedback, an automated writing evaluation (AWE) system for the RTA (Zhang et al., 2019) was developed that generated formative feedback based on rubric-based AES features. These AES features were computed by recognizing when a set of manually created ***Topical Components*** (TCs) from the source text were used by students in their essays. The TCs represent a comprehensive list of topics related to evidence in the source article, which include: 1) important keywords indicating the set of topics (denoted as *topic words*), and 2) phrases representing specific examples for each topic (denoted as *specific examples*). The grading rubric encourages students to mention and elaborate topics and specific examples from the source article as much as possible in their essays. Therefore, the RTA AES and AWE systems use rubric-based features based on the TCs in order to follow the grading rubric.

Previously, human effort was required to manually create TCs based on expert knowledge of the source text. To eliminate this effort, Zhang and Litman (2020) used the attention layer output of a co-attention neural network to automatically extract TCs. Their experimental results showed that automated TCs performed equally well as manual TCs on a downstream, rubric-based AES task. However, to eliminate the human effort for creating TCs, they introduced a different human evidence score grading effort to train the co-attention neural network. Unfortunately, we believe that the effort to grade student essays is more than the original effort to create the TCs. Our goal is to remove both sources of human effort.

To do so, we introduce two simple essay quality signals, word count and topic distribution similarity, which can be generated automatically and used as weak supervision for training the neural AES. Although the learned AES model outperforms simple baselines, weak supervision is not enough to yield a state-of-the-art AES model. Nonetheless, the proposed essay quality signals can be successfully used to generate TCs for a downstream rubric-based AES task. By using auto-generated essay quality signals, we can thus eliminate all human effort for generating TCs. We evaluate the generated TCs using a rubric-based AES requiring TCs, for two RTA source articles. Results show that our simple signals for training a neural AES to create TCs automatically do not degrade performance compared to using manually constructed TCs, whether for 1) representing essays as rubric-based features, 2) grading essays.

2 Related Work

The majority of research in the AES area uses supervised machine learning techniques that require a large number of human-graded essays for training. However, graded essay corpora are usually missing in real classroom scenarios, and annotating a corpus to train an AES model is labor-intensive. A prior proposal to address this problem used an unsupervised-learning approach based on a voting algorithm (Chen et al., 2010). The area of short answer scoring has also faced a similar problem. Zesch et al. (2015a) presented a semi-supervised method to reduce the size of the required human-labeled corpus. Meanwhile, Ramachandran et al. (2015) proposed a graph-based lexico-semantic text matching for pattern identification. These works reduce human effort, but do not eliminate them. In contrast, our AES work fully replaces human graded evidence scores with essay quality signals that are easy to extract automatically and to use during training. Although our results show that the signals are not effective for the AES task itself, they are useful for extracting Topical Components (TCs).

Previously, human expert effort was required to extract TCs. Specifically, experts read through the source article and created lists of topic words and of specific examples that students were expected to use in their essays (Rahimi et al., 2017). In order to eliminate this human effort, three systems were later developed. An LDA-based system (Rahimi and Litman, 2016) used a LDA topic model (Blei et al., 2003) and TurboTopic algorithm (Blei and Lafferty, 2009) for TC extraction. Zhang and Litman (2020) proposed another system based on the PositionRank (Florescu and Caragea, 2017) algorithm. While these two TC extraction systems did not require any human coding, they also did not match prior performance. The state-of-the-art system (Zhang and Litman, 2020) extracted TCs by exploiting the attention weights of a neural AES model. However, human grading effort was needed for model training. In our work, we replace hu-

Prompt	RTA_{MVP}	RTA_{Space}
Score 1	852 (29%)	538 (26%)
Score 2	1197 (40%)	789 (38%)
Score 3	616 (21%)	512 (25%)
Score 4	305 (10%)	237 (11%)
Total	2970	2076

Table 1: The Evidence score distribution of RTA.

man scores with automated essay quality signals for training, while still achieving state-of-the-art TC extraction.

We believe that many predictive features used in the traditional feature-based AES systems can be useful signals for our weak supervision approach to TC extraction. For example, length-based features (Attali and Burstein, 2006; Chen and He, 2013; Östling et al., 2013; Phandi et al., 2015; Zesch et al., 2015b), prompt-relevant features (Louis and Higgins, 2010; Klebanov et al., 2016), or semantic features (Klebanov and Flor, 2013; Persing and Ng, 2013) all weakly relate to the quality of an essay's content. In this paper, we examine two such signals, word count and topic distribution similarity, and show that with these simple essay quality signals, human-labeled essay scores are unnecessary for TC extraction.

3 Corpora

Our work focuses on a specific source-based essay writing task named the response-to-text assessment (RTA) (Correnti et al., 2013). The corpora were all collected from upper elementary level classrooms. Based on different articles that students read before writing their essays, two forms of the RTA were developed. RTA_{MVP} is based on an article from *Time for Kids* about an effort by the United Nations to end poverty in a rural village in Sauri, Kenya, named the Millennium Villages Project (MVP). RTA_{Space} is based on an article which discusses the importance of space exploration. After reading an RTA article, there is a prompt that asks students to write an essay in response to the prompt. The prompt encourages students to use evidence from the source article to support their claims. Table 2 shows a source article excerpt, the corresponding prompt, and a student essay of RTA_{MVP}. The bolded phrases in the source excerpt are evidence examples manually labeled by human experts, which are essential to be discussed in the student essay.

All collected essays (2970 essays for RTA_{MVP} and 2076 essays for RTA_{Space}) were manually graded on a scale of 1 to 4 (low to high) in five dimensions: Analysis, Evidence, Organization, Style, and MUGS (Mechanics, Usage, Grammar, and Spelling). Each dimension evaluates one aspect of students' writing skills. We focus on the Evidence dimension , which evaluates students' ability to find and use evidence from the source article to support their ideas. This dimension is also directly related to the final output of this work, Topical Components. Table 1 shows the distribution of Evidence scores for both forms of the RTA. Table 2 shows an essay with an evidence score of 3. Phrases semantically related to the TCs from the source article are shown in **boldface**. The average essay word counts for each prompt are 180 and 220, respectively.

4 Prior AES Systems for the RTA

Two approaches to AES have been developed for the RTA: 1) a feature-based supervised learning approach (with the features aligned to the Evidence rubric criteria), which we refer to as AES_{rubric}, and 2) a neural network approach, which we refer to as AES_{neural}.

AES_{rubric} (Rahimi et al., 2017; Zhang and Litman, 2017) used a traditional supervised learning framework with hand-crafted, rubric-based features that require knowledge of TCs to compute. That is, a set of interpretable features were carefully designed to capture the relation between student essays and the two aspects of TCs described above (*topic words* and *specific examples*):

Number of Pieces of Evidence (NPE): an integer feature based on the list of *topic words* for each topic that indicates the number of topics (semantically) mentioned in the essay.

Concentration (CON): a binary feature that indicates if an essay elaborates on topics, again based on the list of *topic words*.

Specificity (SPC): a vector of integer values indicating the number of *specific examples* (semantically) mentioned in the essay per topic.

Word Count (WOC): number of words.

To support the needs of the AWE system for the RTA (Zhang et al., 2019), the feature values and predicted evidence scores from AES_{rubric} are passed to the AWE system to select formative feed-

Source Excerpt: Today, Yala Sub-District **Hospital has medicine, free of charge, for all of the most common diseases. Water is connected to the hospital**, which also has a **generator for electricity**. **Bed nets are used** in every sleeping site in Sauri...
Essay Prompt: The author provided one specific example of how the quality of life can be improved by the Millennium Villages Project in Sauri, Kenya. Based on the article, did the author provide a convincing argument that winning the fight against poverty is achievable in our lifetime? Explain why or why not with 3-4 examples from the text to support your answer.
Essay: In my opinion I think that they will **achieve it in lifetime**. During the years threw **2004 and 2008 they made progress**. People didn't have the money to buy the stuff in 2004. **The hospital was packed with patients** and they didn't have alot of treatment in 2004. In 2008 it changed the **hospital had medicine, free of charge**, and **for all the common dieases**. **Water was connected to the hospital** and has a **generator for electricity**. **Everybody has net** in their site. **The hunger crisis has been addressed** with **fertilizer and seeds**, as well as the **tools needed to maintain the food**. **The school has no fees** and **they serve lunch**. To me that's sounds like it is going achieve it in the lifetime.

Table 2: A source excerpt for the RTA_{MVP} prompt and an essay with an evidence score of 3.

Topic	Keywords
Hospital	care, health, hospital, treatment, doctor, electricity, disease, water, ...
Malaria	bed, net, malaria, infect, bed-net, mosquito, bug, sleeping, die, cheap, ...
Farming	farmer, fertilizer, irrigation, dying, crop, seed, water, harvest, hungry, ...
School	school, supplies, fee, student, midday, meal, lunch, supply, book, paper, ...

Table 3: The partial list of topic words of RTA_{MVP}.

Category 1	Category 5	Category 7
unpaved roads	crops dying	progress just four years
tattered clothing	not afford fertilizer irrigation	medicine free charge
bare feet	outcome poor crops	no midday meal lunch
less than 1 dollar day	lack fertilizer water	kids go school now
	...	...

Table 4: The partial list of specific examples of RTA_{MVP}.

back messages such as "Use more evidence from the article" (based on NPE values) or "Provide more details for each piece of evidence you use" (based on NPE and SPC values).

Although AES_{rubric} thus provides useful information for the AWE system, in order to improve the stand-alone AES performance, AES_{neural} (Zhang and Litman, 2018) was later developed. AES_{neural} used a hierarchical neural network model with a self-attention mechanism in the phrase level and a co-attention mechanism in the sentence level. The self-attention layer captures the importance of each individual phrase, while the co-attention layer captures the relationship between the source article and the essay. In terms of the essay score prediction task, AES_{neural} significantly outperforms AES_{rubric}, and no human effort for either TC extraction or feature engineering is required. However, the essay representations created by AES_{neural} cannot be directly used by the AWE system, which depends on the rubric-based features to provide formative feedback in terms of the grading criteria.

5 Prior TC Extraction Methods

To develop AES_{rubric}, human expert effort was first required to manually extract TCs (TC_{manual}) in the form of two lists related to evidence in the source text: 1) a *topic words list* of important keywords that indicate the main set of article topics, and 2) a *specific examples* list that includes phrases representing specific examples for article topics. Table 3 shows a partial topic words list for RTA_{MVP}, where the four topics ("hospital", "malaria", "farming", and "school") and the associated keywords were manually created by a human expert. Table 4 shows a partial specific examples list for RTA_{MVP}. The full list has 8 categories. Some categories are similar to Category 1, which is not related to the 4 main topics, but the human expert thought they were important to be mentioned in the essay. Other categories are similar to Category 5, in being directly related to one of the main topics. Other categories are similar to Category 7, in being directly related to multiple main topics.

To replace the need for the human expert in creating such TCs, Zhang and Litman (2020) developed a method for TC extraction using AES_{neural}. Their algorithm was based on the observations that the co-attention layer on the sentence level assigned higher attention scores to important sentences, while the self-attention layer on the word (phrase) level assigned higher attention scores to important words (phrases). Therefore, their system extracted important words from important

Prompt	WC	TDS
RTA_{MVP}	0.480	0.359
RTA_{Space}	0.489	0.253

Table 5: Pearson's r comparing different essay quality signals with evidence score.

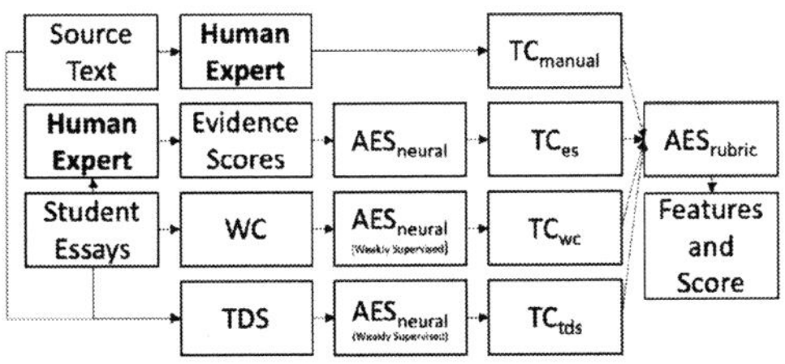

Figure 1: An overview of four TC extraction systems.

sentences based on attention scores and used k-medoids to cluster all words. Finally, it extracted TCs from each cluster. Since human-labeled evidence scores of each essay were required for the neural network training, we denote this method by TC_{es}. Note that TC_{es} replaced the human effort needed to extract TCs with the human effort needed to create the AES_{neural} training supervision signal.

6 Weak Essay Quality Signals

Currently, TC_{es} reaches the top performance for automated TC extraction (Zhang and Litman, 2020) when compared to the LDA-based and Position-Rank methods discussed in the Related Work section. However, TC_{es} requires extra human effort for essay grading, a barrier to making the system useful in real classroom scenarios. Therefore, in this work, we aim to explore essay quality signals other than gold-standard evidence scores in order to eliminate the remaining human effort in the TC extraction process.

6.1 Word Count (WC)

Most intuitively, word count is usually highly positively correlated with essay quality, especially with the holistic score of an essay. Most feature-based AES systems use word count as one of the features (Attali and Burstein, 2006; Chen and He, 2013; Östling et al., 2013; Phandi et al., 2015; Zesch et al., 2015b). Since the word count is highly predictive of essay score on its own, some models even manually assign a lower weight to this feature to prevent it from dominating the final model (Burstein et al., 2004). Therefore, we believe the word count is a good indicator of overall essay quality. In addition, per the grading rubric of the evidence dimension, an essay with a higher evidence score should mention more topics and elaborate more specific examples. Therefore, we also believe that the word count should be correlated with the RTA evidence score as well. Table 5 shows that the correlations between word count and evidence score on our two corpora are 0.480 and 0.489 for RTA_{MVP} and RTA_{Space}, respectively.

6.2 Topic Distribution Similarity (TDS)

Although the LDA-based TC extraction system (Rahimi and Litman, 2016) did not outperform TC_{es} on a downstream AES_{rubric} task, the generated TCs still seemed to be of reasonable quality. One possible reason is that the quality of the LDA model trained on student essays is good enough to extract important information. Since an essay with a higher evidence score should mention topics and specific examples from the source article as much as possible, we hypothesize that the topic distribution of a good essay should be similar to the source article. Therefore, the second weak essay quality signal we explore is the similarity between the topic distribution of the student essay and the source article.

More specifically, we first train an LDA model on both student essays and the source article. We believe that including the source article into the LDA training process will provide more information to learn from, even if the influence is minor. We then use the LDA model to infer the topic distribution of each essay and the source article. Finally, we calculate the similarity between the topic distribution of a student essay and the source article as the essay's quality signal for the proposed weakly-supervised approach for co-attention neural network training.

Since LDA is an unsupervised method and it is hard to know how many topics exist in a corpus, we use the Topic Coherence score (Röder et al., 2015) to select the best number of topics in an automated manner. Topic Coherence measures whether a topic is semantically interpretable by computing the semantic similarity between important words in the topic. We use C_V measurement because it reaches the best performance in the original paper. C_V measurement is based on a sliding window, and combines the indirect cosine measure with the normalized pointwise mutual information (NPMI).

Layer	Parameter Name	Value
Embedding	Embedding dimension	50
Word-CNN	Kernel size	5
	Number of filters	100
Sent-LSTM	Hidden units	100
Modeling	Hidden units	100
Dropout	Dropout rate	0.5
Others	Epochs	100
	Batch size	100
	Initial learning rate	0.001
	Momentum	0.9

Table 6: Hyper-parameters for neural training.

Prompt	Component	Parameter	TC_{es}	TC_{wc}	TC_{tds}
RTA_{MVP}	Topic Words	# of Topics	16	13	5
		# of Words	25	10	25
	Examples	# of Topics	18	14	20
		# of Examples	15	15	30
RTA_{Space}	Topic Words	# of Topics	10	18	16
		# of Words	20	30	25
	Examples	# of Topics	9	19	16
		# of Examples	20	15	20

Table 7: Selected parameters for different models.

Since a good topic model should have as many semantically interpretable topics as possible, a good topic model should receive high topic coherence scores. We train multiple LDA models with different numbers of topics for each individual form of RTA, and select the number of topics resulting in the best coherence scores. The best number of topics for RTA_{MVP} is 7, and the best number of topics for RTA_{Space} is 14.

Once we use the pre-trained LDA model to infer topic distributions for each essay and the source article, we calculate the similarity between them to get topic distribution similarity. We select cosine similarity rather than dot product similarity since the grading rubric encourages students to mention more topics rather than go deep into one topic. A full elaboration of evidence is only required for essays with a high evidence score, although the rubric encourages all students to elaborate evidence as much as possible. Therefore, in geometrical terms, we care about angle difference more than magnitude difference. In other words, we measure how many topics from the source article are mentioned in an essay. Table 5 shows that the correlations between topic distribution similarity and evidence scores are 0.359 and 0.253 for RTA_{MVP} and RTA_{Space}, respectively.

7 Experimental Setup

Figure 1 shows an overview of usage of AES_{neural} and four TC extraction systems to be evaluated. TC_{manual} lets human experts extract TCs from each source article, and is thus the upper bound for evaluating the other (automated) TC extraction systems. TC_{es} is our baseline automated model, which builds on AES_{neural} and a clustering algorithm to extract TCs from student essays and the source article, using the gold-standard evidence score of each essay for AES_{neural} training. TC_{wc} and TC_{tds} are methods proposed by this work that are instead based on weakly-supervised AES_{neural} training. TC_{wc} replaces evidence score with the word count of each essay, while TC_{tds} uses topic distribution similarity with the number of topics.

Our experiments are designed to test two hypotheses related to the alternative AES and TC methods shown in Figure 1. The first hypothesis, denoted by H1, is that while weakly supervised training might not yield state-of-the-art, AES_{neural} performance when evaluated as an end in itself, the use of automated essay quality signals nonetheless can outperform weak baselines such as random and majority score prediction. Our second hypothesis, denoted by H2, is that weakly supervised training can nonetheless yield versions of AES_{neural} that are still useful for automated TC extraction. All neural network models are built with TensorFlow 2.2.0, and trained on an RTX 5000 GPU.

7.1 $\mathbf{AES_{neural}}$ Performance (H1)

Our experiment for H1 tests the impact of replacing human-labeled evidence scores with our proposed weak essay quality signals when training the AES_{neural} model. Specifically, we train AES_{neural} models on human-labeled evidence score, word count, and topic distribution similarity. Then, we calculate the Quadratic Weighted Kappa (QWK) between predicted scores of AES_{neural} and human evidence scores. We also compare these scoring results to random and majority prediction baselines.

Following Zhang and Litman (2018), we use 5-fold cross-validation in this experiment. We split both corpora into 5 folds, the partition is the same as the setting presented by Zhang and Litman (2018). In each fold, 60% of the data are used for training, 20% of the data are the development set, and 20% of the data are used for testing. All essay

Prompt	Majority (1)	Random (2)	Evidence Score (3)	WC (4)	TDS (5)
RTA_{MVP}	0.000	0.016	**0.697 (1,2,4,5)**	0.366 (1,2)	0.440 (1,2)
RTA_{Space}	0.000	0.016	**0.684 (1,2,4,5)**	0.380 (1,2)	0.386 (1,2)

Table 8: The performance (QWK) of AES_{neural} using different essay quality signals for training. The numbers in the parentheses show the model numbers over which the current model performs significantly better ($p \leq 0.05$). The best results in each row are in bold.

scores and WC are scaled to the range [0, 1] for training. Since TDS is topic distribution similarity between essays and the source article, the score range is [0, 1], so we do not scale it in the experiments. The scaled essay scores or essay quality signals are only used for training. When calculating the Quadratic Weighted Kappa, we scaled the predicted score back to the original score range, which is $[1, 4]$. All hyper-parameters for the AES_{neural} training are shown in Table 6. Please note that we used essay scores for the development set to determine early stopping. Therefore, we assume a small amount of graded essays is available for this purpose in experiment of H1. Since all hyper-parameters are inherited from prior work, they are not selected based on the development set.

7.2 Extracted TCs (H2)

We configure experiments to evaluate the four TC extraction methods in Figure 1 both extrinsically and intrinsically. We thus break H2 into two sub-hypotheses: H2a) the AES_{rubric} model for scoring Evidence will perform comparably when extracting features using TC extraction methods involving either human (TC_{manual}, TC_{es}) or automated (TC_{wc}, TC_{tds}) methods; H2b) the correlation between the human evidence score and the TC-dependent feature values will be comparable when extracting features using either TC_{manual}, TC_{es}, TC_{wc}, and TC_{tds}. Extrinsically, the experiment for H2a examines the impact of using our proposed TC extraction methods on the downstream AES_{rubric} task. Intrinsically, the experiment for H2b measures the impact on the essay representation itself. For H2a, we calculate the Quadratic Weighted Kappa (QWK) between predicted scores of AES_{rubric} and human evidence scores. For H2b, we compare the correlation between human evidence score with NPE feature and sum of SPC features, because both features are integer features and are extracted based on TCs.

For these experiments, we stratify essay corpora following Zhang and Litman (2020): 40% for training word embeddings and extracting TCs, 20% for selecting the best embedding and parameters, and 40% for testing. We use the same hyper-parameters from Zhang and Litman (2018) for the co-attention neural network training as shown in Table 6. Table 7 show all other parameters selected using the development sets for all models.

8 Results and Discussion

Table 8, which addresses H1, shows the Quadratic Weighted Kappa between human evidence scores and predicted scores by AES_{neural} using different essay quality signals for training, as well as random prediction and majority prediction. Unsurprisingly, the models trained on human scores significantly outperform our proposed weaker essay quality signals on both prompts, even though we assume a small amount of graded essays is available for early stopping. Although QWK of WC and TDS are lower than Evidence Score, they still significantly outperform random and majority prediction baselines. The results support H1 that while weak supervision signals such as word count and topic distribution similarity are not enough for training AES_{neural} to reach a state-of-the-art QWK, they still provide some predictive utility.

Although both WC and TDS underperform the human-generated Evidence Scores, TDS constantly outperforms WC, despite the fact that WC has higher correlations with Evidence Score than TDS (recall Table 5). One possible reason is that the human evidence score assesses if an essay mentions and elaborates evidence from the source article, which measures the relationship between the essay and the source article. TDS is topic distribution similarity between student essays and the source article, so the AES model learns more relations between student essays and the source article. However, WC only contains length information of essays but no relation between essays and the source article.

Table 9, which addresses H2a, shows the Quadratic Weighted Kappa between human evidence scores and predicted scores by AES_{rubric} when using different TCs. On RTA_{MVP}, TC_{wc}

Prompt	TC_{manual} (1)	TC_{es} (2)	TC_{wc} (3)	TC_{tds} (4)
RTA_{MVP}	0.643	0.648 (1)	0.645	**0.652 (1,2,3)**
RTA_{Space}	0.609 (4)	**0.622 (1,4)**	**0.622 (1,4)**	0.599

Table 9: The performance (QWK) of AES_{rubric} using different TCs extraction methods for feature creation. The numbers in the parentheses show the model numbers over which the current model performs significantly better ($p < 0.05$). The best results between automated methods in each row are in bold.

Prompt	Feature	TC_{manual}	TC_{es}	TC_{wc}	TC_{tds}
RTA_{MVP}	NPE	0.542	**0.639**	**0.560**	0.533
	SPC (sum)	0.689	0.679	0.653	0.674
RTA_{Space}	NPE	0.484	**0.625**	**0.615**	**0.599**
	SPC (sum)	0.601	0.598	0.485	0.438

Table 10: Pearson's r comparing feature values computed using each TCs extraction method with human (gold-standard) Evidence essay scores. All correlation values are significant ($p \leq 0.05$). Bolding indicates that the automated method is better than TC_{manual}.

yields statistically similar performance compared to TC_{manual} and TC_{es}, while TC_{tds} significantly outperforms all other methods. The story is different when switching to RTA_{Space}, where TC_{tds} is now outperformed by all other methods. Considering that the two proposed methods based on weak supervision do not require human expert effort for either TC extraction (TC_{manual}) or for grading evidence score for neural training (TC_{es}), we believe the results support H2a.

Table 10 shows Pearson's r comparing feature values computed using each TC extraction method with human (gold-standard) Evidence essay scores, and partially support H2b. For NPE feature, TC_{wc} always yields better performance than TC_{manual}. TC_{tds} yields better performance than TC_{manual} on RTA_{Space} only. However, for SPC features, there is no automated method that outperforms TC_{manual}. On RTA_{MVP}, the proposed methods yield similar performance as TC_{es}.

A very interesting finding is that both WC and TDS underperform Human Score on AES_{neural} task, while TC_{wc} and TC_{tds} help AES_{rubric} reach an even higher QWK. This result shows that while learning using weak supervision is not enough for AES_{neural} training, with post-processing the intermediate output, the neural predictions can still help to generate useful TCs for the AES_{rubric} task.

Since word count is highly positively correlated with evidence score for both RTA_{MVP} and RTA_{Space}, TC_{wc} works well on average compared to TC_{tds}. Extrinsically, it outperforms TC_{manual} on both corpora. It also matches TC_{es} on RTA_{Space}, and has similar performance on RTA_{MVP}. Intrinsically, TC_{wc} yields higher correlations for the NPE feature when comparing to TC_{manual}. Although correlations for SPC are worse than TC_{es}, considering word count is the most intuitive signal without the needs of human effort, it performs surprisingly well.

Moving to topic distribution similarity, TC_{tds} shows worse extrinsic performance on RTA_{Space} comparing to RTA_{MVP}. To figure out the reason, we take a deep dive into the TCs generated by both methods. We consider that good automated TCs should cover topics in TC_{manual} as many as possible. Therefore, we manually label a topic for each of the manual topic words. For RTA_{MVP}, TC_{tds} has 4 related topics out of 5 (**80%**), while there are 10 related topics out of 16 (62.50%) for RTA_{Space}. Obviously, TC_{tds} preserves more related topics in RTA_{MVP}. Similarly, we also manually compare specific examples of both automated TCs with TC_{manual}. For examples rather than keywords, TC_{tds} has 16 out of 20 related categories (**80%**) for RTA_{MVP}, while there are 11 out of 16 related categories (68.75%) for RTA_{Space}. TC_{tds} again preserves more related categories in RTA_{MVP}.

We also observe that we can always find a better QWK using an automated TC method compared to TC_{manual} (Table 9). It is typically assumed that humans are the upper bound, but they do not seem to do an optimal job when creating TCs. One possible reason is that the human expert is subjective when creating TCs, and they add words and examples they thought necessary. However, some words or examples may not be as important as humans thought. Meanwhile, AES_{neural} is objective. TCs generated by TC_{es}, TC_{wc}, and TC_{tds} directly extract important words and examples that

AES_{neural} considers essential, and they are highly related to its essay score or essay quality signals. Therefore, TC_{es}, TC_{wc}, and TC_{tds} are more suitable for AES_{rubric}, which heavily relies on feature values extracted based on TCs.

A concern that might be raised about our work is that our essay quality signals have the potential to be gamed by students. For example, our signals could assign high scores to long essays with no relation to the prompt or to essays with replicated words of the source article. However, in our experiments, both essay quality signals are only used for training AES_{neural} and extracting Topical Components. For experiments of H1, essay quality signals are used as the label for training the AES_{neural} model instead of used as features during testing (when gaming would be expected). The trained AES_{neural} is in fact tested on the human-graded evidence scores, not word count nor topic distribution similarity. For experiments of H2, essay quality signals are only used as the label for training AES_{neural} and extracting Topical Components. AES_{rubric} extracts features based on the Topical Components, and are then trained and tested on evidence scores. The purpose of this experiment is to show that the Topical Components extracted from the AES_{neural} are useful for another downstream AES model, even though the QWK of the AES_{neural} trained on essay quality signals is low. In sum, since essay quality signals are not used as predictive features in our system and only used as the label for training, we believe that our proposed method for Topical Components extraction is hard to be gamed – assuming adverserial essays only appear in the testing set. However, if such essays appear in the training data the risk of the manipulation of both AES_{neural} and AES_{rubric} based on word count, topic distribution similarity, or other essay quality signals is still possible (Lochbaum et al., 2013). A future deep analysis of both AES models would be necessary to address this problem.

Another limitation of our research is that to date, our approach has only been tested on two RTA corpora. This is because Topical Components have only been used in AES_{rubric} until now. Furthermore, although Word Count shows a high correlation with evidence scores in our RTA corpora, this high correlation could easily disappear in tasks in which the prompt specifies the expected word count (Weiss et al., 2019). Similarly, topic distribution similarity might not a good essay quality signal if a prompt is not source-based, or does not expect similar topics in content.

9 Conclusion and Future Work

This paper presented an investigation of replacing human-labeled evidence scores with other automated essay quality signals, such as word count and topic distribution similarity. These signals are easy to be calculated and integrated into existing systems in order to eliminate human effort. Not surprisingly, these weak supervised signals are not enough for training a useable AES_{neural} model. However, they still help generate TCs, which is required by AES_{rubric}. We observe that even a simple signal like word count does not hurt the state-of-the-art baseline (TC_{es}). Since there is no need for human effort, we believe that our work brings AES technology closer to being useful in real classroom scenarios.

In our future work on using weak supervision for AES training, we would like to explore other possible essay quality signals beyond the two investigated here, again drawing on machine learning features used in prior work. It would also be interesting to examine whether our two existing signals might yield better AES results when training other types of neural algorithms and/or when applied to different datasets. Moreover, the impact of data size for training on this model is worth exploration. Finally, with respect to TC generation, because the specific examples are generated from clustering results, words in a specific example are not in readable orders. This leads to another interesting future investigation into making all examples in the specific examples list more human-understandable, although this would not affect the system performance due to the nature of the AES_{rubric}.

Acknowledgments

We would like thank members of the PETAL group as well as reviewers for comments on an earlier version of the paper. We would also like to thank Adriana Kovashka for originally suggesting that we explore weak supervision.

The research reported here was supported, in whole or in part, by the Institute of Education Sciences, U.S. Department of Education, through Grant R305A160245 to the University of Pittsburgh. The opinions expressed are those of the authors and do not represent the views of the Institute or the U.S. Department of Education.

References

Dimitrios Alikaniotis, Helen Yannakoudakis, and Marek Rei. 2016. Automatic text scoring using neural networks. In *Proceedings of the 54th Annual Meeting of the Association for Computational Linguistics (Volume 1: Long Papers)*, volume 1, pages 715–725.

Evelin Amorim, Marcia Cançado, and Adriano Veloso. 2018. Automated essay scoring in the presence of biased ratings. In *Proceedings of the 2018 Conference of the North American Chapter of the Association for Computational Linguistics: Human Language Technologies, Volume 1 (Long Papers)*, pages 229–237.

Yigal Attali and Jill Burstein. 2006. Automated essay scoring with e-rater® v. 2. *The Journal of Technology, Learning and Assessment*, 4(3).

David M Blei and John D Lafferty. 2009. Visualizing topics with multi-word expressions. *arXiv preprint arXiv:0907.1013*.

David M Blei, Andrew Y Ng, and Michael I Jordan. 2003. Latent dirichlet allocation. *Journal of machine Learning research*, 3(Jan):993–1022.

Jill Burstein, Martin Chodorow, and Claudia Leacock. 2004. Automated essay evaluation: The criterion online writing service. *Ai magazine*, 25(3):27–27.

Hongbo Chen and Ben He. 2013. Automated essay scoring by maximizing human-machine agreement. In *Proceedings of the 2013 Conference on Empirical Methods in Natural Language Processing*, pages 1741–1752.

Yen-Yu Chen, Chien-Liang Liu, Chia-Hoang Lee, Tao-Hsing Chang, et al. 2010. An unsupervised automated essay-scoring system. *IEEE Intelligent systems*, 25(5):61–67.

Richard Correnti, Lindsay Clare Matsumura, Laura Hamilton, and Elaine Wang. 2013. Assessing students' skills at writing analytically in response to texts. *The Elementary School Journal*, 114(2):142–177.

Madalina Cozma, Andrei Butnaru, and Radu Tudor Ionescu. 2018. Automated essay scoring with string kernels and word embeddings. In *Proceedings of the 56th Annual Meeting of the Association for Computational Linguistics (Volume 2: Short Papers)*, pages 503–509.

Ronan Cummins, Meng Zhang, and Edward John Briscoe. 2016. Constrained multi-task learning for automated essay scoring. Association for Computational Linguistics.

Fei Dong and Yue Zhang. 2016. Automatic features for essay scoring–an empirical study. In *Proceedings of the 2016 Conference on Empirical Methods in Natural Language Processing*, pages 1072–1077.

Fei Dong, Yue Zhang, and Jie Yang. 2017. Attention-based recurrent convolutional neural network for automatic essay scoring. In *Proceedings of the 21st Conference on Computational Natural Language Learning (CoNLL 2017)*, pages 153–162.

Youmna Farag, Helen Yannakoudakis, and Ted Briscoe. 2018. Neural automated essay scoring and coherence modeling for adversarially crafted input. In *Proceedings of the 2018 Conference of the North American Chapter of the Association for Computational Linguistics: Human Language Technologies, Volume 1 (Long Papers)*, pages 263–271.

Noura Farra, Swapna Somasundaran, and Jill Burstein. 2015. Scoring persuasive essays using opinions and their targets. In *Proceedings of the Tenth Workshop on Innovative Use of NLP for Building Educational Applications*, pages 64–74.

Corina Florescu and Cornelia Caragea. 2017. Position-rank: An unsupervised approach to keyphrase extraction from scholarly documents. In *Proceedings of the 55th Annual Meeting of the Association for Computational Linguistics (Volume 1: Long Papers)*, pages 1105–1115.

Debanjan Ghosh, Aquila Khanam, Yubo Han, and Smaranda Muresan. 2016. Coarse-grained argumentation features for scoring persuasive essays. In *Proceedings of the 54th Annual Meeting of the Association for Computational Linguistics (Volume 2: Short Papers)*, pages 549–554.

Cancan Jin, Ben He, Kai Hui, and Le Sun. 2018. Tdnn: a two-stage deep neural network for prompt-independent automated essay scoring. In *Proceedings of the 56th Annual Meeting of the Association for Computational Linguistics (Volume 1: Long Papers)*, pages 1088–1097.

Beata Beigman Klebanov and Michael Flor. 2013. Word association profiles and their use for automated scoring of essays. In *Proceedings of the 51st Annual Meeting of the Association for Computational Linguistics (Volume 1: Long Papers)*, pages 1148–1158.

Beata Beigman Klebanov, Michael Flor, and Binod Gyawali. 2016. Topicality-based indices for essay scoring. In *Proceedings of the 11th Workshop on Innovative Use of NLP for Building Educational Applications*, pages 63–72.

Xia Li, Minping Chen, Jianyun Nie, Zhenxing Liu, Ziheng Feng, and Yingdan Cai. 2018. Coherence-based automated essay scoring using self-attention. In *Chinese Computational Linguistics and Natural Language Processing Based on Naturally Annotated Big Data*, pages 386–397. Springer.

Karen E Lochbaum, Mark Rosenstein, Peter Foltz, Marcia A Derr, et al. 2013. Detection of gaming in automated scoring of essays with the iea. In *National Council on Measurement in Education Conference (NCME)*.

Annie Louis and Derrick Higgins. 2010. Off-topic essay detection using short prompt texts. In *proceedings of the NAACL HLT 2010 fifth workshop on innovative use of NLP for building educational applications*, pages 92–95.

Elijah Mayfield and Alan W Black. 2020. Should you fine-tune bert for automated essay scoring? In *Proceedings of the Fifteenth Workshop on Innovative Use of NLP for Building Educational Applications*, pages 151–162.

Danielle S McNamara, Scott A Crossley, Rod D Roscoe, Laura K Allen, and Jianmin Dai. 2015. A hierarchical classification approach to automated essay scoring. *Assessing Writing*, 23:35–59.

Farah Nadeem, Huy Nguyen, Yang Liu, and Mari Ostendorf. 2019. Automated essay scoring with discourse-aware neural models. In *Proceedings of the Fourteenth Workshop on Innovative Use of NLP for Building Educational Applications*, pages 484–493.

Huy V Nguyen and Diane J Litman. 2018. Argument mining for improving the automated scoring of persuasive essays. In *Thirty-Second AAAI Conference on Artificial Intelligence*.

Robert Östling, Andre Smolentzov, Björn Tyrefors Hinnerich, and Erik Höglin. 2013. Automated essay scoring for swedish. In *Proceedings of the Eighth Workshop on Innovative Use of NLP for Building Educational Applications*, pages 42–47.

Isaac Persing, Alan Davis, and Vincent Ng. 2010. Modeling organization in student essays. In *Proceedings of the 2010 Conference on Empirical Methods in Natural Language Processing*, pages 229–239. Association for Computational Linguistics.

Isaac Persing and Vincent Ng. 2013. Modeling thesis clarity in student essays. In *Proceedings of the 51st Annual Meeting of the Association for Computational Linguistics (Volume 1: Long Papers)*, pages 260–269.

Isaac Persing and Vincent Ng. 2015. Modeling argument strength in student essays. In *Proceedings of the 53rd Annual Meeting of the Association for Computational Linguistics and the 7th International Joint Conference on Natural Language Processing (Volume 1: Long Papers)*, pages 543–552.

Peter Phandi, Kian Ming A Chai, and Hwee Tou Ng. 2015. Flexible domain adaptation for automated essay scoring using correlated linear regression. In *Proceedings of the 2015 Conference on Empirical Methods in Natural Language Processing*, pages 431–439.

Zahra Rahimi and Diane Litman. 2016. Automatically extracting topical components for a response-to-text writing assessment. In *Proceedings of the 11th Workshop on Innovative Use of NLP for Building Educational Applications*, pages 277–282.

Zahra Rahimi, Diane Litman, Richard Correnti, Elaine Wang, and Lindsay Clare Matsumura. 2017. Assessing students' use of evidence and organization in response-to-text writing: Using natural language processing for rubric-based automated scoring. *International Journal of Artificial Intelligence in Education*, 27(4):694–728.

Lakshmi Ramachandran, Jian Cheng, and Peter Foltz. 2015. Identifying patterns for short answer scoring using graph-based lexico-semantic text matching. In *Proceedings of the Tenth Workshop on Innovative Use of NLP for Building Educational Applications*, pages 97–106.

Michael Röder, Andreas Both, and Alexander Hinneburg. 2015. Exploring the space of topic coherence measures. In *Proceedings of the eighth ACM international conference on Web search and data mining*, pages 399–408.

Kaveh Taghipour and Hwee Tou Ng. 2016. A neural approach to automated essay scoring. In *Proceedings of the 2016 Conference on Empirical Methods in Natural Language Processing*, pages 1882–1891.

Yi Tay, Minh C Phan, Luu Anh Tuan, and Siu Cheung Hui. 2018. Skipflow: incorporating neural coherence features for end-to-end automatic text scoring. In *Thirty-Second AAAI Conference on Artificial Intelligence*.

Zarah Weiss, Anja Riemenschneider, Pauline Schröter, and Detmar Meurers. 2019. Computationally modeling the impact of task-appropriate language complexity and accuracy on human grading of german essays. In *Proceedings of the Fourteenth Workshop on Innovative Use of NLP for Building Educational Applications*, pages 30–45.

Helen Yannakoudakis and Ted Briscoe. 2012. Modeling coherence in esol learner texts. In *Proceedings of the Seventh Workshop on Building Educational Applications Using NLP*, pages 33–43. Association for Computational Linguistics.

Torsten Zesch, Michael Heilman, and Aoife Cahill. 2015a. Reducing annotation efforts in supervised short answer scoring. In *Proceedings of the Tenth Workshop on Innovative Use of NLP for Building Educational Applications*, pages 124–132.

Torsten Zesch, Michael Wojatzki, and Dirk Scholten-Akoun. 2015b. Task-independent features for automated essay grading. In *Proceedings of the Tenth Workshop on Innovative Use of NLP for Building Educational Applications*, pages 224–232.

Haoran Zhang and Diane Litman. 2017. Word embedding for response-to-text assessment of evidence. In *Proceedings of ACL 2017, Student Research Workshop*, pages 75–81.

Haoran Zhang and Diane Litman. 2018. Co-attention based neural network for source-dependent essay scoring. In *Proceedings of the Thirteenth Workshop on Innovative Use of NLP for Building Educational Applications*, pages 399–409.

Haoran Zhang and Diane Litman. 2020. Automated topical component extraction using neural network attention scores from source-based essay scoring. In *Proceedings of the 58th Annual Meeting of the Association for Computational Linguistics*, pages 8569–8584.

Haoran Zhang, Ahmed Magooda, Diane Litman, Richard Correnti, Elaine Wang, LC Matsmura, Emily Howe, and Rafael Quintana. 2019. erevise: Using natural language processing to provide formative feedback on text evidence usage in student writing. In *Proceedings of the AAAI Conference on Artificial Intelligence*, volume 33, pages 9619–9625.

Parsing Argumentative Structure in English-as-Foreign-Language Essays

Jan Wira Gotama Putra[†], **Simone Teufel**[‡†], **Takenobu Tokunaga**[†]
[†]Tokyo Institute of Technology, Japan
[‡]University of Cambridge, United Kingdom
{gotama.w.aa@m, take@c}.titech.ac.jp, simone.teufel@cl.cam.ac.uk

Abstract

This paper presents a study on parsing the argumentative structure in English-as-foreign-language (EFL) essays, which are inherently noisy. The parsing process consists of two steps, linking related sentences and then labelling their relations. We experiment with several deep learning architectures to address each task independently. In the sentence linking task, a biaffine model performed the best. In the relation labelling task, a fine-tuned BERT model performed the best. Two sentence encoders are employed, and we observed that non-fine-tuning models generally performed better when using Sentence-BERT as opposed to BERT encoder. We trained our models using two types of parallel texts: original noisy EFL essays and those improved by annotators, then evaluate them on the original essays. The experiment shows that an end-to-end in-domain system achieved an accuracy of .341. On the other hand, the cross-domain system achieved 94% performance of the in-domain system. This signals that well-written texts can also be useful to train argument mining system for noisy texts.

1 Introduction

Real-world texts are not always well-written, especially in the education area where students are still learning how to write effectively. It has been observed that student texts often require improvements at the discourse-level, e.g., in persuasiveness and content organisation aspects (Bamberg, 1983; Zhang and Litman, 2015; Carlile et al., 2018). Worse still, texts written by non-native speakers are also less coherent, exhibit less lexical richness and more unnatural lexical choices and collocations (Johns, 1986; Silva, 1993; Rabinovich et al., 2016). Our long-term goal is to improve EFL essays from the discourse perspective. One way to do this is by recommending a better arrangement of sentences, which enhances text coherence and comprehension (Connor, 2002; Bacha, 2010). This may serve as feedback for students in the educational setting (Ivanic, 2004). The first step to achieve this goal, which is discussed in the current paper, is parsing argumentative structure in terms of dependencies between sentences. This is because the relationships between sentences are crucial to determine the proper order of sentences (Grosz and Sidner, 1986; Hovy, 1991; Webber and Joshi, 2012).

This paper describes the application of Argument Mining (AM) to EFL essays. AM is an emerging area in computational linguistics which aims to explain how argumentative discourse units (e.g., sentences, clauses) function and relate to each other in the discourse, forming an argument as a whole (Lippi and Torroni, 2016). AM has broad applications in various areas, such as in the legal (Ashley, 1990) and news (Al-Khatib et al., 2016) domains. Also in the education domain, AM is beneficial for many downstream tasks such as text assessment (Wachsmuth et al., 2016), text improvement (as described above) and teaching (Putra et al., 2020). It is common in AM to use well-written texts written by proficient authors, as do Peldszus and Stede (2016), Al-Khatib et al. (2016), among others. However, there are more non-native speakers of English than native speakers in the world, and their writings are often noisy as previously described. Yet, EFL is a niche domain in AM.

This paper presents three contributions. First, this paper presents an application of AM to EFL essays. We parse the argumentative structure in two steps: (i) a ***sentence linking*** step where we identify related sentences that should be linked, forming a tree structure, and (ii) a ***relation labelling*** step, where we label the relationship between the sentences. Several deep learning models were evaluated to address each step. We do not only evaluate the model performance based on individual links

Proceedings of the 16th Workshop on Innovative Use of NLP for Building Educational Applications, pages 97–109
April 20, 2021 ©2021 Association for Computational Linguistics

but also perform a structural analysis, giving more insights into the models' ability to learn different aspects of the argumentative structure.

The second contribution is showing the effectiveness of well-written texts as training data for argumentative parsing of noisy texts. Many AM corpora exist for well-written texts because past studies typically assumed well-written input. Corpora with noisy texts, such as the EFL one we use here, exist, but are far more infrequent. In the past, well-written and noisy texts have been treated as two separate domains, and AM systems were trained separately on each domain. We want to investigate how far the existing labelled corpora for well-written texts can also be useful for training parsers for noisy texts. To this end, we train parsers on both in-domain and out-of-domain texts and evaluate them on the in-domain task. For our out-of-domain texts, we use the improved versions of noisy EFL texts. These improvements were produced by an expert annotator and have a quality closer to those of proficient authors.

The third contribution of this paper is an evaluation of Sentence-BERT (SBERT, Reimers and Gurevych (2019)) in AM as a downstream application setting. BERT (Devlin et al., 2019) is a popular transformer-based language model (LM), but as it is designed to be fine-tuned, it can be suboptimal in low-resource settings. SBERT tries to alleviate this problem by producing a more universal sentence embeddings, that can be used as they are in many tasks. The idea of training embeddings on the natural language inference (NLI) task goes back to Conneau et al. (2017), and this is the SBERT variant we use here. The NLI task involves recognising textual entailment (TE), and a TE model has been previously used by Cabrio and Villata (2012) for argumentation. We will quantify how the two encoders perform in our task. All resources of this paper are available on github.[1]

2 Related Work

Argumentative structure analysis consists of two main steps (Lippi and Torroni, 2016). The first step is *argumentative component identification* (ACI), which segments a text into argumentative discourse units (ADUs); then differentiates them into argumentative (ACs) and non-argumentative components (non-ACs). ACs function argumentatively while non-ACs do not, e.g., describing a personal episode in response to the given writing prompt. ACs can be further classified according to their communicative roles, e.g., *claim* and *premise*. The second step is *argumentative structure prediction*, which contains two subtasks: (1) *linking* and (2) *relation labelling*. In the linking task, directed relations are established from *source* to *target* ACs to form a structured representation of the text, often in the form of a tree. In the relation labelling task, we identify the relations that connect them, e.g., *support* and *attack*.

In the education domain, argumentative structure interrelates with text quality, and it becomes one of the features that go into automatic essay scoring (AES) systems (Persing et al., 2010; Song et al., 2014; Ghosh et al., 2016; Wachsmuth et al., 2016). End-to-end AES systems also exist, but hybrid models are preferred for both performance and explainability reasons (Uto et al., 2020).

Eger et al. (2017) formulated AM in three ways: as relation extraction, as sequence tagging and as dependency parsing. They performed end-to-end AM at token-level, executing all subtasks in AM all at once. Eger et al. achieved the highest performance in their experiments with the relation extraction model LSTM-ER (Miwa and Bansal, 2016). We instead use their sequence tagging formulation, which adapts the existing vanilla **B**idirectional **L**ong-**s**hort-**t**erm **m**emory (BiLSTM) network (Hochreiter and Schmidhuber, 1997; Huang et al., 2015), as it can be straightforwardly applied to our task. The dependency parsing formulation is also a straightforward adaptation as it models tree structures. The biaffine model is the current state-of-the-art of syntactic dependency parsing (Dozat and Manning, 2017), and it has been adapted to relation detection and labelling tasks in AM by Morio et al. (2020). In a similar way, we also adapt the biaffine model to our argumentative structure. However, we use sentences instead of spans as ADU, trees instead of graphs.

Most work in AM uses well-written texts in the legal (e.g., Ashley, 1990; Yamada et al., 2019) and news (e.g., Al-Khatib et al., 2016) domains, but there are several AM studies that concentrate on noisy texts. For example, Habernal and Gurevych (2017) focused on the ACI task in web-discourse. Morio and Fujita (2018) investigated how to link arguments in discussion threads. In the education domain, Stab and Gurevych (2017) studied the argumentation in persuasive essays. One of the prob-

[1] https://github.com/wiragotama/BEA2021

lems with the existing corpora is the unclear distinction between native and non-native speakers. Additionally, to investigate and bridge the gap of performance between AM systems on noisy and well-written texts, it is necessary to use a parallel corpus containing both versions of texts. However, none of the above studies did.

3 Dataset

We use part of the "International Corpus Network of Asian Learners of English" (Ishikawa, 2013, 2018), which we annotated with Argumentative Structure and Sentence Reordering ("ICNALE-AS2R" corpus).[2] This corpus contains 434 essays written by college students in various Asian countries. They are written in response to two prompts: (1) about banning smoking and (2) about students' part-time jobs. Essays are scored in the range of $[0, 100]$. There are two novelties in this corpus: (1) it uses a new annotation scheme as described below and (2) contains a parallel version of essays which have been improved from the discourse perspective. Therefore, this corpus can be used in many downstream tasks, e.g., employing argumentative structures for assessing and improving EFL texts. It is also possible to extend the improved version of texts on other linguistic aspects.

The corpus was annotated at sentence-level, i.e., a sentence corresponds to an ADU.[3] In our annotation scheme, we first differentiate sentences as ACs and non-ACs, without further classification of AC roles. Annotators then establish links from source to target ACs, forming tree-structured representations of the texts. Then, they identify the relations that connect ACs. We instructed annotators to use the *major claim*, the statement that expresses the essay author's opinion at the highest level of abstraction, as the *root* of the structure. As there are no further classification of AC roles, the term "major claim" here refers to a concept, not an explicitly annotated category. As the last step, annotators rearrange sentences and performed *text repair* to improve the texts from a discourse perspective.

There are four relations between ACs: SUPPORT (sup), ATTACK (att), DETAIL (det) and RESTATEMENT (res). SUPPORT and ATTACK relations are common in AM. They are used when the source sentence supports or attacks the argument in the target sentence (Peldszus and Stede, 2013; Stab and Gurevych, 2014). We use the DETAIL relation in two cases. First, when the source presents additional details (further explanations, descriptions or elaborations) about the target sentence, and second, when the source introduces a topic of the discussion in a neutral way by providing general background. From the organisational perspective, the differentiation between DETAIL and SUPPORT is useful. While the source sentence in a SUPPORT relation *ideally* follows its target, the DETAIL relation has more flexibility. We also use a relation called RESTATEMENT for those situations where high-level parts of an argument are repeated or summarised for the second time, e.g., when the major claim is restated in the conclusion of the essay. DETAIL and RESTATEMENT links are not common in AM; the first was introduced by Kirschner et al. (2015) and the second by Skeppstedt et al. (2018), but both work on well-written texts. The combination of these four relations is unique in AM.

To improve the texts, annotators were asked to rearrange sentences so that it results in the most logically well-structured texts they can think of. This is the second annotation layer in our corpus. No particular reordering strategy was instructed. Reordering, however, may cause irrelevant or incorrect referring and connective expressions (Iida and Tokunaga, 2014). To correct these expressions, annotators were instructed to minimally *repair* the text where this is necessary to retain the original meaning of the sentence. For instance, they replaced pronouns with their referents, and removed or replaced inappropriate connectives. Text repair is also necessary to achieve standalone major claims. For example, "*I think so*" with *so* referring to the writing prompt (underlined in what follows) can be rephrased as "*I think smoking should be banned at all restaurants*."

Figure 1 shows an example of our annotation scheme using a real EFL essay. Figure 2 then illustrates how the reordering operation produced an improved essay. The annotator recognised that (16) is the proper major claim of the essay in Figure 1. However, this essay is problematic because the major claim is not introduced at the beginning of the essay. Thus, the annotator moved (16) to the beginning, and the whole essay is concluded by sentence

[2]A full description of the corpus and the annotation study we performed is available in a separate submission.

[3]Texts written by proficient authors may contain two or more ideas per sentence. However, our targets are EFL learners; pedagogically, they are often taught to put one idea per sentence.

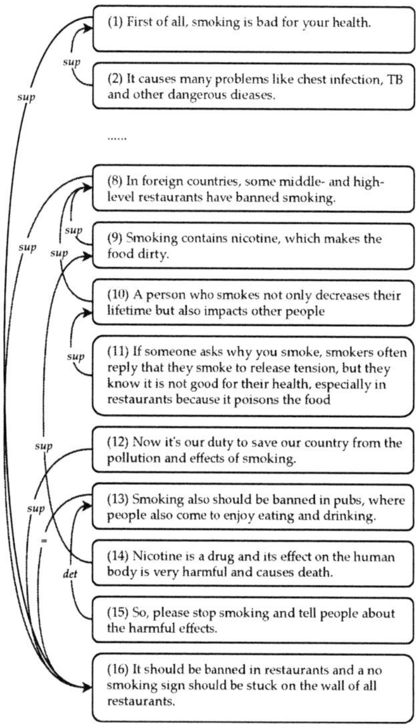

Figure 1: A snippet of argumentative structure annotation for essay code "W_PAK_SMK0_022_B1_1_EDIT" by our expert annotator. The essay discusses banning smoking in restaurants.

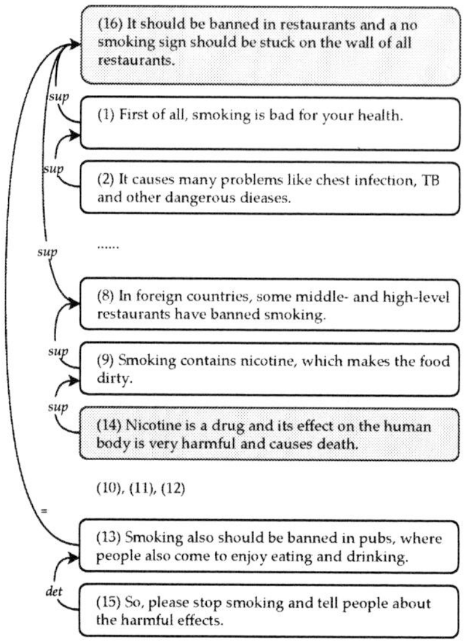

Figure 2: The improved version of essay Figure 1.

(13) in Figure 2. We also observe that crossing links happen in Figure 1, and they may suggest the jump of ideas, indicating coherence breaks. For example, sentence (14) describes nicotine and the annotator thinks that it properly connects to (9) which also talks about nicotine. Therefore, it is more desirable to place sentences (9) and (14) close to each other, as shown in Figure 2. The reordered version is arguably better since it is more consistent with the argumentative-development-strategy prescribed in teaching, i.e., introduce a topic and state the author's stance on that topic, support the stance by presenting more detailed reasons, and finally concludes the essay at the end (Silva, 1993; Bacha, 2010).

We performed an inter-annotator agreement (IAA) study on 20 essays, using as annotators a PhD student in English education (also an EFL teacher – *expert annotator*) and the first author, both having a near-native English proficiency. We found the agreement to be Cohen's κ=.66 for ACI; κ=.53 for sentence linking; and κ=.61 for relation labelling (Cohen, 1960). The sentence linking task was the most difficult one, and it is understandable since a text may have multiple acceptable structures. The relation labels hardest to distinguish were between SUPPORT and DETAIL.

This kind of annotation is expensive. Also, there is no metric to measure the agreement on reordering. Therefore, we chose to have the expert annotator annotate all essays in the production for the purpose of consistency. There are 6,021 sentences in the ICNALE-AS2R corpus; 5,799 (96%) of these are ACs and 222 (4%) are non-ACs. An essay contains 14 sentences on average, and the average structural depth is 4.3 (counting the root at depth = 0). The corpus does not contain paragraph breaks. The most frequent relation label is SUPPORT (3,029–56%), followed by DETAIL (1,585–30%), ATTACK (437–8%), and RESTATEMENT (314–6%). In total, 105 out of 434 essays were rearranged (1-3 sentences were moved on average). As we have explained before, the expert annotator reordered a scattered set of sentences which logically form a sub-argument to be close in position to each other. They also placed the major claim at the beginning as opposed to the middle or the end of the essay. In general, the expert arranges the essays to be more consistent with the typical argumentative-development strategy prescribed in teaching. The text repair was done on 181 sentences, 123 (71%) of which attempt to repair the prompt-type error of the major claim. The remaining 58 sentences concern changes in connectives and referring expressions.

4 Parsing Models

We adopt a pipeline approach by using independent models for sentence linking, which includes the ACI task, and relation labelling. Although a pipeline system may fall prey to error propagation, for a new scheme and corpus, it can be advantageous to look at intermediate results.

4.1 Sentence Linking

Given an entire essay as a sequence of sentences $s_1, ..., s_N$, our sentence linking model outputs the distance $d_1, ..., d_N$ between each sentence s_i to its target; if a sentence is connected to its preceding sentence, the distance is $d = -1$. We consider those sentences that have no explicitly annotated outgoing links as linked to themselves ($d = 0$); this concerns major claims (roots) and non-ACs.

≤ -5	-4	-3	-2	-1	0
16.6	3.9	5.2	8.3	37.0	10.9
$\geq +5$	$+4$	$+3$	$+2$	$+1$	
1.0	0.6	0.9	2.3	13.4	

Table 1: Distribution of distance (in percent) between source and target sentences in the corpus.

Table 1 shows the distribution of distance between the source and target sentences in the corpus, which ranges $[-26, ..., +15]$. Adjacent links predominate (50.4%). Short-distance links ($2 \leq |d| \leq 4$) make up 21.2% of the total. Backward long distance links at $d \leq -5$ are 16.6%, whereas forward long distance links are rare (1.0%).

We follow the formulation by Eger et al. (2017), where AM is modelled as sequence tagging (4.1.1) and as dependency parsing (4.1.2).

4.1.1 Sequence Tagger Model

Figure 3 shows our sequence tagging architecture ("SEQTG"). We adapt the vanilla BiLSTM with softmax prediction layers (as Eger et al. (2017) similarly did), training the model in a multi-task learning (MTL) setup. There are two prediction layers: (1) for sentence linking as main task and (2) for ACI as an auxiliary task.

The input sentences $s_1, ..., s_N$ are first encoded into their respective sentence embeddings (using either BERT or SBERT as encoder).[4] We do not fine-tune the encoder because our dataset is too small for it.[5] The resulting sentence embeddings are then fed into a dense layer for dimensionality reduction. The results are fed into a BiLSTM layer (#$stack = 3$) to produce contextual sentence representations, then fed into prediction layers.

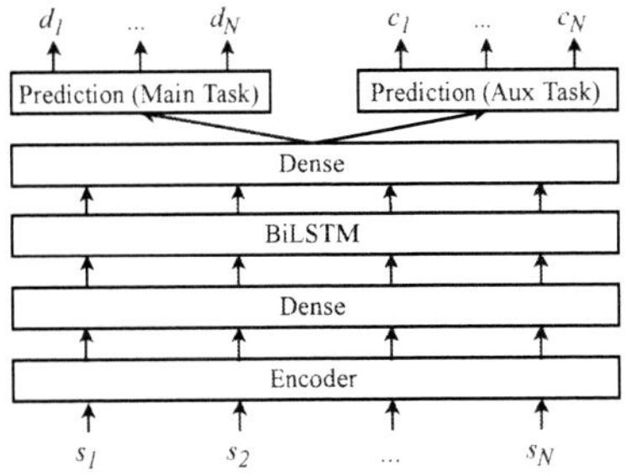

Figure 3: BiLSTM-softmax ("SEQTG").

Main Task: The model predicts the probability of link distances, in the range $[-26, ..., +15]$. To make sure there is no out-of-bound prediction, we perform a constrained argmax during prediction time. For each sentence s_i, we compute the argmax only for distances at $[1 - i, ..., N - i]; i \geq 1$.

Auxiliary Task: As the auxiliary task, the model predicts *quasi*-argumentative-component type c for each input sentence. Our scheme does not assign AC roles per se, but we can compile the following sentence types from the tree typology:

- *major claim (root)*: only incoming links,
- *AC (non-leaf)*: both outgoing and incoming links,
- *AC (leaf)*: only outgoing links, and
- *non-AC*: neither incoming nor outgoing links.

These four labels should make a good auxiliary task as they should help the model to learn the placement of sentences in the hierarchical structure.

We use the dynamic combination of loss as the MTL objective (Kendall et al., 2018). To evaluate whether the auxiliary task does improve the model performance, we also experiment only on the main task (single-task learning–STL).

4.1.2 Biaffine Model

We adapt the biaffine model ("BIAF") by Dozat and Manning (2017), treating the sentence linking task as sentence-level dependency parsing (Figure 4).

The first three layers produce contextual sentence representations in the same manner as in the

[4] By averaging subword embeddings.

[5] We conducted a preliminary fine-tuning experiment on sentence linking task, but the performance did not improve.

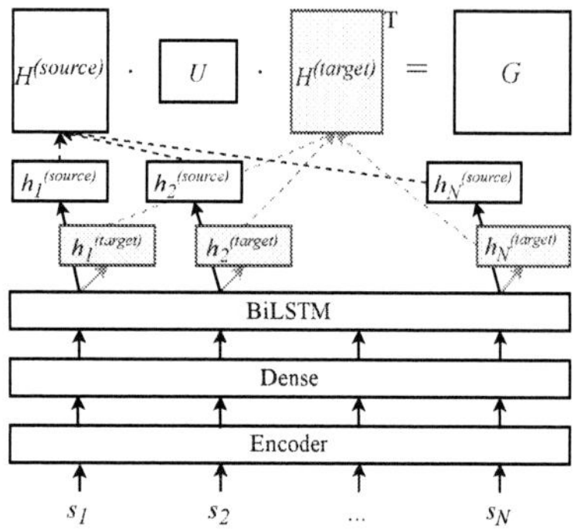

Figure 4: Biaffine Model ("BIAF").

SEQTG model. These representations are then fed into two different dense layers, in order to encode the corresponding sentence when it acts as a source $\left(h^{(source)}\right)$ or target $\left(h^{(target)}\right)$ in a relation. Finally, a biaffine transformation is applied to all source and target representations to produce the final output matrix $G \in \mathbb{R}^{N \times N}$, in which each row g_i represents where the source sentence s_i should point to (its highest scoring target).

When only considering the highest scoring or most probable target for each source sentence in isolation, the output of the models (SEQTG and BIAF) does not always form a tree (30-40% non-tree outputs in our experiment). In these cases, we use Chu-Liu-Edmonds algorithm (Chu and Liu, 1965; Edmonds, 1967) to create a minimum spanning tree out of the output.

4.2 Relation Labelling

In the relation labelling task, given a pair of *linked* source and target sentences $\langle s_{source}, s_{target}\rangle$, a model outputs the label that connects them, i.e., one of {SUPPORT, ATTACK, DETAIL, RESTATEMENT}. We use non-fine-tuning models with feed-forward architecture and fine-tuning transformer-based LMs.

4.2.1 Non-fine-tuning Models

In non-fine-tuning models, both source and target sentences $\langle s_{source}, s_{target}\rangle$ are encoded using BERT or SBERT to produce their respective embeddings. We then pass these embeddings into respective dense layers for a dimensionality reduction and transformation step, producing $\langle r_{source}, r_{target}\rangle$. As the first option ("FFCON", Figure 5a), r_{source} and r_{target} are concatenated, passed to a dense layer for a further transformation, and finally fed into a prediction layer. As the second option (FFLSTM, Figure 5b), we feed r_{source} and r_{target} to an LSTM layer, and the hidden units of LSTM are concatenated before being sent to a dense layer (Deguchi and Yamaguchi, 2019).

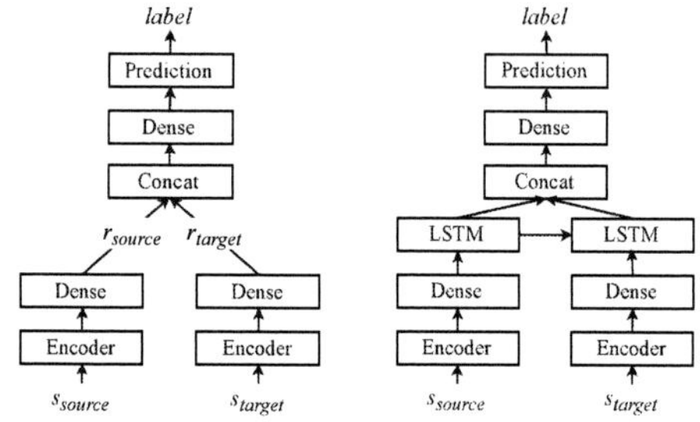

(a) FFCON model. (b) FFLSTM model.

Figure 5: Non-finetuning relation labelling models.

4.2.2 Fine-tuning Models

Unlike sentence linking, where an entire essay is taken as input, the relation labelling task takes a pair of sentences. There are 5,365 of such pairs in the ICNALE-AS2R corpus. We fine-tune BERT and DISTILBERT (Sanh et al., 2019) on the resulting sentence pair classification task. The pair is fed into the transformer model, and then the `[CLS]` token representation is passed into a prediction layer.

5 Experimental Results and Discussion

The dataset is split into 80% training set (347 essays , 4,841 sentences) and 20% testing set (87 essays, 1,180 sentences), stratified according to prompts, scores and country of origin of the EFL learners. We are interested in how the AM models trained on well-written texts may perform on more noisy texts. To find out, we train the models on both the original EFL texts (in-domain) and the parallel improved texts (out-of-domain), then evaluated on the original EFL texts. The difference between in- and out-of-domain data lies on the textual surface, i.e., sentence rearrangement, the use of connectives, referring expressions, and textual repair for major claims. Since not all essays undergo any reordering, the out-of-domain data is roughly 75% the same as the in-domain data.

The number of hidden units and learning rates (alongside other implementation notes) to train our models can be found in Appendix A. We run the experiment for 20 times,[6] and report the average

[6]Using the same dataset split. This is to account for ran-

performance. The relation labelling models are trained and evaluated using sentence pairs according to the gold-standard. In the end-to-end evaluation (Section 5.3), however, the input to the relation labelling model is the automatic prediction. Statistical testing, whenever possible, is conducted using the student's t-test (Fisher, 1937) on the performance scores of the 20 runs, with a significance level of $\alpha = 0.05$.

5.1 Sentence Linking

We first report our in-domain before turning to the cross-domain results.

Table 2 shows our experimental result on the prediction of individual links. The best model is a biaffine model, namely SBERT-BIAF, statistically outperforming the next-best non-biaffine model (accuracy .471 vs .444 and F1-macro .323 vs .274; significant difference on both metrics). Training the SEQTG model in the MTL setting did not improve the performance on these standard metrics.

Model	**Accuracy**	**F1-macro**
BERT-SEQTG [STL]	.436	.274
BERT-SEQTG [MTL]	.431	.242
BERT-BIAF	.446	.310
SBERT-SEQTG [STL]	.444	.229
SBERT-SEQTG [MTL]	.438	.220
SBERT-BIAF	**.471**†	**.323**†

Table 2: In-domain results of individual-link predictions in the sentence linking task. Best result shown in **bold-face**. The † symbol indicates that the difference to the second-best result (underlined) is significant.

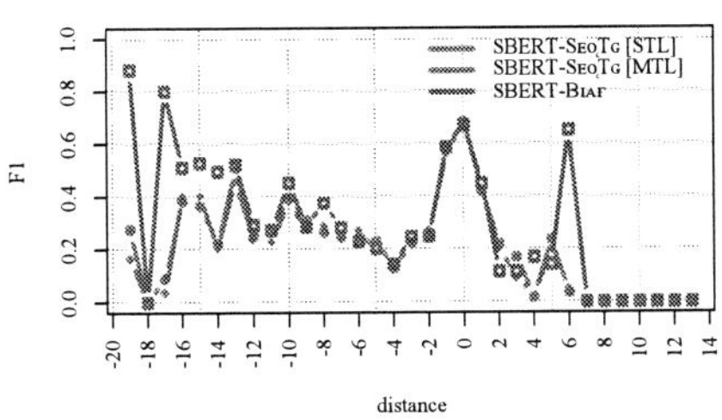

Figure 6: Models' performance across distances for in-domain evaluation using SBERT encoder.

To gain deeper insights into model quality, we also considered the models' F1 score per target distance (Figure 6). All models, and in particular BIAF, are better at predicting long-distance links ($d \leq -5$, avg. F1 = [0.22, 0.41]) than short distance links ($2 \leq |d| \leq 4$, avg. F1 = [0.16, 0.24]) when using SBERT encoder (the same trend goes when using BERT encoder). Long-distance links tend to happen at the higher tree level, e.g., the links from nodes at depth=1 to the root, while short-distance links tend to happen at the deeper level, e.g., within a sub-argument at depth≥2. As deep structures seem to be harder to parse, we would expect longer texts to suffer more.

dom initialisation in neural networks.

Next, we look at the models' ability to perform *quasi* argumentative component type (QACT) classification: whether they can correctly predict the role of major claim, AC (non-leaf), AC (leaf) and non-AC, as defined in our auxiliary task described in Section 4.1.1, based on the topology of argumentative structures. This evaluates whether the models place sentences properly in the hierarchical structure. Table 3 shows the result. SBERT-SEQTG [MTL] performed the best, significantly outperforming the second-best SBERT-BIAF (F1-macro=.609 vs .601). We now see the gain of training in the MTL setup as all SEQTG [MTL] models produce better hierarchical arrangements of nodes compared to the STL models; the F1-macro when using BERT encoder is .599 vs .592 (not significant) and SBERT .609 vs .596 (significant).

We notice that BIAF works acceptably well (F1-macro of .601) only when paired with the SBERT encoder. When using the BERT encoder, it has great difficulty in producing *any* non-AC nodes at all (Non-AC F1=.058; F1-macro=.493), despite its good performance on individual links. This result seems to suggest that SBERT is a better encoder than BERT for non-fine-tuning models. This also proves the importance of the evaluation of AM models beyond standard metrics, e.g., in terms of their structural properties as we do here. Prediction performance on individual links does not guarantee the quality of the whole structure. Considering the entire situation, SBERT-BIAF is our preferred model because its performance on standard metrics is substantially better than non-biaffine models. It also performs reasonably well on the hierarchical arrangement of nodes.

We next look at the cross-domain performance of the best sentence linking model, namely SBERT-BIAF. It achieves an accuracy of .459 and an F1-macro of .270 for the prediction of individual links. The F1-macro for QACT classification is .565. These scores are somewhat lower compared to the in-domain performance (significant difference). This means that the modifications of even

Model	Major claim	AC (non-leaf)	AC (leaf)	non-AC	F1-macro
BERT-SEQTG [STL]	.695	.603	.584	.486	.592
BERT-SEQTG [MTL]	.704	.594	.592	**.507**†	.599
BERT-BIAF	**.730**	.609	.573	.058	.493
SBERT-SEQTG [STL]	.705	.616	.590	.471	.596
SBERT-SEQTG [MTL]	.725	.622	**.611**†	.477	**.609**†
SBERT-BIAF	**.730**	**.639**†	.599	.437	.601

Table 3: In-domain results of *quasi* argumentative component type classification (node labels identified by topology). We show F1 score per node label and F1-macro. **Bold-face**, †, and underline as above.

25% of essays (in terms of rearrangement) in the out-of-domain data may greatly affect the linking performance, in the cross-domain setting.

5.2 Relation Labelling

	Sup	Det	Att	Res	F1-m
(B)-FFCON	.698	.433	.282	.594	.502
(B)-FFLSTM	.695	.434	.277	.600	.502
(S)-FFCON	.719	.479	.372	.558	.532
(S)-FFLSTM	.722	**.481**	.396	.574	.543
DISTILBERT	.741	.426	.431	.631	.557
BERT	**.760**†	.468	**.478**†	**.673**†	**.595**†

Table 4: In-domain relation labelling results, showing F1 score per class and F1-macro. "(B)" for BERT and "(S)" for SBERT. **Bold-face**, underline and † as above.

Table 4 shows our experimental results for the in-domain relation labelling task, when gold-standard links are used. BERT model achieves the significantly best performance (F1-macro = .595). Non-fine-tuning models performed better when using SBERT than BERT encoder (F1-macro=.532 vs. .502; .543 vs. .502; both having significant difference). This further confirms the promising potential of SBERT and might suggest that the NLI task is suitable for pre-training a relation labelling model; we plan to investigate this further.

We can see from the results that the ATTACK label is the most difficult one to predict correctly, presumably due to its infrequent occurrence. However, the RESTATEMENT label, which is also infrequent, is relatively well predicted by all models. We think that has to do with all models' ability to recognise semantic similarity. Recall that the RESTATEMENT label is used when a concluding statement rephrases the major claim. SUPPORT and DETAIL are often confused. Note that they are also the most confusing labels between human annotators. Sentence pairs that should be classified as having ATTACK and RESTATEMENT labels are also often classified as SUPPORT.

We also performed our cross-domain experiment for this task. Our best relation labelling model, BERT, achieves the cross-domain F1-macro of .587 (the difference is not significant to in-domain performance). Although not currently shown, the change of performance in other models are also almost negligible (up to 2% in F1-macro).

5.3 End-to-end Evaluation

For end-to-end evaluation, we combine in a pipeline system the best models for each task: SBERT-BIAF for sentence linking and fine-tuned BERT for relation labelling.

	Accuracy	ACI	SL	RL
Human-human (IAA)	.474	.66	.53	.61
In-domain	.341	.42	.41	.43
Cross-domain	.321	.36	.40	.39

Table 5: End-to-end results. κ scores are used for "ACI" (argument component identification), "SL" (sentence linking) and "RL" (relation labelling).

Table 5 shows the evaluation results of the average of 20 runs. Accuracy measures whether the pipeline system predicts all of the following correctly for each source sentence in the text: the correct ACI label (AC vs. non-AC), the correct target distance and the correct relation label. In addition, we also calculated the Cohen's κ score between the system's output and the gold annotation for annotation subtasks in our scheme.

The accuracy of the in-domain system is .341, and that of the cross-domain system .321 (significant difference). When compared to human performance on all metrics (in the IAA study), there is still a relatively big performance gap. In an end-to-end setting, the cross-domain system is able to perform at 94% of the in-domain performance. As we feel that this performance drop might well be acceptable in many real-world applications, this signals the potential of training an AM model for noisy texts using the annotated corpora for well-written texts alongside those more infrequent annotations for noisy text, at least as long as the genre stays the same.

We conducted an error analysis on some random end-to-end outputs. The system tends to fail to identify the correct major claim when it is not placed at the beginning of the essay. For example, the major claim can be pushed into the middle of the essay when an essay contains a lot of background about the discussion topic. Cultural preferences might also play a role. In writings by Asian students, it has been often observed that reasons for a claim are presented before, not after the claim as is more common in anglo-Saxon cultures (Kaplan, 1966; Silva, 1993; Connor, 2002) (as illustrated in Figure 1). The BiLSTM-based models, which are particularly sensitive to order, can be expected to be thrown off by such effects.

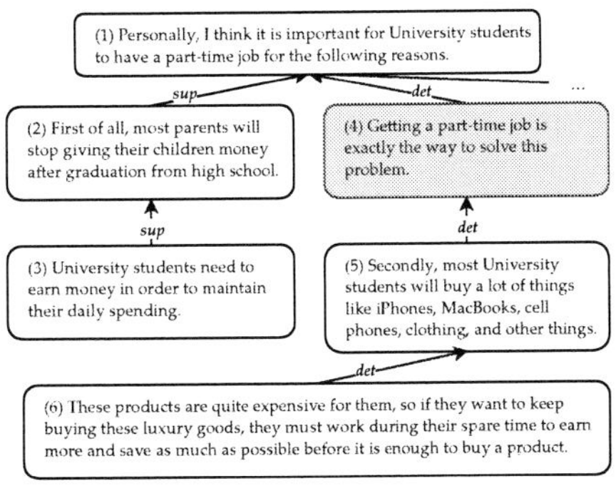

Figure 7: An example snippet of the in-domain system output for the essay code "W_HKG_PTJ0_021_B1_1."

Another source of error concerns placing a sub-argument into the main argument's sibling position instead of that of its child. In general, the systems also have some problems to do with clustering, i.e, splitting a group of sentences that should belong together into separate sub-arguments, or reversely, grouping together sentences that do not belong together. Thus, in order to move forward, the system needs improvement concerning the hierarchical arrangement of sentences in the structure. Figure 7 illustrates this problem. In the gold structure, sentence (4) points at (2), forming a sub-argument (sub-tree) of $\{2, 3, 4\}$. However, the system puts sentence (4) in the inappropriate sub-tree. This kind of cases often happens at group boundaries.

We also found that the system may erroneously use the RESTATEMENT label when connecting claims (at depth = 1) and major claims, when the claims include almost all tokens that present in the major claim. We suspect that our model learned to depend on lexical overlaps to recognise RESTATEMENT as this type of relation concerns paraphrasing. However, we cannot perform an error analysis to investigate to what extent this has affected the performance on each of the other relation labels, which concern entailment and logical connections.

6 Conclusion

This paper presents a study on parsing argumentative structure in the new domain of EFL essays, which are noisy by nature. We used a pipelined neural approach, consisting of a sentence linking and a relation labelling module. Experimental result shows that the biaffine model combined with the SBERT encoder achieved the best overall performance in the sentence linking task (F1-macro of .323 on individual links). We also investigated MTL, which improved the sequence tagger model in certain aspects. In the sentence linking task, we observed that all models produced more meaningful structures when using SBERT encoder, demonstrating its potential for downstream tasks. In the relation labelling task, non-fine tuning models also performed better when using SBERT encoder. However, the best performance is achieved by a fine-tuned BERT model at F1-macro of .595.

We also evaluated our AM parser on a cross-domain setting, where training is performed on both in-domain (noisy) and out-of-domain (cleaner) data, and evaluation is performed on the in-domain test data. We found that the best cross-domain system achieved 94% (Acc of .321) of the in-domain system (Acc of .341) in terms of end-to-end performance. This signals the potential to use well-written texts, together with noisy texts, to increase the size of AM training data. The main challenge of argument parsing lies in the sentence linking task: the model seems to stumble when confronted with the hierarchical nature of arguments, and we will further tackle this problem in the future.

Acknowledgements

This work was partially supported by Tokyo Tech World Research Hub Initiative (WRHI), JSPS KAKENHI grant number 20J13239 and Support Centre for Advanced Telecommunication Technology Research. We would like to thank anonymous reviewers for their useful and detailed feedback.

References

Khalid Al-Khatib, Henning Wachsmuth, Johannes Kiesel, Matthias Hagen, and Benno Stein. 2016. A news editorial corpus for mining argumentation strategies. In *Proceedings of COLING 2016, the 26th International Conference on Computational Linguistics: Technical Papers*, pages 3433–3443, Osaka, Japan. The COLING 2016 Organizing Committee.

Kevin D. Ashley. 1990. *Modeling legal argument - reasoning with cases and hypotheticals*. Artificial intelligence and legal reasoning. MIT Press.

Nahla Nola Bacha. 2010. Teaching the academic argument in a university efl environment. *Journal of English for Academic Purposes*, 9(3):229 – 241.

Betty Bamberg. 1983. What makes a text coherent. *College Composition and Communication*, 34(4):417–429.

Elena Cabrio and Serena Villata. 2012. Combining textual entailment and argumentation theory for supporting online debates interactions. In *Proceedings of the 50th Annual Meeting of the Association for Computational Linguistics (Volume 2: Short Papers)*, pages 208–212, Jeju Island, Korea. Association for Computational Linguistics.

Winston Carlile, Nishant Gurrapadi, Zixuan Ke, and Vincent Ng. 2018. Give me more feedback: Annotating argument persuasiveness and related attributes in student essays. In *Proceedings of the 56th Annual Meeting of the Association for Computational Linguistics (Volume 1: Long Papers)*, pages 621–631, Melbourne, Australia. Association for Computational Linguistics.

Y. Chu and T. Liu. 1965. On the shortest arborescence of a directed graph.

Jacob Cohen. 1960. A coefficient of agreement for nominal scales. *Educational and Psychological Measurement*, 20(1):37–46.

Alexis Conneau, Douwe Kiela, Holger Schwenk, Loïc Barrault, and Antoine Bordes. 2017. Supervised learning of universal sentence representations from natural language inference data. In *Proceedings of the 2017 Conference on Empirical Methods in Natural Language Processing*, pages 670–680, Copenhagen, Denmark. Association for Computational Linguistics.

Ulla Connor. 2002. New directions in contrastive rhetoric. *TESOL Quarterly*, 36(4):493–510.

Mamoru Deguchi and Kazunori Yamaguchi. 2019. Argument component classification by relation identification by neural network and TextRank. In *Proceedings of the 6th Workshop on Argument Mining*, pages 83–91, Florence, Italy. Association for Computational Linguistics.

Jacob Devlin, Ming-Wei Chang, Kenton Lee, and Kristina Toutanova. 2019. BERT: Pre-training of deep bidirectional transformers for language understanding. In *Proceedings of the 2019 Conference of the North American Chapter of the Association for Computational Linguistics: Human Language Technologies, Volume 1 (Long and Short Papers)*, pages 4171–4186, Minneapolis, Minnesota. Association for Computational Linguistics.

Timothy Dozat and Christopher D. Manning. 2017. Deep biaffine attention for neural dependency parsing. In *Proceedings of the International Conference on Learning Representations (ICLR)*.

Jack Edmonds. 1967. Optimum branchings. *Journal of Research of the National Bureau of Standards - B. Mathematics and Mathematical Physics*, 71B:233–240.

Steffen Eger, Johannes Daxenberger, and Iryna Gurevych. 2017. Neural end-to-end learning for computational argumentation mining. In *Proceedings of the 55th Annual Meeting of the Association for Computational Linguistics (Volume 1: Long Papers)*, pages 11–22, Vancouver, Canada. Association for Computational Linguistics.

Ronald Aylmer Fisher. 1937. *The design of experiments*. Oliver and Boyd, Edinburgh.

Matt Gardner, Joel Grus, Mark Neumann, Oyvind Tafjord, Pradeep Dasigi, Nelson F. Liu, Matthew E. Peters, Michael Schmitz, and Luke Zettlemoyer. 2018. Allennlp: A deep semantic natural language processing platform. *CoRR*, abs/1803.07640.

Debanjan Ghosh, Aquila Khanam, Yubo Han, and Smaranda Muresan. 2016. Coarse-grained argumentation features for scoring persuasive essays. In *Proceedings of the 54th Annual Meeting of the Association for Computational Linguistics (Volume 2: Short Papers)*, pages 549–554, Berlin, Germany. Association for Computational Linguistics.

Barbara J. Grosz and Candace L. Sidner. 1986. Attention, intentions, and the structure of discourse. *Computational Linguistics*, 12(3):175–204.

Ivan Habernal and Iryna Gurevych. 2017. Argumentation mining in user-generated web discourse. *Computational Linguistics*, 43(1):125–179.

Sepp Hochreiter and Jürgen Schmidhuber. 1997. Long short-term memory. *Neural Computation*, 9(8):1735–1780.

Eduard H. Hovy. 1991. *Approaches to the Planning of Coherent Text*, pages 83–102. Springer US, Boston, MA.

Zhiheng Huang, Wei Xu, and Kai Yu. 2015. Bidirectional LSTM-CRF models for sequence tagging. *CoRR*, abs/1508.01991.

Ryu Iida and Takenobu Tokunaga. 2014. Building a corpus of manually revised texts from discourse perspective. In *Proceedings of the Ninth International Conference on Language Resources and Evaluation (LREC'14)*, pages 936–941, Reykjavik, Iceland. European Language Resources Association (ELRA).

Roz Invanic. 2004. Discourses of writing and learning to write. *Language and Education*, 18:220–245.

Shinichiro Ishikawa. 2013. The icnale and sophisticated contrastive interlanguage analysis of asian learners of english. *Learner Corpus Studies in Asia and the World*, 1:91–118.

Shinichiro Ishikawa. 2018. The icnale edited essays: A dataset for analysis of 12 english learner essays based on a new integrative viewpoint. *English Corpus Linguistics*, 25:1–14.

Ann M. Johns. 1986. The esl student and the revision process: Some insights from schema theory. *Journal of Basic Writing*, 5(2):70 – 80.

Robert B. Kaplan. 1966. Cultural thought patterns in inter-cultural education. *Language Learning*, 16(1-2):1–20.

Alex Kendall, Yarin Gal, and Roberto Cipolla. 2018. Multi-task learning using uncertainty to weigh losses for scene geometry and semantics. In *Proceedings of the International Conference on Learning Representations (ICLR)*.

Diederik P. Kingma and Jimmy Lei Ba. 2015. Adam: a method for stochastic optimization. In *Proceedings of International Conference on Learning Representations (ICLR)*.

Christian Kirschner, Judith Eckle-Kohler, and Iryna Gurevych. 2015. Linking the thoughts: Analysis of argumentation structures in scientific publications. In *Proceedings of the 2nd Workshop on Argumentation Mining*, pages 1–11, Denver, CO. Association for Computational Linguistics.

Marco Lippi and Paolo Torroni. 2016. Argumentation mining: State of the art and emerging trends. *ACM Trans. Internet Technol.*, 16(2).

Makoto Miwa and Mohit Bansal. 2016. End-to-end relation extraction using LSTMs on sequences and tree structures. In *Proceedings of the 54th Annual Meeting of the Association for Computational Linguistics (Volume 1: Long Papers)*, pages 1105–1116, Berlin, Germany. Association for Computational Linguistics.

Gaku Morio and Katsuhide Fujita. 2018. End-to-end argument mining for discussion threads based on parallel constrained pointer architecture. In *Proceedings of the 5th Workshop on Argument Mining*, pages 11–21, Brussels, Belgium. Association for Computational Linguistics.

Gaku Morio, Hiroaki Ozaki, Terufumi Morishita, Yuta Koreeda, and Kohsuke Yanai. 2020. Towards better non-tree argument mining: Proposition-level biaffine parsing with task-specific parameterization. In *Proceedings of the 58th Annual Meeting of the Association for Computational Linguistics*, pages 3259–3266, Online. Association for Computational Linguistics.

Adam Paszke, Sam Gross, Francisco Massa, Adam Lerer, James Bradbury, Gregory Chanan, Trevor Killeen, Zeming Lin, Natalia Gimelshein, Luca Antiga, Alban Desmaison, Andreas Kopf, Edward Yang, Zachary DeVito, Martin Raison, Alykhan Tejani, Sasank Chilamkurthy, Benoit Steiner, Lu Fang, Junjie Bai, and Soumith Chintala. 2019. Pytorch: An imperative style, high-performance deep learning library. In H. Wallach, H. Larochelle, A. Beygelzimer, F. d'Alché-Buc, E. Fox, and R. Garnett, editors, *Advances in Neural Information Processing Systems 32*, pages 8024–8035. Curran Associates, Inc.

Andreas Peldszus and Manfred Stede. 2013. From argument diagrams to argumentation mining in texts: A survey. *International Journal of Cognitive Informatics and Natural Intelligence*, 7(1):1–31.

Andreas Peldszus and Manfred Stede. 2016. An annotated corpus of argumentative microtexts. In *Argumentation and Reasoned Action - Proceedings of the 1st European Conference on Argumentation, Lisbon, 2015.*

Isaac Persing, Alan Davis, and Vincent Ng. 2010. Modeling organization in student essays. In *Proceedings of the 2010 Conference on Empirical Methods in Natural Language Processing*, pages 229–239, Cambridge, MA. Association for Computational Linguistics.

Jan Wira Gotama Putra, Simone Teufel, Kana Matsumura, and Takenobu Tokunaga. 2020. TIARA: A tool for annotating discourse relations and sentence reordering. In *Proceedings of the 12th Language Resources and Evaluation Conference*, pages 6912–6920, Marseille, France. European Language Resources Association.

Ella Rabinovich, Sergiu Nisioi, Noam Ordan, and Shuly Wintner. 2016. On the similarities between native, non-native and translated texts. In *Proceedings of the 54th Annual Meeting of the Association for Computational Linguistics (Volume 1: Long Papers)*, pages 1870–1881, Berlin, Germany. Association for Computational Linguistics.

Nils Reimers and Iryna Gurevych. 2019. Sentence-BERT: Sentence embeddings using Siamese BERT-networks. In *Proceedings of the 2019 Conference on Empirical Methods in Natural Language Processing and the 9th International Joint Conference on Natural Language Processing (EMNLP-IJCNLP)*, pages 3982–3992.

Victor Sanh, Lysandre Debut, Julien Chaumond, and Thomas Wolf. 2019. Distilbert, a distilled version of bert: smaller, faster, cheaper and lighter. In *Proceedings of 5th Workshop on Energy Efficient Machine Learning and Cognitive Computing, NeurIPS*.

Tony Silva. 1993. Toward an understanding of the distinct nature of l2 writing: The esl research and its implications. *TESOL Quarterly*, 27(4):657–677.

Maria Skeppstedt, Andreas Peldszus, and Manfred Stede. 2018. More or less controlled elicitation of argumentative text: Enlarging a microtext corpus via crowdsourcing. In *Proceedings of the 5th Workshop on Argument Mining*, pages 155–163, Brussels, Belgium. Association for Computational Linguistics.

Yi Song, Michael Heilman, Beata Beigman Klebanov, and Paul Deane. 2014. Applying argumentation schemes for essay scoring. In *Proceedings of the First Workshop on Argumentation Mining*, pages 69–78, Baltimore, Maryland. Association for Computational Linguistics.

Christian Stab and Iryna Gurevych. 2014. Annotating argument components and relations in persuasive essays. In *Proceedings of COLING 2014, the 25th International Conference on Computational Linguistics: Technical Papers*, pages 1501–1510, Dublin, Ireland. Dublin City University and Association for Computational Linguistics.

Christian Stab and Iryna Gurevych. 2017. Parsing argumentation structures in persuasive essays. *Computational Linguistics*, 43(3):619–659.

Masaki Uto, Yikuan Xie, and Maomi Ueno. 2020. Neural automated essay scoring incorporating handcrafted features. In *Proceedings of the 28th International Conference on Computational Linguistics*, pages 6077–6088, Barcelona, Spain (Online). International Committee on Computational Linguistics.

Henning Wachsmuth, Khalid Al-Khatib, and Benno Stein. 2016. Using argument mining to assess the argumentation quality of essays. In *Proceedings of COLING 2016, the 26th International Conference on Computational Linguistics: Technical Papers*, pages 1680–1691, Osaka, Japan. The COLING 2016 Organizing Committee.

Bonnie Webber and Aravind Joshi. 2012. Discourse structure and computation: Past, present and future. In *Proceedings of the ACL-2012 Special Workshop on Rediscovering 50 Years of Discoveries*, pages 42–54, Jeju Island, Korea. Association for Computational Linguistics.

Hiroaki Yamada, Simone Teufel, and Takenobu Tokunaga. 2019. Building a corpus of legal argumentation in japanese judgement documents: towards structure-based summarisation. *Artificial Intelligence and Law*, 27(2):141–170.

Fan Zhang and Diane Litman. 2015. Annotation and classification of argumentative writing revisions. In *Proceedings of the Tenth Workshop on Innovative Use of NLP for Building Educational Applications*, pages 133–143.

Appendix A. Implementation Notes

BERT encoder We use bert-base-multilingual-cased (https://github.com/google-research/bert#pre-trained-models) and bert-as-a-service (https://github.com/hanxiao/bert-as-service). When using BERT, the sentence embedding is created by averaging subword embeddings composing the sentence in question.

SBERT encoder We use SBERT model fine-tuned on the NLI dataset ("bert-base-nli-mean-tokens"), https://github.com/UKPLab/sentence-transformers.

Sequence Tagger Dropout is applied between each layer, except between encoder and the dimensionality reduction layer because we do not want to lose any embedding information. We train this model using the cross-entropy loss for each prediction layer. The MTL loss is defined as $L = \sum_t \frac{1}{2\sigma_t^2} L_t + \ln(\sigma_t)$, where the loss L_t of each task t is dynamically weighted, controlled by a learnable parameter σ_t.

Biaffine We apply dropout between all layers, following Dozat and Manning (2017). We use the max-Margin criterion to train the biaffine model.

Principally, we can model the whole AM pipeline using the biaffine model by predicting links and their labels at once (e.g., in Morio et al., 2020). This is achieved by predicting another output graph $X \in \mathbb{R}^{N \times N \times L}$, denoting the probability of each node x_i pointing to x_j on a certain relation label l_i. However, we leave this as another MTL experiment for future work.

Relation Labelling Models We train the relation labelling models with the cross-entropy loss. Dropout is applied between the final dense layer and the prediction layer.

Hidden Units and Learning Rates The number of hidden units and learning rates to train our models are shown in Table 6. All models are trained using Adam optimiser (Kingma and Ba, 2015). Our experiment is implemented in PyTorch (Paszke et al., 2019) and AllenNLP (Gardner et al., 2018).

Hyperparameter Tuning Before training our models, we first performed the hyperparameter tuning step. To find the best hyperparameter (e.g., batch size, dropout rate, epochs) of each architecture, in combination with each encoder (BERT/SBERT) and each input type (in- or out-of-domain), we perform 5-fold-cross validation on the training set for 5 times, and select the hyperparameter set that produces the best F1-macro score. During the hyperparameter tuning step, we do not coerce the output to form a tree, i.e., only taking the argmax results.

	Dense1	LSTM	Dense2	LR
SEQTG	512	256	256	.001
BIAF	512	256	256	.001
FFLSTM	256	128	256	.001
FFCON	256	-	256	.001
(DISTIL)BERT	-	-	-	$2e^{-5}$

Table 6: The number of hidden units and learning rates (LR) of our models. "Dense1" denotes the dimensionality reduction layer (after encoder). "Dense2" denotes the dense layer after BiLSTM (before prediction).

Training and Domain Adaptation for Supervised Text Segmentation

Goran Glavaš[1] **Ananya Ganesh**[2] **Swapna Somasundaran**[2]

[1]Data and Web Science Group, University of Mannheim
goran@informatik.uni-mannheim.de

[2]Educational Testing Service
{aganesh002,ssomasundaran}@ets.org

Abstract

Unlike traditional unsupervised text segmentation methods, recent supervised segmentation models rely on Wikipedia as the source of large-scale segmentation supervision. These models have, however, predominantly been evaluated on the in-domain (Wikipedia-based) test sets, preventing conclusions about their general segmentation efficacy. In this work, we focus on the domain transfer performance of supervised neural text segmentation in the educational domain. To this end, we first introduce K12SEG, a new dataset for evaluation of supervised segmentation, created from educational reading material for grade-1 to college-level students. We then benchmark a hierarchical text segmentation model (HITS), based on RoBERTa, in both in-domain and domain-transfer segmentation experiments. While HITS produces state-of-the-art in-domain performance (on three Wikipedia-based test sets), we show that, subject to the standard full-blown fine-tuning, it is susceptible to domain overfitting. We identify adapter-based fine-tuning as a remedy that substantially improves transfer performance.

1 Introduction

Organizing long texts into coherent segments facilitates human text comprehension as well as downstream tasks like text summarization (Angheluta et al., 2002; Bokaei et al., 2016), passage retrieval (Huang et al., 2003; Prince and Labadié, 2007; Shtekh et al., 2018), and sentiment analysis (Xia et al., 2010; Li et al., 2020). Text segmentation is very important in the educational domain as it enables large-scale passage extraction. Educators, for example, need to extract coherent passage segments from books to create reading materials for students. Similarly, test developers must create reading assessments at scale by extracting coherent segments from a variety of sources.

Most segmentation models allow for (i.e., sequential) segmentation (Hearst, 1994; Choi, 2000; Riedl and Biemann, 2012; Glavaš et al., 2016; Koshorek et al., 2018; Glavaš and Somasundaran, 2020), though methods for hierarchical segmentation have been proposed as well (Eisenstein, 2009; Du et al., 2013; Bayomi and Lawless, 2018). Owing to the absence of large annotated datasets, (linear) text segmentation has long been limited to unsupervised models, relying on various measures of lexical and semantic sentence overlap (Hearst, 1994; Choi, 2000; Utiyama and Isahara, 2001; Fragkou et al., 2004; Glavaš et al., 2016) and topic modeling (Brants et al., 2002; Misra et al., 2009; Riedl and Biemann, 2012). More recently, Koshorek et al. (2018) automatically created a large segment-annotated dataset WIKI727 by leveraging the headings structure in Wikipedia articles, effectively enabling supervised text segmentation; they then trained a hierarchical recurrent neural segmentation model on WIKI727. In subsequent work, Glavaš and Somasundaran (2020) improved on their segmentation performance by (i) replacing recurrent components of the hierarchical model with transformer networks (Vaswani et al., 2017) and (ii) adding an auxiliary self-supervised coherence objective. Although both Koshorek et al. (2018) and Glavaš and Somasundaran (2020) report massive gains over unsupervised baselines, their models have mostly been subject to *in-domain* evaluation on test sets also derived from Wikipedia.

In this work, in contrast, we concern ourselves with domain transfer of supervised text segmentation models, with a focus on the educational domain. To investigate the effects of domain transfer in supervised text segmentation, we first introduce K12SEG – a segment-annotated dataset which we automatically created from educational texts designed for grade-1 to college-level student population. We then benchmark a hierarchical neural

Proceedings of the 16th Workshop on Innovative Use of NLP for Building Educational Applications, pages 110–116
April 20, 2021 ©2021 Association for Computational Linguistics

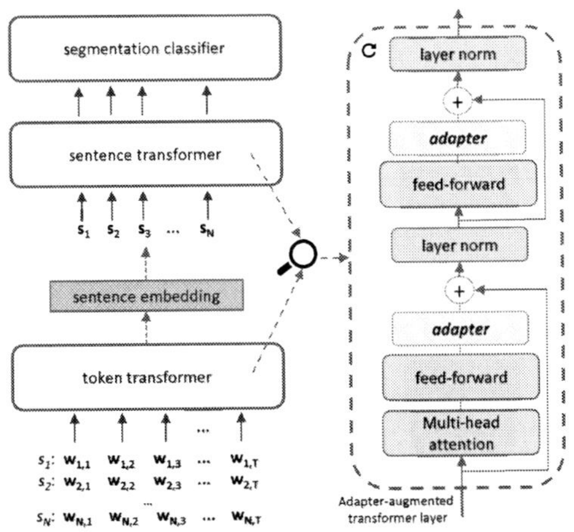

Figure 1: Architecture of the adapter-augmented hierarchical model for supervised text segmentation.

text segmentation model (HITS) in a range of in-domain and domain-transfer segmentation experiments involving WIKI727 (Koshorek et al., 2018) and our new K12SEG dataset.

Our HITS model, illustrated in Figure 1, though similar to the hierarchical segmentation models of Glavaš and Somasundaran (2020), differs in two crucial aspects. First, we initialize the parameters of the lower (token-level) transformer with the weights of the pretrained RoBERTa (Liu et al., 2019). Secondly, aiming to prevent both (1) forgetting of distributional information captured in RoBERTa's parameters and (2) overfitting to the training domain – we augment the layers of the token-level transformer with adapter parameters (Rebuffi et al., 2018; Houlsby et al., 2019) before segmentation training. Adapter-based fine-tuning only updates the additional adapter parameters and the original transformer parameters are frozen: this fully preserves the distributional knowledge obtained in transformer's pretraining. Encoding out-of-domain segmentation knowledge (e.g., from the WIKI727 dataset) separately from the distributional information (original RoBERTa parameters) allows to combine the two types of information more flexibly during the secondary segmentation training in the target domain (e.g., on K12SEG), resulting in more effective domain transfer.

Experimental results confirm the above expectations. Our adapter-augmented HITS model trained on WIKI727, besides yielding state-of-the-art in-domain (Wikipedia) segmentation performance, facilitates domain transfer and leads to substantial gains in our target educational domain (K12SEG).

2 Segmentation Model

Hierarchical Transformer-Based Model. Our base segmentation model (Figure 1) consists of two hierarchically linked transformers: the lower transformer contextualizes tokens within sentences and yields sentence embeddings; the upper transformer then contextualizes sentence representations. An individual training instance is a sequence of N sentences, $\{s_1, \ldots, s_N\}$, each consisting of T (subword) tokens, $s_i = \{w_{i,1}, \ldots, w_{i,T}\}$. We initialize the lower transformer with the pretrained RoBERTa weights (Liu et al., 2019).[1] We then use the transformed vector of the sentence start token (<s>), $\mathbf{s}_i$, as the embedding of the sentence s_i. The purpose of the randomly initialized upper sentence-level transformer is to contextualize the sentences in the sequence with one another. Let $\mathbf{x}_i$ be the transformed representation of the sentence s_i, produced by the upper transformer. The segmentation prediction for the sentence s_i is then made by the simple feed-forward softmax classifier: $\mathbf{y}_i = softmax\,(\mathbf{W}\mathbf{x}_i + \mathbf{b})$. We minimize the binary cross-entropy loss.

Adapter-Based Training. Unlike Koshorek et al. (2018); Glavaš and Somasundaran (2020), we initialize the lower transformer with RoBERTa weights, encoding general-purpose distributional knowledge. Full fine-tuning, in which all transformer parameters are updated in downstream training, may overwrite useful distributional signal with domain-specific artefacts, overfit the model to the training domain, and impede domain transfer for the downstream task (Rücklé et al., 2020). Alternative, adapter-based fine-tuning (Rebuffi et al., 2018; Houlsby et al., 2019; Pfeiffer et al., 2020), injects additional adapter parameters into transformer layers and updates only them during downstream fine-tuning, keeping the original transformer parameters unchanged. We adopt the bottleneck adapter architecture of Houlsby et al. (2019), reported effective for a wide range of downstream task. Concretely, in each layer of the lower transformer, we insert two bottleneck adapters: one after the multi-head attention sublayer and another after the feed-forward sublayer. Let $\mathbf{X} \in \mathbb{R}^{T \times H}$ stack contextualized vectors for the sequence of T tokens in one of the transformer layers, input to the adapter layer. The adapter then yields the following output:

[1]We use the 12-layer *Base* RoBERTa model

$$\mathbf{X}' = \mathbf{X} + g\left(\mathbf{X}\mathbf{W}_d + \mathbf{b}_d\right)\mathbf{W}_u + \mathbf{b}_u.$$

The parameter matrix $\mathbf{W}_d \in \mathbb{R}^{H\times a}$ down-projects the token vectors from $\mathbf{X}$ to the *adapter size* $a < H$, and $\mathbf{W}_u \in \mathbb{R}^{a\times H}$ up-projects the activated down-projections back to transformer's hidden size H; g is the non-linear activation function.

Training Instances and Inference. We train the model with sequences of N sentences as instances which we create by sliding the window of size N over document's sentences, with a sliding step of $N/2$. At inference, for each sentence s, we make predictions for all of the windows that contain s. This means that we obtain (at most) N segmentation probabilities for each sentence (for the i-th sentence, we get predictions from windows $[i-N+1:i], [i-N+2:i+1], \ldots, [i:i+N-1]$). We average the sentence's segmentation probabilities obtained across different windows and predict that it starts a new segment if the average is above the threshold t. We treat the sequence length N and threshold t as hyperparameters and optimize them using the development datasets. For brevity, we describe the optimization details in the Appendix.

3 Evaluation

3.1 Data

WIKI727. To the best of our knowledge, WIKI727 (Koshorek et al., 2018) is the only large segment-annotated dataset designed for supervised text segmentation. It consists of 727K Wikipedia articles (train portion: 582K articles), automatically segmented according to the articles' heading structure.

K12SEG. To empirically evaluate domain transfer in supervised text segmentation, we introduce a new dataset, dubbed K12SEG, created from educational reading material designed for grade-1 to college-level students (Zeno et al., 1995). The original dataset, the *Educators Word Frequency*, was created by standardized sampling of reading materials from a variety of content areas (e.g. science, social science, home economics, fine arts, health, business etc.). Each sample is 250-325 words long. We create one synthetic K12SEG instance by selecting and concatenating two samples from (a) the same book, (b) different books from the same content area (e.g., science) or (c) different books from different content areas. In contrast to WIKI727, in which the number and sizes of segments greatly vary across Wikipedia articles, K12SEG documents are more uniform: with two segments (samples) each and minor variation in sentence length (mean: 30 sentences). Besides the different genre between WIKI727 and K12SEG, this stark difference between their distributions of segment numbers and sizes poses an additional challenge for the domain transfer. We split the total of 18,906 K12SEG documents into train (15,570 documents), development (3,000), and test portions (336). An example 2-segment document from from K12SEG is shown in Table 1.

Wikipedia-Based Test Sets. For the in-domain (Wikipedia) evaluation, we use three small-sized test sets. WIKI50 is an additional test set consisting of 50 documents, created by Koshorek et al. (2018) in the same manner as WIKI727. Chen et al. (2009) similarly created the CITIES (64 articles) and ELEMENTS (117) from Wikipedia pages of world cities and chemical elements, respectively.

3.2 Experimental Setup

Experiments. We carry out two sets of experiments. We first benchmark the performance of our HITS model "in domain", i.e., by training it on WIKI727 and evaluating it on WIKI50, ELEMENTS, and CITIES. Here we directly compare HITS (with full and adapter-based fine-tuning) with state-of-the-art segmentation models: the hierarchical Bi-LSTM (HBi-LSTM) model of Koshorek et al. (2018), and two hierarchical transformer variants of Glavaš and Somasundaran (2020) – with (CATS) and without (TLT-TS) the auxiliary coherence objective. The second set of experiments quantifies the efficacy of HITS in transfer for the educational domain. We compare the performance of "in-domain" training on K12SEG with transfer strategies: (i) *zero-shot transfer*: HITS variants (full and adapter-based fine-tuning) trained on WIKI727 and evaluated on the K12SEG test set and (ii) *sequential training*: HITS variants sequentially trained first on WIKI727 and then on the train portion of K12SEG.

Training and Optimization Details. We initialize the weights of the lower transformer network in all HITS variants with the pretrained RoBERTa Base model, having $L_L = 12$ layers (with 12 attention heads each) and hidden representations

First segment	Second segment
Traveling familiar routes in our family cars we grow so accustomed to crossing small bridges and viaducts that we forget they are there. We have to stop and think to remember how often they come along. Only when a bridge is closed for repairs and we have to take a long detour do we realize how difficult life would be without it. Try to imagine our world with all the bridges removed. In many places life would be seriously disrupted, traffic would be paralyzed, and business would be terrible. Bridges bring us together and keep us together. They are a basic necessity for civilization. The first structures human beings built were bridges. Before prehistoric people began to build even the crudest shelter for themselves, they bridged streams. Early prehistoric tribes were wanderers. Since they did not stay in one place they did not think of building themselves houses. But they could not wander far without finding a stream in their way. Nature provided the first bridges. Finding themselves confronted with some narrow but rapid river, humans noticed a tree that had fallen across the river from bank to bank. The person who first scrambled across a fallen log, perhaps after watching monkeys run across it, was the first human being to cross a bridge. Eventually, when they had learned how to chop down a tree, they also learned how to make a tree fall in the direction they wanted it to fall. The wandering tribe that first deliberately made a tree fall across a stream were the first bridge-builders.	Working in the mud and water of a river bottom was difficult and dangerous. People were often crushed or maimed by the pile driver or the piles. But the work on the foundations is the most important part of bridge-building. The part of a bridge that is underwater, the part we never see, is more important than the part we do see, because no matter how well made the superstructure may be, if the foundation is not solid the bridge will fall. Not only did the pier foundations have to be solid, they also had to be protected as much as possible from wear. A flowing river constantly stirs up the bottom, so that the water's lower depths are a thick soup filled with mud and sand and pebbles which grind against anything in the path of the current. This action is called scour. to reduce the wear and tear of the current, the Romans built the fronts of their piers in the shape of a boat's prow. The Romans used only one kind of arch, the semicircular. The arch describes a full half-circle from pier to pier. Each end of the half-circle rests on a pier, and the two piers will hold the arch up by themselves, even before the rest of the bridge is built, provided each pier is at least one third as thick as the width of the arch. Thus a bridge could be built one arch at a time, and if the work had to stop the partial structure would stay in place until work could be resumed. The Romans built their bridges during the summer and fall, when the weather was best and the water level was generally lowest, and stopped during winter and spring.

Table 1: An example 2-segment document from the K12SEG dataset.

of size $H = 768$. Our upper-level transformer for sentence contextualization has $L_U = 6$ layers (with 6 attention heads each), and the same hidden size $H = 768$. We apply a dropout ($p = 0.1$) on the outputs of both the lower and upper transformer outputs. In adapter-based fine-tuning we set the adapter size to $a = 64$ and use GeLU (Hendrycks and Gimpel, 2016) as the activation function. In all experiments, we limit the sentence input to $T = 128$ subword tokens (shorter sentences are padded, longer sentences trimmed). We optimize models' parameters using the Adam algorithm (Kingma and Ba, 2015) with the initial learning rate of 10^{-5}. We train for at most 30 epochs over the respective training set (WIKI727 or K12SEG), with early stopping based on the loss on the respective development set. We train in batches of 32 instances (i.e., 32 sequences of N sentences) and have found (via cross-validation on respective development sets) the optimal sequence length to be $N = 16$ sentences and the optimal average segmentation probability threshold at inference time to be $t = 0.35$.

3.3 Results and Discussion

We report the results in terms of P_K, the standard evaluation metric for text segmentation (Beeferman et al., 1999). P_K is the percentage of wrong predictions on whether or not the first and last sentence in a sequence of K consecutive sentences belong to the same segment. As in previous work (Koshorek et al., 2018; Glavaš and Somasundaran, 2020), we set K to one half of the average gold-standard segment size of the evaluation dataset.

In-Domain Wikipedia Evaluation. We report the results of the in-domain Wikipedia evaluation on WIKI50, CITIES, and ELEMENTS in Table 2. Our HITS model variants, which we start training with the pretrained RoBERTa as the token-level transformer, outperform the hierarchical neural models from (Koshorek et al., 2018) and (Glavaš

Model	Fine-tuning	WIKI50	CITIES	ELEM.
HBi-LSTM	–	18.24	19.68	41.63
TLT-TS	–	17.47	19.21	20.33
CATS	–	16.53	16.85	18.41
HITS (ours)	Full	**14.50**	15.03	17.06
HITS (ours)	Adapter	15.17	**14.11**	**14.67**

Table 2: "In-domain" performance of hierarchical neural segmentation models, trained on the large WIKI727 dataset, on three Wikipedia-based test sets (smaller values of the error measure P_K mean better performance).

and Somasundaran, 2020), which start from a randomly initialized token-level encoder. This is consistent with findings from many other tasks: fine-tuning pretrained transformers yields better results than task-specific training from scratch, even if the dataset is large (as is the case with WIKI727). Full fine-tuning produces better results on WIKI50, whereas adapter-based fine-tuning exhibits stronger performance on CITIES and ELEMENTS. Since the articles in WIKI50 come from a range of Wikipedia categories, much like in the training set WIKI727, whereas CITIES and ELEMENTS each contain articles from a single category, we believe these results already indicate that full fine-tuning is more prone to domain (genre, topic) overfitting than adapter-based tuning. Remarkably, HITS (Full) surpasses the human WIKI50 performance, reported to stand at 14.97 P_K points (Koshorek et al., 2018).

Domain Transfer Results. Table 3 shows the performance of both in-domain and transferred HITS model variants on the K12SEG test set. Interestingly, with Full fine-tuning, we observe the same performance regardless of whether we train the model on the out-of-domain (but much larger) WIKI727 dataset or the (smaller) in-domain K12SEG training set. More interestingly, adapter-based fine-tuning in the zero-shot domain transfer yields better performance than in-domain adapter fine-tuning. Poor performance of in-domain training could mean that K12SEG is either (a) insufficiently large or (b) contains such versatile segmentation examples over which it is hard to generalize. Gains from *sequential* domain transfer, in which the model is exposed to exactly the same K12SEG training set but only *after* it was trained on a much larger out-of-domain WIKI727 dataset, point to (a) as the more likely explanation. In both in-domain and zero-shot setups, adapter-based fine-tuning produces better segmentation than full fine-tuning, contributing to the conclusion that adapter-based fine-tuning curbs overfitting to domain-specific artefacts, improving the model's generalization ability. Finally, the sequential training in which we freeze the lower transformer's parameters (including the adapters) during the (secondary) in-domain training, gives the best result overall. We speculate that the relatively small K12SEG train set gives the advantage to the model variant that uses that limited-size data to fine-tune fewer parameters (i.e., only the upper, sentence-level transformer).

Setup	Fine-tuning	Freeze	K12SEG (test)
In domain	Full	–	25.5
	Adapter	–	23.9
Zero-shot	Full	–	25.5
	Adapter	–	20.7
Sequential	Full	No	12.9
	Full	Yes	14.8
	Adapter	No	13.3
	Adapter	Yes	**10.4**

Table 3: Segmentation performance in domain transfer. Evaluation on K12SEG test set. *In domain*: training on the K12SEG train set; *Zero-shot*: training on the train portion of WIKI727; *Sequential*: sequential training, first on WIKI727 and then on the train portion of K12SEG. For *Sequential* training, the column *Freeze* specifies whether the the lower transformer's parameters were frozen during secondary, in-domain fine-tuning (on the train portion of K12SEG).

4 Conclusion

Supervised text segmentation has been limited to a single large-scale segmentation dataset, WIKI727, built automatically from Wikipedia. In this work, we studied domain transfer for supervised text segmentation: we introduce K12SEG, a new dataset for supervised text segmentation built from educational reading materials (grade-1 to college-level students), and use it together with WIKI727 in our domain transfer experiments. Our hierarchical segmentation model (HITS) couples the pretrained RoBERTa with the upper-level transformer that provides sentence contextualization. We show that HITS obtains state-of-the-art performance on standard Wikipedia-based evaluation datasets, but overfits to the training domain (Wikipedia). We finally substantially improve model's transfer capabilities through adapter-based fine-tuning.

References

Roxana Angheluta, Rik De Busser, and Marie-Francine Moens. 2002. The use of topic segmentation for automatic summarization. In *Proc. of the ACL-2002 Workshop on Automatic Summarization*, pages 11–12.

Mostafa Bayomi and Séamus Lawless. 2018. C-hts: A concept-based hierarchical text segmentation approach. In *Proceedings of the Eleventh International Conference on Language Resources and Evaluation (LREC 2018)*.

Doug Beeferman, Adam Berger, and John Lafferty. 1999. Statistical models for text segmentation. *Machine learning*, 34(1-3):177–210.

Mohammad Hadi Bokaei, Hossein Sameti, and Yang Liu. 2016. Extractive summarization of multi-party meetings through discourse segmentation. *Natural Language Engineering*, 22(1):41–72.

Thorsten Brants, Francine Chen, and Ioannis Tsochantaridis. 2002. Topic-based document segmentation with probabilistic latent semantic analysis. In *Proc. of CIKM*, pages 211–218. ACM.

Harr Chen, SRK Branavan, Regina Barzilay, and David R Karger. 2009. Global models of document structure using latent permutations. In *Proc. of Human Language Technologies: The 2009 Annual Conference of the North American Chapter of the Association for Computational Linguistics*, pages 371–379. Association for Computational Linguistics.

Freddy YY Choi. 2000. Advances in domain independent linear text segmentation. In *1st Meeting of the North American Chapter of the Association for Computational Linguistics*.

Lan Du, Wray Buntine, and Mark Johnson. 2013. Topic segmentation with a structured topic model. In *Proc. of the 2013 Conference of the North American Chapter of the Association for Computational Linguistics: Human Language Technologies*, pages 190–200.

Jacob Eisenstein. 2009. Hierarchical text segmentation from multi-scale lexical cohesion. In *Proc. of HLT-NAACL*, pages 353–361. Association for Computational Linguistics.

Pavlina Fragkou, Vassilios Petridis, and Ath Kehagias. 2004. A dynamic programming algorithm for linear text segmentation. *Journal of Intelligent Information Systems*, 23(2):179–197.

Goran Glavaš, Federico Nanni, and Simone Paolo Ponzetto. 2016. Unsupervised text segmentation using semantic relatedness graphs. In *Proc. of the Fifth Joint Conference on Lexical and Computational Semantics*, pages 125–130.

Goran Glavaš and Swapna Somasundaran. 2020. Two-level transformer and auxiliary coherence modeling for improved text segmentation. In *Proceedings of the The Thirty-Fourth AAAI Conference on Artificial Intelligence (AAAI)*, pages 7797–7804.

Marti A Hearst. 1994. Multi-paragraph segmentation of expository text. In *Proc. of the 32nd annual meeting on Association for Computational Linguistics*, pages 9–16. Association for Computational Linguistics.

Dan Hendrycks and Kevin Gimpel. 2016. Gaussian error linear units (GELUs). *CoRR*, abs/1606.08415.

Neil Houlsby, Andrei Giurgiu, Stanislaw Jastrzebski, Bruna Morrone, Quentin De Laroussilhe, Andrea Gesmundo, Mona Attariyan, and Sylvain Gelly. 2019. Parameter-efficient transfer learning for nlp. In *International Conference on Machine Learning*, pages 2790–2799.

Xiangji Huang, Fuchun Peng, Dale Schuurmans, Nick Cercone, and Stephen E Robertson. 2003. Applying machine learning to text segmentation for information retrieval. *Information Retrieval*, 6(3-4):333–362.

Diederik P Kingma and Jimmy Ba. 2015. Adam: A method for stochastic optimization. In *Proceedings of ICLR*.

Omri Koshorek, Adir Cohen, Noam Mor, Michael Rotman, and Jonathan Berant. 2018. Text segmentation as a supervised learning task. In *Proc. of the 2018 Conference of the North American Chapter of the Association for Computational Linguistics: Human Language Technologies, Volume 2 (Short Papers)*, pages 469–473.

Jing Li, Billy Chiu, Shuo Shang, and Ling Shao. 2020. Neural text segmentation and its application to sentiment analysis. *IEEE Transactions on Knowledge and Data Engineering*.

Yinhan Liu, Myle Ott, Naman Goyal, Jingfei Du, Mandar Joshi, Danqi Chen, Omer Levy, Mike Lewis, Luke Zettlemoyer, and Veselin Stoyanov. 2019. Roberta: A robustly optimized bert pretraining approach. *arXiv preprint arXiv:1907.11692*.

Hemant Misra, François Yvon, Joemon M Jose, and Olivier Cappe. 2009. Text segmentation via topic modeling: An analytical study. In *Proc. of CIKM*, pages 1553–1556. ACM.

Jonas Pfeiffer, Ivan Vulić, Iryna Gurevych, and Sebastian Ruder. 2020. Mad-x: An adapter-based framework for multi-task cross-lingual transfer. *arXiv preprint arXiv:2005.00052*.

Violaine Prince and Alexandre Labadié. 2007. Text segmentation based on document understanding for information retrieval. In *International Conference on Application of Natural Language to Information Systems*, pages 295–304. Springer.

Sylvestre-Alvise Rebuffi, Hakan Bilen, and Andrea Vedaldi. 2018. Efficient parametrization of multi-domain deep neural networks. In *CVPR*.

Martin Riedl and Chris Biemann. 2012. Topictiling: a text segmentation algorithm based on lda. In *Proc. of ACL 2012 Student Research Workshop*, pages 37–42. Association for Computational Linguistics.

Andreas Rücklé, Jonas Pfeiffer, and Iryna Gurevych. 2020. Multicqa: Zero-shot transfer of self-supervised text matching models on a massive scale.

Gennady Shtekh, Polina Kazakova, Nikita Nikitinsky, and Nikolay Skachkov. 2018. Exploring influence of topic segmentation on information retrieval quality. In *International Conference on Internet Science*, pages 131–140. Springer.

Masao Utiyama and Hitoshi Isahara. 2001. A statistical model for domain-independent text segmentation. In *Proc. of ACL*.

Ashish Vaswani, Noam Shazeer, Niki Parmar, Jakob Uszkoreit, Llion Jones, Aidan N Gomez, Łukasz Kaiser, and Illia Polosukhin. 2017. Attention is all you need. In *Advances in neural information processing systems*, pages 5998–6008.

Huosong Xia, Min Tao, and Yi Wang. 2010. Sentiment text classification of customers reviews on the web based on svm. In *2010 Sixth International Conference on Natural Computation*, volume 7, pages 3633–3637. IEEE.

Susan Zeno, Stephen H Ivens, Robert T Millard, and Raj Duvvuri. 1995. *The educator's word frequency guide*. Touchstone Applied Science Associates.

Data Strategies for Low-Resource Grammatical Error Correction

Simon Flachs[2,3]*, **Felix Stahlberg**[1], and **Shankar Kumar**[1]

[1]Google Research, [2]University of Copenhagen, [3]Siteimprove
flachs@di.ku.dk,
{fstahlberg, shankarkumar}@google.com

Abstract

Grammatical Error Correction (GEC) is a task that has been extensively investigated for the English language. However, for low-resource languages the best practices for training GEC systems have not yet been systematically determined. We investigate how best to take advantage of existing data sources for improving GEC systems for languages with limited quantities of high quality training data. We show that methods for generating artificial training data for GEC can benefit from including morphological errors. We also demonstrate that noisy error correction data gathered from Wikipedia revision histories and the language learning website Lang8, are valuable data sources. Finally, we show that GEC systems pre-trained on noisy data sources can be fine-tuned effectively using small amounts of high quality, human-annotated data.

1 Introduction

Grammatical Error Correction (GEC) research has thus far been mostly focused on the English language. One reason for this narrow focus is the difficulty of the task – even for English, which has a reasonable amount of high quality data, the task is challenging. Another reason for the English-centric research has been the lack of available GEC benchmark datasets in other languages, which has made it harder to develop GEC systems on these languages.

In the past few years, there are several languages for which GEC benchmarks have become available (Davidson et al., 2020; Boyd et al., 2014; Rozovskaya and Roth, 2019; Náplava and Straka, 2019). Simultaneously, there has been considerable progress in GEC for English using cheap data sources such as artificial data and revision logs (Grundkiewicz et al., 2019; Grundkiewicz and Junczys-Dowmunt, 2014; Lichtarge et al., 2019). Since these resources are language-agnostic, the time is ripe for investigating these techniques for other languages.

Pretraining GEC systems on artificially generated errors is now common practice for English. Grundkiewicz and Junczys-Dowmunt (2019) showed good results on English, Russian, and German, using a rule-based error generation approach that Náplava and Straka (2019) extended to Czech. This approach employed the Aspell dictionary to create confusion sets of phonologically and lexically similar words. In this work, we additionally investigate the usefulness of morphology-based confusion sets. For English, model-based error generation approaches have also been shown to be useful (Kiyono et al., 2019; Stahlberg and Kumar, 2021).

State-of-the-art English GEC systems also make use of lower quality data sources, such as Wikipedia revision histories and crowd-sourced corrections from the language learning website Lang8 (Mizumoto et al., 2011; Lichtarge et al., 2019). Given that it is possible to extract data from both Wikipedia and Lang8 in multiple languages, it would be interesting to determine if this data will help improve GEC for non-English languages. Boyd (2018) have already shown promising results for German using Wikipedia revisions with a custom language-specific filtering method.

Contributions In this work we investigate data strategies for Grammatical Error Correction on languages without large quantities of high quality training data. In particular we answer the following questions: i) Can artificial error generation methods benefit from including morphological errors?; ii) How can we best make use of noisy GEC data when other data is limited?; iii) How much gold training data is necessary?

*Research conducted at Google Research.

Proceedings of the 16th Workshop on Innovative Use of NLP for Building Educational Applications, pages 117–122
April 20, 2021 ©2021 Association for Computational Linguistics

	Gold			WikiEdits	Lang8
	Train	Dev	Test		
es	10,143	1,408	1,127	4,871,833	1,214,781
de	19,237	2,503	2,337	9,160,287	863,767
ru	4,980	2,500	5,000	8,482,683	684,936
cs	42,210	2,485	2,676	1,193,447	17,061

Table 1: Number of sentences for each language.

2 GEC data sources

2.1 Gold data

In recent years, high quality GEC datasets have been made available in several languages – in this work we look into Spanish (es), German (de), Russian (ru), and Czech (cs). An overview of the number of sentences for each language is shown in Table 1.

Spanish COWS-L2H (Davidson et al., 2020) is a corpus of learner Spanish corrected for grammatical errors, gathered from essays written by mostly beginner level Spanish students at the University of California at Davis.

German Falko-Merlin (Boyd, 2018) is a parallel error-correction corpus generated by merging two German learner corpora, the Falko (Reznicek et al., 2012) and Merlin (Boyd et al., 2014) corpus. The Falko part of the corpora is gathered from essays from advanced German learners, while Merlin consists of essays from a wider range of proficiency levels.

Russian RULEC-GEC (Rozovskaya and Roth, 2019) is a GEC-annotated subset of the RULEC corpus. The sources of the corpora are essays and papers written in a university setting by non-native Russian speakers of various levels.

Czech AKCES-GEC (Náplava and Straka, 2019) is a GEC corpus generated from a subset of the AKCES corpora, which consists of texts written by non-native speakers of Czech.

2.2 Artificial data

Text can be easily manipulated to destroy its grammatical structure, for example by deleting a word, or swapping the order of two words. Given that large quantities of text in multiple languages are available on the internet it is easy to produce large amounts of artificial training data. Even though these types of rule-based corruption methods do not always simulate realistic errors by human writers, they are still very useful for pre-training GEC models (Grundkiewicz et al., 2019; Grundkiewicz and Junczys-Dowmunt, 2014; Lichtarge et al., 2019).

Both rule-based and model-based methods for generating artificial data have been shown to be important components of top-performing GEC systems for English, with model-based methods currently yielding the best results (Kiyono et al., 2019). However, model-based methods typically need a large amount of training data to be able to produce an errorful data set that matches the distribution of human writers. For our low-resource setting we therefore employ a rule-based approach.

Rule-based error creation approaches using insertion, deletion and replacement operations to corrupt sentences have given good results on both English and other languages (Grundkiewicz and Junczys-Dowmunt, 2019; Náplava and Straka, 2019). Here, for word replacement operations, the Aspell dictionary is commonly used to generate confusion sets of lexically and phonetically similar words that are plausible real-world confusions (Grundkiewicz et al., 2019). Another potential source of confusion sets, which we explore in this work, is Unimorph, a database of morphological variants of words available for many languages[1] (Kirov et al., 2018).

2.3 Noisy data

Wikipedia edits Wikipedia is a publicly available, online encyclopedia for which all content is communally created and curated, and is currently available for 316 languages.[2] Wikipedia maintains a revision history of each page, making it possible to extract edits made between subsequent revisions. A subset of the edits contain corrections for grammatical errors. However there are many other types of edits unrelated to the GEC task, such as stylistic changes, vandalism etc. This noise poses a challenge for training GEC systems.

Wikipedia edit history is commonly used for training English GEC systems (Grundkiewicz and Junczys-Dowmunt, 2014; Lichtarge et al., 2019), and has also been shown useful for German, when using a custom language-specific filtering method (Boyd, 2018). To keep our experiments language-independent, we do not use this filtering method. Instead, we expect that the effects of noise in the Wikipedia data would be mitigated by subsequent

[1] http://unimorph.org

[2] https://meta.wikimedia.org/wiki/List_of_Wikipedias

finetuning on gold data. For our experiments, we use the data generation scripts from Lichtarge et al. (2019) to gather training examples from the Wikipedia edit history (see Table 1); we refer to this data source as WIKIEDITS.

Lang8 Lang8 is a social language learning website, where users can post texts in a language they are learning, which are then corrected by other users who are native or proficient speakers of the language. The website contains relatively large quantities of sentences with their corrections (Table 1) which can be used for training GEC models (Mizumoto et al., 2011). Lang8, however, also contains considerable noise. The corrections may include additional comments. Also, there is high variability in the language proficiency of users providing the corrections.

3 Systems

For all experiments we use the *Transformer* sequence-to-sequence model (Kiyono et al., 2019) available in the Tensor2tensor library.[3] The model is trained with early stopping, using Adafactor as optimizer with inverse square root decay (Shazeer and Stern, 2018). A detailed overview of hyperparameters is listed in Appendix A.[4]

We compare our results to two baseline GEC systems, Grundkiewicz and Junczys-Dowmunt (2019) (G&J) and Náplava and Straka (2019) (N&S), which have both been evaluated on Russian and German, and for Náplava and Straka (2019) additionally on Czech. Both of these systems are pretrained on artificial data and finetuned on gold data. When training the models several strategies were used: source and target word dropouts, edit-weighted maximum likelihood estimation and checkpoint averaging. In this work we do not employ these techniques because our focus is on comparing methods for data collection and generation and less on surpassing the state-of-the-art.

4 Experiments

We evaluate our models using $F_{0.5}$ score computed using the MaxMatch scorer (Dahlmeier and Ng, 2012). For all experiments, the reported scores are computed for the model trained on the specified data source, further finetuned on the gold training data.

[3]https://github.com/tensorflow/tensor2tensor

[4]We used the "transformer_clean_big_tpu" setting

	cs	de	ru	es
		Artificial		
Unimorph	71.08	60.87	32.91	44.68
Aspell	71.53	**63.49**	32.86	**48.22**
Aspell+Unimorph	**71.90**	62.55	**35.95**	48.20
		WikiEdits		
WikiEdits	55.14	58.00	23.92	47.35
Artificial→WikiEdits	**74.64**	**66.74**	40.68	**52.56**
Artificial+WikiEdits	72.91	66.66	**42.80**	51.55
		Summary		
N&S (2019)	**80.17**	**73.71**	**50.20**	-
G&J (2019)	-	70.24	34.46	-
Artificial	71.90	63.49	35.95	48.22
+ WikiEdits	74.64	66.74	42.80	52.56
+ Lang8	75.07	69.24	44.72	**57.32**

Table 2: $F_{0.5}$ scores of experiments on the ARTIFICIAL, WIKIEDITS, and LANG8 data sources.

4.1 Creating artificial data

We first investigate if artificial data creation methods can benefit from the inclusion of morphology-based confusion sets generated from Unimorph.

We train the systems on 10 million examples generated from the WMT News Crawl using the rule-based method from Náplava and Straka (2019) which is a modification of the method presented by Grundkiewicz and Junczys-Dowmunt (2019).

First, for each sentence a word-level (or character-level) error probability is sampled from a normal distribution with a predefined mean and standard deviation. The number of words (or characters) to corrupt are then decided by multiplying the probability by the number of words (or characters) in the sentence. Each corruption is then performed using one of the following operations: insert, swap-right, substitute and delete. Furthermore, at the word level an operation to change the casing is included and at the character level an operation to replace diacritics is included. The operation to apply is selected based on probabilities estimated from the development sets. All parameters used in our experiments are presented in Appendix B.

When creating the artificial data we report three experiments – for the word substitution operation a replacement word is chosen from a confusion set generated by either 1) Aspell; 2) Unimorph; or 3) Aspell or Unimorph with equal likelihood (Aspell + Unimorph).

Table 2 shows that using only Unimorph performs the worst. This is expected since the system would only learn to correct morphological substitution errors. Mixing Aspell and Unimorph works better for Russian and Czech but for the other languages, using Aspell alone performs better. Thus including Unimorph can help for morphological rich languages, such as Russian and Czech. We will refer to the best performing artificially created dataset for each language as ARTIFICIAL.

4.2 Including noisy data

We next investigate whether data extracted from Wikipedia revisions and Lang8 can improve our systems even further.

WIKIEDITS We perform three experiments: 1) training on WIKIEDITS from scratch; 2) fine-tuning on WIKIEDITS, starting from models pre-trained on ARTIFICIAL (ARTIFICIAL→WIKIEDITS); and 3) training on an equal-proportion mix of ARTIFICIAL and WIKIEDITS (ARTIFICIAL + WIKIEDITS). From Table 2, training only on WIKIEDITS performs worse than the models trained solely on ARTIFICIAL. However, finetuning the ARTIFICIAL-trained model on WIKIEDITS gives a large improvement. This suggests that the model primed for the GEC task by pre-training on ARTIFICIAL can better handle the noise in WIKIEDITS. Mixing the two sources is generally worse, indicating that WIKIEDITS, despite its noise, is of a higher quality and contains realistic GEC errors. However, this is not the case for Russian, where it is better to mix the two data sources. This suggests that Russian Wikipedia revisions are more likely to be unrelated to GEC, and mixing it with ARTIFICIAL regularizes this noise.

LANG8 Fine-tuning the best model from the WIKIEDITS experiments on LANG8 improves performance on all languages (Table 2), which confirms the utility of this data source as a valuable source of grammatical corrections.

4.3 How much gold data do we need?

Human annotated (Gold) data is a scarce resource, as human annotations are expensive. Therefore it is important to determine how much data is necessary to train useful GEC systems in new languages. We analyze the performance of systems finetuned on increasingly larger subsets of available data.

We investigate two scenarios: 1) finetuning a model pretrained only on ARTIFICIAL, and 2) finetuning a model pretrained on ARTIFICIAL,

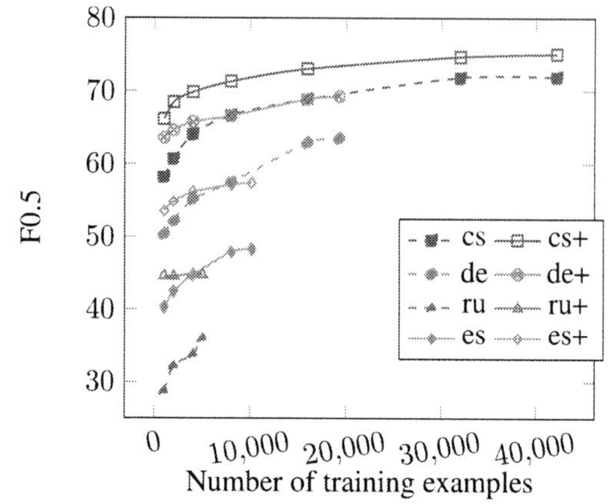

Figure 1: GEC performance ($F_{0.5}$) for different amounts of gold training data. Systems have been pretrained on ARTIFICIAL. The + denotes system has additionally been pretrained on WIKIEDITS and LANG8

WIKIEDITS, and LANG8 (using the best method from previous experiments). This ablation allows us to assess whether noisy data sources can ameliorate the need for gold data.

Performance curves (Figure 1) flatten out quickly at around 15k sentences, suggesting that not much data is needed. This is especially the case when the system has additionally been trained on WIKIEDITS and LANG8. This demonstrates that it is possible to obtain a reasonable quality without much human-annotated data in new languages.

5 Conclusion

In this paper we have investigated how best to make use of available data sources for GEC in low resource scenarios. We have shown a set of best practices for using artificial data, Wikipedia revision data and Lang8 data, that gives good results across four languages.

We show that using Unimorph for generating artificial data is useful for Russian and Czech, which are morphologically rich languages. Using Wikipedia edits is a valuable source of data, despite its noise. Lang8 is an even better source of high-quality GEC data, despite its smaller size and uncertainties associated with crowdsourcing. When using gold data for fine-tuning, even small amounts of data can yield good results. This is especially true when the initial model has been pretrained on Wikipedia edits and Lang8. We expect this work to provide a good starting point for developing GEC systems for a wider range of languages.

References

Adriane Boyd. 2018. Using Wikipedia edits in low resource grammatical error correction. In *Proceedings of the 2018 EMNLP Workshop W-NUT: The 4th Workshop on Noisy User-generated Text*, pages 79–84, Brussels, Belgium. Association for Computational Linguistics.

Adriane Boyd, Jirka Hana, Lionel Nicolas, Detmar Meurers, Katrin Wisniewski, Andrea Abel, Karin Schöne, Barbora Štindlová, and Chiara Vettori. 2014. The MERLIN corpus: Learner language and the CEFR. In *Proceedings of the Ninth International Conference on Language Resources and Evaluation (LREC'14)*, pages 1281–1288, Reykjavik, Iceland. European Language Resources Association (ELRA).

Daniel Dahlmeier and Hwee Tou Ng. 2012. Better evaluation for grammatical error correction. In *Proceedings of the 2012 Conference of the North American Chapter of the Association for Computational Linguistics: Human Language Technologies*, pages 568–572, Montréal, Canada. Association for Computational Linguistics.

Sam Davidson, Aaron Yamada, Paloma Fernandez Mira, Agustina Carando, Claudia H. Sanchez Gutierrez, and Kenji Sagae. 2020. Developing NLP tools with a new corpus of learner Spanish. In *Proceedings of the 12th Language Resources and Evaluation Conference*, pages 7238–7243, Marseille, France. European Language Resources Association.

Roman Grundkiewicz and Marcin Junczys-Dowmunt. 2014. The wiked error corpus: A corpus of corrective wikipedia edits and its application to grammatical error correction. In *International Conference on Natural Language Processing*, pages 478–490. Springer.

Roman Grundkiewicz and Marcin Junczys-Dowmunt. 2019. Minimally-augmented grammatical error correction. In *Proceedings of the 5th Workshop on Noisy User-generated Text (W-NUT 2019)*, pages 357–363, Hong Kong, China. Association for Computational Linguistics.

Roman Grundkiewicz, Marcin Junczys-Dowmunt, and Kenneth Heafield. 2019. Neural grammatical error correction systems with unsupervised pre-training on synthetic data. In *Proceedings of the Fourteenth Workshop on Innovative Use of NLP for Building Educational Applications*, pages 252–263, Florence, Italy. Association for Computational Linguistics.

Christo Kirov, Ryan Cotterell, John Sylak-Glassman, Géraldine Walther, Ekaterina Vylomova, Patrick Xia, Manaal Faruqui, Sebastian Mielke, Arya McCarthy, Sandra Kübler, David Yarowsky, Jason Eisner, and Mans Hulden. 2018. UniMorph 2.0: Universal morphology. In *Proceedings of the Eleventh International Conference on Language Resources and Evaluation (LREC-2018)*, Miyazaki, Japan. European Languages Resources Association (ELRA).

Shun Kiyono, Jun Suzuki, Masato Mita, Tomoya Mizumoto, and Kentaro Inui. 2019. An empirical study of incorporating pseudo data into grammatical error correction. In *Proceedings of the 2019 Conference on Empirical Methods in Natural Language Processing and the 9th International Joint Conference on Natural Language Processing (EMNLP-IJCNLP)*, pages 1236–1242, Hong Kong, China. Association for Computational Linguistics.

Jared Lichtarge, Chris Alberti, Shankar Kumar, Noam Shazeer, Niki Parmar, and Simon Tong. 2019. Corpora generation for grammatical error correction. In *Proceedings of the 2019 Conference of the North American Chapter of the Association for Computational Linguistics: Human Language Technologies, Volume 1 (Long and Short Papers)*, pages 3291–3301, Minneapolis, Minnesota. Association for Computational Linguistics.

Tomoya Mizumoto, Mamoru Komachi, Masaaki Nagata, and Yuji Matsumoto. 2011. Mining revision log of language learning SNS for automated Japanese error correction of second language learners. In *Proceedings of 5th International Joint Conference on Natural Language Processing*, pages 147–155, Chiang Mai, Thailand. Asian Federation of Natural Language Processing.

Jakub Náplava and Milan Straka. 2019. Grammatical error correction in low-resource scenarios. In *Proceedings of the 5th Workshop on Noisy User-generated Text (W-NUT 2019)*, pages 346–356, Hong Kong, China. Association for Computational Linguistics.

Marc Reznicek, Anke Lüdeling, Cedric Krummes, Franziska Schwantuschke, Maik Walter, Karin Schmidt, Hagen Hirschmann, and Torsten Andreas. 2012. Das falko-handbuch. korpusaufbau und annotationen version 2.01.

Alla Rozovskaya and Dan Roth. 2019. Grammar error correction in morphologically rich languages: The case of Russian. *Transactions of the Association for Computational Linguistics*, 7:1–17.

Noam Shazeer and Mitchell Stern. 2018. Adafactor: Adaptive learning rates with sublinear memory cost. *arXiv:1804.04235*.

Felix Stahlberg and Shankar Kumar. 2021. Synthetic data generation for grammatical error correction with tagged corruption models. In *Proceedings of the Sixteenth Workshop on Innovative Use of NLP for Building Educational Applications*, Online. Association for Computational Linguistics.

A Model hyperparameters

An overview of model hyperparameters used for our GEC system:

- 6 layers for both the encoder and the decoder.
- 8 attention heads.
- A dictionary of 32k word pieces.
- Embedding size $d_{model} = 1024$.
- Position-wise feed forward network at every layer of inner size $d_{ff} = 4096$.
- Batch size = 4096.
- For inference we use beam search with a beam width of 4.
- When pretraining we set the learning rate to 0.2 for the first 8000 steps, then decrease it proportionally to the inverse square root of the number of steps after that.
- When finetuning, we use a constant learning rate of 3×10^{-5}.

B Artificial data parameters

Language	Token-level operations					Character-level operations				
	sub	ins	del	swap	recase	sub	ins	del	swap	toggle diacritics
es	0.69	0.17	0.11	0.01	0.02	0.25	0.25	0.25	0.25	0
cs	0.7	0.1	0.05	0.1	0.05	0.2	0.2	0.2	0.2	0.2
de	0.64	0.2	0.1	0.01	0.05	0.25	0.25	0.25	0.25	0
ru	0.65	0.1	0.1	0.1	0.05	0.25	0.25	0.25	0.25	0

Table 3: Language specific parameters for token- and character-level noising operations. For all languages word error rate is set to 0.15 and character error rate to 0.02

Towards a Data Analytics Pipeline for the Visualisation of Complexity Metrics in L2 writings

Thomas Gaillat
University Rennes 2 / France
thomas.gaillat@univ-rennes2.fr

Anas Knefati
ENSAI / France
@ensai.fr

Antoine Lafontaine
University Rennes 1 / France
@univ-rennes1.fr

Abstract

In this paper, we present the design of a tool for the visualisation of linguistic complexity in second language (L2) learner writings. We show how metrics can be exploited to visualise complexity in L2 writings in relation to CEFR levels.

1 Introduction

The analysis of educational data has been a growing field in the last decade. Learning Content Management Software (LCMS) platforms in education have provided the opportunity to collect and process large quantities of educational data supporting both data mining and analytics (Baker et al., 2016). As far as we know, the field of foreign language learning has not availed yet of projects with data analytics at their core. The proceedings from the Visualisation and Digital Humanities workshop series[1] and those of the Learning Analytics and Knowledge conference[2] fall short of studies focused on the automatic exploitation of linguistic data for learners of a language. This problem may be linked to the complexity of apprehending learner writings due to the multidimensional nature of this type of language (errors, usage, phraseology ...)

One way to approach the problem is to use data analytics methods in order to bridge the gap between the collection of learner productions and their automatic analysis resulting in meaningful feedback. To this end, it is necessary to identify quantifiable features of learner writings. Data could be sourced in one of the three dimensions of language proficiency, *i.e.,* Complexity, Accuracy and Fluency (CAF) (Housen et al., 2012). A data analytics framework could rely on measures that operationalise these three theoretical constructs. A selection of CAF measures could be the source of automatically generated linguistic profile reports of L2 writings.

As part of CAF, linguistic complexity is one of the constructs that lends itself well to computational methods. At theoretical level it informs on the elaborateness of the learner language. At operational level there are a number of statistical measures in the form of frequencies, ratios and indices (Bulté and Housen, 2012). The construct is already used in combination with corpora to achieve different tasks such as automatic proficiency level prediction. In these tasks, complexity metrics are exploited with supervised learning methods to predict levels (Ballier et al., 2020; Venant and D'Aquin, 2019; Pilán and Volodina, 2018; Yannakoudakis et al., 2011).Among all the metrics that have been tested (see (Bulté and Housen, 2012, p.31-33) for a review), several have been reported as predictive of proficiency (Kyle, 2016; Lu, 2012; Vajjala and Meurers, 2012). Some readability metrics have also been used in L2 studies (Lissón, 2017; Pilán et al., 2014).

A number of text analysis tools exist in education but are not focused on L2 learning. They provide environments for reading or writing assessment and training (Dascalu et al., 2013; McNamara et al., 2007; Roscoe et al., 2014; Attali and Burstein, 2006; Napolitano et al., 2015). They focus on providing quantified results in relation to internal scales for first language (L1) learning. In addition, and to the best of our knowledge, the tools do not provide visualisations for the textual measurements. In the field of L2 learning a tool called *FeedBook* (Rudzewitz et al., 2019) provides visualisations of linguistic features as part of the feedback given to students. One need that remains to be addressed is the ability for learners to position the linguistic properties of their productions with regard to proficiency levels.

[1] See http://vis4dh.org/

[2] See https://lak20.solaresearch.org/

Proceedings of the 16th Workshop on Innovative Use of NLP for Building Educational Applications, pages 123–129
April 20, 2021 ©2021 Association for Computational Linguistics

CEFR levels	Number of texts
A1	23
A2	72
B1	102
B2	43
C1	18
C2	16

Table 1: Cohorts in the CEFR-annotated corpus

Our proposal is to exploit state-of-the-art linguistic complexity metrics in the automatic analysis of L2 writings. NLP tools are used to annotate, compute metrics and display visualisations of learner productions compared with writings classified according to the CEFR[3] levels (European Council, 2001). Section 2 describes the method. Section 3 covers visualisation interpretation. Learner engagement is presented in section 4. We discuss issues and perspectives in Section 5.

2 Methodology

2.1 A CEFR-based reference data set

To compare new texts with existing texts, we exploit a learner corpus of written productions. Texts from English for Specific Purposes (ESP) university students are used. This corpus includes 274 third-level education writings. Two language certification experts assessed the writings in terms of CEFR proficiency levels. The first production task for learners consisted in describing an experiment/discovery/invention/technology of their choice and the second task was to give their opinion on the impact of the previously described item. Learners had 45 minutes to complete both tasks. Table 1 shows the breakdown of the texts according to the CEFR levels.

CEFR annotation was evaluated with a measurement of inter-rater agreement (Cohen's weighted Kappa = 0.71). Complexity metrics were computed and six subsets or cohorts were created according to the six CEFR levels. A comparative data set of metrics and CEFR levels was thus created[4].

2.2 Metrics

Three groups of metrics are computed at processing time. Syntactic complexity is operationalised with fourteen metrics. These metrics are grouped in five different types (Lu, 2014): Length of production unit (e.g. sentence), sentence complexity, subordination, coordination and particular structures (e.g.complex nominals). Each metric is a ratio of a frequency of a constituent over the frequency of all constituents of a higher-level scope.

Readability is operationalised with forty eight metrics. They are based on the morphological features of words used to compute different indicator values. The assumption is that indicators operationalise the level of maturity required for reading a specific text. This includes indicators such as the Coleman Liau, the Dale Chall readability score and the Flesch kincaid grade. They all rely on word length in terms of characters and syllables as well as predetermined lists of words judged as difficult[5].

Lexical richness is operationalised with thirteen metrics which provide information on lexical diversity, *i.e.*, the range of different words used in a text. Two types of lexical diversity are included. Diversity based on word type variation is accounted for with TTR based formulae. Diversity based on type repetition is accounted for with Yule's K and similar formulae in which the frequency of word types in a sample of size n is relative to the total number of words in a text[6]. We acknowledge that lexical sophistication and lexical density (content vs grammar words) are not taken into account.

The metrics were selected for two reasons. Firstly, their significance is reported in the literature on L2 criterial features (Hawkins and Filipović, 2012; Lu, 2014; Kyle, 2016; Lissón, 2017) and analysing it in terms of CEFR levels is outside the scope of this paper. Secondly, it was decided to also include metrics linked to descriptive syntactic information. Complex Nominal and Coordinated Phrase indices were selected due to their meaningfulness. In total, 83 metrics are computed[7].

2.3 Data collection and cleaning

The learners' productions are collected via two types of MOODLE activities (Dougiamas and Taylor, 2003), *i.e.*, *Assignment* and *Database*. The *Assignment* activity allows teachers to collect written assignments as they see fit within their course scenario. They can download all the assignments as

[3]Common European Framework of Reference in languages

[4]Available from IRIS database at `https://www.iris-database.org/iris/`

[5]For a detailed description of the formulae refer to `https://quanteda.io/reference/textstat_readability.html?q=reada`

[6]For the formulae see `https://quanteda.io/reference/textstat_lexdiv.html`

[7]A list of metrics is available as supplementary material

a batch file and transfer them as input into the data processing pipeline. The texts can also be collected via a learner-corpus building interface alongside student metadata. A file includes all the texts and metadata and can be imported into the pipeline.

Prior to processing the files, the texts are cleaned. All special characters are deleted. Punctuation symbols are spaced consistently. Accents (from expressions of other languages for instance) are removed. The pronoun "I" is upper-cased for each text. The negative modal verb "can't" is replaced by "cannot". It permits to ensure a better parsing and a more accurate computation of the metrics.

2.4 The pipeline

The pipeline[8] is implemented in R (R Core Team, 2012) with a Creative Commons Share Alike licence. It includes our R implementation of L2SCA[9] (Lu, 2010) for syntactic complexity metrics. It also relies on Quanteda (Benoit et al., 2018) an R package used to compute readability and lexical diversity with `textstat\_lexdiv()` and `textstat\_readability()`.

The data workflow functions as described in Figure 1. Firstly, the input data is made up of new learner texts which are passed through the aforementioned processing tools to compute the metrics. Secondly, the reference corpus mentioned in Section 2.1 is also passed through the same processing tools. As a result, new texts can be compared with existing texts on the basis of the computed metrics. These can be visualised as of box-plots and radar charts.

2.5 Data transformation for visualisations

Prior to displaying metric values to users, these values are transformed to ensure comparability. First all the metric values are normalised to constrain them in a [0,1] interval for the radar chart. Yule's K is transformed into its inverse for the radar chart to avoid confusions by learners. This is because, as opposed to all other indicators, K's values drop as CEFR levels get higher. All the normalised indicators finally displayed, show increasing values as CEFR levels increase. In terms of statistics, the median and a shaded-grey strip for first and third quartiles are used to describe the control cohorts. Using an interval aims to show the variability of a metric within a CEFR level. Using the mean was not favoured to ensure robustness to outliers. Provision is also made for the rare cases in which metric values fall out of the interval. In this case, the value is not visualised on the graph and a warning is displayed: "You are off radar for the following indicators:".

3 Interpreting visualisations

In this section, we conduct an illustrative analysis of a sample text and compare some of its features with the visualised metrics. It was written by a French learner of English as part of the French National Language Certification Proficiency exam[10]. It was classified as B2 or higher. For reasons of space, we only provide the following exerpt.

> *With the development of new technologies such as smartphones, new questions are being caused about how to evaluate students. Indeed, using cellphones to cheat is common in high-schools. The first question we have to ask ourselves is wether we should authorize students to access their phone or not. Arguments against are well-know: ... But we also have to consider arguments in favor of it, in order to do what is best for our students. First, they will be working with these technologies in their professional lives, and we should be preparing them for that, by teaching them a proper use of smartphones and computers...*

In Figure 2 the metrics are compared with those of the cohort of B2 learners (see Section 2.1). The learner's individual report is divided in two parts. On the left, a radar chart displays ratio-based metrics and, on the right, raw frequencies are reported. In addition to the metric acronym a categorisation label is provided in order to indicate the word, sentence or text scope (Anonymised reference 2019b) of the metric. For instance the Number of Different Words (NDW) is labeled *Text.size.type* and can be interpreted at text level in terms of types as a unit. The radar chart displays the cohort in a grey-shaded area representing the two central quartiles. The dark line represents the median of the cohort. The boxplots show the position of the learner's metric in relation to the full B2 cohort.

The indicators in the radar chart show that the learner's ratios globally correspond to those of the B2 cohort. For instance, the learner makes use of Complex Nominals in her text. This includes

[8] Available at `https://github.com/LIDILE/VizLing`

[9] Available at `http://www.personal.psu.edu/xxl13/downloads/l2sca.html`

[10] See CLES certification at `https://www.certification-cles.fr/en/`

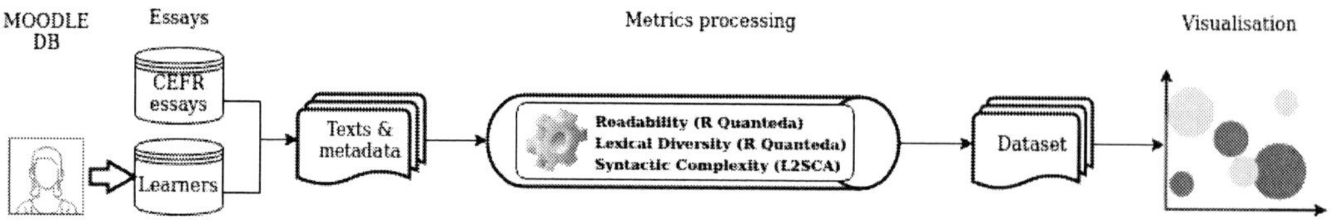

Figure 1: NLP pipeline - from data collection to visualisation

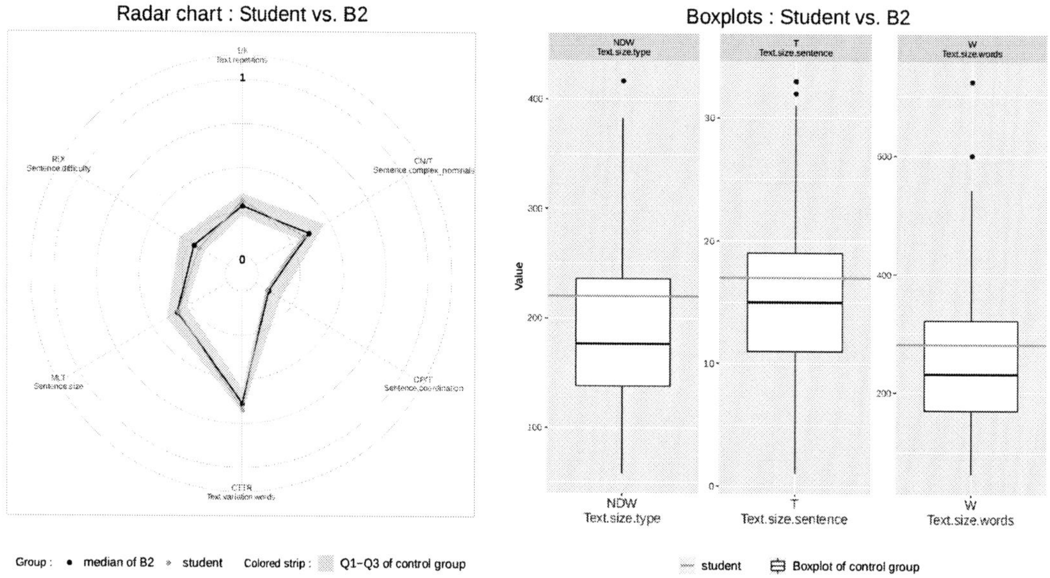

Figure 2: Individual report of a learner in comparison with a cohort of B2 learners

the adverbial clause "With the development of new technologies such as smartphones" which is used in apposition to the main clause. It also includes the nominal clause "The first question we have to ask ourselves" used in subject position of BE. The use of *adjective + noun* as in "proper use" is another more simple example of nominal complexity. The three different cases are all accounted for by the system. It appears that the learner's level of use is slightly under the B2 median (C1 and C2 radar charts show even higher values for the two central quartiles). The teacher and learner can analyse such structures more into details. The teacher could in turn note the lack of use of compounds and genitives in the text. In short, the metric helps learners and teachers identify an issue related to an objective criterion of linguistic complexity. Specific feedback and actions can then be undertaken.

4 Learner engagement

The efficacy of the tool needs to be evaluated. Learner engagement remains to be assessed thoroughly but a preliminary qualitative assessment was conducted in a class setting environment. We show results about the impact of the tool on learners' engagement. Fifty-four first year higher-level students were given five individual writing tasks in five weekly waves. After each wave they were provided feedback within 24 hours. Notwithstanding the results, we measured the number of submitted writings (Figure 3) and the frequency of consultation of feedback reports (Figure 4). We use these measurements as a rough proxy to measuring learner engagement, i.e. how they respond to the feedback they receive (Ellis, 2010). The statistics are assumed to tap into the intensity of learners' interest in the reports. Over time the number of submitted papers did not decrease in spite of the lockdown imposed on students in the midst of the COVID crisis. Following detailed explanations from their teacher to ensure comprehension, a majority of students consulted their reports three times or more, showing continuous interest.

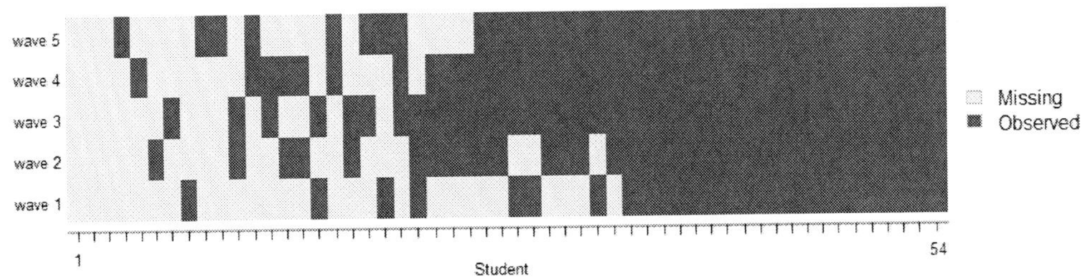

Figure 3: Writings available for each student

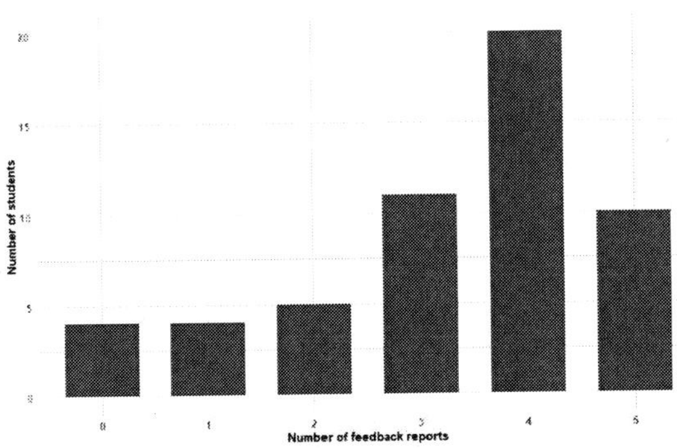

Figure 4: Consultation of feedback reports

5 Discussion and perspectives

In this paper we have presented a linguistic complexity visualisation tool. It displays learner writings according to several criteria and positions them in relation to cohorts of specific CEFR levels. More work remains to be done. Firstly, the visualizations used may be difficult to understand for learners who are not used to such types as radar charts. The tool aims primarily at helping trained language teachers analyse their students' writings in order to give them objective and specific feedback (Shute, 2008). By gaining access to these features, teachers can give specific answers regarding the mastery of certain concepts. They also become aware of features of language use that need to be addressed. Teachers can then provide evidence-based advice.

Secondly, the collected data shows limitations. The metrics on which the visualisations rely need to be evaluated on the data in terms of proficiency predictive power. Correlation analysis remains to be conducted in order to validate significant metrics to be displayed. The reference corpus is small and at the same time lacks diversity. All the texts belong to university students of specific fields, which may impact vocabulary and syntactic structures. More data needs to be collected in each field in order to support finer-grained analysis of third level education writings.

One last limitation is that some metrics remain difficult to interpret linguistically as argued by (Biber et al., 2020). For instance, readability formulas combine different features such as morphology and most common words. Specific advice on one of the features is therefore near impossible. Nevertheless, by interpreting the linguistic scopes (whether the measures apply at word, sentence or text level), it is possible to provide a certain degree of feedback.

The tool could be exploited in the learner module of an Intelligent Tutoring System dedicated to language learning. Because linguistic complexity measurements keep track of the evolution of systemic syntactic and lexical complexity, these data constitute part of the knowledge representation of the learner.

The tool gives access to learning analytics at linguistic level. In a context of distance learning, teachers are empowered with a rapid diagnostics tool that gives them an objective, although reduced, view of some of the features of their learners' language. Further developments will focus on identifying and evaluating more significant metrics in terms of proficiency and meta-linguistic influence on learners. Other types of charts could also be explored, and an aggregation functionality could provide group visualisations to reveal linguistic class patterns for teachers.

References

Yigal Attali and Jill Burstein. 2006. Automated Essay Scoring With e-rater® V.2. *The Journal of Technology, Learning and Assessment*, 4(3):3–29.

Ryan S. Baker, Taylor Martin, and Lisa M. Rossi. 2016. Educational Data Mining and Learning Analytics.

In *The Wiley Handbook of Cognition and Assessment*, pages 379–396. John Wiley & Sons, Ltd.

Nicolas Ballier, Stéphane Canu, Caroline Petitjean, Gilles Gasso, Carlos Balhana, Theodora Alexopoulou, and Thomas Gaillat. 2020. Machine learning for learner English. *International Journal of Learner Corpus Research*, 6(1):72–103.

Kenneth Benoit, Kohei Watanabe, Haiyan Wang, Paul Nulty, Adam Obeng, Stefan Müller, and Akitaka Matsuo. 2018. quanteda: An R package for the quantitative analysis of textual data. *Journal of Open Source Software*, 3(30):774.

Douglas Biber, Bethany Gray, Shelley Staples, and Jesse Egbert. 2020. Investigating grammatical complexity in L2 English writing research: Linguistic description versus predictive measurement. *Journal of English for Academic Purposes*, 46:100869.

Bram Bulté and Alex Housen. 2012. *Defining and Operationalising L2 Complexity*. John Benjamins Publishing Company.

Mihai Dascalu, Philippe Dessus, Stefan Trausan-Matu, Maryse Bianco, Aurélie Nardy, Mihai Dascălu, and Ştefan Trăuşan-Matu. 2013. ReaderBench, an Environment for Analyzing Text Complexity and Reading Strategies. In *AIED 13 - 16th International Conference on Artificial Intelligence in Education*, volume 7926 of *Lecture Notes in Computer Science (LNCS)*, pages 379–388, Memphis, TN, United States. Springer.

Martin Dougiamas and Peter Taylor. 2003. Moodle: Using Learning Communities to Create an Open Source Course Management System. In *Proceedings of the EDMEDIA 2003 Conference, Honolulu, Hawaii*, pages 171–178, Hawaii. Association for the Advancement of Computing in Education (AACE).

Rod Ellis. 2010. EPILOGUE: A Framework for Investigating Oral and Written Corrective Feedback. *Studies in Second Language Acquisition*, 32(2):335–349. Publisher: Cambridge University Press.

European Council. 2001. *Common European Framework of Reference for Languages: Learning, teaching, assessment*. Cambridge University Press, Cambridge.

John A. Hawkins and Luna Filipović. 2012. *Criterial Features in L2 English: Specifying the Reference Levels of the Common European Framework*, volume 1 of *English Profile Studies*. Cambridge University Press, United Kingdom.

Alex Housen, Folkert Kuiken, and Ineke Vedder, editors. 2012. *Dimensions of L2 performance and proficiency: complexity, accuracy and fluency in SLA*, volume 32 of *Language Learning & Language Teaching (LL&LT)*. John Benjamins Publishing Company, Amsterdam, The Netherlands, USA.

Kristopher Kyle. 2016. *Measuring Syntactic Development in L2 Writing: Fine Grained Indices of Syntactic Complexity and Usage-Based Indices of Syntactic Sophistication*. Ph.D. thesis, Georgia State University.

Paula Lissón. 2017. Investigating the use of readability metrics to detect differences in written productions of learners : a corpus-based study. *Bellaterra journal of teaching and learning language and literature*, 10(4):0068–86.

Xiaofei Lu. 2010. Automatic analysis of syntactic complexity in second language writing. *International Journal of Corpus Linguistics*, 15(4):474–496.

Xiaofei Lu. 2012. The Relationship of Lexical Richness to the Quality of ESL Learners' Oral Narratives. *The Modern Language Journal*, 96(2):190–208.

Xiaofei Lu. 2014. *Computational Methods for Corpus Annotation and Analysis*. Springer, Dordrecht.

Danielle S. McNamara, Chutima Boonthum, Irwin Levinstein, and Keith Millis. 2007. Evaluating self-explanations in iSTART: Comparing word-based and LSA algorithms. In *Handbook of latent semantic analysis*, pages 227–241. Lawrence Erlbaum Associates Publishers, Mahwah, NJ, US.

Diane Napolitano, Kathleen Sheehan, and Robert Mundkowsky. 2015. Online Readability and Text Complexity Analysis with TextEvaluator. In *Proceedings of the 2015 Conference of the North American Chapter of the Association for Computational Linguistics: Demonstrations*, pages 96–100, Denver, Colorado. Association for Computational Linguistics.

Ildikó Pilán and Elena Volodina. 2018. Investigating the importance of linguistic complexity features across different datasets related to language learning. In *Proceedings of the Workshop on Linguistic Complexity and Natural Language Processing*, pages 49–58, Santa Fe, New-Mexico. Association for Computational Linguistics.

Ildikó Pilán, Elena Volodina, and Richard Johansson. 2014. Rule-based and machine learning approaches for second language sentence-level readability. In *Proceedings of the Ninth Workshop on Innovative Use of NLP for Building Educational Applications*, pages 174–184, Baltimore, Maryland. Association for Computational Linguistics.

R Core Team. 2012. *R: A language and environment for statistical computing*. R Foundation for Statistical Computing, Vienna, Austria.

Rod D. Roscoe, Laura K. Allen, Jennifer L. Weston, Scott A. Crossley, and Danielle S. McNamara. 2014. The Writing Pal Intelligent Tutoring System: Usability Testing and Development. *Computers and Composition*, 34:39–59.

Björn Rudzewitz, Ramon Ziai, Florian Nuxoll, Kordula De Kuthy, and Walt Detmar Meurers. 2019. Enhancing a Web-based Language Tutoring System with Learning Analytics. In *Proceedings of the Workshops of the 12th International Conference on Educational Data Mining (EDM 2019)*, volume 2592, pages 1–7, Montréal, Canada.

Valerie J. Shute. 2008. Focus on formative feedback. *Review of Educational Research*, 78(1):153–189.

Sowmya Vajjala and Detmar Meurers. 2012. On Improving the Accuracy of Readability Classification Using Insights from Second Language Acquisition. In *Proceedings of the Seventh Workshop on Building Educational Applications Using NLP*, pages 163–173, Stroudsburg, PA, USA. Association for Computational Linguistics.

Rémi Venant and Mathieu D'Aquin. 2019. Towards the Prediction of Semantic Complexity Based on Concept Graphs. In *12th International Conference on Educational Data Mining (EDM 2019)*, pages 188–197, Montreal, Canada.

Helen Yannakoudakis, Ted Briscoe, and Ben Medlock. 2011. A New Dataset and Method for Automatically Grading ESOL Texts. In *Proceedings of the 49th Annual Meeting of the Association for Computational Linguistics: Human Language Technologies - Volume 1*, HLT '11, pages 180–189, Stroudsburg, PA, USA. Association for Computational Linguistics.

Estonian as a Second Language Teacher's Tools

Tiiu Üksik, Jelena Kallas, Kristina Koppel, Katrin Tsepelina, Raili Pool
The Institute of the Estonian Language / Roosikrantsi 6, 10119 Tallinn, Estonia
(tiiu.yksik, jelena.kallas, kristina.koppel)@eki.ee,
katrin.tsepelina@eki.ee, raili.pool@ut.ee

Abstract

The paper describes "Teacher's Tools" (et *Õpetaja tööriistad*) developed by the Institute of the Estonian Language for teachers and specialists of Estonian as a Second Language. The toolbox includes four modules: vocabulary, grammar, communicative language activities and text evaluation. The vocabulary module provides graded word lists for young (CEFR levels pre-A1–C1) and adult (CEFR levels A1–C1) learners. The grammar module provides descriptions of young learners' grammar competence. The communicative language activities module gives teachers an overview of the typical situations that learners should be able to cope with. The text evaluation module marks lemmas in texts according to their CEFR assignment in the vocabulary module. So far the grammar and the communicative language activities modules have been developed only for young learners (CEFR levels pre-A1–B2). The toolbox is aimed at providing support for the development of Estonian as an L2 courses, educational materials, exercises and tests within a CEFR-based framework. The project started in 2017 and is ongoing.

1 Introduction

"Teacher's Tools" is a compatible toolkit developed for teachers and specialists of Estonian as a Second Language, providing an extensive overview of the development of lexical and grammatical competence in Estonian among L2 learners. The toolkit is accessible as a sub-page of the language portal Sõnaveeb[1]. The framework of the project is based on the Common European Framework of Reference for Languages: Learning, Teaching, Assessment (CEFR, 2001), its Companion Volume with New Descriptors (CEFR/CV, 2018) and the Collated Representative Samples of Descriptors of Language Competences Developed for Young Learners for Ages 7–10 (Szabo, 2018a) and 11–15 (Szabo, 2018b). The toolkit distinguishes between adult (CEFR levels A1–C1) and young learners (CEFR levels pre-A1–C1). The methodology of the project is adapted from similar projects for other languages (e.g. Capel, 2010, 2012; O'Keeffe and Geraldine 2017; Alfter et al., 2019).

2 Resources of Estonian as an L2

There are quite a few corpora available for the research of the Estonian Language (the biggest Estonian corpus is the "Estonian National Corpus 2019" (1,5 billions words))[2]. However, at the beginning of the project in 2017 there was a clear lack of resources available for the research of Estonian as an L2. In order to fill this gap, the Institute of Estonian Language compiled two types of corpora: 1) coursebook corpora and 2) learner corpora. As Volodina and Kokkinakis (2013) point out, the first type of corpora provides information about what and when education professionals found important for students to learn (passive linguistic competence), while learner corpora provide an indication of active linguistic competence. Both need to be studied since the second is directly influenced by the first. The coursebook corpora were compiled in several stages and resulted in two groups of corpora: "Estonian as a Second Language Coursebook Content Corpus 2017"[3] (contains eight coursebooks for adult learners at levels A1–C1; 500 000 tokens) and "Estonian as a Second Language School Coursebook Content Corpus 2021"[4] (contains 27 school coursebooks for grades 1–12; 1 300 000 tokens). The learner corpus was compiled in 2019–2021 and contains 6700 Estonian as an L2 young learner's texts. These are texts written mostly as state standard-determining tests (grades 3 and 6), basic school final examinations

[1] https://sonaveeb.ee/teacher-tools

[2] DOI: 10.15155/3-00-0000-0000-0000-08489L
[3] DOI: 10.15155/3-00-0000-0000-0000-06ADEL
[4] DOI: 10.15155/3-00-0000-0000-0000-0888BL

Proceedings of the 16th Workshop on Innovative Use of NLP for Building Educational Applications, pages 130–134
April 20, 2021 ©2021 Association for Computational Linguistics

Figure 1: Vocabulary module

(grade 9) and state exams (grade 12) for 2017–2021. The data is available for analysis through the interface of the Estonian Learner Language Corpus EMMA[5]. The texts were not corrected or altered. Both types of corpora were used for the development of "Teacher's Tools". The coursebook corpora were used primarily to create passive vocabulary word lists and for the analysis of explicit and implicit grammar teaching. The learner corpus was used for the creation and analysis of active vocabulary word lists and the dynamics of grammar acquisition.

3 Modules of "Teacher's Tools"

"Teacher's Tools" consists of four modules: vocabulary, grammar, communicative language activities and text evaluation.

3.1 Vocabulary

The vocabulary module includes young and adult learners' word lists compiled on the basis of coursebook and learner corpus word lists in comparison with frequency distribution in the "Estonian National Corpus 2017"[6]. Currently, the vocabulary list for adult learners includes about 12 500 words for levels A1–C1. The young learners' word list includes approx. 9000 words for levels pre-A1–B2. All words are presented as lemmas. Users can generate word lists based on learner type (young or adult) and POS. In addition, 24 topics (*clothes*, *furniture*, *birds* etc.) are compiled. The search results can be sorted alphabetically, by level or by POS (see Figure 1).

[5]DOI: 10.15155/1-00-0000-0000-0000-001A5L

[6]DOI: 10.15155/3-00-0000-0000-0000-071e7l

3.2 Grammar

The grammar module is the first attempt to create a systematic overview of Estonian L2 learner's grammar competence development. The general methodology was adopted from the English Grammar Profile[7] project (O'Keeffe and Geraldine, 2017). Currently, the grammar module provides descriptions of grammar competence on the morphology, derivation, phrase and sentence levels, from level pre-A1 up to level B2 (see Figure 2). The same grammatical category (e.g. the use of the genetive case for nouns or the use of imperative mood for verbs) may be described at all levels, but the functions and usage (how often the learner makes mistakes and what kinds of mistakes) are level-specific. Search options offer users choices of four main categories: morphology, derivation, phrase formation and sentence formation. The main categories contain 19 subcategories. For example, subcategories of *morphology* are *verb*, *noun*, *adjective*, *numeral*, *pronoun*, *adverb*. Every subcategory has grammatical markers (e.g. *number* and *case* for *noun*). The grammatical markers have values, for example *number* has values *singular* and *plural*. All descriptions are equipped with example sentences compiled either by experts or taken from coursebook and learner's corpora.

3.3 Communicative language activities

The communicative language activities module is based on CEFR/CV descriptor scales, and examples are taken from Szabo (2018a,b), which include reception processes and strategies of written

[7]https://www.englishprofile.org/english-grammar-profile/egp-online (13.01.2021)

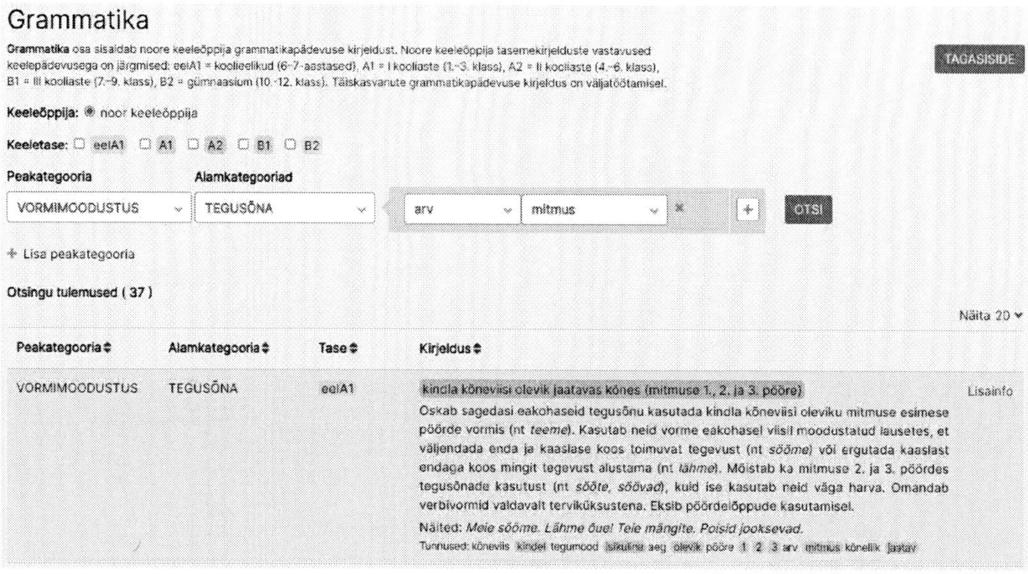

Figure 2: Grammar module

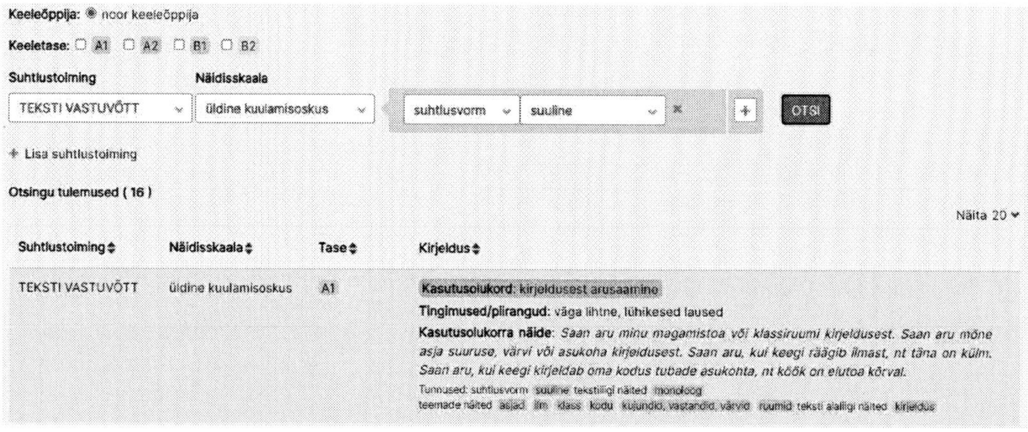

Figure 3: Communicative language activities module

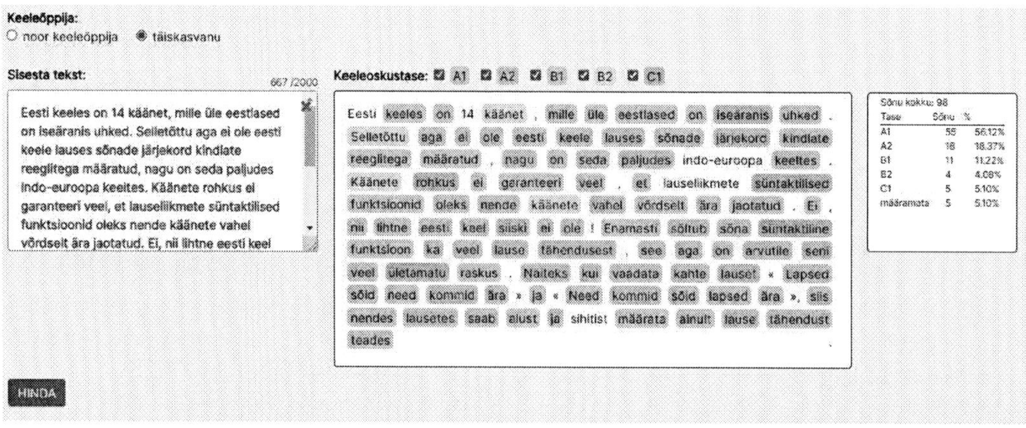

Figure 4: Text evaluation module

and spoken texts (listening and reading), written and oral text production and production strategies, and written and spoken interaction and interaction strategies. It covers young learners at levels A1–B2. The architecture of the module is similar to that of the grammar module, containing main categories (reception, production, interaction and mediation) and subcategories, which are followed by detailed descriptions, including limitations: when and how well the language user can manage certain communicative activities (see Figure 3). For example, by choosing the main category *reception* and the subcategory *overall listening comprehension*, a teacher can see that at the A1 level the learner should be able to understand a simple description with short sentences, for example about the weather or how big a certain object is.

3.4 Text evaluation

The text evaluation tool helps to assess Estonian texts for their degrees of complexity according to the CERF (see Figure 4). Currently, the tool takes into account only lexical information and defines the CEFR level of each particular lemma based on CEFR vocabulary lists (see Chapter 3.1). Similar tools have also been developed for many other languages (see e.g. Alfter, 2021). The program runs on EstNLTK v 1.6, which offers functionality to lemmatise and perform morphological analysis. The tool needs to be developed further. First, there is a need to implement methods for the improvement of the analysis of homonyms (for example *tamm* can mean either an *oak* or a *dam*, which is assigned different levels in word lists) and multi-word expressions. So far, the analysis is based only on single word lists, which is not sufficient.

4 Summary

"Teacher's Tools" is the first attempt to provide a systematic overview of the development of lexical and grammatical competence in Estonian as a Second Language. The project is a work in progress and further development of the toolkit is foreseen. We plan to add descriptions of the development of grammar competence and communicative language activities for adult learners. The enrichment of the text evaluation module with the possibility of measuring grammatical difficulty and readability (by for example adding Lix-index value) is under development. "Teacher's Tools" as a resource can be used for different CALL tasks, including automatic CEFR-related vocabulary and grammar exercise generation or lexical simplification tasks. The use of NLP for the development of such computer-assisted tools has enormous potential for enhancing the teaching and learning of Estonian as an L2.

References

Estonian Learner Language Corpus EMMA = Eesti keele õppija korpus EMMA. University of Tartu.

Language portal Sõnaveeb. The Institute of the Estonian Language.

CEFR = the common european framework of reference for languages: Learning, teaching, assessment. 2001. Council of Europe, Strasbourg.

Estonian as a Second Language Coursebook Content Corpus 2017. 2017. The Institute of the Estonian Language.

Estonian National Corpus 2017. 2017. The Institute of the Estonian Language.

CEFR/CV = Common European Framework of Reference for Languages: Learning, teaching, assessment. Companion Volume with New Descriptors. 2018. Council of Europe, Strasbourg.

Estonian National Corpus 2019 (.vrt format). 2019. The Institute of the Estonian Language.

Estonian as a Second Language School Coursebook Content Corpus 2021. 2021. The Institute of the Estonian Language.

David Alfter. 2021. *Exploring natural language processing for single-word and multi-word lexical complexity from a second language learner perspective*. Ph.D. thesis, University of Gothenburg, Faculty of Humanities.

David Alfter, Lars Borin, Ildiko Pilán, Therese Lindström Tiedemann, and Elena Volodina. 2019. *Lärka: From Language Learning Platform to Infrastructure for Research on Language Learning*, Linköping Electronic Conference Proceedings. Linköping University Press. CLARIN Annual Conference ; Conference date: 08-10-2018 Through 10-10-2018.

Annette Capel. 2010. A1-B2 vocabulary: Insights and issues arising from the English Profile Wordlists project. *English Profile Journal*, 1(1):1–11.

Annette Capel. 2012. Completing the English Vocabulary Profile: C1 and C2 vocabulary. *English Profile Journal*, 1(2):1–14.

Anne O'Keeffe and Mark Geraldine. 2017. The english grammar profile of learner competence: Methodology and key findings. *International Journal of Corpus Linguistics*, 4(22):457–489.

Tunde Szabo. Collated Representative Samples of Descriptors of Language Competences Developed for Young – Volume 2: Ages 11-15. 2018a. Council of Europe.

Tunde Szabo. Collated Representative Samples of Descriptors of Language Competences Developed for Young – Volume 2: Ages 11-15. 2018b. Council of Europe.

Elena Volodina and Sofie Johansson Kokkinakis. 2013. Compiling a corpus of CEFR-related texts. Antwerpen, Belgium. May 27–29.

Assessing Grammatical Correctness in Language Learning

Anisia Katinskaia[†*] and **Roman Yangarber**[†]
University of Helsinki, Finland
*Department of Computer Science
†Department of Digital Humanities
first.last@helsinki.fi

Abstract

We present experiments on assessing the grammatical correctness of learner answers in the Revita language-learning platform.[1] In particular, we explore the problem of detecting *alternative-correct answers*: when more than one inflected form of a lemma fits syntactically and semantically in a given context. This problem was formulated as *Multiple Admissibility* (MA) in (Katinskaia et al., 2019). We approach the problem from the perspective of grammatical error detection (GED), since we hypothesize that models for detecting grammatical mistakes can assess the correctness of potential alternative answers in the language-learning setting. Due to the paucity of training data, we explore the ability of pre-trained BERT to detect grammatical errors and then fine-tune it using *synthetic* training data. In this work, we focus on errors in inflection. Our experiments A. show that pre-trained BERT performs worse at detecting grammatical irregularities for Russian than for English; B. show that fine-tuned BERT yields promising results on assessing correctness in grammatical exercises; and C. establish new GED benchmarks for Russian. To further investigate its performance, we compare fine-tuned BERT with one a state-of-the-art model for GED (Bell et al., 2019) on our dataset, and on RULEC-GEC (Rozovskaya and Roth, 2019). We release our manually annotated learner dataset, used for testing, for general use.

1 Introduction

Many intelligent tutoring systems (ITS) and computer-aided language learning systems (CALL) generate exercises and try to assess the learner's answers automatically. Providing feedback to the learner is difficult, due to the critical requirement of very high precision—providing incorrect feedback is much more harmful than no feedback at all. For this reason, most existing systems have pre-fabricated sets of exercises, with possible expected answers and prepared feedback.

Revita is an online L2 learning system for learners beyond the beginner level, which can be used in the classroom and for self-study (Katinskaia et al., 2017; Katinskaia and Yangarber, 2018; Katinskaia et al., 2018). It covers several languages, most of which are highly inflectional, with rich morphology. In contrast to the pre-fabricated approach, Revita allows the learner to upload *arbitrary* texts to be used as learning content, and automatically creates exercises based on the chosen content. At practice time, Revita presents the text one paragraph at a time with some words hidden and used as fill-in-the-blank (*cloze*) exercises. For each hidden word, Revita provides a hint—the base form (*lemma*) of the word. The learner should insert the inflected form of the lemma, given the context.

Continuous assessment of the user's answers is also performed automatically (Hou et al., 2019). Revita checks the learner's answer by comparing it with the *expected* answer—the one found in the original text. The problem arises when, for some exercise, besides the expected answer, another answer is also valid in the context. As a result, Revita may provide undesirable feedback by flagging answers that are not expected, but nonetheless correct, as "errors"—this can strongly mislead, confuse and discourage the learner. For example, both highlighted answers in the example below can be considered correct, but Revita expects the learner to use only the past tense form "сдавал" ("took"):

*"Мне приснилось, как я **сдавал** экзамены."*
*("I saw a dream how I **took** exams.")*
*"Мне приснилось, как я **сдаю** экзамены."*
*("I saw a dream how I **take** exams.")*

Hence, detecting alternative-correct answers is essential in the learning context. We manually checked a large set of answers, which were marked

[1] revita.cs.helsinki.fi

Proceedings of the 16th Workshop on Innovative Use of NLP for Building Educational Applications, pages 135–146
April 20, 2021 ©2021 Association for Computational Linguistics

Learner level	Advanced	Others
Gram. error	649 (62.2%)	4777 (72.8%)
Alternative corr.	395 (37.8%)	1024 (15.6%)

Table 1: Percentage of answers with real grammatical errors and alternative-correct answers for advanced and other learners among all answers which were automatically marked by Revita as incorrect.

by Revita as "erroneous" and discovered that the percentage of alternative-correct answers for advanced learners is more than double the percentage for other learners (see Table 1).

To address this problem, we build a model, which takes a paragraph with learner answers and decides whether they are *grammatically* correct. If the model is not certain about a user's answer, we can fall back on the "default" method—comparing to the expected answer. For evaluation, we created a dataset of paragraphs containing answers given by real learners, manually annotated for acceptability in their context.[2] Additionally, we do not focus on semantics, due to the current setup of the exercises—if a learner inserts an answer with a lemma that is different from the given hint, that is always considered erroneous. Learners may give such answers, but they are easily identified and are not considered and are not annotated in this set of experiments.

The paper is organized as follows. In section 2, we review prior work on GED, with a focus on limited training data. In section 3, we describe the learner corpora collected by Revita and used for evaluation and propose a novel method for generating data with *simulated* grammatical errors. In section 4, we first experiment with a pre-trained BERT as a masked language model (MLM). We fine-tune the pre-trained BERT on synthetic data and measure its ability to assess grammatical correctness on the learner data. In section 5, we discuss the results of the experiments. In section 6, we summarize our contribution and discuss future work.

2 Related Work

Early experiments with GED utilized rules (Foster and Vogel, 2004) and supervised learning from error-annotated corpora (Chodorow et al., 2007). Much work focused on detection of particular types of errors, e.g., verb forms (Lee and Seneff, 2008). Later work is mostly independent of the type of errors, and explores various neural architectures.

Rei and Yannakoudakis (2016) first approach error detection by bi-LSTM models, which achieved strong results on in-domain data. Rei et al. (2016) added character-level embeddings to capture morphological similarities between words. Rei (2017) experiment with using a secondary language modeling (LM) objective. Rei and Yannakoudakis (2017) perform experiments with adding multiple auxiliary tasks for error detection. The best result was achieved by combining the main error detection task with predicting error types, POS tags, and types of grammatical relations. In subsequent experiments, the architecture was modified for jointly learning to label tokens and sentences (Rei and Søgaard, 2019). Bell et al. (2019) extended the above model by incorporating contextualized word embeddings produced by BERT, ELMO, and Flair (Peters et al., 2017; Devlin et al., 2018; Akbik et al., 2018). BERT embeddings produced the best performance across all test sets.

Previous work on GED mostly uses bi-LSTM as a classification model, combined with various approaches for augmenting the training data (Liu and Liu, 2017; Kasewa et al., 2018), or creating new, grammatically-specific word embeddings (Kaneko et al., 2017). More recent work utilizes transformer models (Kaneko and Komachi, 2019; Kaneko et al., 2020; Li et al., 2020; Chen et al., 2020).

Several works on GEC focus on lower-resource languages, including Russian, using the RULEC-GEC dataset for training or fine-tuning (Rozovskaya and Roth, 2019; Náplava and Straka, 2019; Katsumata and Komachi, 2020). Náplava and Straka (2019) outperformed results of Rozovskaya and Roth (2019) by over 100% on $F_{0.5}$, but still showed poor performance compared with other languages in the experiment. GEC for Russian is demonstrated to be the most challenging task, which is explained in part by the small size of RULEC-GEC.

The problem of scarce training data for GED can be approached by using pre-trained language models. Linzen et al. (2016) explored the ability of a LSTM model trained without grammatical supervision to detect grammatical errors by performing an *unsupervised cloze test*. The authors use a dataset of sentence pairs: an error-free original and an erroneous one. The erroneous sentence can be built manually or automatically, and differs from the original by only one word—the target position. They

[2]The annotated data is released with this paper. The dataset contains only *replacement* errors due to the current design of the practice mode in Revita.

feed complete sentences into the model, collect all predictions for the target position, and compare the scores assigned to the original correct word and the incorrect one, e.g., *write* vs. *writes*. Errors should have a lower probability than correct forms. The LM performs much worse than supervised models, especially in case of long syntactic dependencies (Jozefowicz et al., 2016; Marvin and Linzen, 2018; Gulordava et al., 2018). This work was done on Italian, Hebrew, and Russian.

Goldberg (2019) adapted the described evaluation methods and applied them to pre-trained BERT models by masking out the target words. BERT showed high scores on all test cases with subject-verb agreement and reflexive anaphora, except for sentences with relative clauses. The experiments were extended by Wolf (2019) by evaluating the OpenAI Generative Pre-trained Transformer (GPT) of Radford et al. (2018). BERT outperformed the OpenAI GPT on the datasets from Linzen et al. (2016) and Goudalova et al. (2018), but not on the dataset from Marvin and Linzen (2018).

The problem of data scarcity can be addressed by generating artificial training data. Among the existing approaches are oversampling a small learner corpus (Junczys-Dowmunt et al., 2018; Aprosio et al., 2019), utilizing additional resources, such as Wikipedia edits (Grundkiewicz and Junczys-Dowmunt, 2014; Boyd, 2018), or introducing *natural* and *synthetic* noise into error-free data (Belinkov and Bisk, 2017; Felice and Yuan, 2014). *Natural noise* means harvesting naturally occurring errors from the available corpora and creating a look-up table of possible replacements. Using natural noise also tries to imitate the distribution of errors in the available learner corpora. *Synthetic noise* can be generated by probabilistically injecting character-level or word-level noise into the source sentence, as shown in (Lichtarge et al., 2019; Kiyono et al., 2019; Zhao et al., 2019).

Synthetic error generation based on confusion sets extracted from a spellchecker was used by one of the top-scoring systems at the Restricted and the Low Resource tracks at the BEA-2019 Shared task (Grundkiewicz et al., 2019). Both tracks suppose limited use of available learner corpora. This method was compared in (White and Rozovskaya, 2020) with another top scoring approach (Choe et al., 2019) which relies on token-based and POS-based confusion sets extracted from a small annotated sample of the W&I +LOCNESS dataset (Yannakoudakis et al., 2018). Extensive evaluation showed that the methods are better suited for correcting different types of errors. In general, the token- and POS-based pattern method demonstrated stronger results.

If enough training data is available, errors can be generated by back-translation from correct data to data with errors (reverse error correction), which can be modified by additional random noise (Rei et al., 2017; Kasewa et al., 2018; Xie et al., 2018; Kiyono et al., 2019).

3 Data

First, we describe our real learner data. This data was used as the test set for all experiments presented below. Then, we present the method for generating ungrammatical data for training.

3.1 Learner Data

While students perform exercises using the Revita language-learning platform, it continuously collects[3] and automatically annotates *ReLCo*—the longitudinal Revita Learner Corpus (Katinskaia et al., 2020), where each record includes:

- an authentic learner error in the context;
- unique anonymized internal identifiers (ID) of the learner;
- the type of exercise which was practiced.
- the timestamp;

Error category	%
Noun: Case	32.1
Noun: Number	16.4
Adj.: Case	13.0
Verb: Number	10.7
Verb: Tense	10.4
Adj.: Gender	8.8
Verb form	8.2
Verb: Person	6.0
Pron.: Case	7.9
Adj.: Number	7.0

AC category	%
Verb: Tense	31.3
Noun: Number	27.2
Noun: Case	17.5
Verb: Gender	14.7
Verb: Number	13.0
Adj.: Case	10.0
Verb form	9.0
Verb: Mood	6.8
Adj.: Gender	5.9
Pron.: Case	2.3

Table 2: Most frequent grammatical errors and alternative-correct (AC) answers in the annotated dataset.

Revita generates exercises—"cloze", multiple-choice, listening, etc.—with hidden words in each paragraph. Learner answers that differ from the expected answers but have the same lemma are automatically flagged as grammatical errors, e.g., ел

[3] Students are aware that data is collected when they register on the platform.

Data	Sentences	Tokens	Errors per sentence	Grammatical errors	Correct
Real	7 869	120 420	1.9	4 704	693
Simulated	6 891 517	106 767 033	1.7	11 510 977	—

Table 3: The real dataset collected from learners, and the simulated dataset. The column "Correct" shows learner answers, which were manually labeled as correct by the annotators.

"(he) ate" in place of ест "(she/he/it) eats". Our goal is to improve this step—we aim to provide to the learners better feedback on the grammatical correctness of their answers, and in addition to improve the quality of automatic annotation.

Exercises include words of various parts of speech (POS); in this work, we focus only on the inflected POSs. A total of 10K of such flagged answers were manually checked, and annotated as correct or incorrect. Annotation was performed by two native speakers, with 91% agreement. Cases where annotators did not agree were resolved by consensus. Answers with spelling errors or with incorrect lemmas are ignored, since we focus only on grammatical errors (see the most frequent types in Table 2). We label as "unsure" cases when we could not decide whether the answer is correct. There were 194 such answers (2% of the annotated data), and they were not used for evaluation.

We assume that the context for annotation is *one paragraph*—earlier text is not used; all following sentences are also ignored (because they are not seen by the learner at the time of practice).[4] It is important to note that we annotate *jointly* all answers—which may affect each other—given by the learner in the paragraph at the same time during practice. In total, we have collected 3004 paragraphs, with an average of 2.6 sentences per paragraph. We include the same paragraph in the data multiple times if it had different exercises when it was shown to the learners, or if the same exercises were given, but they were answered differently. Statistics about this dataset of real errors are given in Table 3.

The manually annotated data is released to the community.[5] It includes the answers to exercises practiced in 2017–2020 by 150 learners, user IDs (anonymized), timestamps, and the corresponding correct sentences.

[4]For example, if the gender of a pronoun in the current paragraph is answered as feminine, but from the previous paragraph we know that it should be masculine, we do not mark such an answer as an error, if it suits the context of the *current* paragraph.

[5]github.com/Askinkaty/Russian_learner_corpora

3.2 Generating Training Data

As the source of error-free data, we used the open-source "Taiga" Russian corpus (Shavrina and Shapovalova, 2017), which is arranged into several segments based on genre. We used all news segments and a part of a literary text segment. Details about the data are presented in Table 3.

Keeping in line with the current design of Revita's practice mode—where the learner may not change the word order, nor the number of words in the sentence, nor the lemma of the hidden word—we generate errors by replacing some of the words by other random forms from their paradigms. During the pre-processing all sentences are parsed by a rule-based shallow parser, which is implemented as a component of Revita. It identifies which words belong to *chunks*—constructions based on syntactic agreement and government. We use about 30 types of chunks, e.g., `Prep+Adj+Noun` or `Noun+Conj+Noun`.[6]

A synthetic sentence $\widetilde{X}$ is produced from a source sentence $X = (x_1, x_i, ..., x_n)$ with n words by replacing the i-th word x_i by a form from the paradigm of x_i. The word is replaced, if: it has a valid morphological analysis; it is present in a frequency dictionary, which was computed from the entire "Taiga" corpus; and it has an inflected POS. Paradigms are generated by pymorphy2 (Korobov, 2015). Using the paradigm as a confusion set is similar to the approach in (Yin et al., 2020).

For every x_i, we pick a random sample from the uniform distribution. The word x_i is replaced, if it does not belong to a chunk and the picked value is above the threshold $\theta_p = p(error)$ = 0.1. The word x_i is also replaced, if it belongs to a chunk and the picked value is above the threshold $\theta_{p,c} = p(error, chunk)$ = 0.04. The thresholds denote a probability of inserting an error, and their values were chosen to reflect the distributions of errors in chunks and single tokens in the learner data.

[6]For example, in Russian, as in many languages, prepositions govern nouns in a specific case; adjective and noun must agree in gender, number and case; etc.

4 Models

We explore two ways to tackle the problem of scarce data: 1. use a LM in an unsupervised fashion to detect grammatical irregularities; 2. train GED models with supervision on synthetic data.

4.1 BERT as a Masked Language Model

We evaluate BERT as a masked language model (MLM)—to check how well it can distinguish correct answers from grammatical errors in the annotated learner data by performing an unsupervised cloze test, similar to that described by Goldberg (2019). The pre-trained BERT Base[7](Kuratov and Arkhipov, 2019) is used for all experiments.

Joint assessment of answers: We need to assess more than one target word *jointly*, because correctness depends on the joint fills in *all* exercises in a paragraph. Experiments described by Linzen et al. (2016) and Goldberg (2019) mask only *one* target word at a time in the original sentence and the sentence with the error. However, as the following example shows, two different sets of answers can suit the same context, as long as they are considered *jointly*. The words in the brackets are the hints (lemmas), which the user should replace:
"*Я [идти] по улице и [увидеть] пуделя.*"
("*I [walk] down the street and [see] a poodle.*")
The expected answers may be: "***Я иду** по улице и **вижу** пуделя.*"
("***I walk** down the street and **see** a poodle.*") But the learner may provide different answers, which are *alternatively correct*, if inserted jointly:
"***Я шёл** по улице и **увидел** пуделя.*"
("***I walked** down the street and **saw** a poodle.*")

We adapted the approach of (Linzen et al., 2016; Goldberg, 2019) to our setup and applied two masking strategies: 1. mask *one target* token in a sentence (Table 4, left side) before feeding it to BERT, and 2. mask *multiple targets* to be predicted jointly (right side). We use WordPiece (Schuster and Nakajima, 2012) to segment tokens for BERT, so some target words missing in the pre-trained model's vocabulary are split into sub-tokens. Because of this, we compared the mean log-probabilities of all of the target's sub-tokens. Acc_{err} denotes accuracy calculated on MLM predictions for only erroneous answers. We also evaluated predictions using different BERT layers.

Alternative-correct answers: The method of Linzen et al. (2016) and Goldberg (2019) is based on comparing the model's probabilities predicted for the original word and for the replacement, with the assumption that the replacement is incorrect. This gives us only the absolute difference in probabilities returned by the LM, which cannot be used to determine whether the learner's answer is also correct in the context. When comparing BERT's predictions for the masked original word and the masked alternative-correct word, we conjecture that the model recognizes an alternative answer as grammatical if its predicted probability is *at least as high* as the probability of the expected answer. We also applied two masking strategies (*one target* vs. *multiple targets*), see accuracy Acc_{corr} in Table 4.

4.2 Supervised Model Architecture

Following prior experiments—which show that fine-tuning BERT for NER (Peters et al., 2019) and error detection (Kaneko et al., 2020) gives better performance than using the contextual representation of words from pre-trained BERT—we also fine-tune the pre-trained model. We modified the Huggingface Pytorch implementation of BERT for token classification and the code for the NER task[8] (Debut et al., 2019). Hyper-parameters for fine-tuning BERT are the same as for the NER task: maximum number of epochs is 3, maximum input sequence length is 256, dropout rate is 0.1, batch size is 32, Adam optimizer, and the initial learning rate is set to 5E-5. We split the generated dataset into a training set, a development set, and a test set. Real learner data was *not* used for optimizing hyper-parameters or regularization—only for the final testing.

Tokens: To process words, we did not use the only first sub-token per token, as is usually done when fine-tuning BERT for NER, but assigned the error/correct label of the entire token to all of its sub-tokens. We also tried labeling as errors only those sub-tokens that are actually erroneous, but that did not improve performance. This may be due to the segmentation and BERT's deficiency in capturing morphological features.

Training sequence: We experimented with using one sentence as the training instance (padded or cut to the maximum input length). However, using a paragraph as input decreases training time and gives better performance (see Table 5, where s denotes *sentence instances* and p means *paragraph instances*). The results were the same with

[7]docs.deeppavlov.ai/en/master/features/models/bert.html

[8]github.com/huggingface/transformers

BERT Layers	One target word			Multiple target words		
	Acc_{err}	Acc_{corr}	$bAcc$	Acc_{err}	Acc_{corr}	$bAcc$
all layers	64.5	61.4	63.0	65.7	57.8	61.8
layer 10	50.9	59.0	55.0	51.9	55.9	53.9
layer 9	50.2	58.4	54.3	51.7	55.8	53.8
layer 8	49.4	60.1	54.8	51.5	57.1	54.3

Table 4: Accuracy of BERT as a MLM on detecting errors. The 3 left columns present results on masking only one target word in the sentence; the 3 right columns present masking multiple learner answers jointly; err and $corr$ denote accuracy for masked grammatical errors and alternative-correct answers, respectively. Balanced accuracy ($bAcc$) is calculated for both classes: errors and alternative-correct answers.

paragraph length from 128 up to 256.

Layers: As multiple studies show that syntactic information is most prominent in the *middle* layers (6-9 for BERT-base), while the final layer is the most task-specific (Rogers et al., 2020; Yin et al., 2020), we also experimented with middle layers from several models with 12, 8, and 6 layers. For the classification task, we use a softmax output layer.

Loss: The training data is very skewed—over 90% of tokens are correct words, so negative examples far outnumber the positive ones. This particularly complicates the process of training and evaluation. To handle this, we use the weighted cross-entropy loss, wCE. It is a variant of cross-entropy where all classes are given weight coefficients:

$$wCE = -\sum_{c=1}^{C} w_c p_c \log \hat{p}_c$$

where the weight of a class c is calculated as: $w_c = \frac{N}{CN_c}$, where N is the total number of samples in the dataset, C is the number of classes, and N_c is the number of samples within the class.

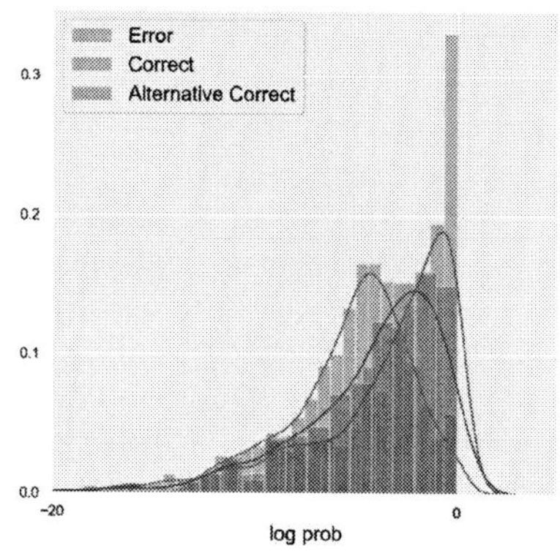

Figure 1: Histograms and kernel density estimations of log-probabilities assigned by BERT as MLM to: grammatical errors, randomly chosen correct words (not used in exercises), and alternative-correct answers.

5 Results and Discussion

BERT as MLM: We calculated balanced accuracy scores $bAcc$ for both classes—grammatical errors and alternative-correct answers (see Table 4). The results for the one-target approach are not strictly comparable with the results in Goldberg (2019) because our data includes grammatical errors in many syntactic relations, not only in subject-verb agreement or reflexive anaphora. However, we can conclude that the pre-trained BERT models capture syntactic-sensitive dependencies markedly worse for Russian than for English, especially if multiple target words are masked. Exploring different layers showed that the lower layers of the pre-trained model are weaker at detecting the errors. Figure 1 presents histograms and kernel density estimation over log-probabilities that BERT as MLM assigns to a. errors, b. correct words sampled randomly from the learner corpus (which were not exercised) and c. alternative-correct answers. These three groups of words clearly have different distributions, but they are not easily separable to assess the learner answers in a reliable fashion.

Fine-tuned BERT: Table 5 presents the metrics calculated on *all words* in the test set and only on the *target words* (with superscript T)—i.e., words which were inserted by the learner: errors or alternative-correct answers. MCC ranges between $[-1, 1]$, and is high if the model correctly predicts a high percentage of negative *and* positive instances (Powers, 2020). We use $F_{0.5}$ because it favors precision over recall; this is important for our task, since providing incorrect feedback on learner answers is far more harmful than no feedback at all. MCC and $F_{0.5}$ do not completely agree, be-

Model	MCC	P	R	$F_{0.5}$	F_1	P^T	R^T	$F^T_{0.5}$	F^T_1	$bAcc^T$
CE+12+p	**63.7**	79.3	84.6	**80.3**	81.9	68.0	77.6	**69.7**	72.5	77.6
CE+12+s	58.5	77.6	81.0	78.2	79.3	66.8	76.9	68.6	71.5	76.9
CE+8+p	**63.4**	79.2	84.4	**80.2**	81.7	68.2	78.1	**70.0**	72.8	78.1
CE+8+s	58.9	77.6	81.4	78.3	79.5	67.1	77.4	68.9	71.9	77.4
wCE+12+p	**55.1**	70.0	87.9	**73.0**	77.9	68.8	74.5	**69.9**	71.5	74.5
wCE+12+s	50.0	68.2	84.4	70.9	75.4	65.9	73.2	67.2	69.4	73.2
wCE+8+p	**56.1**	70.6	88.1	**73.5**	78.4	69.5	75.5	**70.6**	72.4	75.5
wCE+8+s	48.2	67.1	83.9	69.9	74.6	66.3	73.9	67.9	70.0	73.9
CE+12+p+t	66.4	86.3	80.3	85.0	83.2	68.0	77.6	69.7	72.5	77.6
CE+8+p+t	**66.8**	86.5	80.6	**85.3**	83.4	68.4	78.7	**70.2**	73.2	78.7
wCE+12+p+t	65.5	87.2	78.9	85.4	82.8	68.7	76.6	70.1	72.4	76.6
wCE+8+p+t	**66.7**	87.7	79.5	**85.9**	83.4	68.6	77.3	**70.2**	72.7	77.3

Table 5: Results of evaluation of fine-tuned BERT models on assessing grammatical correctness: CE—*cross-entropy loss*, wCE—*weighted cross-entropy*; the numbers denote the number of layers; s—*sentence training instance*, p—*paragraph training instance*, t—scores after moving decision thresholds. MCC—Matthews correlation coefficient, P and R—macro-averaged precision and recall, $F_{0.5}$ and F_1—macro F-measures, $bAcc$—balanced accuracy. Metrics are calculated for *all* tokens, except where superscript^T—calculated only for the *target* words.

cause $F_{0.5}$ does not take into account the true negatives. We report macro-averaged scores, as they reflect how well the model performs for all classes, which is important for our task—assessing the erroneous vs. the alternative-correct answers. Macro-averaging treats all classes as equal, including the minority class—grammatical errors. We calculate the balanced accuracy $bAcc^T$ on the target tokens (errors and alternative-correct) for the fine-tuned models for comparison with BERT as MLM. We consider a word to be tagged as an error if at least one of its sub-segments was tagged as an error.

The fine-tuned models show better results on evaluating the correctness of learner answers. The best performing models are highlighted. We also report the metrics for the best 4 models after moving the decision thresholds (denoted by t in the model name), chosen based on the highest values of $F_{0.5}$ and MCC. The thresholds are shown in Table 6. All evaluation methods show that training with paragraphs outperforms training with sentence instances. This may be due to the wider context available during training and evaluation.

On the target positions, the fine-tuned models perform better with 8 layers, regardless of the loss function, which is consistent with experiments for English (Yin et al., 2020).[9] Performance on the target positions is worse than for all tokens because all

[9]Results with 6 layers are the worst for all models and are not reported in Table 5.

Model	All words	Targets
CE+12+p+t	0.83	0.50
CE+8+p+t	0.83	0.56
wCE+12+p+t	0.98	0.75
wCE+8+p+t	0.98	0.85

Table 6: Decision thresholds for best fine-tuned BERT models.

models, even trained considering unbalanced data, tend to predict more often that a word is correct, which is true for most of the tokens in a paragraph.

Comparison with other models: We use the model proposed for GED by (Bell et al., 2019) as the *baseline*—a bi-LSTM trained with a second LM objective and combined with a character-level bi-LSTM model. We took the best performing configuration, which utilizes BERT contextual embeddings. The baseline was trained only on the real learner datasets with cross-validation (CV).

We used RULEC-GEC (see Table 9) as a second dataset to evaluate how well our fine-tuned model can generalize on other learner corpora, despite the fact that the synthetic training dataset was generated to imitate our learner data. RULEC-GEC is a corrected and error-tagged corpus of learner writing. It is almost double in size, has different error types and higher error rate than in our learner dataset. We performed evaluation on all types of

Model	Our dataset P	R	$F_{0.5}$	F_1	RULEC-GEC P	R	$F_{0.5}$	F_1
Baseline	82.9	70.1	80.0	76.0	84.5	63.4	79.2	72.4
BERT + synthetic data	79.3	84.6	80.3	81.9	72.3	62.4	70.5	68.0
BERT + synthetic data + spellchecker	-	-	-	-	82.1	91.5	83.8	86.5
BERT + real learner data	85.2	78.1	83.7	81.5	96.5	90.9	95.3	93.6

Table 7: Macro precision, recall, $F_{0.5}$, and F_1 evaluated on our learner dataset and RULEC-GEC. "Baseline" refers to a retrained model by (Bell et al., 2019), with using BERT contextualized embeddings. BERT refers to the fine-tuned models, with CE-loss and 12 layers.

Model	Noun	Adj.	Verb	Pron.	Num.
CE+12+p	82.0	79.7	67.9	77.9	73.2
CE+8+p	82.6	79.9	67.9	77.2	70.7
wCE+12+p	86.7	84.3	68.9	87.8	73.2
wCE+8+p	87.9	85.1	70.0	85.1	80.5

Table 8: Accuracy of predicting correctness on the target positions for different parts of speech by the models fine-tuned on synthetic data.

Tokens	Sentences	Errors	Total error rate
206 258	12 480	13 047	6.3%

Table 9: Statistics for the data in RULEC-GEC.

replacement and deletion errors in RULEC-GEC, not only inflection errors.

BERT, fine-tuned on synthetic data, performs comparably with the baseline (see Table 7). It has worse results on RULEC-GEC; however, it is mostly unable to detect spelling errors, as well as other error types, which were not present in the synthetic dataset (preposition, conjunction, and insertion/deletion errors). In combination with the Deep Pavlov spelling correction pipeline,[10] the fine-tuned model can achieve much higher performance without any additional training.

We also experimented with fine-tuning BERT on original learner data with CV. For our dataset, results of the model fine-tuned solely on synthetic data are comparable with the model fine-tuned and tested on the original data with CV. Moreover, recall is better for the model trained on synthetic data. The reason for this might be that our learner data is too scarce. The BERT model fine-tuned and tested solely on RULEC-GEC with CV achieves much better results than any of the other tested systems. We performed this evaluation primarily to compare the performance of fine-tuned BERT and the baseline on the same dataset.

[10]docs.deeppavlov.ai

Model confidence: To evaluate confidence of the fine-tuned models, we apply the method of Monte Carlo dropout (Gal and Ghahramani, 2016). By keeping dropout activated at test time, we can repeatedly sample T predictions for every input and estimate the predictive uncertainty by measuring the variance and entropy of the scores. We sampled $T = 20$ scores of the BERT model (CE-loss, 12 layers) fine-tuned on synthetic data for each test input and calculated their variance and entropy.

A deeper analysis is beyond the scope of the paper, but we observe that the scores have higher uncertainty when the models make mistakes in the predictions, see Figure 2. To use the model in Revita, we can compute the entropy of predicted scores and disregard the predictions when the entropy is high. In that case, we can fall back on our standard procedure of evaluation of learner answers. One disadvantage of this method is that it increases the inference time by a factor of T.

Error Analysis: Analysis of errors shows multiple problems experienced by all fine-tuned BERT models. The most prominent are due to inverted word order and long-range dependencies; many verb forms are classified incorrectly (see Table 8), rare names and non-Cyrillic words are mostly classified as errors as well. This result is consistent with the previous research, which showed that fine-tuned BERT struggles with word order errors and verb forms for English (Yin et al., 2020).

Errors are frequently related to conjoined elements in the sentence. For instance, in case of two subjects with one common predicate (e.g., "Peter and John talk on the phone every day."), BERT cannot detect errors in the number of the predicate ("talk" vs. "talks"). Moreover, BERT often marks

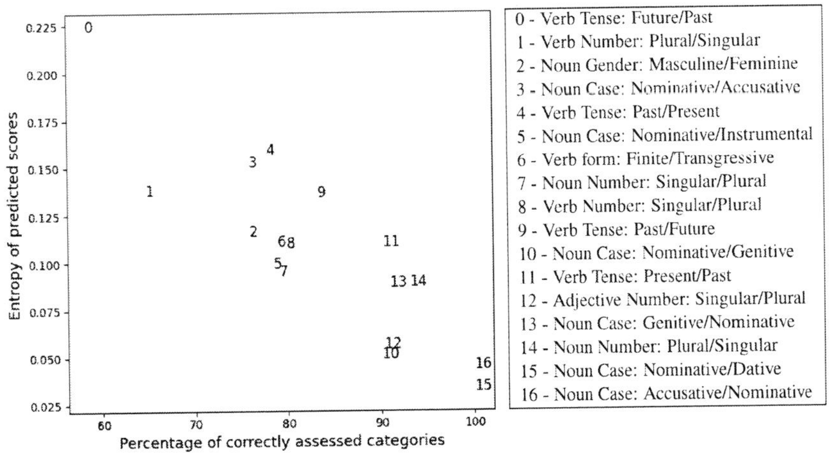

Figure 2: Percentage of 17 the most frequent correctly assessed categories in alternative-correct answers (X-axis) vs. entropy of predicted scores (Y-axis), sampled from 20 BERT models fine-tuned on synthetic data.

an erroneous word as an error along with other words syntactically related to it. This applies to both shallow and long-range relations. So, the presence of an error affects other words which are syntactically related to the erroneous one.

Another interesting problem related to multiple valid possibilities to correct an erroneous sentence. The models for GED, which we have been experimenting with, have no information about where the learners' answers are located in the sentence. In some erroneous sentences, it is possible to correct a hypothetical error (not a wrong learner's answer) and to obtain a corrected sentence with a meaning which is different from the original one but also grammatically valid. When labeling such sentences, fine-tuned BERT can consider an erroneous answer as correct and predict other words in the sentence as errors, which do not agree with the inserted form. For example: "*Я был в Африке и меня там* ***крокодила*** *съел.*" ("*I was in Africa and I was eaten by a* ***crocodile.***"). The highlighted word "crocodile" should be in the nominative rather than accusative case. However, BERT predicts the word "*меня*" ("*me*") as error, likely expecting the nominative "*я*" ("*I*"), i.e., changing the meaning of the sentence to *"I was in Africa and I ate a crocodile."*

6 Conclusions and Future Work

We present a study on assessing grammatical correctness in the context of language learning. Our focus is on assessing *alternative-correct* answers to cloze exercises—such answers are given more frequently by the more advanced learners. This work was done with the Russian version of Revita, using a learner corpus collected automatically and annotated manually. We release the corpus to the research community with this paper.

The motivation behind approaching the problem of alternative-correct answers as GED is based on the hypothesis that models for error detection can assess the correctness of potentially valid answers. Because learner data is limited, we experimented with pre-trained BERT as a MLM, and with several BERT models fine-tuned on *synthetic* data, which we generated for the task. The evaluation shows that the pre-trained BERT is not able to assess grammatical correctness of learner answers; the performance for Russian is considerably lower than for similar experiments with English. Comparison with a baseline model and evaluation on another leaner corpus demonstrates that fine-tuning on synthetic data is a promising approach and generalizes well.

We plan to improve the generation of synthetic data based on error analysis, to cover a wider range of error types, and continue work on estimation of the confidence of the model predictions, since it is critical to provide reliable feedback to the learners. We also plan to specify the *positions* of answers as part of the model's input, which is natural for the exercise-oriented set-up in Revita.

Acknowledgements

This work was supported in part by the Academy of Finland, HIIT—Helsinki Institute for Information Technology, and Tulevaisuus Rahasto (Future Development Fund), University of Helsinki.

References

Alan Akbik, Duncan Blythe, and Roland Vollgraf. 2018. Contextual string embeddings for sequence labeling. In *Proceedings of the 27th International Conference on Computational Linguistics*, pages 1638–1649.

Alessio Palmero Aprosio, Sara Tonelli, Marco Turchi, Matteo Negri, and Mattia A Di Gangi. 2019. Neural text simplification in low-resource conditions using weak supervision. In *Proceedings of the Workshop on Methods for Optimizing and Evaluating Neural Language Generation*, pages 37–44.

Yonatan Belinkov and Yonatan Bisk. 2017. Synthetic and natural noise both break neural machine translation. *arXiv preprint arXiv:1711.02173*.

Samuel Bell, Helen Yannakoudakis, and Marek Rei. 2019. Context is key: Grammatical error detection with contextual word representations. *arXiv preprint arXiv:1906.06593*.

Adriane Boyd. 2018. Using wikipedia edits in low resource grammatical error correction. In *Proceedings of the 2018 EMNLP Workshop W-NUT: The 4th Workshop on Noisy User-generated Text*, pages 79–84.

Mengyun Chen, Tao Ge, Xingxing Zhang, Furu Wei, and Ming Zhou. 2020. Improving the efficiency of grammatical error correction with erroneous span detection and correction. *arXiv preprint arXiv:2010.03260*.

Martin Chodorow, Joel R Tetreault, and Na-Rae Han. 2007. Detection of grammatical errors involving prepositions. In *Proceedings of the fourth ACL-SIGSEM workshop on prepositions*, pages 25–30. Association for Computational Linguistics.

Yo Joong Choe, Jiyeon Ham, Kyubyong Park, and Yeoil Yoon. 2019. A neural grammatical error correction system built on better pre-training and sequential transfer learning. *arXiv preprint arXiv:1907.01256*.

Lysandre Debut, Victor Sanh, Julien Chaumond, Clement Delangue, Anthony Moi, Pierric Cistac, Tim Rault, Rémi Louf, Morgan Funtowicz, , Jamie Brew, and Thomas Wolf. 2019. Huggingface's transformers: State-of-the-art natural language processing. *arXiv preprint arXiv:1910.03771*.

Jacob Devlin, Ming-Wei Chang, Kenton Lee, and Kristina Toutanova. 2018. BERT: Pre-training of deep bidirectional transformers for language understanding. *arXiv preprint arXiv:1810.04805*.

Mariano Felice and Zheng Yuan. 2014. Generating artificial errors for grammatical error correction. In *Proceedings of the Student Research Workshop at the 14th Conference of the European Chapter of the Association for Computational Linguistics*, pages 116–126.

Jennifer Foster and Carl Vogel. 2004. Parsing ill-formed text using an error grammar. *Artificial Intelligence Review*, 21(3-4):269–291.

Yarin Gal and Zoubin Ghahramani. 2016. Dropout as a bayesian approximation: Representing model uncertainty in deep learning. In *international conference on machine learning*, pages 1050–1059.

Yoav Goldberg. 2019. Assessing BERT's syntactic abilities. *arXiv preprint arXiv:1901.05287*.

Roman Grundkiewicz and Marcin Junczys-Dowmunt. 2014. The WikEd error corpus: A corpus of corrective wikipedia edits and its application to grammatical error correction. In *International Conference on Natural Language Processing*, pages 478–490. Springer.

Roman Grundkiewicz, Marcin Junczys-Dowmunt, and Kenneth Heafield. 2019. Neural grammatical error correction systems with unsupervised pre-training on synthetic data. In *Proceedings of the Fourteenth Workshop on Innovative Use of NLP for Building Educational Applications*, pages 252–263.

Kristina Gulordava, Piotr Bojanowski, Edouard Grave, Tal Linzen, and Marco Baroni. 2018. Colorless green recurrent networks dream hierarchically. *arXiv preprint arXiv:1803.11138*.

Jue Hou, Maximilian W Koppatz, José Marıa Hoya Quecedo, Nataliya Stoyanova, Mikhail Kopotev, and Roman Yangarber. 2019. Modeling language learning using specialized Elo ratings. In *Proceedings of the Fourteenth Workshop on Innovative Use of NLP for Building Educational Applications, ACL: 56th annual meeting of the Association for Computational Linguistics*, pages 494–506.

Rafal Jozefowicz, Oriol Vinyals, Mike Schuster, Noam Shazeer, and Yonghui Wu. 2016. Exploring the limits of language modeling. *arXiv preprint arXiv:1602.02410*.

Marcin Junczys-Dowmunt, Roman Grundkiewicz, Shubha Guha, and Kenneth Heafield. 2018. Approaching neural grammatical error correction as a low-resource machine translation task. *arXiv preprint arXiv:1804.05940*.

Masahiro Kaneko and Mamoru Komachi. 2019. Multi-head multi-layer attention to deep language representations for grammatical error detection. *arXiv preprint arXiv:1904.07334*.

Masahiro Kaneko, Masato Mita, Shun Kiyono, Jun Suzuki, and Kentaro Inui. 2020. Encoder-decoder models can benefit from pre-trained masked language models in grammatical error correction. *arXiv preprint arXiv:2005.00987*.

Masahiro Kaneko, Yuya Sakaizawa, and Mamoru Komachi. 2017. Grammatical error detection using error-and grammaticality-specific word embeddings.

In *Proceedings of the Eighth International Joint Conference on Natural Language Processing (Volume 1: Long Papers)*, pages 40–48.

Sudhanshu Kasewa, Pontus Stenetorp, and Sebastian Riedel. 2018. Wronging a right: Generating better errors to improve grammatical error detection. *arXiv preprint arXiv:1810.00668*.

Anisia Katinskaia, Sardana Ivanova, and Roman Yangarber. 2020. Toward a paradigm shift in collection of learner corpora. In *Proceedings of The 12th Language Resources and Evaluation Conference*, pages 386–391.

Anisia Katinskaia, Sardana Ivanova, Roman Yangarber, et al. 2019. Multiple admissibility in language learning: Judging grammaticality using unlabeled data. In *The 7th Workshop on Balto-Slavic Natural Language Processing Proceedings of the Workshop*. The Association for Computational Linguistics.

Anisia Katinskaia, Javad Nouri, and Roman Yangarber. 2017. Revita: a system for language learning and supporting endangered languages. In *6th Workshop on NLP for CALL and 2nd Workshop on NLP for Research on Language Acquisition, at NoDaLiDa*, Gothenburg, Sweden.

Anisia Katinskaia, Javad Nouri, Roman Yangarber, et al. 2018. Revita: a language-learning platform at the intersection of ITS and CALL. In *Proceedings of the Eleventh International Conference on Language Resources and Evaluation (LREC 2018)*. European Language Resources Association (ELRA).

Anisia Katinskaia and Roman Yangarber. 2018. Digital cultural heritage and revitalization of endangered Finno-Ugric languages. In *Proceedings of the 3rd Conference on Digital Humanities in the Nordic Countries*, Helsinki, Finland.

Satoru Katsumata and Mamoru Komachi. 2020. Stronger baselines for grammatical error correction using pretrained encoder-decoder model. *arXiv preprint arXiv:2005.11849*.

Shun Kiyono, Jun Suzuki, Masato Mita, Tomoya Mizumoto, and Kentaro Inui. 2019. An empirical study of incorporating pseudo data into grammatical error correction. *arXiv preprint arXiv:1909.00502*.

Mikhail Korobov. 2015. Morphological analyzer and generator for Russian and Ukrainian languages. In *International Conference on Analysis of Images, Social Networks and Texts*, pages 320–332. Springer.

Yuri Kuratov and Mikhail Arkhipov. 2019. Adaptation of deep bidirectional multilingual transformers for Russian language. *arXiv preprint arXiv:1905.07213*.

John Lee and Stephanie Seneff. 2008. Correcting misuse of verb forms. In *Proceedings of ACL-08: HLT*, pages 174–182.

Yiyuan Li, Antonios Anastasopoulos, and Alan W Black. 2020. Towards minimal supervision BERT-based grammar error correction. *arXiv preprint arXiv:2001.03521*.

Jared Lichtarge, Chris Alberti, Shankar Kumar, Noam Shazeer, Niki Parmar, and Simon Tong. 2019. Corpora generation for grammatical error correction. *arXiv preprint arXiv:1904.05780*.

Tal Linzen, Emmanuel Dupoux, and Yoav Goldberg. 2016. Assessing the ability of LSTMs to learn syntax-sensitive dependencies. *Transactions of the Association for Computational Linguistics*, 4:521–535.

Zhuo-Ran Liu and Yang Liu. 2017. Exploiting unlabeled data for neural grammatical error detection. *Journal of Computer Science and Technology*, 32(4):758–767.

Rebecca Marvin and Tal Linzen. 2018. Targeted syntactic evaluation of language models. *arXiv preprint arXiv:1808.09031*.

Jakub Náplava and Milan Straka. 2019. Grammatical error correction in low-resource scenarios. *arXiv preprint arXiv:1910.00353*.

Matthew E Peters, Waleed Ammar, Chandra Bhagavatula, and Russell Power. 2017. Semi-supervised sequence tagging with bidirectional language models. *Proceedings of the 55th Annual Meeting of the Association for Computational Linguistics*, page 1756–1765.

Matthew E Peters, Sebastian Ruder, and Noah A Smith. 2019. To tune or not to tune? Adapting pretrained representations to diverse tasks. *arXiv preprint arXiv:1903.05987*.

David MW Powers. 2020. Evaluation: from precision, recall and F-measure to ROC, informedness, markedness and correlation. *arXiv preprint arXiv:2010.16061*.

Alec Radford, Karthik Narasimhan, Tim Salimans, and Ilya Sutskever. 2018. Improving language understanding by generative pre-training. *URL https://s3-us-west-2. amazonaws. com/openai-assets/researchcovers/languageunsupervised/language understanding paper. pdf*.

Marek Rei. 2017. Semi-supervised multitask learning for sequence labeling. *arXiv preprint arXiv:1704.07156*.

Marek Rei, Gamal KO Crichton, and Sampo Pyysalo. 2016. Attending to characters in neural sequence labeling models. *arXiv preprint arXiv:1611.04361*.

Marek Rei, Mariano Felice, Zheng Yuan, and Ted Briscoe. 2017. Artificial error generation with machine translation and syntactic patterns. *arXiv preprint arXiv:1707.05236*.

Marek Rei and Anders Søgaard. 2019. Jointly learning to label sentences and tokens. In *Proceedings of the AAAI Conference on Artificial Intelligence*, volume 33, pages 6916–6923.

Marek Rei and Helen Yannakoudakis. 2016. Compositional sequence labeling models for error detection in learner writing. *arXiv preprint arXiv:1607.06153*.

Marek Rei and Helen Yannakoudakis. 2017. Auxiliary objectives for neural error detection models. *arXiv preprint arXiv:1707.05227*.

Anna Rogers, Olga Kovaleva, and Anna Rumshisky. 2020. A primer in bertology: What we know about how BERT works. *arXiv preprint arXiv:2002.12327*.

Alla Rozovskaya and Dan Roth. 2019. Grammar error correction in morphologically rich languages: The case of Russian. *Transactions of the Association for Computational Linguistics*, 7:1–17.

Mike Schuster and Kaisuke Nakajima. 2012. Japanese and Korean voice search. In *2012 IEEE International Conference on Acoustics, Speech and Signal Processing (ICASSP)*, pages 5149–5152. IEEE.

Tatiana Shavrina and Olga Shapovalova. 2017. To the methodology of corpus construction for machine learning: "Taiga" syntax tree corpus and parser. *Corpus Linguistics*, page 78.

Max White and Alla Rozovskaya. 2020. A comparative study of synthetic data generation methods for grammatical error correction. In *Proceedings of the Fifteenth Workshop on Innovative Use of NLP for Building Educational Applications*, pages 198–208.

Thomas Wolf. 2019. Some additional experiments extending the tech report "Assessing BERT's syntactic abilities" by Yoav Goldberg. Technical report.

Ziang Xie, Guillaume Genthial, Stanley Xie, Andrew Y Ng, and Dan Jurafsky. 2018. Noising and denoising natural language: Diverse backtranslation for grammar correction. In *Proceedings of the 2018 Conference of the North American Chapter of the Association for Computational Linguistics: Human Language Technologies, Volume 1 (Long Papers)*, pages 619–628.

Helen Yannakoudakis, Øistein E Andersen, Ardeshir Geranpayeh, Ted Briscoe, and Diane Nicholls. 2018. Developing an automated writing placement system for ESL learners. *Applied Measurement in Education*, 31(3):251–267.

Fan Yin, Quanyu Long, Tao Meng, and Kai-Wei Chang. 2020. On the robustness of language encoders against grammatical errors. *arXiv preprint arXiv:2005.05683*.

Wei Zhao, Liang Wang, Kewei Shen, Ruoyu Jia, and Jingming Liu. 2019. Improving grammatical error correction via pre-training a copy-augmented architecture with unlabeled data. *arXiv preprint arXiv:1903.00138*.

On the application of Transformers for estimating the difficulty of Multiple-Choice Questions from text

Luca Benedetto and **Paolo Cremonesi**
Politecnico di Milano, Milan, Italy
{name.surname}@polimi.it

Giovanni Aradelli and **Andrea Cappelli** and **Andrea Giussani** and **Roberto Turrin**
Cloud Academy Sagl, Mendrisio, Switzerland
{name.surname}@cloudacademy.com

Abstract

Classical approaches to question calibration are either subjective or require newly created questions to be deployed before being calibrated. Recent works explored the possibility of estimating question difficulty from text, but did not experiment with the most recent NLP models, in particular Transformers. In this paper, we compare the performance of previous literature with Transformer models experimenting on a public and a private dataset. Our experimental results show that Transformers are capable of outperforming previously proposed models. Moreover, if an additional corpus of related documents is available, Transformers can leverage that information to further improve calibration accuracy. We characterize the dependence of the model performance on some properties of the questions, showing that it performs best on questions ending with a question mark and Multiple-Choice Questions (MCQs) with one correct choice.

1 Introduction

Question Difficulty Estimation (QDE), also referred to as "calibration", is a crucial task in education. Indeed, since question difficulty can be leveraged to assess the skill level of students under examination, wrongly calibrated questions are cause of erroneous estimations. Also, an accurate calibration enables to detect and discard questions that are too easy or too difficult for certain students. Traditionally, QDE is performed manually or with pretesting. Manual calibration is intrinsically subjective and inconsistent. Pretesting leads indeed to an accurate and consistent calibration, but i) introduces a long delay between question generation and when the question can be used to score students, and ii) requires to deploy the new questions before actually using them for scoring. To address the issues of the traditional approaches to calibration, recent research tried to leverage Natural Language Processing (NLP) techniques to perform QDE from question text: the idea is to use some pretested questions to train a model that performs QDE from text and thus eliminates (or at least reduces) the need for pretesting of new questions. Although such works showed promising results, none of them experimented with the latest NLP research, such as Transformer-based models (Vaswani et al., 2017). In this work, we aim at filling that gap, studying how different Transformers, also trained with different approaches, compare with the current state of the art. We evaluate several models built upon the pre-trained BERT (Devlin et al., 2019) and DistilBERT (Sanh et al., 2019) language models on the publicly available *ASSISTments* dataset and the private *CloudAcademy* dataset. By using data from two different domains, we add to the growing body of evidence showing that item text can be used to perform QDE. More precisely, we show that - after being fine-tuned on the task of QDE from text - Transformer models are capable of calibrating newly generated questions more accurately than previously proposed approaches. On top of that, we explore the possibility of leveraging additional textual information which might be available (e.g. transcript of video lectures) to perform an additional pre-training of the Transformers before fine-tuning them for QDE, and show that such approach can be used to further improve the accuracy. Overall, Transformer-based models are capable of reducing the RMSE by up tp 6.5%, with respect to previous approaches. Lastly, we perform an analysis of the best performing model to under-

Proceedings of the 16th Workshop on Innovative Use of NLP for Building Educational Applications, pages 147–157
April 20, 2021 ©2021 Association for Computational Linguistics

stand whether some question characteristics (e.g. text length, question type) particularly affect its performance. Code is available at `https://github.com/aradelli/transformers-for-qde`.

2 Related Work

There is a large interest in understanding how textual features affect item difficulty (El Masri et al., 2017; Hickendorff, 2013), and this is not limited to the educational domain: for instance Wang et al. (2014) focus on difficulty estimation in community question answering systems. The first works addressing QDE from text focused on MCQs and used deterministic approaches based on bag of words and similarities between question, answer, and distractors (Alsubait et al., 2013; Yaneva et al., 2018; Kurdi et al., 2016). Recent works mostly use machine learning approaches.

Huang et al. (2017) proposed a neural network for QDE of "reading" problems, in which the answer has to be found in a text provided together with the question. The model receives as input both the text of the question and the document, thus it actually estimates the difficulty of finding the correct answer in the provided document. This is a major difference from all other works, in which the difficulty depends on the questions only.

Yaneva et al. (2019) introduced a model to estimate the *p-value* of questions from text. The *p-value* of a question is defined as the fraction of students who correctly answered it and does not account for different skill levels. This model was trained using the text of questions and a large dataset of medical documents, thus it cannot be used if an analogous dataset is not available. Similarly, the model proposed in (Qiu et al., 2019) requires for training a dataset of medical documents in addition to the question texts. The model is made of two neural architectures to estimate the *wrongness* (i.e. $1 -$ p-value) of newly-generated MCQs, considering it as made of two components which indicate i) how difficult it is to choose between the possible choices, and ii) how difficult it is to recall the knowledge required to answer the question.

Benedetto et al. (2020b) proposed R2DE, a model that estimates the difficulty and discrimination, as defined in Item Response Theory (IRT) (Hambleton et al., 1991), of newly generated MCQs. R2DE computes TF-IDF features from the text of the questions and the text of the possible choices, and feeds two Random Forest regressors with such features. The performance of R2DE was improved in (Benedetto et al., 2020a), with the addition of readability and linguistics features.

To the best of our knowledge, (Xue et al., 2020) is the first work that explored the effects of transfer learning for QDE from text. Specifically, the authors fine-tune pre-trained ELMo embeddings (Peters et al., 2018) for the task of response time prediction, and subsequently perform a second fine-tuning for the task of *p-value* estimation. Differently from all the other models, this one and R2DE can be trained using only question text, without needing an additional dataset of related documents.

Our approach differs from previous research in several ways. First of all, we adopt transfer learning on Transformers, which are yet to be explored for QDE from text. Secondly, similarly to (Benedetto et al., 2020b,a), we perform the estimation of the IRT difficulty which, differently from *wrongness* and *p-value*, models students' skill levels as well. Specifically, we consider the one-parameter model (Rasch, 1960), a logistic model that associates a skill level to each student and a difficulty level to each question (both represented as scalars). A brief introduction to the one-parameter IRT model is given in Appendix A. Thirdly, the Transformer models presented here do not necessarily require an additional dataset of documents from the same topics as the questions, and they can be trained using only question texts; however, if such dataset is available, it can be leveraged to further improve the accuracy of calibration. Lastly, each previous work experimented on one private dataset; we experiment on two datasets (one being publicly available), showing that Transformers can be successfully used for QDE in different domains.

3 Introduction to BERT and DistilBERT

BERT (Devlin et al., 2019) is a pre-trained language model that reached state of the art performance in many language tasks. Its key technical innovation was the application of the Transformer, a popular self-attention model (Vaswani et al., 2017), to language modeling. BERT is originally trained to address two tasks: Masked Language Modeling (MLM) and Next Sentence Prediction (NSP). MLM consists in removing one word from the input text and asking the model to fill the gap, while in NSP the model is asked - given two input sentences - to tell whether the second sentence is a reasonable continuation to the first one. Crucially,

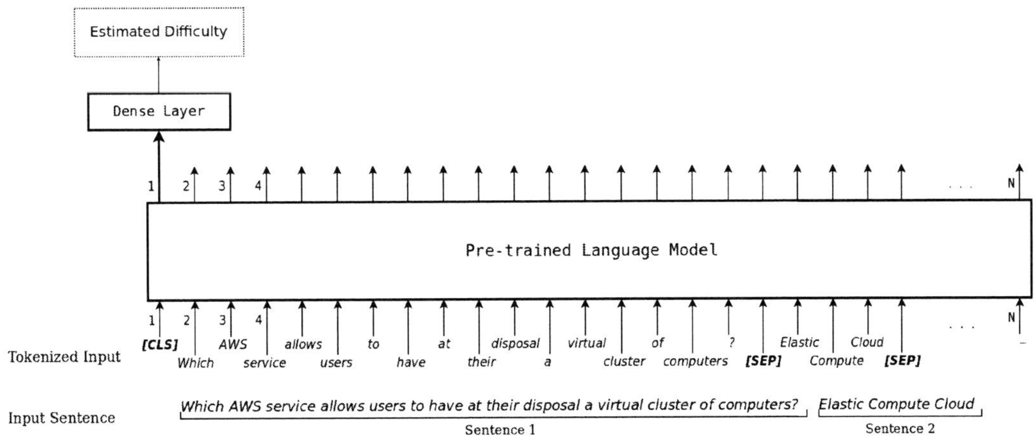

Figure 1: Fine-tuning of the pre-trained language model for the task of question difficulty estimation.

BERT can be used for many different downstream tasks, as we do here for QDE: starting from the pre-trained model, it is sufficient to stack an additional layer on top of the original network and then retrain it on the desired task (process named "fine-tuning"). During fine-tuning, the internal weights of the pre-trained model are updated and adapted to the desired task (together with the weights of the added layer), which is both more efficient than training the whole network from scratch and capable of better results, as the knowledge of the pre-trained model is not discarded.

BERT is a large model and therefore requires many resources for training and fine-tuning. For this reason, we also experiment with DistilBERT (Sanh et al., 2019), which is a language model obtained by distilling BERT. Knowledge distillation is a compression technique in which a small model is trained to reproduce the full output distribution of a larger model (Hinton et al., 2015). With this approach, DistilBERT is able to retain 95% of BERT's performance on several language understanding tasks using about half the number of parameters of BERT. Similarly to BERT, DistilBERT can be fine-tuned on downstream tasks and it is therefore worth exploring for QDE from text.

4 Models

This section describes how we build the different models which are compared with the current state of the art of QDE from text. These models are built upon the two pre-trained language models, fine-tuning them with two different approaches. The first approach consists in directly fine-tuning the pre-trained model for the task of QDE from text. The second approach is made of two steps: we i) further pre-train the pre-trained model on the task of Masked Language Modeling (MLM) to improve domain knowledge, and subsequently ii) fine-tune it on the task of QDE from text. This is all done separately for the two datasets: we do not perform any experiments across the two datasets.

4.1 Fine-tuning for QDE from text

This is the simplest of the two approaches; the architecture used for fine-tuning is shown in Figure 1. Given the pre-trained language model, we stack an additional fully connected layer on top of the network, in order to use that as the new output. Following the fine-tuning guidelines in (Devlin et al., 2019), we use only the first output of the pre-trained language model. This works since the first output correspond to the special token `[CLS]` which is added at the beginning of the input text and is the only one used for regression and classification. Since question calibration is a regression task, the additional output layer has one neuron, and the weights of the connections with the previous layer are randomly initialized. During fine-tuning, both the weights of the additional layer and the internal weights of the pre-trained language model are updated. For the input, we use the same tokenization and the same encoding as the original models. That is, all the input samples start with the special token `[CLS]` and contain two sentences, separated by the `[SEP]` token (another special token): the first sentence is the (tokenized) question while the second one contains the (tokenized) choices' text[1].

[1]It is possible to have a question made of several sentences. In that case, the whole question is considered as "Sentence 1",

Specifically, we experiment with three different encodings for the second sentence: i) *Q only*, we leave it empty, thus considering only the text of the question, ii) *Q+correct*, we use the text of the correct choice(s) (as in Figure 1), iii) *Q+all*, we use the text of all the possible choices, concatenating them in a single sentence. For the *ASSISTments* dataset, only the first encoding is possible as the text of the choices (correct answer and distractors) is not available. We also experimented a fourth approach, considering all the possible choices using several `[SEP]` tokens between each choice; however, this approach performed largely worse that the others, thus we do not report it here. We believe that the model, in that case, does not have enough training questions to learn the meaning of the additional separators (BERT and DistilBERT are pre-trained to use only one `[SEP]` token).

4.2 Pre-training for MLM

Masked Language Modeling (MLM) is a fill-in-the-blank task, where a word of the input text is substituted by a `[MASK]` token and the model is trained to use the surrounding words to predict the word that was masked. We leverage MLM to perform an additional pre-training of the pre-trained language models before the fine-tuning on QDE from text. Our goal is to let the model learn the questions' topics more accurately than how it would do with the fine-tuning on QDE only. In order for MLM to be effective, though, we need an additional dataset of documents about the same topics that are assessed by the questions: this is available only for the *CloudAcademy* dataset, which contains the transcript of some of the video-lectures on the e-learning platform. In practice, we perform pre-training with MLM as follows. We randomly mask 15% of the words of the available lectures, then train the language model to predict the masked words sentence by sentence. The actual prediction is performed by stacking a fully connected layer and a softmax layer on top of the original pre-trained model: for each masked sentence, this additional layer consumes as input the contextual embedding corresponding to the `[MASK]` token, and tries to predict the word that should be inserted in its place. After pre-training the model on the task of MLM, the additional dense and softmax layers are removed from the network, thus leaving us with a pre-trained model which has the same architecture as the original one, with the only difference that all the internal weights were updated during the additional MLM pre-training. The architecture for the final fine-tuning for QDE from text is the same as the one shown in Figure 1.

5 Experimental Datasets

In this work we use the publicly available data collection provided by *ASSISTments* and the private *CloudAcademy* data collection. Both data collections are made of two datasets: i) the *Answers* dataset (referred to as *A*) and ii) the *Questions* dataset (*Q*). It is important to remark that *A* and *Q* are abstract names: we have one *A* dataset for *CloudAcademy* and one *A* dataset for *ASSISTments* (similarly for *Q*). *A* contains the students' answers: for each one, it stores the user ID, the question ID, the correctness of the answer and a timestamp. Importantly, *A* contains only "first timers", meaning that we consider only the first interaction between a student and a question. *Q* contains the textual information about the items: question ID, question text and, in the case of *CloudAcademy*, the text of the possible choices. For the experiments on *CloudAcademy* data, we also have access to an additional dataset - referred to as *Lectures* (*L*) - which contains the transcripts of some online lectures available on the platform and is used for the additional MLM pre-training.

5.1 *ASSISTments* dataset

ASSISTments[2] is an online tutoring system that provides instructional assistance while assessing students (Feng et al., 2009). In practice, this means that questions - called *problems* - can be broken down into steps: if the student does not get the *original* problem correctly, he has to answer a sequence of *scaffolding* questions that break the problem down into steps. In the current work, we consider both original and scaffolding problems for QDE from text. An example problem and the corresponding scaffolding questions are shown in Appendix B. We filter the dataset to keep only questions that are answered by at least 50 students, to improve the reliability of the estimation of ground truth latent traits with IRT; on average, each item is answered by 151 students and each student answers to 64 different items. We also remove the questions that require external resources and the system messages

and the `[SEP]` token is still used only to indicate the end of the question. We use this naming ("Sentence 1" and "Sentence 2") since it is the one used in the original paper.

[2]https://new.assistments.org/

(e.g. "*Submit your answer from the textbook.*", "*Sorry, that is incorrect. Let's go to the next question!*"). After removal of the unsuitable questions, the final dataset used for QDE from text contains 11,393 different items. A is publicly available for download[3]; Q is publicly available under request[4].

5.2 *CloudAcademy* dataset

CloudAcademy[5] is an e-learning provider offering online courses about IT technologies. All the questions are MCQ and we have access to the text of the possible choices. An example question is shown in Appendix B. The dataset used in our experiments is a sub-sample of the *CloudAcademy* data collection and it was generated in order to have only questions answered by at least 50 students. A contains 7,323,502 interactions, involving 34,696 students and 13,603 unique questions; on average, each item is answered by 304 students and each student answers to 115 different items. The overall correctness is 66%. L contains the transcript of some of the online lectures offered by *CloudAcademy* about the same topics (i.e. cloud technologies) assessed by the questions. L contains a total of 159,563 sentences and 3,228,038 words.

6 Experimental Setup

As displayed in Figure 2, training is performed in two steps, repeated for the two datasets: i) the IRT model is trained in order to calibrate the questions and obtain the ground truth difficulties, then ii) these ground truth latent traits are used as target values to train the model on QDE from text.

The first step consists in using A to estimate with IRT the target difficulty of all the questions. Specifically, we use *pyirt*[6] for the estimation and consider $[-5; 5]$ as the possible range of difficulties. Difficulties estimated at this stage will later be used as ground truth and therefore are inserted as target values in Q. Then, Q is split into a train dataset (Q_{TRAIN}), used to train our model on QDE from text, and a test dataset (Q_{TEST}), which is used for the final evaluation of the model; we keep 80% of the questions for training and 20% for testing. At training time, we keep a portion of Q_{TRAIN} (10%) as development set, for hyperparameter tuning.

When L is used for pre-training the model, the setup is very similar. The only difference is that the regression model, before being fine-tuned on the task of QDE from text using Q_{TRAIN}, is pre-trained on the task of MLM on L. Being an unsupervised task, we use the whole L for this.

Transformers are implemented with the *transformers*[7] library from *HuggingFace*; fine-tuning and pre-training are performed with *TensorFlow*[8]. Hyperparameters are shown in Appendix C.

7 Results

7.1 Evaluation of the input configurations

Before comparing the Transformer models with the state of the art, we show here the performance of the different configurations, both with and without the additional pre-training on MLM. Table 1 displays the Mean Absolute Error (MAE) and the Root Mean Squared Error (RMSE) of the different configurations; the error is the difference between the IRT difficulty and the estimation of the Transformer model. The input configurations are the ones presented in Section 4: i) *Q only*, ii) *Q+correct*, iii) *Q+all*. We show the mean of the errors, measured over three independent runs with different random initializations. The results shown here are obtained on Q_{TEST} for *CloudAcademy*; indeed, for *ASSISTments* the text of the possible choices is not avail-

Table 1: Comparison of different Transformer models on *CloudAcademy*, with (Y) and without (N) additional MLM pre-training.

Model (MLM)	Input	MAE	RMSE
DistilBERT (N)	Q only	0.805	1.017
DistilBERT (N)	Q + cor.	0.799	1.019
DistilBERT (N)	Q + all	0.794	1.013
BERT (N)	Q only	0.807	1.022
BERT (N)	Q + cor.	0.789	0.999
BERT (N)	Q + all	0.811	1.027
DistilBERT (Y)	Q only	0.801	1.016
DistilBERT (Y)	Q + cor.	0.788	0.998
DistilBERT (Y)	Q + all	0.795	1.009
BERT (Y)	Q only	0.809	1.023
BERT (Y)	Q + cor.	0.774	0.981
BERT (Y)	Q + all	0.794	1.005

[3]https://sites.google.com/site/assistmentsdata/home/2012-13-school-data-with-affect

[4]https://sites.google.com/site/assistmentsdata/home/assistments-problems

[5]https://cloudacademy.com/

[6]https://pypi.org/project/pyirt/

[7]https://huggingface.co/transformers

[8]https://www.tensorflow.org/

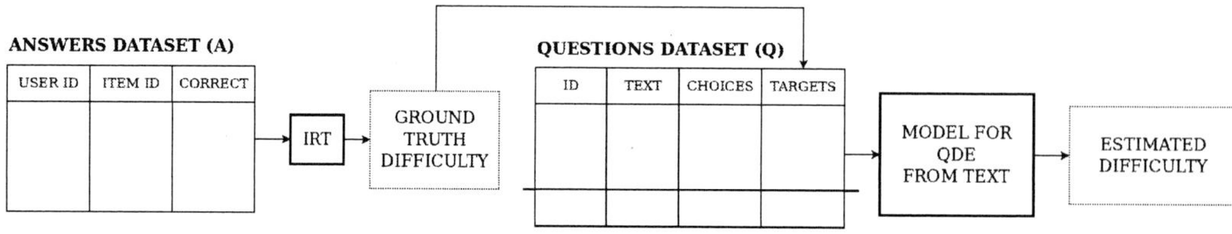

Figure 2: Experimental setup.

able and therefore the only possible input configuration is *Q only*. Even though there is not one model configuration which clearly outperforms all the others, it can be seen that both the additional pre-training and the textual information of the possible choices are helpful in improving the accuracy of the estimation. For DistilBERT without the additional MLM pre-training the best configuration is *Q+all*, while in all the other cases the best input configuration is *Q+correct*.

7.2 Comparison with state of the art

As baselines, we use: i) ZeroR: predicts for all the questions the average difficulty of the training questions. ii) R2DE (Benedetto et al., 2020b): performs difficulty estimation in two steps: the input texts are converted into feature arrays with TF-IDF and then the feature arrays are given as input to a Random Forest regression model, that performs the actual estimation. We implemented R2DE using the available code[9]. iii) ELMo (Xue et al., 2020): we re-implement this model to adapt it to our experimental datasets, and show here the results obtained with all the input configurations (on our dataset, the best performing input configuration is different than the one in the original paper).

Table 2 and Table 3 show the results of the experiments on QDE for *CloudAcademy* and *ASSISTments*, by displaying the MAE and the RMSE obtained on Q_{TEST} by the Transformer models and the chosen baselines (all the possible input configurations are considered for the baselines). For each Transformer model, only one input configuration is shown, as obtained in subsection 7.1. In order to understand how well the models estimate the difficulty of very easy and very challenging questions, we also show the MAE and RMSE measured on the questions whose difficulty b is such that $|b| > 2$ (also referred to as "extreme" questions). The results shown are the mean and the standard deviation of the errors over three independent runs.

Table 2 shows that also R2DE and ELMo are able to leverage the text of the possible choices to improve the accuracy of the estimation; indeed, the best performing input configuration is *Q+all* for R2DE and *Q+correct* for ELMo. The table shows that the Transformer models generally outperform the proposed baselines on both metrics, both with and without the additional pre-training on MLM. The model that consistently and significantly outperforms all the others is BERT with *Q+correct* and the additional MLM pre-training. It is also interesting to remark that ELMo seems to perform estimations a bit biased towards high and low difficulties: indeed, considering overall MAE and RMSE it performs at the same level of R2DE but it is better for the estimation of "extreme" questions. This might also be the reason why ELMo performs better than DistilBERT without MLM on "extreme" questions but worse overall. All models have larger errors on "extreme" questions than on general ones, but the increase is different for each of them: the best performing model has an increase in the MAE of 1.19, which is lower than the other Transformers (from 1.28 to 1.41), ELMo (1.37) and R2DE (1.52). Results are similar for the RMSE: the increase is 1.19 for the best model, between 1.19 and 1.30 for the other Transformers, 1.23 for ELMo (*Q+correct*) and 1.37 for R2DE (*Q+all*).

Table 3 shows results similar to Table 2: BERT is the best performing model and both Transformer models outperform the baselines. However, we can see that the errors are larger than in the previous experiment, thus suggesting that all the models are less capable at estimating the difficulty of the questions in *ASSISTments*. There could be several reasons for this, but we believe that this limitation is mainly due to two aspects: i) the platform allows the creation of question with images (not available to us); ii) the language used in the dataset is "less natural" than in *CloudAcademy* (e.g. many questions are equations with no additional text).

[9] `https://github.com/lucabenedetto/r2de-nlp-to-estimating-irt-parameters`

Table 2: Comparison with the state of the art on *CloudAcademy*.

Model	Input	MLM	MAE	MAE, $\|b\| > 2$	RMSE	RMSE, $\|b\| > 2$
ZeroR	-	-	0.845 $\pm$ 0.000	2.527 $\pm$ 0.000	1.069 $\pm$ 0.000	2.568 $\pm$ 0.000
R2DE	Q only	-	0.826 $\pm$ 0.001	2.397 $\pm$ 0.004	1.051 $\pm$ 0.001	2.468 $\pm$ 0.005
R2DE	Q + cor.	-	0.819 $\pm$ 0.001	2.320 $\pm$ 0.005	1.033 $\pm$ 0.002	2.391 $\pm$ 0.005
R2DE	Q + all	-	0.813 $\pm$ 0.001	2.331 $\pm$ 0.008	1.034 $\pm$ 0.001	2.405 $\pm$ 0.008
ELMo	Q only	-	0.833 $\pm$ 0.002	2.286 $\pm$ 0.032	1.053 $\pm$ 0.002	2.373 $\pm$ 0.025
ELMo	Q + cor.	-	0.831 $\pm$ 0.008	2.184 $\pm$ 0.033	1.048 $\pm$ 0.010	2.276 $\pm$ 0.018
ELMo	Q + all	-	0.839 $\pm$ 0.004	2.213 $\pm$ 0.025	1.057 $\pm$ 0.007	2.308 $\pm$ 0.015
DistilBERT	Q + all	N	0.794 $\pm$ 0.005	2.203 $\pm$ 0.044	1.013 $\pm$ 0.007	2.309 $\pm$ 0.036
BERT	Q + cor.	N	0.789 $\pm$ 0.010	2.118 $\pm$ 0.130	0.999 $\pm$ 0.017	2.222 $\pm$ 0.110
DistilBERT	Q + cor.	Y	0.788 $\pm$ 0.005	2.067 $\pm$ 0.074	0.998 $\pm$ 0.007	2.187 $\pm$ 0.061
BERT	Q + cor.	Y	**0.774** $\pm$ 0.011	**1.962** $\pm$ 0.042	**0.981** $\pm$ 0.015	**2.079** $\pm$ 0.047

Table 3: Comparison with the state of the art on *ASSISTments*.

Model	Input	MLM	MAE	MAE, $\|b\| > 2$	RMSE	RMSE, $\|b\| > 2$
ZeroR	-	-	1.066 $\pm$ 0.000	2.882 $\pm$ 0.000	1.424 $\pm$ 0.000	3.033 $\pm$ 0.000
R2DE	Q only	-	0.966 $\pm$ 0.001	2.408 $\pm$ 0.005	1.304 $\pm$ 0.001	2.700 $\pm$ 0.003
ELMo	Q only	-	0.933 $\pm$ 0.013	2.025 $\pm$ 0.052	1.255 $\pm$ 0.017	2.375 $\pm$ 0.036
DistilBERT	Q only	N	0.919 $\pm$ 0.009	1.864 $\pm$ 0.059	1.239 $\pm$ 0.010	2.259 $\pm$ 0.037
BERT	Q only	N	**0.911** $\pm$ 0.003	**1.849** $\pm$ 0.074	**1.228** $\pm$ 0.003	**2.243** $\pm$ 0.038

7.3 Analysis of the best performing model

We analyze here some of the characteristics of the best performing model (i.e. BERT), trying to understand whether there are some question properties which particularly influence its accuracy. We perform the same analysis for R2DE, to understand whether such characteristics are a peculiarity of BERT or are shared among different models; the choice of R2DE is motivated by the fact that it is the second best performing model on the *CloudAcademy* dataset (excluding the other Transformer models) and it uses TF-IDF to create the features, thus a non-neural approach. We report here the results of three analyses, studying possible differences in the accuracy of QDE depending on i) input length and question difficulty, ii) number of correct choices, and iii) whether it is a cloze question.

First of all, in Figure 3 we show for the two datasets the distribution of questions depending on the input length and the true difficulty; the number of questions in each bin is represented by its color. The two figures show that the distribution is far for uniform and in many areas there are not enough questions to obtain significant results from this analysis. We do not show here the distribution of *CloudAcademy* for the *Q+all* input configuration, which is the one used by R2DE, but it is qualitatively similar to the ones displayed. Considering this distribution, we decided to focus only on some of the questions while analyzing the error depending on the input length and the true difficulty. Specifically, we keep questions i) with $|b| < 3$ and len $<= 110$ for *CloudAcademy* and BERT (96.4% of the questions); ii) with $|b| < 3$ and len $<= 110$ for *CloudAcademy* and R2DE (96.9%); iii) with $|b| < 4$ and len $<= 80$ for *ASSISTments* (94.3%), there is no difference between BERT and R2DE because they use the same input configuration.

Figure 4 shows how the estimation error (represented by the color) of BERT and R2DE depends on the input length and the target difficulty of the questions. The error heavily depends on the target difficulty: this suggests that the two models tend to estimate difficulties closer to 0 than the target values (especially R2DE). Indeed, we have observed that both the target difficulties and the estimated difficulties follow a Gaussian distribution, with higher variance for the target difficulties. There is no clear correlation between error and input length, but in some cases it seems that the error increases with the input length (e.g. row $b = -1$ in BERT). Figure 5 shows the same analysis as Figure 4 for *ASSIST-*

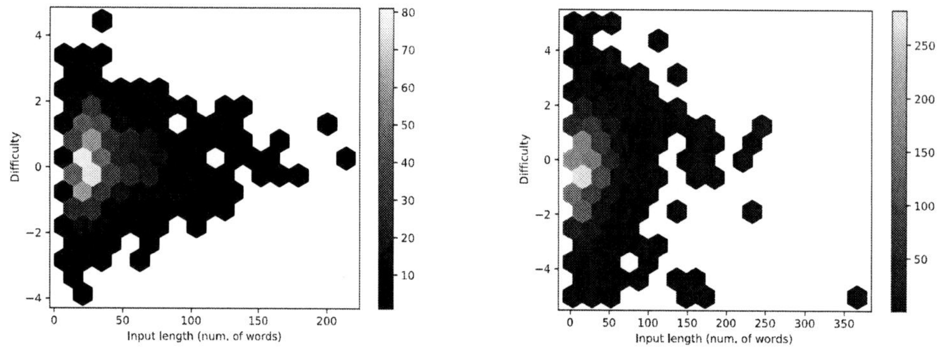

(a) *CloudAcademy*, *Q+correct* configuration.

(b) *ASSISTments*.

Figure 3: Distribution of questions per input length and difficulty.

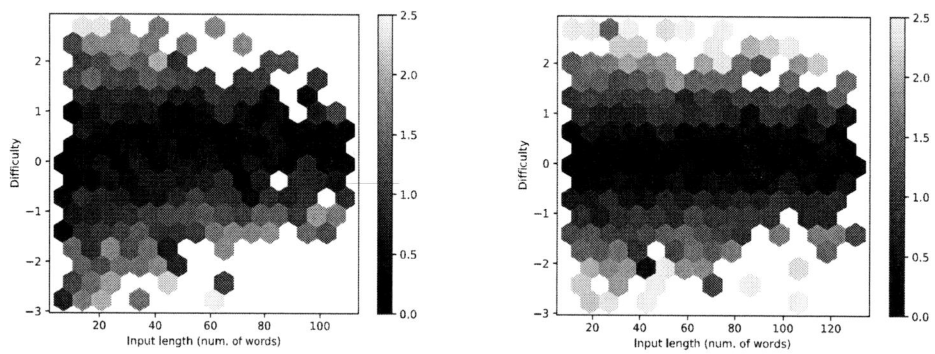

(a) BERT.

(b) R2DE.

Figure 4: *CloudAcademy*, estimation error depending on input length and target difficulty.

ments. The findings are very similar, but it is even more evident the fact that R2DE tends to perform predictions close to 0; the error of BERT depends less heavily on the difficulty. Again, there are no clear correlations between the input length and the accuracy of the estimation.

In *CloudAcademy*, there are i) *cloze* questions, in which the correct choice goes in place of an underscore in the text, and ii) questions with a question mark at the end. Of the 1259 test questions, 222 are cloze questions. From the average errors for the different types of questions, we observed that both BERT and R2DE perform slightly worse on cloze questions: BERT's MAE is 0.804 on cloze questions and 0.756 on the other questions; similarly, R2DE's MAE is 0.893 on cloze questions and 0.794 on the other questions.

Lastly, we looked at the average error depending on the number of correct choices: we compared questions with multiple correct choices (there are 141 of them in the test set) and the questions with one correct choice. For BERT, the overall MAE is 0.774 and on the questions with multiple correct choices it is 0.764; in the case of R2DE, the MAE is 0.813 overall and 0.750 for questions with multiple correct choices. This difference between the two models might be due to the nature of R2DE itself: indeed, it uses a bag of words approach thus it does not care about the position of each word. Instead, BERT uses contextual embeddings which depend on the position of each word and the encoding of multiple correct choices we performed (i.e. concatenation) might not be the better choice, especially considering that probably there are not enough questions to learn the encoding.

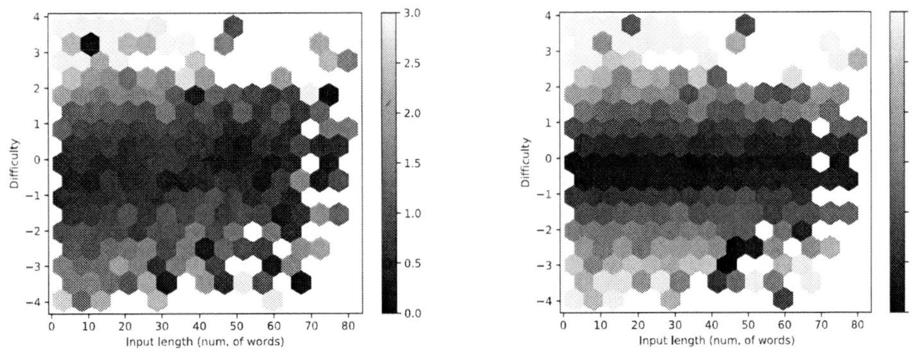

(a) BERT. (b) R2DE.

Figure 5: *ASSISTments*, estimation error depending on input length and target difficulty.

8 Conclusions

In this paper we have performed a study of how Transformer models perform in the task of QDE from text, and have proposed a model which outperforms previous approaches. Specifically, the proposed model is built upon a pre-trained BERT language model, which is fine-tuned for the task of QDE from text. Previous approaches either require an additional dataset of documents about the same topics assessed by the questions or cannot leverage such information; differently from them the proposed model is capable of outperforming state of the art approaches being trained only on the text of the questions, and can be further improved if such additional dataset is available. As an outcome from our analysis, we can say that: i) if an additional dataset is available, BERT with MLM pre-training seems to be the best performing model; ii) if the only available data is the text of the questions, DistilBERT might be a better option, as it has basically the same performance as BERT but at a fraction of the computational cost. Furthermore, we studied the effect of some questions characteristics on BERT and R2DE, comparing the two models. We have observed that the magnitude of the error naturally increases with the magnitude of the difficulty (especially for R2DE), but there is not a clear correlation between the input length and the accuracy of the estimation. We have also observed that both models are less accurate in estimating the difficulty of cloze questions, compared to questions that end with a question mark, and that the decrease in accuracy is lower for BERT. We believe that this happens because underscores are not frequent in natural language and thus the model has a chance of learning them only during the fine-tuning on QDE, not during MLM pre-training. This is probably not enough data for learning (from scratch) the meaning of underscores in exam questions. Lastly, BERT performs better on questions with only one correct choice than on questions with multiple correct choices (for the latter, it is also outperformed by R2DE). This might be due to the encoding we used for multiple correct choices, and it is worth exploring in future research. Future works could continue to dig deeper into the analysis of the model, as we believe that the accuracy of the estimation could be further improved by using an ensemble model in which different sub-models are used depending on some characteristic of the question under calibration. Also, future works will try to explore the attention layers of the proposed model, as it might provide useful information about the reasons why the model works better on some questions.

References

Tahani Alsubait, Bijan Parsia, and Ulrike Sattler. 2013. A similarity-based theory of controlling mcq difficulty. In *2013 second international conference on e-learning and e-technologies in education (ICEEE)*, pages 283–288. IEEE.

Luca Benedetto, Andrea Cappelli, Roberto Turrin, and Paolo Cremonesi. 2020a. Introducing a framework to assess newly created questions with natural language processing. In *International Conference on Artificial Intelligence in Education*, pages 43–54. Springer.

Luca Benedetto, Andrea Cappelli, Roberto Turrin, and Paolo Cremonesi. 2020b. R2de: a nlp approach to estimating irt parameters of newly generated questions. In *Proceedings of the Tenth International Conference on Learning Analytics & Knowledge*, pages 412–421.

Jacob Devlin, Ming-Wei Chang, Kenton Lee, and Kristina Toutanova. 2019. Bert: Pre-training of deep bidirectional transformers for language understanding. In *Proceedings of the 2019 Conference of the North American Chapter of the Association for Computational Linguistics: Human Language Technologies, Volume 1 (Long and Short Papers)*, pages 4171–4186.

Yasmine H El Masri, Steve Ferrara, Peter W Foltz, and Jo-Anne Baird. 2017. Predicting item difficulty of science national curriculum tests: the case of key stage 2 assessments. *The Curriculum Journal*, 28(1):59–82.

Mingyu Feng, Neil Heffernan, and Kenneth Koedinger. 2009. Addressing the assessment challenge with an online system that tutors as it assesses. volume 19, pages 243–266. Springer.

Ronald K Hambleton, Hariharan Swaminathan, and H Jane Rogers. 1991. *Fundamentals of item response theory*. Sage.

Marian Hickendorff. 2013. The language factor in elementary mathematics assessments: Computational skills and applied problem solving in a multidimensional irt framework. *Applied Measurement in Education*, 26(4):253–278.

Geoffrey Hinton, Oriol Vinyals, and Jeff Dean. 2015. Distilling the knowledge in a neural network. *arXiv preprint arXiv:1503.02531*.

Zhenya Huang, Qi Liu, Enhong Chen, Hongke Zhao, Mingyong Gao, Si Wei, Yu Su, and Guoping Hu. 2017. Question difficulty prediction for reading problems in standard tests. In *Thirty-First AAAI Conference on Artificial Intelligence*.

Ghader Kurdi, Bijan Parsia, and Uli Sattler. 2016. An experimental evaluation of automatically generated multiple choice questions from ontologies. In *OWL: Experiences And directions–reasoner evaluation*, pages 24–39. Springer.

Matthew E Peters, Mark Neumann, Mohit Iyyer, Matt Gardner, Christopher Clark, Kenton Lee, and Luke Zettlemoyer. 2018. Deep contextualized word representations. In *Proceedings of NAACL-HLT*, pages 2227–2237.

Zhaopeng Qiu, Xian Wu, and Wei Fan. 2019. Question difficulty prediction for multiple choice problems in medical exams. In *Proceedings of the 28th ACM International Conference on Information and Knowledge Management*, pages 139–148. ACM.

Georg Rasch. 1960. *Probabilistic models for some intelligence and attainment tests*. Danish Institute for Educational Research.

Victor Sanh, Lysandre Debut, Julien Chaumond, and Thomas Wolf. 2019. Distilbert, a distilled version of bert: smaller, faster, cheaper and lighter. *arXiv preprint arXiv:1910.01108*.

Ashish Vaswani, Noam Shazeer, Niki Parmar, Jakob Uszkoreit, Llion Jones, Aidan N Gomez, Łukasz Kaiser, and Illia Polosukhin. 2017. Attention is all you need. In *Advances in neural information processing systems*, pages 5998–6008.

Quan Wang, Jing Liu, Bin Wang, and Li Guo. 2014. A regularized competition model for question difficulty estimation in community question answering services. In *Proceedings of the 2014 Conference on Empirical Methods in Natural Language Processing (EMNLP)*, pages 1115–1126.

Kang Xue, Victoria Yaneva, Christopher Runyon, and Peter Baldwin. 2020. Predicting the difficulty and response time of multiple choice questions using transfer learning. In *Proceedings of the Fifteenth Workshop on Innovative Use of NLP for Building Educational Applications*, pages 193–197.

Victoria Yaneva, Peter Baldwin, Janet Mee, et al. 2019. Predicting the difficulty of multiple choice questions in a high-stakes medical exam. In *Proceedings of the Fourteenth Workshop on Innovative Use of NLP for Building Educational Applications*, pages 11–20.

Victoria Yaneva et al. 2018. Automatic distractor suggestion for multiple-choice tests using concept embeddings and information retrieval. In *Proceedings of the thirteenth workshop on innovative use of NLP for building educational applications*, pages 389–398.

A Introduction to IRT

We model question difficulty as defined in the one-parameter IRT model (also named Rasch model (Rasch, 1960)), which associates a skill level θ to each student and a difficulty level b to each question. For a given question j, its latent trait b_j define the item response function (i.r.f.), which indicates the probability ($\mathrm{P_C}$) that a student i with skill level θ_i correctly answers the question. The formula of the i.r.f. is as follows:

$$\mathrm{P_C} = \frac{1}{1 + e^{-1.7 \cdot (\theta_i - b_j)}} \tag{1}$$

According to the intuition, a student with a given skill θ_i has a lower probability of correctly answering more difficult questions. Also, if a question is too difficult or too easy (i.e. $b_j \to \infty$ or $b_j \to -\infty$), all the students will answer in the same way (i.e. $\mathrm{P_C} \to 0$ or $\mathrm{P_C} \to 1$) regardless of θ_i. Given some students' answers to a set of questions, with IRT it is possible to estimate both the

Table 4: Example questions from *ASSISTments*.

ID	Question	Type
330	*The computer game Peter wants to buy will cost at least \$50 and not more than \$70. He earns \$3 an hour running errands for his grandmother. Which inequality shows the number of hours, n, he will have to work to pay for the game?*	Original
326	*What is the minimum cost of the game?*	Scaffolding
327	*What is the maximum cost of the game?*	Scaffolding
328	*Write an expression that represents the amount of money Peter earns in n hours.*	Scaffolding
329	*Which inequality shows the number of hours, n, Peter will have to work to pay for the game?*	Scaffolding

Table 5: Example question from *CloudAcademy*.

Role	Text
Question	*A user has launched an EBS backed EC2 instance in the US-East-1 region. The user wants to implement a disaster recovery (DR) plan for that instance by creating another instance in a European region. How can the user accomplish this?*
Correct choice	*Create an AMI of the instance and copy the AMI to the EU region. Then launch the instance from the EU AMI.*
Distractor	*Use the "Launch more like this" option to copy the instance from one region to another.*
Distractor	*Copy the instance from the US East region to the EU region.*
Distractor	*Copy the running instance using the "Instance Copy" command to the EU region.*

skill levels of the students and the difficulty of the questions via likelihood maximization, by selecting the configuration (i.e.the θs and bs) that maximizes the probability of the observed results. Also, it is possible to assess the knowledge level $\tilde{\theta}_i$ of a student i from the correctness of its answers to a set of calibrated assessment items $Q = q_1, q_2, ..., q_{N_q}$. This is done by maximizing the results of the multiplication between the i.r.f. of the questions that were answered correctly and the complementary (i.e. $1 - P_C$) of the i.r.f. of the questions that were answered erroneously.

B Example questions

An example problem from *ASSISTments* and the corresponding scaffolding questions are shown in Table 4.

An example question from *CloudAcademy*, with its correct answer and distractors, is given in Table 5.

C Hyperparameters

For fine-tuning on QDE from text we select the hyperparameters from the following pool of candidates:

- *batch size = 16, 32, 64*;
- *learning rate = 1e-5, 2e-5, 3-5*;
- *patience early stopping = 10 epochs*;
- *dropout additional layer = 0.1, 0.2, 0.3, 0.4, 0.5*;
- *internal dropout = 0.1, 0.2, 0.3, 0.4, 0.5.*

For the additional pre-training on MLM, the hyperparameters are selected between the following candidates:

- *batch size = 64*;
- *learning rate = 1e-5*;
- *number of epochs = 4, 12, 24, 36*;
- *dropout = 0.1.*

In both cases we use *sequence length = 256* and the *Adam* optimizer.

Automatically Generating Cause-and-Effect Questions from Passages

Katherine Stasaski, Manav Rathod, Tony Tu, Yunfang Xiao, Marti A. Hearst
UC Berkeley
{katie_stasaski, manav.rathod, tonytu16,
emily.xiao, hearst}@berkeley.edu

Abstract

Automated question generation has the potential to greatly aid in education applications, such as online study aids to check understanding of readings. The state-of-the-art in neural question generation has advanced greatly, due in part to the availability of large datasets of question-answer pairs. However, the questions generated are often surface-level and not challenging for a human to answer. To develop more challenging questions, we propose the novel task of cause-and-effect question generation. We build a pipeline that extracts causal relations from passages of input text, and feeds these as input to a state-of-the-art neural question generator. The extractor is based on prior work that classifies causal relations by linguistic category (Cao et al., 2016; Altenberg, 1984). This work results in a new, publicly available collection of cause-and-effect questions. We evaluate via both automatic and manual metrics and find performance improves for both question generation and question answering when we utilize a small auxiliary data source of cause-and-effect questions for fine-tuning. Our approach can be easily applied to generate cause-and-effect questions from other text collections and educational material, allowing for adaptable large-scale generation of cause-and-effect questions.

Original Passage	Injuries can also be prevented by proper rest and recovery. If you do not get enough rest, your body will become injured and will not react well to exercise, or improve. You can also rest by doing a different activity.
Extracted Cause	you do not get enough rest
Extracted Effect	your body will become injured and will not react well to exercise, or improve
Generated Cause Q	why will your body become injured and not react well to exercise?
Generated Effect Q	what happens if you don't get enough rest?

Table 1: Example passage (taken from the TQA dataset), extracted cause/effect, and generated questions. The Extracted Cause is the intended answer for the Generated Cause Question; similarly for Effect.

1 Introduction

Automated question generation (QG) can have a large educational impact since questions can be generated to check learners' comprehension and understanding of textbooks or other reading materials (Thalheimer, 2003; Kurdi et al., 2020). A high-quality QG system could reduce the costly human effort required to generate questions as well as free up teachers' time to focus on other instructional activities (Kurdi et al., 2020). Furthermore, a robust QG system could also expand the variety of educational material used for formative assessment, allowing students more opportunities to cement their understanding of concepts.

To be truly effective, automated question generation for education must have the ability to ask questions for students at different levels of development. A frequently used measure of question difficulty is Bloom's taxonomy (Bloom et al., 1956; Anderson et al., 2001), which defines a framework of how to assess types of questions across different levels of mastery, progressing from simplest to most complex. Factual questions, which involve recalling information, fall on the lowest level (Recall) (Beatty Jr, 1975; Anderson et al., 2001). By contrast, cause and effect questions are categorized at level 6 – Analysis – according to the original Bloom's taxonomy (Beatty Jr, 1975) or level 2 –

Proceedings of the 16th Workshop on Innovative Use of NLP for Building Educational Applications, pages 158–170
April 20, 2021 ©2021 Association for Computational Linguistics

Understanding – in the commonly used revised model (Anderson et al., 2001).

The rise of large question answering datasets, such as SQuAD (Rajpurkar et al., 2016), NewsQA (Trischler et al., 2017), and HotPotQA (Yang et al., 2018), have created the ability to train well-performing neural QG systems. However, due to the nature of their training data, current question generation systems mainly generate factual questions characteristic of Bloom's level 1.

Questions which test knowledge of a causal relation can assess a deeper level of mastery beyond surface-level factual questions. Altenberg (1984) states that "[a] causal relation can be said to exist between two events or states of affairs if one is understood as the cause of or reason for the other." We aim to generate cause-and-effect questions, which test knowledge of the relationship between these two events or states. An example of our generated questions along with corresponding input, cause, and effect can be seen in Table 1.

To address this task, we propose a novel pipeline to generate and evaluate cause-and-effect questions directly from text. We improve upon a pre-existing causal extraction system (Cao et al., 2016), which uses a series of syntactic rules to extract causes and effects from unstructured text. We utilize the resulting *cause* and *effect* as *intended answers* for a neural question generation system. For each cause and effect, we generate one question, to test each direction of the causal relationship.

Our work sets the stage for *scalable* generation of cause-and-effect questions because it automatically generates causal questions and answers from freeform text. In this paper, we evaluate our approach on two English datasets: SQuAD Wikipedia articles (Rajpurkar et al., 2018) and middle school science textbooks in the Textbook Question Answering (TQA) dataset (Kembhavi et al., 2017).

Our research contributions include:

- A novel cause-and-effect question generation pipeline, including an improved causal extraction system based on a linguistic typology (Cao et al., 2016; Altenberg, 1984),
- An evaluation framework, accompanied by preliminary experimental results showing that fine-tuning on a small, auxiliary dataset of cause-and-effect questions substantially improves both question generation and question answering models,
- A novel collection of 8,808 cause-and-effect questions, with open source code to apply the pipeline to other text collections, allowing for future work to examine the educational impact of automatically-generated cause-and-effect questions.[1]

2 Related Work

In this section, we discuss past work in causal extraction, question answering, question generation, and applications of generated questions.

2.1 Causal Extraction

Causal extraction systems aim to identify whether a causal relation is expressed in text and to identify the cause and effect if so. However, the use of neural techniques in causal extraction is sparse and thus most of the work is still tied to a focus on extracting relations based on specific linguistic features (Asghar, 2016). We utilize Cao et al. (2016), which is aimed at extracting causal relations from academic papers via a series of structured syntactic patterns tied to a linguistic typology (Altenberg, 1984).

Causal relation extraction has been applied to inform question answering models (Girju, 2003; Breja and Jain, 2020). Some work has used neural networks to generate explanations from open-domain "why" questions without using external knowledge sources (Nie et al., 2019).

2.2 Question Answering

Neural question answering (QA) is a widely-explored area with many large datasets of crowdworker-created questions. SQuAD (Rajpurkar et al., 2016) and NewsQA (Trischler et al., 2017) each include over 100,000 crowdworker-created questions from Wikipedia and CNN articles, respectively. NarrativeQA includes questions aimed at larger narrative events, which require reading an entire novel or movie script in order to answer (Kočiský et al., 2018). However, cause-and-effect questions are infrequent ("why" questions compose 9.78% of the dataset), and questions are paired with long documents.

HotPotQA includes over 100,000 questions spanning multiple passages, where questions require combining multiple facts in order to correctly answer the question (Yang et al., 2018). However, HotPotQA is still primarily a factual recall task. For instance, our inspection of the dataset finds

[1] https://github.com/kstats/CausalQG

that 30% of the questions expect a Person entity as an answer. The three most common question types are "what," "which," and "who," which suggest a factual, information lookup style answer. While HotPotQA questions are potentially more difficult for machines to answer than questions from other QA datasets, the resulting questions are overwhelmingly factual and include entities as the intended answer.

Question answering approaches trained on these datasets include gated attention-based methods (Wang et al., 2017b) as well as transformer-based methods (Yang et al., 2019; Lan et al., 2020). Models which augment QA data with automatically-generated questions have also been explored (Duan et al., 2017).

2.3 Question Generation

Past work has utilized purely syntactic cues to generate questions (Heilman and Smith, 2010). However, these systems rely on rules which may be brittle. More recent work has combined a syntactic question generator with backtranslation, to improve robustness and reduce grammatical errors of generated questions (Dhole and Manning, 2020). While Syn-QG is able to reliably generate types of causal questions using two specific patterns, the system is limited in diversity of question wording by syntactic rules.

Question answering datasets have been used to train neural models to generate questions directly from input text. Question generation approaches include specialized attention mechanisms (Zhao et al., 2018) as well as generating via large transformer models (Qi et al., 2020; Chan and Fan, 2019). Jointly training QA and QG models have also been explored (Wang et al., 2017a). Past work has also trained neural QG systems on questions generated via a rule-based system (De Kuthy et al., 2020).

2.4 Question Generation Applications

Past work has explored educational applications of question generation (Kurdi et al., 2020). QG-Net utilizes a pointer-generator model trained on SQuAD to automatically generate questions from textbooks (Wang et al., 2018). Additional work has aimed at generating educational questions from a structured ontology (Stasaski and Hearst, 2017). QuizBot exposes students to questions via a dialogue interface, where pre-set questions are chosen in an intelligent order (Ruan et al., 2019).

3 Cause-and-Effect Question Generation Pipeline

We propose a novel pipeline which combines a causal extractor with a neural question generation system to produce cause-and-effect questions. The entire pipeline can be seen in Figure 1.

3.1 Datasets

Our pipeline can take in freeform text and automatically extract a cause and effect to generate questions. We feed passages from the SQuAD 2.0 development set (Rajpurkar et al., 2018) and the Textbook Question Answering (Kembhavi et al., 2017) datasets into our causal extraction pipeline for evaluation experiments.

SQuAD 2.0 consists of over 100,000 questions from over 500 Wikipedia articles. This dataset is standard to train both QA and QG systems; we do not use the question portion of this dataset because it consists primarily of straightforward factual questions. A heuristic to determine the proportion of cause-and-effect questions in SQuAD is the number of questions in the dataset which begin with "why." While this does not capture all possible ways of expressing causality, this can serve as a signal for the prevalence of cause-and-effect questions in each dataset. In SQuAD, only 1.3% of questions begin with "why," indicating cause-and-effect questions are not a significant component of this dataset. A more extensive analysis which examines hand-labeled question n-grams finds similar results (Appendix A).

TQA consists of 26,260 questions from Life Science, Earth Science and Physical Science textbooks. We choose this dataset because it contains educational textbook text, which often express causal relationships; however, we do not use the TQA questions since many are tied to an entire lesson in the textbook and include visual diagrams.

3.2 Causal Extraction

We use and improve a pre-existing causal extractor to identify cause and effect pairs in unstructured input text, see Causal Extractor in Figure 1 (Cao et al., 2016).[2] The system achieves approximately 0.85 recall of hand-labeled cause-and-effect relationships over 3 academic articles, as reported in Cao et al. (2016). The extractor relies on a series of hand-crafted patterns based on syntax cues and

[2] `https://github.com/Angela7126/CE_extractor--Patterns_Based`

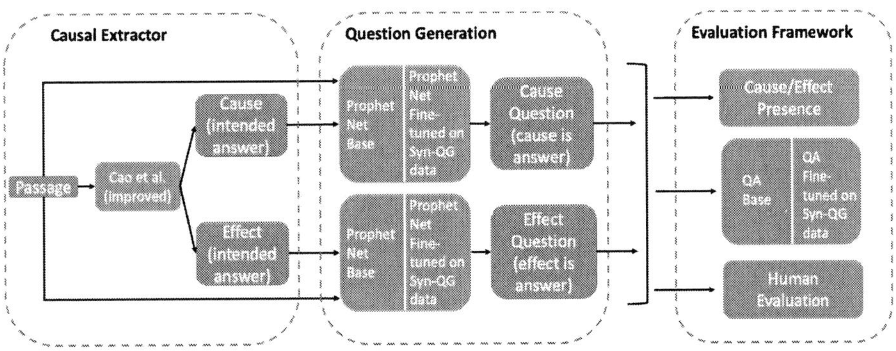

Figure 1: Causal extraction and question generation pipeline. Input passage is passed to the causal extractor, which identifies a cause and effect. The cause and effect are each passed into the Question Generator as intended answers, to generate a resulting question. Questions are evaluated using automatic and human metrics. Example passages and questions can be seen in in Table 1.

part-of-speech tags. An example pattern, where & indicates a class of tokens defined by Cao et al. (2016), $\&C$ is the cause, $\&R$ is the effect, and optional arguments are shown in parentheses is:

&C (,/;/./–) (&AND) as a (&ADJ) result (,) &R

A match to this pattern from the TQA dataset (**cause bolded**, *effect italicized*, and other matched terms underlined) is:

> **Unsaturated fatty acids have at least one double bond between carbon atoms**. As a result, *some carbon atoms are not bonded to as many hydrogen atoms as possible*. They are unsaturated with hydrogens.

We pass 2 or 3 sentence passages into the causal extractor, since a cause and effect may span across adjacent sentences. We always try to select a 3-sentence passage, but when a paragraph boundary would be crossed, we reduce to 2-sentence passage. We use a sliding 3-sentence window to examine all possible sentence combinations. Multiple causal relationships may be found in a single passage; the sliding window captures the multiple relationships across different passages.

3.2.1 Adjustments to Cao et al.'s Extractor

After an examination of 160 extracted causal relationships from SQuAD and TQA, we implement targeted modifications to improve the quality of extracted causal relationships. We omit causal relationships which include direct reference to a figure in a textbook or are part of a question. We additionally find that ambiguous causal linking phrases ("as," "so," and "since") are prevalent but have lower accuracy than more direct phrases ("because"). Thus, we filter out "as," "so," and "since" patterns where "as," "so," or "since" is not labeled as a conjunction or subordinate conjunction by the part-of-speech tagger. Further details are described in Appendix B. This modification reduces the total number of extracted relations from 3,976 to 3,359 for TQA and from 1,105 to 1,045 for SQuAD. Evaluation of these changes appears in Section 4.

3.2.2 Causal Link Typology

One motivation for choosing the Cao et al. system is that each pattern is tied to a typology of causal links (Altenberg, 1984). The typology contains 4 main categories, based on the causal link which is utilized to express the causal relationship: Adverbial ("so", "hence", "therefore"), Prepositional ("because of", "on account of"), Subordination ("because", "as", "since"), and Clause-integrated linkage ("that's why", "the result was"). Examples of causal relations extracted using each part of the typology, using the TQA dataset, can be seen in Table 2. By incorporating these patterns in our evaluation framework, we can examine potential gaps in model performance that might be tied to syntactic cues, allowing for the design of improved models.

3.3 Cause-and-Effect Question Generation

After extracting causes and effects from input text, we use each as an intended answer for a neural question generation system (see Question Generation in Figure 1). This results in two output questions

Type	Example
Adverbial	**Different energy levels in the cloud have different numbers of orbitals**. Therefore, *different energy levels have different maximum numbers of electrons*. Table 5.1 lists the number of orbitals and electrons for the first four energy levels.
Prepositional	The function of these scales is for protection against predators. *The shape of sharks teeth differ* according to **their diet**. Species that feed on mollusks and crustaceans have dense flattened teeth for crushing, those that feed on fish have needle-like teeth for gripping, and those that feed on larger prey, such as mammals, have pointed lower teeth for gripping and triangular upper teeth with serrated edges for cutting.
Subordination	The spoon particles started moving faster and became warmer, causing the temperature of the spoon to rise. Because **the coffee particles lost some of their kinetic energy to the spoon particles**, *the coffee particles started to move more slowly*. This caused the temperature of the coffee to fall.
Clause-Integration	**The stars outer layers spread out and cool**. The result is *a larger star that is cooler on the surface, and red in color*. Eventually a red giant burns up all of the helium in its core.

Table 2: Examples of causal relationships from different typology categories (Altenberg, 1984), from the TQA dataset, with causes bolded, effects italicized, and causal link words underlined.

for each causal relationship (one corresponding to cause, and one to effect). We use ProphetNet, a state-of-the-art question generation model, to generate these questions (Qi et al., 2020).[3] The novelty of ProphetNet is its ability to generate text by predicting the next n-gram instead of just the next token, which helps to prevent overfitting on strong local correlations. ProphetNet is fine-tuned for question generation using SQuAD 1.1 (Rajpurkar et al., 2016). Models specifications are described in Section 5, and model evaluation is described in Sections 6 and 7.

4 Evaluating Extracted Causal Relations

In order to ensure the extracted causes and effects are suitable to generate questions from, we evaluated the original Cao et al. (2016) and our improved causal extractor for accuracy via a crowdworking task. Workers evaluated if an extracted cause and effect were causal or not, judged from a passage with the extracted cause and effect highlighted (see Appendix C).

We utilized Amazon Mechanical Turk to recruit crowdworkers for data labeling. We required crowdworkers to have a 98% HIT approval rating, have completed at least 5,000 past HITs, and be located in the United States. We estimated the task would require no more than 10 minutes to complete; therefore, we paid $1.66, equivalent to $10 per hour. We asked crowdworkers to provide a one-sentence explanation for their classification decision for the first and last item in the HIT, which we manually checked to ensure quality. To increase confidence in the labels and to tiebreak disagreements, we acquired 5 labels for every passage.

[3] https://github.com/microsoft/ProphetNet

Type	TQA	SQuAD
Adverbial	87.1%	84.6%
Prepositional	92.3%	72.7%
Subordination	77.1%	75.7%
Clause-Int	83.3%	86.7%

Table 3: Percent of extractions labeled as causal by crowdworkers, for samples of 100 each from TQA and SQuAD datasets, by linguistic category, for our improved sytsem.

We sampled 100 passages from TQA and 100 from SQuAD for both the original causal extraction system and our improved system. We used proportionate stratified sampling where the size of sample typology group is proportional to the size of population typology group, while also ensuring that all typology groups are represented in the sample.

After tiebreaking using majority vote, for the original Cao et al. (2016) causal extraction system we find an overall 70% of TQA and 68% of SQuAD are rated as causal. In comparison, for our improved system, we find an overall 83% of TQA and 79% of SQuAD are rated as causal. Results segmented by typology for our improved system can be seen in Table 3 (results for the original Cao et al. (2016) system can be seen in Appendix C). While the accuracies are higher for TQA than SQuAD, all accuracies range from 72 to 92%. This provides evidence that the extractor is able to reliably identify causes and effects, which we can utilize as intended answers for the downstream question generation system.

Fleiss's kappa (Fleiss et al., 1971) however, is only slight to fair for this evaluation (0.21 for base extractor and 0.10 for our improved extractor). This could be due to a high prior probability of an extracted cause and effect being causal (62% of questions have 4 or 5 annotators in agreement) (Falotico and Quatto, 2015). However, future work should additionally investigate alternatives to this task to achieve higher agreement. Overall, the high accuracy of our improved extractor provides evidence that we can reliably extract a cause and effect to pass into a question generation system.

5 QG and QA Models

This section describes the design of both the question generation (QG) and question answering (QA) models, which occur in the Question Generation and Evaluation Framework components of Figure 1, respectively. We describe them together because they share an auxiliary data source. The QG models are evaluated in Sections 6 (automated) and 7 (manual).

To generate cause-and-effect questions where the intended answers are the causes and effects from our improved extractor, we train and evaluate two question generation models based on ProphetNet. We also make use of question answering models to assess the quality of the generated questions. We choose a transformer-based QA model from the Huggingface Transformers library (Wolf et al., 2020) which is BERT-large fine-tuned on SQuAD 2.0 with whole-word masking.[4] F1 performance for this model on the original SQuAD 2.0 test set is 0.93.

For both QA and QG, we utilize an additional data source for fine-tuning, to examine the effect of augmenting the models with additional cause-and-effect question data. We use a syntactic question generation system combined with backtranslation, Syn-QG[5] (Dhole and Manning, 2020), to generate questions and answers for fine-tuning. We limit Syn-QG to two patterns, Purpose (PNC and PRP) and Cause (CAU), which generate cause-and-effect questions. We input three-sentence passages which our system has identified as including a cause and effect to Syn-QG, resulting in 2,082 questions from TQA and 1,753 from SQuAD. While the wording and syntactic structure of Syn-QG questions lack diversity, we hypothesize that ProphetNet will benefit from fine-tuning on a set of cause-and-effect questions as this question type was not well-represented in the SQuAD training set.

Additionally, while Syn-QG uses its own syntactic patterns to generate cause-and-effect questions directly from text, we observe their system is not able to cover all causal relationships included in Cao et al. (2016). From randomly-sampled passages which our improved extractor has identified as including a cause and effect, Syn-QG is able to generate cause-and-effect questions for 309 out of 500 passages for SQuAD and 233 out of 500 passages for TQA.

We compare two models for QG and QA experiments in Sections 6 and 7: Base (with no fine-tuning) and Syn-QG fine-tuned to explore the effect of fine-tuning QG and QA models on a small auxiliary dataset of cause-and-effect questions. For all experiments, we split the Syn-QG auxiliary dataset into 80% training and 20% test data. The QG models' resulting questions are fed as input into the QA models (see Figure 1). Additional model specifications are in Appendix D. Table 4 contains generated questions for each typology category for both the base and the Syn-QG fine-tuned QG models.

6 Automated Evaluation of Generated Questions

As part of our Evaluation Framework, we develop two automated metrics to evaluate the generated cause-and-effect questions: (i) cause/effect presence, which measures whether the cause or effect is present in the question, and (ii) QA system performance, which measures whether a question answering system can answer the generated question.

6.1 Cause/Effect Presence

Because causal relationships contain both a cause and an effect, we assume that a question which assesses understanding of this relationship would include a direct mention of one of the two. For instance, a question which has the cause as the

[4] https://huggingface.co/deepset/bert-large-uncased-whole-word-masking-squad2

[5] https://bitbucket.org/kaustubhdhole/syn-qg

Category	Passage	ProphetNet Base		ProphetNet Syn-QG	
		Cause Question	Effect Question	Cause Question	Effect Question
Adv	Myopia is corrected with a concave lens, which curves inward like the inside of a bowl. **The lens changes the focus**, so *images fall on the retina as they should*. Generally, nearsightedness first occurs in school-age children.	what causes images to fall on the retina as they should?	what happens when the concave lens changes the focus?	why do images fall on the retina as they should?	why does the lens change the focus?
Prep	Their activity at night. *An elongated, toothed snout used* for **slashing the fish that they eat**, as seen in sawsharks. Teeth used for grasping and crushing shellfish, a characteristic of bullhead sharks.	what is the snout used for?	what is used for slashing the fish that they eat?	for what purpose is an elongated, toothed snout used?	what is used for slashing the fish that they eat?
Sub	The droplets gather in clouds, which are blown about the globe by wind. As **the water droplets in the clouds collide and grow**, *they fall from the sky as precipitation*. Precipitation can be rain, sleet, hail, or snow.	how do droplets fall from the sky as precipitation?	what happens when water droplets in the clouds collide and grow?	why do they fall from the sky as precipitation?	what happens as the water droplets in the clouds collide and grow?
C-I	**Some mixtures are heterogeneous**. This means *they* vary in their composition. An example is trail mix.	what means some mixtures vary in their composition?	some mixtures are heterogeneous in what way?	why do some mixtures vary in their composition?	some mixtures are heterogeneous in their composition?

Table 4: Randomly sampled generated question from each typology category from TQA, with corresponding base and Syn-QG questions. Passages include causes in **bold** (which are the intended answers for Cause Questions) and effects *italicized* (which are the intended answers for Effect Questions).

intended answer would contain the effect in the question text, and vice versa. Thus, we propose the Cause/Effect Presence metric: for questions where the cause is the intended answer, we measure the recall of the words in the extracted effect present in the question. Likewise, for questions where the effect is the intended answer, we measure the recall of the words in the extracted cause present in the question. Because the question could contain a subset of words expected for the cause/effect, we measure this in terms of recall. Furthermore, a question is necessarily going to have additional words, such as the opening phrase, e.g. "why," which we do not want to penalize. Formally defined:

$$Recall_{cause} = \frac{|Q_e \cap C|}{|C|}$$

$$Recall_{effect} = \frac{|Q_c \cap E|}{|E|}$$

where C is a bag of all words in the cause extracted from the passage, E is a bag of all words in the effect extracted from the passage, Q_e is a bag of all words in the effect question, and Q_c is a bag of all words in the cause question. For words that appear n times in an extracted cause or effect, we give credit for each appearance in the question, up to n times.

Results for Cause/Effect Presence on SQuAD and TQA can be seen in Table 5. Results stratified by typology for the best performimg model (fine-tuned Syn-QG) can be seen in Appendix E.

We note that after fine-tuning ProphetNet on Syn-QG data, performance increases from 0.55 to 0.72 for TQA and 0.37 to 0.56 for SQuAD. This is somewhat expected, as Syn-QG's syntax rules result in questions that are similarly-structured and include the cause or effect. We also note slightly higher scores when an effect is the intended answer. Future work should isolate whether this is due to the model's ability to generate better questions from effects or whether the extractor is better at extracting effects than causes from passages. In Section 7, we explore this further by having humans label the quality of the QG model's output.

6.2 Question Answering System Performance

Following past work on evaluating QG models (Yuan et al., 2017), we measure whether a QA system is able to accurately answer the generated cause-and-effect questions from the passage. If the QG model produces an ill-formed or incorrect ques-

Model	TQA			SQuAD		
	C	E	T	C	E	T
Base	0.52	0.57	0.55	0.32	0.42	0.37
Syn-QG	0.71	0.72	0.72	0.54	0.57	0.56

Table 5: Average cause and effect recall in questions generated by ProphetNet Base and fine-tuned on Syn-QG (out of 1.0, higher is better). C indicates questions where a cause is the intended answer, E indicates questions where the effect is the intended answer, and T indicates the total for both.

QG	QA	Textbook			SQuAD		
		C	E	T	C	E	T
Base	**Base**	0.24	0.18	0.21	0.22	0.15	0.18
	Syn-QG	0.60	0.49	0.54	0.60	0.46	0.53
Syn-QG	**Base**	0.24	0.16	0.20	0.19	0.13	0.16
	Syn-QG	0.57	0.48	0.53	0.58	0.43	0.51

Table 6: F1 results for base and fine-tuned QA on questions generated from base and fine-tuned ProphetNet. C indicates questions where a cause is the intended answer, E indicates questions where the effect is the intended answer, and T indicates the total between both.

tion, the QA model will be less likely to produce the correct answer. The QA model must answer a cause question with an effect, and an effect question with a cause. We report the QA model's F1 performance on the set of cause-and-effect questions in Table 6.

Fine-tuning the QA model with the Syn-QG data provides a large F1 improvement over the base model (0.21 to 0.54 for TQA, 0.18 to 0.53 for SQuAD), showing the benefit of fine-tuning on an auxiliary cause-and-effect dataset. However, the QA models do not perform as well at answering cause-and-effect questions as they do at answering factual ones; we see a 0.4-0.7 drop in F1 values from factual to causal questions. Future work can explore using our dataset to further improve QA performance on cause-and-effect questions.

Results stratified by typology for the best-performing QG and QA pair (both fine-tuned on Syn-QG) can be seen in Table 7. The lowest-performing category for both TQA and SQuAD is Adverbial. However, Adverbial was ranked the second-highest for correct causal links by crowdworkers (in Section 4). It is unexpected that one of the more reliable extraction types resulted in the lowest QA performance. Future work can explore why QA models are not adept at handling this linguistic phrasing and how to improve model performance in this category.

Type	F1	#TQA	F1	#SQuAD
Adv.	0.50	2,868	0.47	510
Prep.	0.57	940	0.56	550
Sub.	0.53	2,546	0.47	870
C-I	0.59	364	0.63	160

Table 7: F1 scores of best QG-QA pair (both fine-tuned on Syn-QG) broken down by typology.

7 Human Evaluation of Generated Questions

While automated metrics are scalable, they may not be as reliable as human evaluation. Thus, we conducted a crowdworker task to evaluate generated questions. To ensure we provide the model with high-quality causal relations, we evaluated questions generated from the extracted relations that were labeled as Causal in Section 4 (83 from TQA and 79 for SQuAD). We performed human evaluation for base ProphetNet, to establish a baseline human-rating of generated questions.

Crowdworkers were presented with a passage (with the intended answer highlighted) and a generated question (see Appendix C). Workers were asked to label (1) if the question is a *causal* question and (2) whether the answer highlighted in the passage correctly answers the question. If a question was too ill-formed or ungrammatical to provide these classifications, crowdworkers were asked to select a checkbox and provide a text justification. The conditions for this task were the same as in Section 4.

Results can be seen in Table 8. These high accuracy ratings (80%-90%) indicate ProphetNet is able to reliably generate questions which are correct for the intended answer and are valid cause-and-effect questions. For both tasks, questions generated from the TQA dataset were higher-ranked than those generated from SQuAD. For the task of determining whether a question was causal, there is not a consistent winner between the set of cause and effect questions. This indicates ProphetNet is consistently better at generating questions for both directions of the cause-and-effect relationship.

For the task of determining whether an intended answer is correct, when the effect is the intended answer, the proportion that are rated as correct is higher than for cause. This is consistent with the higher performance for effect questions on the Cause/Effect Presence metric.

Results stratified by typology can be seen in Table 9. For rating answer correctness, the Preposi-

Condition	% Causal	% Answer
TQA Cause	96%	90%
TQA Effect	98%	93%
TQA Total	**97%**	**92%**
SQuAD Cause	89%	90%
SQuAD Effect	82%	87%
SQuAD Total	**85%**	**89%**
Overall Cause	93%	90%
Overall Effect	90%	90%
Overall Total	**91%**	**90%**

Table 8: Percentage of Base ProphetNet generated questions (n=324) classified by crowdworkers as causal (% Causal) and matching the intended answer (% Answer), by dataset and whether the intended answer was cause or effect. "Total" indicates the combination of cause and effect questions and "Overall" indicates the combination of datasets.

	TQA			SQuAD		
Category	**%C**	**%A**	**Tot**	**%C**	**%A**	**Tot**
Adv.	97%	91%	70	84%	86%	44
Prep.	96%	83%	24	91%	84%	32
Sub.	96%	96%	52	82%	95%	56
C-I	100%	100%	20	85%	85%	26

Table 9: Percentage of crowdworking ratings indicating a cause-and-effect question (% C), a correct answer (% A), and the total number of questions evaluated segmented by typology category.

tional category was the lowest for both datasets, indicating a potential model shortcoming. The Subordination questions from SQuAD were the least causal over all categories.

In 22 cases out of 1,620, a crowdworker indicated that a generated question was too ill-formed to provide a rating. Fleiss's kappa for determining whether a question was causal was 0.07 and for determining whether the answer was correct was 0.14, both slight agreement. However, this is likely due to the high prior probability distribution (Falotico and Quatto, 2015). For 74.1% of questions, 4 or 5 annotators all agreed on the same rating for determining whether a question was causal; likewise, 80.9% of the time 4 or 5 annotators all agreed for determining whether an answer is correct.

Overall, human ratings indicate that 80%-90% of the time, the generated question is both causal and correct for the intended answer.

8 Future Work

Our proposed pipeline is generalizable to a wide range of corpora, allowing for the generation of cause-and-effect questions from other educational texts at-scale. Human evaluation ratings indicate our model can reliably generate questions which are both causal and correct for the intended answer. However, more work needs to be done to generate questions which sound more natural and are less reliant on the wording of the input passage. The types of grammar errors made should also be examined before assessing the educational benefits of the generated questions.

Additionally, our goal in generating cause-and-effect questions was to generate questions which fall higher on Bloom's taxonomy. While our results indicate cause-and-effect questions are more challenging than straightforward factual questions for a QA model, further work should assess the difficulty of these questions in an educational setting.

The complexity of causal relationships can be further explored. We observe instances of overlapping causal relationships extracted from our system, such as the Subordination example in Table 2. This can be leveraged to generate questions which require knowledge of longer logic chains to answer, similar to past work which accomplished this (Stasaski and Hearst, 2017).

Future work can also examine diversifying question wording. By generating multiple questions testing the same causal relationship, students can have multiple opportunities to solidify their knowledge. Our pipeline allows for straightforward experimentation with the question generation model.

9 Conclusion

We propose a new task, cause-and-effect question generation, along with a novel pipeline to utilize extracted causes and effects as intended answers for a question generation system. We provide automatic and manual evaluation metrics and show that fine-tuning QG and QA models on an auxiliary dataset of cause-and-effect questions improves performance. Our publicly-released pipeline can automatically generate cause-and-effect questions for educational resources at scale.

Acknowledgements

This work was supported by an AWS Machine Learning Research Award, an NVIDIA Corporation GPU grant, an AI2 Key Scientific Challenge Proposal grant, and a National Science Foundation (NSF) Graduate Research Fellowship (DGE 1752814). We thank the three anonymous reviewers as well as Nate Weinman, Philippe Laban, Dongyeop Kang, and the Hearst Lab Research Group for their helpful comments.

References

Bengt Altenberg. 1984. Causal linking in spoken and written english. *Studia Linguistica*, 38(1):20–69.

Lorin W Anderson, Benjamin Samuel Bloom, et al. 2001. *A taxonomy for learning, teaching, and assessing: A revision of Bloom's taxonomy of educational objectives*. Longman,.

Nabiha Asghar. 2016. Automatic extraction of causal relations from natural language texts: a comprehensive survey. *arXiv preprint arXiv:1605.07895*.

Ross Beatty Jr. 1975. Reading comprehension skills and bloom's taxonomy. *Literacy Research and Instruction*, 15(2):101–108.

Benjamin S. Bloom, David Krathwohl, and Bertram B. Masia. 1956. *Taxonomy of educational objectives: The classification of educational goals. Handbook I: Cognitive domain*. Green.

Manvi Breja and Sanjay Kumar Jain. 2020. Causality for question answering. In *COLINS*, pages 884–893.

Mengyun Cao, Xiaoping Sun, and Hai Zhuge. 2016. The role of cause-effect link within scientific paper. *12th International Conference on Semantics, Knowledge and Grids (SKG)*, pages 32–39.

Ying-Hong Chan and Yao-Chung Fan. 2019. A recurrent BERT-based model for question generation. In *Proceedings of the 2nd Workshop on Machine Reading for Question Answering*, pages 154–162, Hong Kong, China. Association for Computational Linguistics.

Jacob Cohen. 1960. A coefficient of agreement for nominal scales. *Educational and psychological measurement*, 20(1):37–46.

Kordula De Kuthy, Madeeswaran Kannan, Haemanth Santhi Ponnusamy, and Detmar Meurers. 2020. Towards automatically generating questions under discussion to link information and discourse structure. In *Proceedings of the 28th International Conference on Computational Linguistics*, pages 5786–5798, Barcelona, Spain (Online). International Committee on Computational Linguistics.

Kaustubh Dhole and Christopher D. Manning. 2020. Syn-QG: Syntactic and shallow semantic rules for question generation. In *Proceedings of the 58th Annual Meeting of the Association for Computational Linguistics*, pages 752–765, Online. Association for Computational Linguistics.

Nan Duan, Duyu Tang, Peng Chen, and Ming Zhou. 2017. Question generation for question answering. In *Proceedings of the 2017 Conference on Empirical Methods in Natural Language Processing*, pages 866–874, Copenhagen, Denmark. Association for Computational Linguistics.

Rosa Falotico and Piero Quatto. 2015. Fleiss' kappa statistic without paradoxes. *Quality & Quantity*, 49(2):463–470.

J.L. Fleiss et al. 1971. Measuring nominal scale agreement among many raters. *Psychological Bulletin*, 76(5):378–382.

Roxana Girju. 2003. Automatic detection of causal relations for question answering. In *Proceedings of the ACL 2003 Workshop on Multilingual Summarization and Question Answering*, pages 76–83, Sapporo, Japan. Association for Computational Linguistics.

Michael Heilman and Noah A. Smith. 2010. Good question! statistical ranking for question generation. In *Human Language Technologies: The 2010 Annual Conference of the North American Chapter of the Association for Computational Linguistics*, pages 609–617, Los Angeles, California. Association for Computational Linguistics.

Aniruddha Kembhavi, Minjoon Seo, D. Schwenk, Jonghyun Choi, Ali Farhadi, and Hannaneh Hajishirzi. 2017. Are you smarter than a sixth grader? textbook question answering for multimodal machine comprehension. *2017 IEEE Conference on Computer Vision and Pattern Recognition (CVPR)*, pages 5376–5384.

Tomáš Kočiský, Jonathan Schwarz, Phil Blunsom, Chris Dyer, Karl Moritz Hermann, Gábor Melis, and Edward Grefenstette. 2018. The NarrativeQA reading comprehension challenge. *Transactions of the Association for Computational Linguistics*, 6:317–328.

Ghader Kurdi, Jared Leo, Bijan Parsia, Uli Sattler, and Salam Al-Emari. 2020. A Systematic Review of Automatic Question Generation for Educational Purposes. *International Journal of Artificial Intelligence in Education*, 30(1):121–204.

Zhenzhong Lan, Mingda Chen, Sebastian Goodman, Kevin Gimpel, Piyush Sharma, and Radu Soricut. 2020. Albert: A lite bert for self-supervised learning of language representations. In *International Conference on Learning Representations*.

Allen Nie, Erin Bennett, and Noah Goodman. 2019. Learning to explain: Answering why-questions via rephrasing. In *Proceedings of the First Workshop on NLP for Conversational AI*, pages 113–120, Florence, Italy. Association for Computational Linguistics.

Myle Ott, Sergey Edunov, Alexei Baevski, Angela Fan, Sam Gross, Nathan Ng, David Grangier, and Michael Auli. 2019. fairseq: A fast, extensible toolkit for sequence modeling. In *Proceedings of NAACL-HLT 2019: Demonstrations*.

Kishore Papineni, Salim Roukos, Todd Ward, and Wei-Jing Zhu. 2002. Bleu: a method for automatic evaluation of machine translation. In *Proceedings of the*

40th annual meeting of the Association for Computational Linguistics, pages 311–318.

Weizhen Qi, Yu Yan, Yeyun Gong, Dayiheng Liu, Nan Duan, Jiusheng Chen, Ruofei Zhang, and Ming Zhou. 2020. ProphetNet: Predicting future n-gram for sequence-to-sequence pre-training. In *Proceedings of the 2020 Conference on Empirical Methods in Natural Language Processing: Findings*, pages 2401–2410, Online. Association for Computational Linguistics.

Pranav Rajpurkar, Robin Jia, and Percy Liang. 2018. Know what you don't know: Unanswerable questions for SQuAD. In *Proceedings of the 56th Annual Meeting of the Association for Computational Linguistics (Volume 2: Short Papers)*, pages 784–789, Melbourne, Australia. Association for Computational Linguistics.

Pranav Rajpurkar, Jian Zhang, Konstantin Lopyrev, and Percy Liang. 2016. SQuAD: 100,000+ questions for machine comprehension of text. In *Proceedings of the 2016 Conference on Empirical Methods in Natural Language Processing*, pages 2383–2392, Austin, Texas. Association for Computational Linguistics.

Sherry Ruan, Liwei Jiang, Justin Xu, Bryce Joe-Kun Tham, Zhengneng Qiu, Yeshuang Zhu, Elizabeth L. Murnane, Emma Brunskill, and James A. Landay. 2019. Quizbot: A dialogue-based adaptive learning system for factual knowledge. In *Proceedings of the 2019 CHI Conference on Human Factors in Computing Systems*, CHI '19, page 1–13, New York, NY, USA. Association for Computing Machinery.

Katherine Stasaski and Marti A. Hearst. 2017. Multiple choice question generation utilizing an ontology. In *Proceedings of the 12th Workshop on Innovative Use of NLP for Building Educational Applications*, pages 303–312, Copenhagen, Denmark. Association for Computational Linguistics.

Will Thalheimer. 2003. *The learning benefits of questions*. Work Learning Research.

Adam Trischler, Tong Wang, Xingdi Yuan, Justin Harris, Alessandro Sordoni, Philip Bachman, and Kaheer Suleman. 2017. NewsQA: A machine comprehension dataset. In *Proceedings of the 2nd Workshop on Representation Learning for NLP*, pages 191–200, Vancouver, Canada. Association for Computational Linguistics.

Tong Wang, Xingdi (Eric) Yuan, and Adam Trischler. 2017a. A joint model for question answering and question generation. In *Learning to generate natural language workshop, ICML 2017*.

Wenhui Wang, Nan Yang, Furu Wei, Baobao Chang, and Ming Zhou. 2017b. Gated self-matching networks for reading comprehension and question answering. In *Proceedings of the 55th Annual Meeting of the Association for Computational Linguistics (Volume 1: Long Papers)*, pages 189–198, Vancouver, Canada. Association for Computational Linguistics.

Zichao Wang, Andrew S. Lan, Weili Nie, Andrew E. Waters, Phillip J. Grimaldi, and Richard G. Baraniuk. 2018. Qg-net: A data-driven question generation model for educational content. In *Proceedings of the Fifth Annual ACM Conference on Learning at Scale*, L@S '18, New York, NY, USA. Association for Computing Machinery.

Thomas Wolf, Lysandre Debut, Victor Sanh, Julien Chaumond, Clement Delangue, Anthony Moi, Pierric Cistac, Tim Rault, Remi Louf, Morgan Funtowicz, Joe Davison, Sam Shleifer, Patrick von Platen, Clara Ma, Yacine Jernite, Julien Plu, Canwen Xu, Teven Le Scao, Sylvain Gugger, Mariama Drame, Quentin Lhoest, and Alexander Rush. 2020. Transformers: State-of-the-art natural language processing. In *Proceedings of the 2020 Conference on Empirical Methods in Natural Language Processing: System Demonstrations*, pages 38–45, Online. Association for Computational Linguistics.

Zhilin Yang, Zihang Dai, Yiming Yang, Jaime Carbonell, Russ R Salakhutdinov, and Quoc V Le. 2019. Xlnet: Generalized autoregressive pretraining for language understanding. In *Advances in Neural Information Processing Systems*, volume 32, pages 5753–5763. Curran Associates, Inc.

Zhilin Yang, Peng Qi, Saizheng Zhang, Yoshua Bengio, William W. Cohen, Ruslan Salakhutdinov, and Christopher D. Manning. 2018. HotpotQA: A dataset for diverse, explainable multi-hop question answering. In *Conference on Empirical Methods in Natural Language Processing (EMNLP)*.

Xingdi Yuan, Tong Wang, Caglar Gulcehre, Alessandro Sordoni, Philip Bachman, Saizheng Zhang, Sandeep Subramanian, and Adam Trischler. 2017. Machine comprehension by text-to-text neural question generation. In *Proceedings of the 2nd Workshop on Representation Learning for NLP*, pages 15–25, Vancouver, Canada. Association for Computational Linguistics.

Yao Zhao, Xiaochuan Ni, Yuanyuan Ding, and Qifa Ke. 2018. Paragraph-level neural question generation with maxout pointer and gated self-attention networks. In *Proceedings of the 2018 Conference on Empirical Methods in Natural Language Processing*, pages 3901–3910, Brussels, Belgium. Association for Computational Linguistics.

A Manual Analysis of SQuAD Questions

We conduct a manual analysis of the 68 most-frequent n-gram question openers from SQuAD, to investigate the prevalence of causal questions which exist. We restrict the question openers to the most frequent n-grams which cover 80% of the dataset, excluding unigrams other than "why" because they were uninformative. Two researchers hand-labeled each opener as one of: cause-and-effect, not cause-and-effect, and unknown, where unknown question openers could be the start of cause-and-effect questions but would require reading the entire question to determine. A third researcher tie-broke disagreements. The average Cohen's Kappa (Cohen, 1960) is 0.72 (substantialagreement). Of the 87,599 questions in SQuAD which could be labeled by the 68 most-frequent n-gram question openers, 1,194 (1.4%) were cause-and-effect, 29,540 (33.7%) were not cause-and-effect, and 56,865 (64.9%) were unknown. The full list of labeled question openers is found in our Github repo.

B Causal Extraction Details

For the causal extraction section of the pipeline, we modified the "as" pattern. The original pattern is formulated as:

> &R@Complete@ (,) (-such/-same/-seem/-regard/-regards/-regarded/-view/-views/-viewed/-denote/-denoted/-denotes) as (-if/-follow/-follows/-&adv) &C@Complete@

Where @Complete@ indicates that the text piece is a clause which must have predicate and subject, "-" indicates tokens followed should not be matched, and "()" indicates tokens that are not required. &R and &C represent the extracted cause and effect. However, the original pattern assumes that the cause is always before "as." In reality, "as" can be included before both the cause and the effect, such as in the following example:

> Some renewable resources are too expensive to be widely used. As the technology improves and more people use renewable energy, the prices will come down. The cost of renewable resources will go down relative to fossil fuels as we use fossil fuels up.

For this example, the causal phrase extracted by original pattern is "Some renewable resources are too expensive to be widely used." The effect phrase extracted by original pattern is "The technology improves and more people use renewable energy, the prices will come down."

We implement a new pattern (pattern-id = 145): ",/;/./– As &C , &R". For each cause-and-effect extracted in the original pattern, if the new pattern is also a match, we replace the cause and effect with the output from the new pattern. For the example sentences above, the causal phrases extracted by our new pattern is "the technology improves and more people use renewable energy." The corresponding effect phrase extracted by new pattern is "The prices will come down."

C Crowdworking Task Interface

Figure 2 contains the cause (bolded and highlighted in orange) and effect (underlined and highlighted in blue) shown to workers when evaluating the quality of an extracted cause and effect. Figure 3 contains a sample stimulus showing the intended answer and generated question.

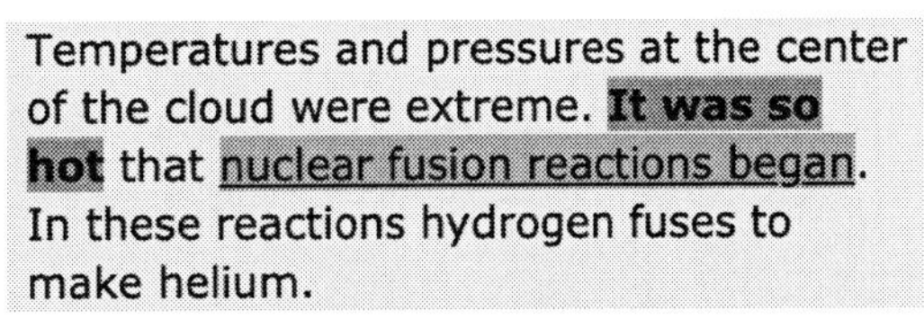

Figure 2: Example crowdworking presentation of passage, cause, and effect, from TQA dataset.

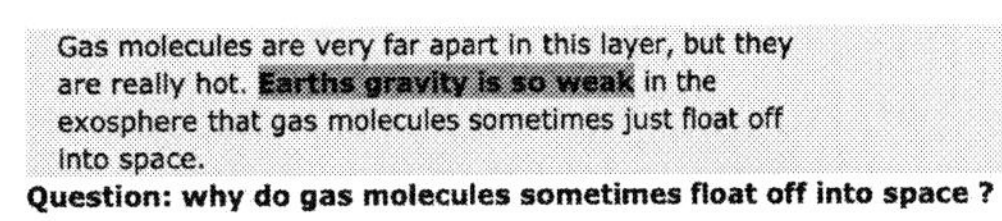

Figure 3: Example crowdworking presentation of passage, intended answer, and generated question, from TQA dataset.

Table 10 contains the crowdworker ratings for the Cao et al. (2016) causal extraction system, stratified by typology. Each main typology category is further stratified by the type and sub-type of link. For example, the Adverbial link category contains two types: (A) Anaphoric and (B) Cataphoric. The Anaphoric category is further segmented into three sub-types: (1) Implicit Cohesion (e.g.,"therefore") (2) Pronominal Cohesion (e.g., "for this reason"), and (3) Pronominal + Lexical Cohesion (e.g., "because of" *NP*) (Altenberg, 1984). We refer to the main category by name, with the subcategories denoted with codes, e.g., Adv.1.a.

Category	TQA	#T	SQuAD	#S
Adv.1.a	33	34	16	21
Adv.1.b	2	3	2	2
Adv.1.c	0	4	1	3
Adv.2.a	2	2	1	2
Prep.1.a	8	11	16	21
Sub.1.a	12	27	18	29
Sub.2.a	2	3	0	4
Sub.3.a	2	3	3	3
C-I.1.a	3	4	3	5
C-I.1.b	3	3	2	3
C-I.1.c	2	3	2	3
C-I.1.e	*	0	1	1
C-I.1.f	1	1	*	0
C-I.1.h	*	0	1	1
C-I.2.a	0	2	2	2

Table 10: Number of extracted relations that were labeled as causal by crowdworkers for original Cao et al. (2016) system, organized by linguistic category. #T is total number in TQA and #S is total number in SQuAD. '*' indicates no relation found.

D Model specifics

Causal Extraction: The approximate runtime for this algorithm on an Intel(R) Core(TM) i7-6850K CPU machine is 72 hours for the TQA dataset and 24 hours for SQuAD.

Question Generation: ProphetNet has 391,324,672 parameters; our version is unchanged from Qi et al. (2020). We finetune the provided question generation model checkpoint, which is a 16 GB model fine-tuned on SQuAD. The approximate runtime to fine tune this model on an auxiliary dataset on a p3.2xlarge AWS ec2[6] machine is 0.5 hours. For our fine-tuning process, we train for 3 epochs with a learning rate of 1e-6 with a batch size of 1. The rest of parameters are kept the same as what is found in the examples provided by the ProphetNet GitHub repository README. Approximate inference time is 10 minutes for TQA and 5 minutes for SQuAD. We utilize the Fairseq library (Ott et al., 2019) to facilitate the training and inference processes. Comparing the fine-tuned model's generated questions to the Syn-QG questions, the fine-tuned QG model achieves 57.01 training BLEU and 53.89 test BLEU (Papineni et al., 2002).

Question Answering: The QA model we utilize has 334,094,338 parameters. The approximate runtime to fine tune this model on an auxiliary dataset on a p3.2xlarge AWS ec2 machine is 0.5 hours. For our fine-tuning process, we train for 10 epochs with an initial learning rate of 1e-5, a batch size of 4, 500 warm-up steps, and a weight decay of 0.01. The rest of the parameters are the defaults set by the HuggingFace TrainingArguments class. We also truncate each example to a max of 512 tokens. Approximate inference time is 1 minutes for TQA and 1 minute for SQuAD. On the Syn-QG dataset, the fine-tuned QA model achieves 0.97 training F1 and 0.95 test F1.

[6]https://aws.amazon.com/ec2/

Type	Recall	#T	Recall	#S
Adv.1.a	0.76	1309	0.60	229
Adv.1.b	0.55	28	0.32	8
Adv.1.c	0.37	94	0.39	15
Adv.2.a	0.45	3	0.67	3
Total Adv.	0.73	1434	0.58	255
Prep.1.a	0.72	470	0.56	275
Total Prep.	0.72	470	0.56	275
Sub.1.a	0.69	1146	0.52	385
Sub.2.a	0.73	57	0.54	35
Sub.3.a	0.78	70	0.59	15
Total Sub.	0.70	1273	0.53	435
C-I.1.a	0.71	99	0.57	48
C-I.1.b	0.61	33	0.56	11
C-I.1.c	0.79	29	0.90	13
C-I.1.e	*	0	0.12	1
C-I.1.f	1	1	*	0
C-I.1.h	*	0	0.14	1
C-I.2.a	0.61	20	0.32	6
Total C-I	0.69	182	0.59	80

Table 11: Average cause/effect presence recall in the TQA and SQuAD datasets, categorized by typology. Questions are generated by ProphetNet fine-tuned on Syn-QG. #T refers to number of questions in TQA; #S the same for SQuAD. '*' indicates no relation found.

E Cause/Effect Present Results

Table 11 shows the results for the automatic cause/effect present metric segmented by typology categories. For SQuAD, the lowest-performing category is Subordination, which corresponds to the category with the lowest proportion of extracted relationships labeled as causal by crowdworkers (Section 4).

Interventions Recommendation: Professionals' Observations Analysis in Special Needs Education

Javier Muñoz[1], **Felipe Bravo-Marquez**[1,2]
[1]Department of Computer Science, University of Chile
[2]Millennium Institute for Foundational Research on Data, IMFD-Chile
jmunoz@dcc.uchile.cl, fbravo@dcc.uchile.cl,

Abstract

This paper presents a new task in educational NLP, recommending professional interventions for Special Needs Education (SNE) students using NLP techniques. The task is formulated as a multi-label classification problem in which each training example is formed by the student's diagnosis along with various free text observations made by teachers and professionals, and the target classes correspond to a set of interventions recommended based on that information. Using the previously mentioned structure, we build the Special Needs Education Corpus (SNEC), a new corpus of over 3,000 Chilean special needs students. We also train several machine learning models using different settings and feature representations of our data. Our results indicate that textual features are the most useful in terms of classification performance and that other non-textual features, such as diagnosis and other chosen interventions, are also beneficial. We also observed a positive effect of representing text inputs with a dense BERT-based representation over using sparse n-grams and non-contextual word embeddings. Our corpus and source code are available at https://github.com/dccuchile/SNEC.

1 Introduction

One consequence of the adoption of digital technologies in schools is the wide availability of data records associated with their enrolled students. These records have been successfully employed in many ways to help students improve their school performance. For example, Romero and Ventura (2010) present different projects that use student records, such as their grades in different subjects, to help them in different ways, for example recommending activities or books that can help them to improve their grades.

These investigations focus on, for example, correction of grammatical errors, automated writing evaluation, automated content evaluation, vocabulary analysis, among others. These tasks use free text pieces written by students as inputs to develop different kinds of outputs, allowing students to improve their grammar together with reading and writing skills (Costa-jussà and Alfonseca, 2019).

Another important task is to analyze free text observations and reports made by teachers and other professionals (e.g., physiologists, speech therapists) that have worked with the students to decide certain strategies or interventions that can help students improve their school performance and social skills.

This task is especially important in "Special Needs Education" (SNE), where students with different disabilities, such as motor disorders, Down's Syndrome, specific language impairment, among others, may need particular interventions, such as access curricular adaptation, involve the family in the educational process, interdisciplinary support, among others (Olakanmi et al., 2020).

As the decisions made by professionals working in SNE usually are more critical than the decisions made in traditional education, teachers and professionals are not always sure about their decisions (Podell and Soodak, 1993). For this reason, different tools have been developed to help SNE professionals diagnosing Special Needs students and performing the chosen interventions with these students (Drigas and Ioannidou, 2011).

In this work we study the problem of recommending the best interventions to students in Special Needs Education considering their diagnosis, professionals' observations and even other applied interventions, formulating this problem as a multi-label text classification task with additional data. We explore different input sets and text transformations that allow a machine learning system to make intervention predictions for each student.

To achieve this, we collected data from differ-

Proceedings of the 16th Workshop on Innovative Use of NLP for Building Educational Applications, pages 171–179
April 20, 2021 ©2021 Association for Computational Linguistics

ent Chilean Special Needs schools to build a new the Special Needs Education Corpus (SNEC). This dataset was built with records from around 3,000 students with different diagnoses, Spanish-written observations by professionals and the best interventions for each of them.

Each student has one of 12 possible diagnoses and has one or more recommended interventions, chosen from a set of 14 possible interventions. The professionals that give their observations of students are in most cases doctors, psychologists and special education teachers, but speech therapists can also observe if the student is required to work with these professionals.

The content of the observations are free text instances and vary according to the professional who issues them. We have therefore designed different experiments to analyze whether these observations should be differentiated or use a simplification such as joining the observations and working with a single joined document and see if it is enough to get correct interventions prediction. As each student might need more than one intervention, we formulate this problem as a multi-label text classification task with additional attributes, such as the diagnosis and other chosen interventions.

We use different sparse bag of n-grams text representations and dense neural text transformers models, such as BERT (Devlin et al., 2019), to analyze which text representation approach is best suited to our problem.

The focus of this paper is therefore to introduce a new task in the Educational Data Mining field, specifically in SNE field using Natural Language Processing (NLP) techniques, together with a our new SNEC corpus with Spanish-written professionals' observations of students with different disabilities and results of several experiments using different approaches and text transformations to predict the best interventions for each one of these students using machine learning techniques.

The remainder of this paper is structured as follows. In Section 2 we present related work to our practical problem, recommending interventions in Special Needs Education, and the technical problem, use different text representations for observations written by professionals and different input sets to make intervention predictions. In Section 3 we propose our task and show the dataset origin and details of each attribute. In Section 4 we present our experiment settings and the evaluation metrics used to analyze the results of the experiments. The details and results of the experiments are shown and discussed in Section 5. Finally, in Section 6 we present our conclusions and future work.

2 Related Work

This work can be viewed from multiple perspectives: from a domain point of view it lies in the fields of Educational Data Mining (EDM) and SNE and from a technical point view we have a text classification problem. In this section we present different tools used both in traditional educational data mining and particularly in SNE and then we also present text classification methods that are relevant to this work.

Educational Data Mining is a specific field that uses computational approaches to analyze educational data in order to study educational questions, as defined in (Romero and Ventura, 2010). Our problem shares features with many tasks defined in the above paper, such as providing feedback for supporting instructors (where the objective is to provide feedback to support course teachers in decision making) and recommendations for the students (where the objective is to make recommendations directly to the students analyzing their personalized activities).

In Special Needs Education there are also different tools that help teachers and other professionals to work with students. Drigas and Ioannidou (2011) show different tools and projects trying to solve particular problems present only in SNE, such as diagnosing SNE students using different A.I. learning methods. This work also presents different instruments that help professionals carry out the interventions chosen for each student.

Our study also analyzes the technical problem of the interventions recommendation - the text classification problem when we use the free text instances, such as the professionals' observations. A relatively recent architecture that has yielded state-of-the-art results in many NLP tasks is the Transformer (Cer et al., 2018), which can be used for training large language models from unalabeled corpora (e.g., BERT (Devlin et al., 2019)). These pre-trained models can be later fine-tuned to almost any target task at hand with successful results. Although most of these large pre-trained models are only available for the English language, several language-specific versions have been made available in recent years, such as BETO (Cañete et al.,

2020), the Spanish version of BERT.

3 Problem Formulation

In this section we present the task studied in this work together with its context and our new corpus.

Our task lies in the field of Educational Data Mining, specifically in the area of Special Needs Education. It consists of automatically recommending interventions for students with different disabilities and behaviors, and its main goal is to help SNE teachers and professionals decide the best interventions for their students.

In Chile, Special Needs Education professionals write different documents that contain observations and relevant information of students they have worked with at the beginning of the school year. In these documents the diagnosis of the SNE students is established and in case students have more than one diagnosis they are diagnosed with 'Multiple cognitive deficit' and more details of the diagnoses are also settled down in the documents. Professionals also give details about the students behavior and relevant observed information together with interventions that can help students with their problems.

With these document professionals then decide the best interventions for each student by analyzing the information of the student's different documents and diagnosis. At the end of the year these professionals write a single document for each student, writing down the interventions that were useful for the student and also interventions that were not applied, but professionals think would have been useful had it been applied. Interventions that did not work are also written, but for this research we use just the interventions that did work.

We built a new Special Needs Education Corpus (SNEC) from the records from around 3,000 students with different disabilities from Chilean SNE schools enrolled between 2018 and 2019. Each student record consists in his or her diagnosis, the observations of the professionals that have worked with each student at the beginning of the year and the interventions that professionals chose as the best for this student (applied or not) at the end of the scholar year.

The students' diagnosis were obtained from a web application that helps teachers store basic student information, such as his or her name and diagnosis, and students' digitized documents.

This web application is used to track the students' progress, both in school performance and evolution of their diagnosis. For this work we summarized the possible diagnosis of a student, grouping the same diagnoses but different severity into a single general diagnosis. This way, students have a diagnosis from 12 possible diagnoses. The number of students per diagnosis are shown in Table 1.

Diagnoses	Number of students
Specific learning disorder	855
Specific language impairment	616
Intellectual disability	566
Borderline intellectual functioning	398
Attention deficit disorder	392
Autism spectrum disorder	111
Down's Syndrome	28
Hearing impairment - Hearing loss	27
Motor disorders	27
Multiple cognitive deficit	6
Global developmental delay	5
Visual impairment	4

Table 1: Number of students per diagnosis.

The professionals observations are free text instances and were obtained from digitized documents required by Chilean laws for Special Needs schools. Depending on the document type there are observations of different professionals that have worked with the student.

The professionals can be doctors, speech therapists, psychologists or Special Needs teachers. Each student can have 0 or more observations of each professional type, but must have at least one observation. A student can also have more than one document containing observations from the same professional, being able to have more than one observation per professional observation type. For this work if the student has more than one observation per observation type, these are joined and used as a single observation. The number of students that have each observation type are shown in Table 2.

Observations type	Number of students
SNE Teacher Observations	2,560
Psychologist Observations	2,523
Doctor Observations	1,884
Speech Therapist Observations	525

Table 2: Number of students per observation type.

The best interventions for each student were obtained from another special document required by Chilean laws named "Formulario Único de reevaluación"[1]. This document is completed at the end of the school year and contains the applied interventions both those that worked and those that did

[1] https://especial.mineduc.cl/implementacion-dcto-supr-no170/formulario-unico/

not. This document also contains not applied interventions that could have worked. For this study, interventions were grouped into larger groups to reduce the label space and get a better understanding of the interventions. This way, students have 1 or more assigned "best interventions" from a set of 14 possible interventions as shown in Table 3.

Interventions	Number of students
Access curricular adaptation	2,264
Involve the family in the process	2,048
Interdisciplinary support	1,441
Pedagogical support in subjects	1,314
Special Needs teacher support	1,311
Personal pedagogical support	1,240
Psychologist support	588
Speech therapist support	378
Peer tutoring	350
Objectives curricular adaptation	281
Occupational therapist support	153
General medical support	64
Neurological monitoring	63
Kinesiologist Support	32

Table 3: Number of students per intervention.

After collecting our data, we cleaned it by removing student records without any intervention or professional observation. This usually occurs when documents are not digitized but scanned versions of a physical document, being impossible to extract the data correctly and easily. In these cases we could not obtain the observations or interventions. We then anonymized our dataset by replacing the names of the students or their relatives in the observations with a special token, depending on who the name refers to, replacing the student name by "[ESTUDIANTE]" token or his or her relative's names by "[OTHER_NAME]" token.

The student data can thus be represented as shown in Figure 1. The student is diagnosed with one of 12 different diagnoses and has different evaluations containing free text observations from a doctor, a psychologist, and a special education teacher observations, also including speech therapist observations if the student requires it. Professionals then choose 1 or more interventions from 14 available.

Based on this, we formulate the task of predicting interventions for a given student as a multi-label classification problem, in which all the free text observations and the student's diagnosis are used as input features.

4 Methods

As we are dealing with a multi-label classification task, we employ the stratification method of (Sechidis et al., 2011) to generate training, validation and testing partitions dividing our data in a ratio of 3:1:1 respectively. For this research we do not use the testing partition as we plan to build more complex architectures in future research. This way, we use 1836 students data for training and 612 for validation.

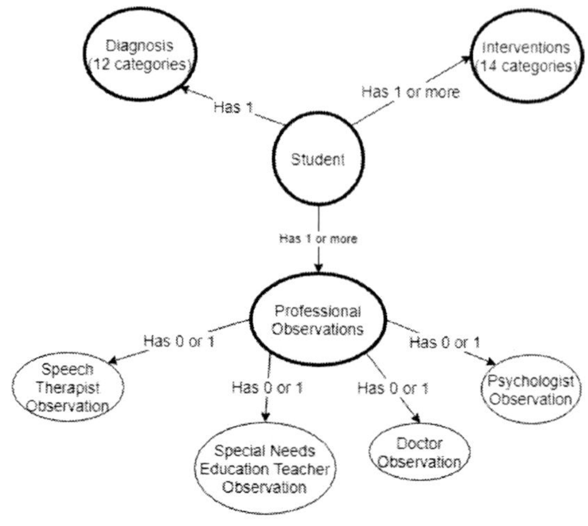

Figure 1: Problem ontology.

We then define general settings and evaluation metrics for all our designed experiments. Our experiments are applied to each intervention, considering a single intervention as output to analyze single intervention behaviors. As behavior of the predictions and possible correlations could be different in well-balanced and unbalanced interventions, we group interventions into two sets: unbalanced interventions (present in less than 15% of the students or in more than 85% of the students) and balanced interventions (not unbalanced interventions).

We consider a dummy majority vote classifier as the baseline. As this study explores the possible correlation between the diagnosis, professional observations or interventions of students and tries different text transformations for the professionals' observations, we use a 'simple' logistic regression classifier with the same settings for all the experiments, only changing the input data (data selection and transformations) for each intervention.

The diagnosis of each student is represented using a One-Hot Encoding (OHE) representation, adding 12 different binary attributes representing each one of them. Interventions are also represented as binary attributes, both when used as input attributes and as output.

In the "simple" text representation experiments we use a sparse bag of n-grams representation of the professional observations, considering from 1 to 3 words as tokens, using unigrams, bigrams and trigrams this way. We also use a simple approach for cases where a student had more than one observation of the same observation type. In these cases we just join the observations and use it as a single observation.

We also design two versions for experiments in which we use the bag of n-grams representation of the observations, first considering the joined different types of observations of each student as a single text input and another version adding a special token to each word of the observations, using a different token depending on the professional that wrote the observation.

Furthermore, we design two versions for experiments using dense neural representations of the observations. As adding a special token to words will cause pre-trained dense transformers generate inaccurate representations, we use each observation type as a different text input and use their representations as different features as input for our classifier.

For this study we use the following metrics: accuracy, Cohen's kappa score (Vieira et al., 2010), F1 score average of positive and negative class and Area Under the Receiver Operating Characteristic Curve (ROC AUC) (Flach, 2016) score of each experiment for each intervention. In this work we report the macro-average of all the interventions.

5 Experiments

For our experiments we train logistic regression models considering different sub-sets of the feature space and also using different representation approaches for our textual features. We also have two groups of experiments: the first one consisted in using sparse n-gram representation of our text inputs, using the bag of n-grams mentioned above, while for experiments of the second group we use dense neural representations of the observations.

5.1 Sparse N-gram Representations Experiments

For these experiments we use a feature ablation technique to design our experiments. Thus, for our first experiment we use the OHE representation of students' diagnosis, bag of n-grams representation of the professionals' observations and all the interventions, except the one we are trying to predict, as binary attributes, using 0 if the intervention is not present and 1 if it is. We train the logistic regression classifier with these features and then we evaluate the performance on our test dataset. This experiment outperformed the dummy classifier mentioned in Section 4 in all the interventions using our both versions, adding special tokens and joining the observations. We also observe that the performance of this experiment is different depending on the intervention we are trying to predict and if we use or do not use the special token. However, this experiment is not realistic since we can try to predict the interventions using a pre-defined order but we cannot know every other predicted intervention always.

Next, we design new experiments using only one of the other interventions as a binary attribute, keeping the OHE representation of the diagnosis and the observations sparse n-grams representation. The performance of these experiments was worse than the obtained in our previous experiment for all the interventions. We analyze the weights the classifier assign to each feature and observe that for certain interventions there are interventions used as binary attributes showing a high positive weight and in the same way, for other interventions some interventions used as a binary attribute with a high negative weight as well, as shown in Table 4 and Table 5, showing the top positive and negative features using 'Special Needs teacher support' intervention as a binary attribute. The interventions with a high negative or positive value were mainly balanced interventions and the interventions that showed a correlation with another intervention were unbalanced and balanced interventions.

Top #	Feature	Weight
1	Specific language impairment (OHE diagnosis)	2.28
2	Special Needs teacher support (Intervention attribute)	0.81
3	'palabra' (Spanish word for 'word')	0.80
4	'buena disposicion' (Spanish phrase for 'readiness')	0.79
5	'estructura' (Spanish word for 'structure')	0.78

Table 4: Top positive features for 'Apoyo fonoaudiólogo(a)' intervention in experiment using all observations joined + OHE diagnosis + presence of 'Special Needs teacher support' intervention as binary feature.

We then remove the interventions as binary attributes and work with OHE representation of the diagnosis and the sparse n-grams representation of professional observations. The performance using these experiment settings are equal to or worse than the obtained using the above settings, with a single intervention as a binary attribute. Depending on the

Top #	Feature	Weight
1	Special Needs teacher support (Intervention attribute)	-1.12
2	'salud' (Spanish word for 'health')	-0.73
3	Specific language impairment (OHE diagnosis)	-0.70
4	'normas' (Spanish word for 'norms')	-0.49
5	'muestra' (Spanish word for 'show')	-0.49

Table 5: Top negative features for 'General medical support' intervention in experiment using all observations joined + OHE diagnosis + presence of 'Special Needs teacher support' intervention as binary feature.

analyzed intervention, the results using the special token approach are better than using the joined observations. However, performance is better using the joined observations approach in most cases.

Our next experiment was using all the interventions, except the one we are trying to predict, as binary attributes, and OHE representation of the diagnosis of students as input for the classifier. The performance of this experiment is worse than the one obtained using the above setting.

We then use only one type of professional observation representation and OHE diagnosis' representation as input for our classifier. Using this setting, the performance is worse than in any of the previous experiments, but we observe that depending on the analyzed intervention, using certain type of observations we obtain better performance than using the other observations. This occurs using the SNE teacher observations in most interventions.

Our lasts experiments use only one of our features: diagnosis, observations or interventions, using also the special token and the joined observations versions when we use the observations as features. The best results using only one attribute are obtained using the professionals' observations, both in balanced and unbalanced interventions.

The results of our sparse n-grams experiments are summarized in Table 6. We present the macro-averaged results of all the interventions and the results of experiments using a single intervention were also summarized. However, as we mentioned before, results are different depending on the analyzed intervention and the intervention we use as binary attribute.

These results show that the observations of the professionals are the most relevant features for predicting interventions using our settings, being SNE teacher observations the most relevant in most cases. We also observe than depending on the analyzed intervention, using a special token to differentiate each type of observation we obtain a better performance than joining the observations and using them as a single text instance. In addition, we observe that diagnosis and interventions are not enough to get better performance than using a majority class algorithm by themselves, but are useful attributes for making better predictions when using the professionals observations. The interventions and diagnosis also presented different weights in our models depending on the analyzed intervention, showing correlation between certain interventions and between interventions and diagnoses.

5.2 Dense Neural Representations Experiments

The focus of these experiments is to use different dense neural representations of the observations as input for our classifier and compare their performance with the previous experiments. This way, in a preliminary experiment we use our own pre-trained embeddings built from our domain data, but the performance using this model to produce representations of the professionals' observations were as bad as the obtained in our sparse n-grams experiments using only the OHE representation of the diagnosis, even using the one-hot encoded diagnosis together with the word embedding representation.

We then use pre-trained frozen BETO transformation of the observations as input together with the one-hot encoded diagnosis. We use our two versions, first joining all the observations and using this joined document as a single text instance, and second encoding each observation and using each type as different features according to the professional who issued them. We also split the observations or joined observations that had more tokens than the allowed by the BETO transformer (512) into smaller pieces and then averaging these representations. This experiment, using observations representation as different features, outperforms all our previous experiments for balanced interventions, except for our first experiment of sparse n-gram representations, where we used all our available data. However, the performance for unbalanced interventions using this approach is worse than the obtained in the experiments using the bag of n-grams representation of the observations.

We also design experiments using a sentence embedding representation, using the cross lingual pre-trained model presented in (Conneau et al., 2020)

Experiment names	Acc	Kappa	F1	AUC
Baseline (Dummy classifier)	0.79	0	0.44	0.5
Only diagnosis	0.8	0.02	0.47	0.51
All other interventions	0.8	0.06	0.51	0.53
All joined observations	0.81	0.27	0.64*	0.62
Observations with special token	0.8	0.25	0.62	0.62
All joined observations + diagnosis	0.81	0.29	0.64	0.63*
Observations with special token + diagnosis	0.81	0.25	0.62	0.62
Doctor observations only + diagnosis	0.79	0.05	0.5	0.52
Psychologist observations only + diagnosis	0.8	0.11	0.55	0.55
Speech therapist observations only + diagnosis	0.8	0.03	0.48	0.51
Special Needs Education teacher observations only + diagnosis	0.81	0.26	0.63	0.61
All other interventions + diagnosis	0.81	0.1	0.53	0.54
All joined observations + diagnosis + 'Single Intervention'	0.81	0.29*	0.64*	0.63*
Observations with special tokens + diagnosis + 'Single Intervention'	0.81	0.26	0.63	0.62
All joined observations + diagnosis + all other interventions	0.82*	0.29*	0.64*	0.63*
Observations with special tokens + diagnosis + all other interventions	0.82*	0.28	0.64*	0.63*

Table 6: Macro-averaged sparse n-grams experiments results of all interventions. Scores with an asterisk correspond to the best macro-average results of each metric.

to make new representations of the professionals observations, but the results are not better than the ones obtained with BETO transformer representations used in the experiment above for any intervention.

Our last experiment consists of using the word embedding representation in the observations from the pre-trained model presented in (Bojanowski et al., 2017) with the "Spanish Billion Word Corpus"[2] embeddings, together with the one-hot encoded diagnosis. The performance using this representation is similar to that obtained with our sparse n-grams experiments where we use OHE representation of the diagnosis only, did not perform further experiments with this approach.

The summarized results of these experiments are presented in Table 7. As in Table 6, we present the macro-average results of all the interventions.

Using these representations we observe that text transformers like BETO also help to get better predictions, while static word embedding representations, where the context of the words is not really taken into account, are not as useful as transformers. We also observe that splitting our text instances into smaller pieces to use the BETO representation the performance of the classifier decrease as more splits are required.

6 Conclusions and Future Work

In this paper we have presented a new task, recommend interventions to professionals to work with Special Needs students using machine learning techniques. We also released SNEC, a new corpus with more than 3,000 students records containing their diagnosis, free text written observations and the best interventions for each of them. Finally, we showed the results of experiments using different text representations.

We observed that the professionals' observations of a student can be used to predict the best interventions for him or her. Besides, the diagnosis and other chosen interventions showed to be valuable in predicting some interventions, but not enough to improve on the predictions made using observations alone.

We also observed that contextualized neural representations of the observations, such as BERT or sentence embeddings, are useful to predict balanced interventions, but not for the unbalanced ones. It is important to remark, though, that, in this study the weights obtained from these pre-trained models were left frozen. The literature suggests that fine-tuning these weights to the task at hand can lead to significant improvements (Cañete et al., 2020).

As a general conclusion we can say that no single approach to represent observations consistently outperformed the others for all the interventions.

We believe that the models trained in this study can be useful to develop new tools to help teachers in deciding which interventions are the best for each student knowing his or her diagnosis, professionals' observations and other possible interventions.

Our next steps are to analyze our results further and find out the limitations of our approach.

We believe that there is plenty of room to im-

[2] `http://crscardellino.github.io/SBWCE/`

Experiment names	Acc	Kappa	F1	AUC
Baseline (Dummy classifier)	0.79	0	0.44	0.5
All observations with new word embedding	0.8	0.02	0.47	0.51
All observations (new word embedding) + diagnosis	0.8	0.04	0.49	0.52
All observations with BETO (average of word representation)	0.82*	0.16	0.57	0.57
All observations (BETO-average representation) + diagnosis	0.82*	0.16	0.58	0.57
Different observations with BETO (average)	0.82*	0.25*	0.62*	0.61
Different observations (BETO-average) + diagnosis	0.82*	0.25*	0.62*	0.62*
All observations (xlm-r-bert sentence embedding)	0.81	0.17	0.57	0.57
All observations (xlm-r-bert sentence embedding) + diagnosis	0.81	0.19	0.59	0.58
Different observations (xlm-r-bert sentence embedding)	0.81	0.19	0.6	0.59
Different observations (xlm-r-bert sentence embedding) + diagnosis	0.81	0.22	0.61	0.6
All observations (fasttext-sbwc) + diagnosis	0.8	0.03	0.48	0.51
Different observations (fasttext-sbwc) + diagnosis	0.82*	0.09	0.53	0.54

Table 7: Macro-averaged dense neural representations experiments results of all interventions. Scores with an asterisk correspond to the best macro-average results of each metric.

prove our results by designing an architecture more tailored to our problem.

For future work, we plan to design an end-to-end neural network architecture for this task and to fine-tune the pre-trained representations employed in this study.

Moreover, we did not experiment with approaches that can more efficiently exploit the multi-label nature of our problem i.e., the correlation between certain interventions. In this direction, we plan to experiment with multi-label loss functions such as the Hamming loss.

Acknowledgments

Felipe Bravo-Marquez was funded by ANID FONDECYT grant 11200290, U-Inicia VID Project UI-004/20 and ANID - Millennium Science Initiative Program - Code ICN17_002.

References

Piotr Bojanowski, Edouard Grave, Armand Joulin, and Tomas Mikolov. 2017. Enriching word vectors with subword information. *Transactions of the Association for Computational Linguistics*, 5:135–146.

José Cañete, Gabriel Chaperon, Rodrigo Fuentes, and Jorge Pérez. 2020. Spanish pre-trained BERT model and evaluation data. In *to appear in PML4DC at ICLR 2020*.

Daniel Cer, Yinfei Yang, Sheng-yi Kong, Nan Hua, Nicole Limtiaco, Rhomni St. John, Noah Constant, Mario Guajardo-Cespedes, Steve Yuan, Chris Tar, Brian Strope, and Ray Kurzweil. 2018. Universal sentence encoder for English. In *Proceedings of the 2018 Conference on Empirical Methods in Natural Language Processing: System Demonstrations*, pages 169–174, Brussels, Belgium. Association for Computational Linguistics.

Alexis Conneau, Kartikay Khandelwal, Naman Goyal, Vishrav Chaudhary, Guillaume Wenzek, Francisco Guzmán, Edouard Grave, Myle Ott, Luke Zettlemoyer, and Veselin Stoyanov. 2020. Unsupervised cross-lingual representation learning at scale. In *Proceedings of the 58th Annual Meeting of the Association for Computational Linguistics*, pages 8440–8451, Online. Association for Computational Linguistics.

Marta R Costa-jussà and Enrique Alfonseca. 2019. Proceedings of the 57th annual meeting of the association for computational linguistics: System demonstrations. In *Proceedings of the 57th Annual Meeting of the Association for Computational Linguistics: System Demonstrations*.

Jacob Devlin, Ming-Wei Chang, Kenton Lee, and Kristina Toutanova. 2019. BERT: Pre-training of deep bidirectional transformers for language understanding. In *Proceedings of the 2019 Conference of the North American Chapter of the Association for Computational Linguistics: Human Language Technologies, Volume 1 (Long and Short Papers)*, pages 4171–4186, Minneapolis, Minnesota. Association for Computational Linguistics.

Athanasios S Drigas and Rodi-Eleni Ioannidou. 2011. A review on artificial intelligence in special education. In *World Summit on Knowledge Society*, pages 385–391. Springer.

Peter A Flach. 2016. Roc analysis. In *Encyclopedia of Machine Learning and Data Mining*, pages 1–8. Springer.

Oluwabunmi Adewoyin Olakanmi, Gokce Akcayir, Oluwbukola Mayowa Ishola, and Carrie Demmans Epp. 2020. Using technology in special education: current practices and trends. *Educational Technology Research and Development*, 68(4):1711–1738.

David M Podell and Leslie C Soodak. 1993. Teacher efficacy and bias in special education referrals. *The Journal of educational research*, 86(4):247–253.

Cristóbal Romero and Sebastián Ventura. 2010. Educational data mining: a review of the state of the art. *IEEE Transactions on Systems, Man, and Cybernetics, Part C (Applications and Reviews)*, 40(6):601–618.

Konstantinos Sechidis, Grigorios Tsoumakas, and Ioannis Vlahavas. 2011. On the stratification of multi-label data. In *Joint European Conference on Machine Learning and Knowledge Discovery in Databases*, pages 145–158. Springer.

Susana M Vieira, Uzay Kaymak, and João MC Sousa. 2010. Cohen's kappa coefficient as a performance measure for feature selection. In *International Conference on Fuzzy Systems*, pages 1–8. IEEE.

C-Test Collector: A Proficiency Testing Application to Collect Training Data for C-Tests

Christian Haring, René Lehmann, Andrea Horbach and Torsten Zesch
Language Technology Lab, University Duisburg-Essen
(christian.haring|rene.lehmann)@stud.uni-due.de
(andrea.horbach|torsten.zesch)@uni-due.de

Abstract

We present the C-Test Collector, a web-based tool that allows language learners to test their proficiency level using c-tests. Our tool collects anonymized data on test performance, which allows teachers to gain insights into common error patterns. At the same time, it allows NLP researchers to collect training data in order to be able to generate c-test variants at the desired difficulty level.

1 Introduction

The c-test (Raatz and Klein-Braley, 1981) is a reduced redundancy exercise frequently used for language proficiency testing. In a c-test, the second half of every second word is replaced by a gap, and the task of the test-taker is to reconstruct the text. For example, the word *redundancy* would be replaced with *redun*___.

C-tests are known to correlate well with general language proficiency (Grotjahn, 2002) and are fast to take and to evaluate. Thus, they are even used in commercial systems such as onDaF (Grotjahn, 2010).

Despite these advantages, the creation of a well-working c-test is a time-consuming task even for language experts. One reason is that the gap scheme is influenced e.g. by Named Entities or other words that would be hard to guess for learners. Improved tool support for curating c-tests has mitigated this problem to some extent (Zesch et al., 2018).

Even with technological support, it is still hard (even for experts) to judge the difficulty of a given test without running a pilot study (Beinborn et al., 2014). Thus, there has been research on predicting (Beinborn et al., 2014) or manipulating (Lee et al., 2019) the difficulty of c-tests. These approaches heavily rely on the availability of training data, i.e. c-tests which have been taken by enough learners so that the solution probability for individual gaps can be reliably estimated. Influencing factors on the part of the student, such as the native language, make the difficulty prediction even more dependent on the availability of the right kind of training data.

In this paper, we present a web-application that makes it easy to collect such training data, by providing an easy-to-use platform for taking a c-test online. In the remainder of this paper, we describe the two ways to interact with the system: (i) as a user taking c-tests and receiving a proficiency assessment, and (ii) as an administrator uploading new tests and accessing the aggregated test results of the users.

2 User Perspective

Figure 1 illustrates the interaction steps of a user with the application.

Self Assessment To allow for an easy start with the tool and to avoid data security issues, we do not create user profiles, but ask users only for the language they want to learn and a self-assessment into one out of six proficiency levels, roughly meant to correspond to the six CEFR levels (Council of Europe, 2009). Optionally, a user can provide age and native language. This meta-information is stored together with the solutions provided by the user for a particular test.

Test Taking After selecting a language and proficiency level, the user is delivered a suitable c-test (see step 2 in Figure 1). Figure 2 gives an example of how a test looks for the user. Tests can be skipped and revisited again at a later stage. If the user has finished a test they are redirected to an evaluation page.

A user may always update their language settings to receive a new test (left-hand side of the upper box). On the right hand side of the upper box, the

Proceedings of the 16th Workshop on Innovative Use of NLP for Building Educational Applications, pages 180–184
April 20, 2021 ©2021 Association for Computational Linguistics

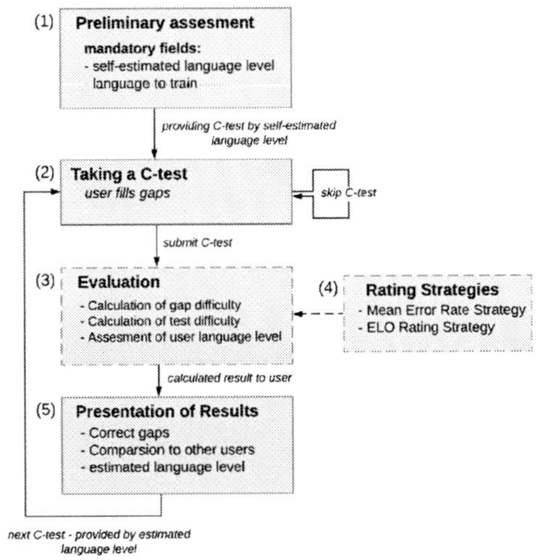

Figure 1: Interaction diagram of the user with the application. Non-interactive sections are marked with dashed lines.

user sees how many tests they have already passed, failed or skipped per level. The system uses this information to update the language proficiency of the user and provides them with new tests whose level matches that of the user.

Presentation of Results Once the user has submitted a c-test for evaluation, the results are presented. For wrongly answered gaps, the correct solution is shown. It is also shown how a user scored in relation to other users who took the same c-test. In addition, they are provided with the current assessment of their language level provided by the application. At this point, the user can either proceed to another c-test (or adjust their settings if they feel the test is too hard or too easy).

3 Admin perspective

The administrator is responsible for adding new tests with pre-set initial difficulty levels and can access the test results of the users. Figure 3 shows the administration view.

Adding Tests A c-test can be added in two ways: First, we support the export format of the C-Test Builder (Zesch et al., 2018), an authoring tool offering technical support for creating a c-test from raw text including automatic detection of Named Entities, numeric expression and other words that should be excluded from the gap scheme.[1] The tool also provides an automatic difficulty assessment as described in Beinborn et al. (2014), the result of which can be used as the initial value for the C-Test Collector. Second, text can be entered manually where those parts of a word that should appear as gaps are manually indicated using a bracket notation, e.g. *redun{dancy}*.

For each newly imported or created test, the admin has to provide the language, a title and an initial difficulty (i.e. a CEFR level). As we have already discussed that it is hard for teachers to correctly assign the difficulty level, this is only used at the beginning and the difficulty is adjusted as soon as more users have taken the test.

Test Overview The administrator is provided with a complete overview of all c-tests currently available in the application, as well as a graphical representation of the language distribution of tests (see Figure 3).

Test Details In the detailed view, information about a particular test is displayed. For each gap, an admin can inspect the distribution of errors made by test takers.

4 Scoring Tests and Users

Adjusting proficiency levels of users and difficulty levels of tests is a cold start problem: In the beginning, each user only has a self-assigned language proficiency and each test has only a rough difficulty level assigned by the administrator. This section describes how tests receive adjusted difficulty ratings and how users' proficiency assignments are adapted throughout their interaction with the system in order to present them with tests of a suitable difficulty.

Whenever a user completes a c-test, their current language level is adjusted. Similarly, the difficulty prediction of the c-test is refined with every new user taking the test, providing a larger basis for the difficulty estimation. We currently use two rating strategies (i) Mean Error Rate and, (ii) the Elo rating system (Elo, 1978).

4.1 Mean Error Rate

Under this strategy, the difficulty of a c-test is determined by the average error rates of the respective

[1] https://github.com/zesch/ctest-builder

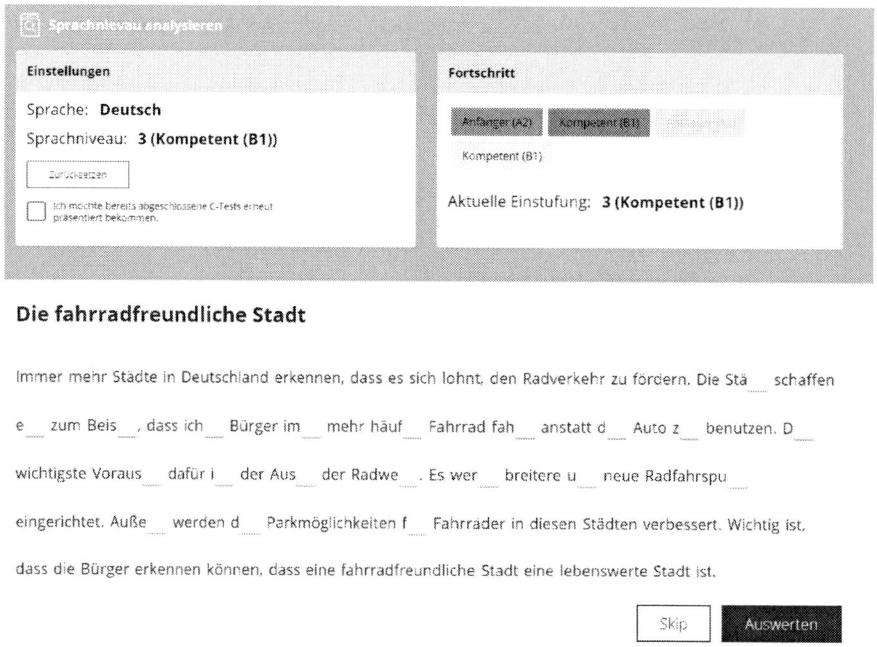

Figure 2: Screenshot from the application during the performance of a c-test. The three integration areas are visible: settings, progress and the actual test.

gaps.

$$MER = \frac{1}{n}\sum_{i=1}^{n} e_i$$

n is the number of gaps in the respective c-test and e is the difficulty of an individual gap. The difficulty of a gap is approximated via the percentage of users who can't solve that gap.

Under this strategy, the user proficiency is only indirectly adapted. A user is only presented with tests matching their current proficiency level. If the user correctly filled more than a certain threshold of gaps from the most recent n tests, their proficiency level is adapted to the next higher level. If they falls below a certain threshold, their proficiency level is adapted to the next lower level.

4.2 Elo Rating

The Elo strategy describes a system for calculating the level of a group of users relative to each other. Usually, the Elo method is applied in competitive sports such as chess or football (Hvattum and Arntzen, 2010). However, the method is also used in research (Lehmann and Wohlrabe, 2017) and adaptive educational settings similar to our case (Pelánek, 2016). In order to use the Elo strategy for our scenario, some adjustments have to be made that we describe in the following. We treat the user and the c-tests like opponents, so that each user and c-test receives a score. Informally speaking: if a user 'beats' a hard test (operationalized in our case as filling at least half of the gaps correctly), their Elo ranking will improve more than if a user correctly solves an easy test. Both ratings are in the range of $[1, 6] \subset \mathbb{N}$

More formally, we define the expectation of success E_U for the user as follows:

$$E_U = \frac{1}{1 + 10^{(R_T - R_U)}}$$

where R_U describes the rating of the user, R_T the rating of the c-test respectively and the success expectation for the test E_T is computed as $1 - E_U$.

Starting from the self-assigned user proficiency and admin assigned test difficulty, the ratings are updated as follows during the evaluation of a user's performance on a c-test:

$$R'_A = R_A + (S_A - E_A), for A \in \{T, U\}$$

R_A defines the old rating and R'_A the updated value. In order to translate the ratings back to the language levels, we round R'_A. In our version, S_A is 1 for winning and 0 for losing. The user "wins" if he has

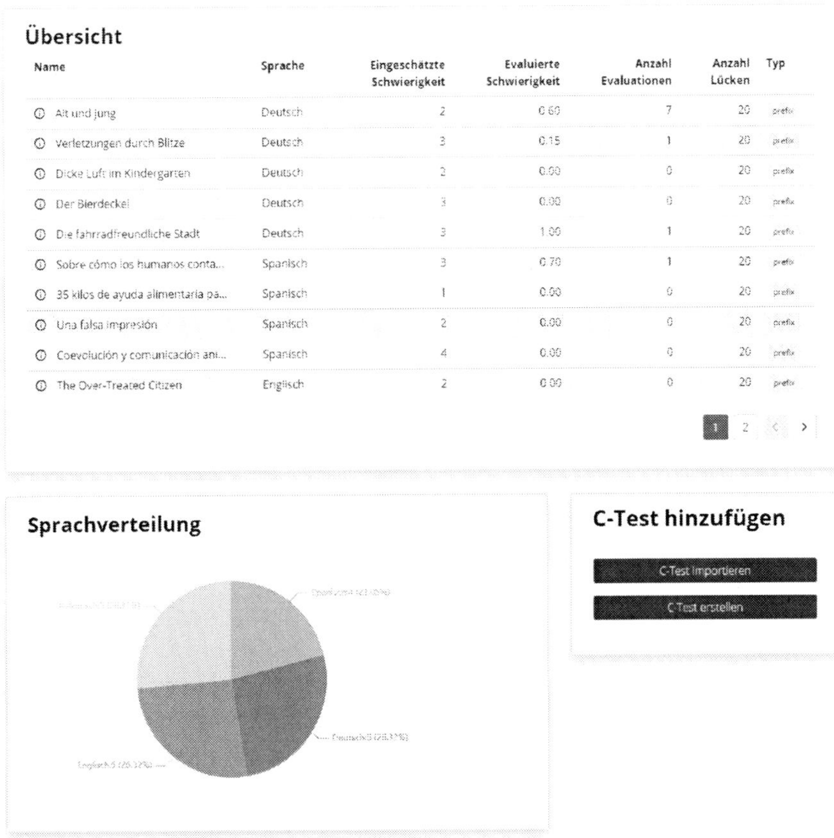

Figure 3: Screenshot of the administration panel. In addition to an overview of all c-tests (*Übersicht*), it is also possible to switch to a detailed view with e.g. language distributions (*Sprachverteilung*) and add new c-tests (*C-Test hinzufügen*.

completed at least 50% correctly. This means, the harder the test, the larger the update if the user can beat it.

5 Implementation Details

Our tool is implemented through a REST backend server and a separated frontend application. The source code is publicly available.[2]

The frontend of the application is provided through a VueJS application that communicates with the provided REST server. The interface provides the functionality to interact with the application and is more or less independent from the backend.

The provided REST server connects and mediates corresponding requests for the creation and evaluation of c-tests. The server was implemented using the Spring Boot Framework.

[2]https://gitlab.com/ctest-evaluator

6 Conclusion and outlook

We have presented an open-source implementation of a data collection tool that provides c-tests for language learners and collects training data for difficulty prediction tasks. The collected data, especially the individual incorrect solution attempts can also be used to study misspellings and cognates for learners of different L1s and L2s. So far, our prototype has only been tested with a small number of users. Next steps thus involve the deployment with a larger user base to start the actual data collection process for c-tests. For many languages, this will provide the first publicly available training data.

References

Lisa Beinborn, Torsten Zesch, and Iryna Gurevych. 2014. Predicting the difficulty of language proficiency tests. *Transactions of the Associ-*

ation for Computational Linguistics 2:517–530. https://www.aclweb.org/anthology/Q14-1040.

Council of Europe, editor. 2009. *Common European Framework of Reference for Languages: learning, teaching, assessment*. Cambridge Univ. Press [u.a.], Cambridge, 10. printing edition. OCLC: 837109490.

Arpad E. Elo. 1978. *The rating of chessplayers, past and present*. Arco Pub., New York. http://www.amazon.com/Rating-Chess-Players-Past-Present/dp/0668047216.

Ruediger Grotjahn. 2002. Konstruktion und Einsatz von C-Tests: Ein leitfaden für die Praxis pages 211–225.

Rüdiger Grotjahn. 2010. *Der C-Test: Beiträge aus der aktuellen Forschung - The C-Test: contributions from current research*. Peter Lang, Bern, Switzerland. https://www.peterlang.com/view/title/12445.

Lars Magnus Hvattum and Halvard Arntzen. 2010. Using ELO ratings for match result prediction in association football. *International Journal of Forecasting* 26(3):460–470. https://doi.org/10.1016/j.ijforecast.2009.10.002.

Ji-Ung Lee, Erik Schwan, and Christian M. Meyer. 2019. Manipulating the difficulty of C-tests. In *Proceedings of the 57th Annual Meeting of the Association for Computational Linguistics*. Association for Computational Linguistics, Florence, Italy, pages 360–370. https://doi.org/10.18653/v1/P19-1035.

Robert Lehmann and Klaus Wohlrabe. 2017. Who is the 'journal grand master'? a new ranking based on the elo rating system. *Journal of Informetrics* 11(3):800–809. https://doi.org/10.1016/j.joi.2017.05.004.

Radek Pelánek. 2016. Applications of the elo rating system in adaptive educational systems. *Computers & Education* 98:169–179.

Ulhich Raatz and Christine Klein-Braley. 1981. The c-test - a modification of the cloze procedure. In *Practice and Problems in Language Testing*. Colchester: University of Essex, Dept. of Language and Linguistics, pages 113–138.

Torsten Zesch, Andrea Horbach, Melanie Goggin, and Jennifer Wrede-Jackes. 2018. *A flexible online system for curating reduced redundancy language exercises and tests*, Research-publishing.net, pages 319–324. https://doi.org/10.14705/rpnet.2018.26.857.

Virtual Pre-Service Teacher Assessment and Feedback via Conversational Agents

Debajyoti Datta [1] *, Maria Phillips [1] *, James P. Bywater [2], Jennifer Chiu [3], Ginger S. Watson [3], Laura Barnes [1] Donald Brown [1]

[1]School of Engineering and Applied Science, University of Virginia
[2]College of Education, James Madison University
[3]School of Education and Human Development, University of Virginia
{dd3ar, mp6kv, jlc4dz, gw2b,lb3dp, deb}@virginia.edu
bywatejx@jmu.edu

Abstract

Conversational agents and assistants have been used for decades to facilitate learning. There are many examples of conversational agents used for educational and training purposes in K-12, higher education, healthcare, the military, and private industry settings. The most common forms of conversational agents in education are teaching agents that directly teach and support learning, peer agents that serve as knowledgeable learning companions to guide learners in the learning process, and teachable agents that function as a novice or less-knowledgeable student trained and taught by a learner who learns by teaching. The Instructional Quality Assessment (IQA) provides a robust framework to evaluate reading comprehension and mathematics instruction. We developed a system for pre-service teachers, individuals in a teacher preparation program, to evaluate teaching instruction quality based on a modified interpretation of IQA metrics. Our demonstration and approach take advantage of recent advances in Natural Language Processing (NLP) and deep learning for each dialogue system component. We built an open-source conversational agent system to engage pre-service teachers in a specific mathematical scenario focused on scale factor with the aim to provide feedback on pre-service teachers' questioning strategies. We believe our system is not only practical for teacher education programs but can also enable other researchers to build new educational scenarios with minimal effort.

1 Introduction

In the era of remote teaching due to governmental regulations and stay-at-home orders for COVID-19, remote teaching methodologies have come to the forefront of education and training. Virtual conversational agents have been used for a variety of training scenarios to train teachers and nurses in many different contexts (Datta et al., 2016). Virtual conversational agents refers to an online interactive system where a user is able to dialogue and receive responses in turn. all future references to conversational agents will refer to this definition of virtual conversational agents. Conversational agents, often characterized as dialogue systems, are common in customer support representative applications (Yan et al., 2017). In education, they have been used extensively for interpreting the content of the conversation, integrating and assimilating information, and providing feedback(Chhibber and Law, 2019). However, as pointed out by Smutny and Schreiberova (2020) very few conversational agents used in education use recent advances in machine learning and deep learning, instead relying on simple decision trees. This reinforces the need for more research and development on artificial intelligence–based methods to support content-specific conversations. A conversational agent deployed through a web interface, as opposed to software implementations, for teacher learning has multiple benefits. Two of the prominent benefits are that this approach can easily be scaled to reach more in-service and pre-service teachers as well while also providing a cost-effective way to build systems that can be scaled to new teaching scenarios as multiple dialogue system components can be reused. The dialogue manager and semantic sentence-level components can be used for different mathematical scenarios as long as the assessment component remains unchanged. In this case the term assessment is referring to pre-service teacher evaluation as opposed to a students understanding of a mathematical topic. In this work, we combine the advances in NLP and deep learning research with a modified version of the Instructional Quality Assessment (IQA) (Boston, 2012) framework to build a scenario to be used in teacher

* First two authors have contributed equally

Proceedings of the 16th Workshop on Innovative Use of NLP for Building Educational Applications, pages 185–198
April 20, 2021 ©2021 Association for Computational Linguistics

education settings. Our goal in this project is to assess and give teachers immediate feedback on the quality of their instructional moves using a specific scenario on a given mathematical topic.

Research demonstrates that the Instructional Quality Assessment provides a robust framework for evaluating teachers' instructional practice in mathematics classrooms. Our demonstration uses a modified version of the IQA that focuses on the strategy of teachers' questions during one-on-one or class discussions through a web-based platform that allows for pre-service teachers to receive real-time feedback on the quality of their questioning. Although our demonstration centers on using an adapted version of IQA as the assessment component, our modular architecture can be used to incorporate alternative evaluation schemes as well.

A critical challenge of developing dialogue systems in a new domain is the requirement of large data sets for the different components of the dialogue system (intent classification, slot filling for dialogue state tracking, and the dialogue policy). In education, where data collection can itself prove a significant challenge, especially given a need for increased domain expert annotations, our system is developed with only a small amount of annotated data: around two thousand sentences that are labeled with one of four adapted IQA classes. Note that this system is not necessarily better than existing approaches that use annotated training data for each component of the dialogue system, rather, this system is a compromise because dialogue systems are challenging to build in low- or no-data amount scenarios. What our system demonstrates is a solution to developing a highly-manipulable scenario given minimal domain-expert annotated data that can be used to support virtual feedback for pre-service teachers.

Our contributions are as follows:

- An open-source web-platform for assessment of the quality of teachers' mathematical questioning
- A process that allows for scenario development with minimal training data
- Direct feedback to pre-service teachers on the quality of mathematical questioning by relying on the state of the art NLP components
- A framework in which new scenarios can be deployed with minimal change in components by relying on transfer learning and weak supervision

2 Related Work

Virtual human-based simulations can provide meaningful, deliberate practice for learning a wide range of teaching skills during teacher preparation as well as extended practice for advanced skills for in-service teachers. Dialogue systems for conversational agents can be built in two different approaches: End-to-end approaches that combine all of the dialogue system stages require large-scaled labeled training data and component-based systems which require less data, but each component needs to be trained separately. Component-based systems have the advantage of allowing certain components to be reused for similar contextual scenarios. Our work utilizes the latter approach leveraging unstructured data collected from web and textbooks as knowledge bases. Our dialogue policy is a combination of handcrafted rules by education domain experts, and dialogue states are tracked through a reading comprehension based approach highlighted by Gao et al. (2019). The most common approach for dialogue state tracking is the "slot-value" pairs approach. In this scenario, different stages of the dialogue are often framed as a multi-class classification task (Mrkšić et al., 2015). While this approach is well-studied, the decision to use the reading comprehension based approach in this system is based on the ability to incorporate pre-trained models for dialogue state tracking.

The assessment component for the pre-service teachers' questioning strategy is an adapted version of IQA. The IQA has been developed by the Learning Research and Developmental Center at the University of Pittsburgh since 2002 (Matsumura et al., 2006). The IQA offers a holistic assessment of mathematical instruction, including the academic rigor of the specific tasks and student and teacher discussion surrounding the task (Pianta and Hamre, 2009). The IQA has been further validated by its developers in subsequent research (Boston and Candela, 2018). More recent developments suggest that the IQA can be used not only as an assessment tool but also as a feedback tool to help teachers actively improve their instruction (Boston and Candela, 2018).

The questions that teachers ask are essential for promoting students' meaningful mathematical discourse. The academic rigor component (Junker et al., 2005; Boston, 2012) of the IQA builds on earlier classifications of teacher questions (e.g. Boaler and Brodie (2004), distinguishes between "probing and exploring" questions that ask students to clarify their ideas or the connections between them, and "procedural and factual" questions that elicit facts or yes/no responses). The IQA is intended to be used in contexts where cognitively demanding mathematical tasks are implemented and is well suited for fine-grained teacher professional development such as that which focuses on teacher questioning (Boston et al., 2015). Another advantage of utilizing IQA is the limited categories as a high number of categories results in very complex dialogue policies (Yan et al., 2017).

Given the limited amount of time domain experts may have for annotating data, several methods to improve label efficiency were explored. Weak supervision techniques, as highlighted by Ratner et al. (2016) provides the two-fold benefit in that it requires less human labeling than would otherwise be required for training. An additional benefit of Weak supervision is that noisy data and the accuracy of each annotator can be taken into account for classification. Ratner et al. (2016) has shown that weak supervision systems are better than generic majority vote approaches. Noisy label data for model classification has also been studied by deep-learning-based approaches (Guan et al., 2018) and proven effective.

3 Data and Tools

3.1 Classification Model Data

A primary purpose of this conversational agent is in its ability to provide feedback for pre-service teachers. This requires the ability to classify each statement or question using the selected assessment rubric which in this implementation is an adapted IQA rubric. The categories of the adapted IQA measure were set by education domain experts and iterated on over the course of several months for the purposes of classification and feedback for pre-service teachers. The adapted IQA measure includes the following categories of questions:

- **Probing and Exploring**: Clarifies student thinking, enables students to elaborate their own thinking for their own benefit and the class. Points to underlying mathematical relationships and meanings and makes links among mathematical ideas. (e.g., Explain to me how you got that expression?)
- **Procedural and Factual**: Elicits a mathematical fact or procedure; Requires a yes/no or single response answer; Requires the recall of a memorized fact or procedure (e.g., What is the square root of 4?)
- **Expository and Cueing**: Provides a mathematical cueing or mathematical information to students. (e.g: To solve this problem you need to double this side, then take that number and multiply it by 3.)
- **Other** This refers to all other conversations not related to the above topics.(e.g: Close your books, Why didn't you use graph paper?)

Annotators also had the opportunity to flag any data as a "data issue" which would represent a transcript preprocessing error or another issue indicating the data could not be labeled such as incoherent text or blank text.

The data used for the adapted IQA evaluation rubric was developed from transcriptions of audio recordings of teachers in whole-class and teacher-student conversations that took place in elementary mathematics classrooms using different mathematics curricula across the United States. The de-identified dataset was shared from an NSF-sponsored project that had previously collected the recordings to answer separate research questions. Students engaged with a project purposed to help them understand different geometry concepts like scale factor, dimensions, surface area, and volume of rectangular prisms. The students recorded the observations from a given visualization and explained the impact of the scale factor. The data collected for the development of this scenario contained 2826 questions. The unique question along with the context, or speaking turn, in which the question was uttered were both provided as reference for the annotators to use during labeling.

We had 5799 total labeled data instances. There were five total annotators: three expert teachers as well as two pre-service teachers. The total number of annotators fluctuated during different stages of the annotation process resulting in varied amounts of labels generated by each annotator. The time to label each data point averaged between 5.2 to 6.7 seconds per annotator. The total number of unique labeled sentences was 2826. The total distribution of labels between the four assessment categories ranged from 856 to 2133. We used weak supervision based approaches to combine the labeled

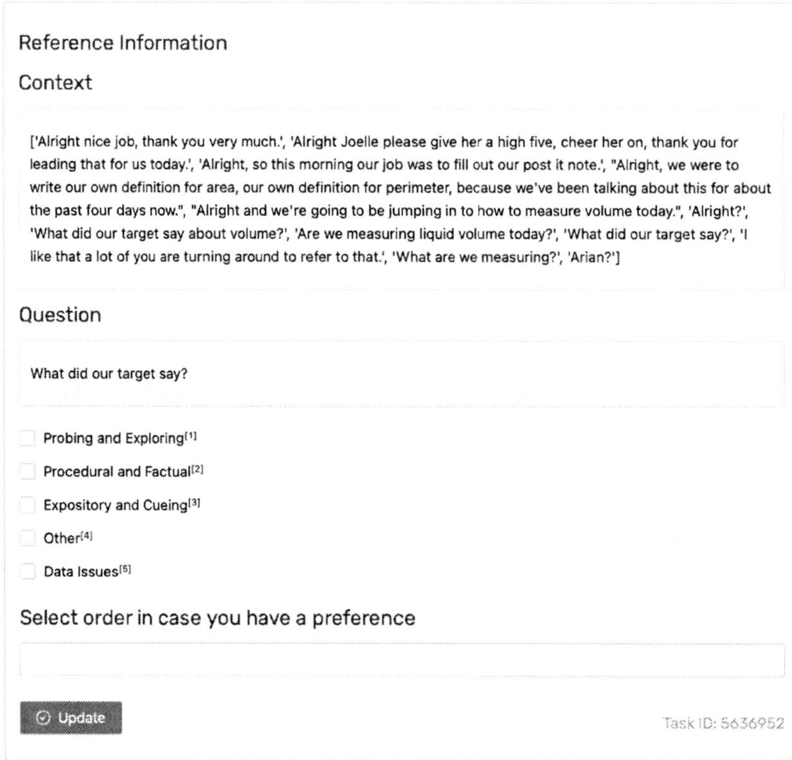

Figure 1: Labeling interface for annotation

data from multiple annotators over majority vote approaches.

3.2 Labeling Platforms

Two labeling platforms were used extensively for this project: Labelbox (Labelbox, 2020) and Label Studio (Tkachenko et al., 2020). While both platforms were simple and straightforward to use, Label Studio enabled the building of custom user interfaces with several improved features such as keyboard shortcuts that allowed annotators to more easily onboard and complete labeling tasks more efficiently.

Each individual question was labeled with a context reference that allowed annotators to see the entire speaking turn of the teacher. The decision to include context came after previous iterations of labeling questions resulted in an inter-annotator agreement of below 0.50, which subsequently increased to 0.66 after including context. An example of the Label Studio labeling interface is shown in Figure 1.

Our data collection approach relied on weak supervision and learning with noisy labels strategies. In this paradigm noisy labels acquired either through human labels or machine learning models are cost effective to acquire. In the scenario in which domain expert annotators are available (in our case, expert teachers), noisy disagreements between annotators can be leveraged to build high accuracy models (Ratner et al., 2016; Guan et al., 2018). Weak supervision approaches are scalable, enabling easy adaptation to multiple mathematical scenarios, one of the key contributions and focuses of this project.

3.3 Knowledge Base Data

The knowledge-base of dialogue systems can be very complex depending on the scenario for which the dialogue system is being built (Yan et al., 2017). For this initial demonstration scenario the conversational agent represents a student with some level of understanding of the topic scale factor. The knowledge base relies on unstructured knowledge about scale factor collected from the web and textbooks in which text compiled is in the format of plain text. As our system is intended to reflect a students understanding of a topic, which is reasonably im-

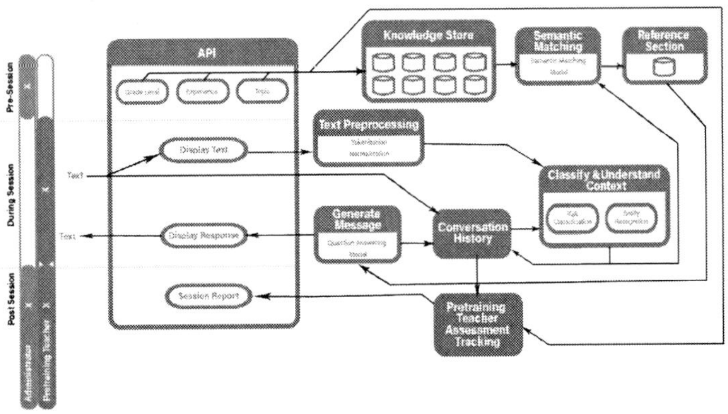

Figure 2: Conversational Agent Implementation Architecture

perfect, contradictory sources of information are not a primary concern. In fact a knowledge base with contradictory information may be leveraged to support more robust answering. Additionally, the expected level of understanding of a student for a given topic is likely to be documented in instructional materials readily available on the web and therefore collecting this data is a simple way to develop a knowledge base. Future efforts will address identifying grade-appropriate filtering that may improve interaction by generating a more realistic student profile with a grade-reflective knowldge-base.

The text collected from the web was not cleaned, labeled, or annotated. Basic pre-processing included removing references to figures or hyperlinks to other web pages. Once the plain text reference base was compiled, we then separated the text into sections of no more than 512 words. This processing step was done so that an entire section could be directly used as the input in the response generation discussed further in the methods section.

Relying on unstructured knowledge bases is critical to rapidly developing and deploying new conversational agent scenarios. Unstructured texts on varying mathematical topics are readily available from websites and video transcripts. Our framework allows for a simple way to incorporate newly generated external knowledge bases as a way to scale to additional scenarios. The ability to use unstructured knowledge as the key input of our knowledge base is possible due to the recent advances in question-answering models, reading comprehension tasks, and readily available libraries such as Huggingface Transformers (Wolf et al., 2020).

3.4 Platform Interface and Hosting

The application was built with Django, a Python web application development framework. Credentials must be generated and are required prior to using the interface. The interface includes an Institutional Review Board (IRB) consent form as well as a description of the scenario to include topic, expected student understanding of topic (Beginner, Intermediate, Advanced), and student grade level. Screenshots of the application are included in the Appendix.

4 Methods

The overall architecture of our conversational agent is depicted in Figure 2. As discussed, a central component of our demonstration is evaluating and providing feedback of pre-service teacher instruction. For this initial version of the scenario, domain experts provided a specified rubric for pre-service teachers to meet that clarifies the types of IQA categories desired within a session. One sample rubric evaluates if the teacher is asking at least one "probing and exploring" question, one "expository and cuing" question, and one "procedural and factual" question. This rubric can be changed easily in the demonstration through a separate JSON file. In our current evaluation, we do not evaluate the order in which the questions are asked, but we plan to include more sophisticated evaluation protocols in future work.

The current implementation incorporates text interactions between a conversational agent, representing a student, and a pre-service teacher. The pre-service teacher can interact with the conversational agent by providing new knowledge and

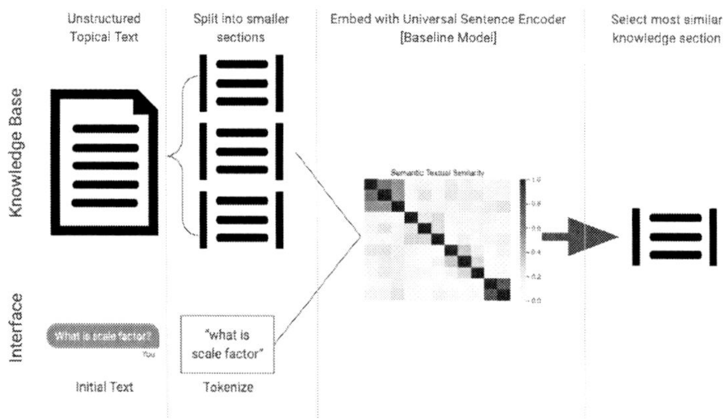

Figure 3: Dialogue System Selection of Knowledge Base Reference Section via Semantic Similarity

testing understanding as well as testing knowledge of the topic "scale factor". The pre-service teacher types a statement, question, multiple statements or multiple questions in the text box, and the conversational agent responds by taking into account the conversation context as well as the pre-service teacher's utterance. Each component of the dialogue system is described in detail in the subsequent subsections.

4.1 Assessment Metric Classifier

In our demonstration, we utilize the entire speaking turn of the pre-service teacher as the input text. This formulation is very similar to the two-sentence classification task like what is used in the Stanford Natural Language Inference corpus (Bowman et al., 2015). We frame our input in a similar format for classification and fine-tuning. The input text undergoes basic cleaning and is tokenized prior to being used as the input to our classifier model. We experimented with multiple text classification approaches to include Convolutional Neural Network (CNN)—based text classification (Kim, 2014), Long Short-Term Memory (LSTM)—based text classification (Liu et al., 2016), and newer approaches that rely on Transformer Architectures (Devlin et al., 2018; Liu et al., 2019) and perform well with small amounts of labeled data. Transfer learning models tend to perform well with less labeled data than other models because of the pretraining with unsupervised text that encodes knowledge and semantic meaning of words and sentences. This demonstration incorporates a fine-tuned Bidirectional Encoder Representations from Transformers (BERT) model for our adapted IQA classification task.

4.2 Semantic Matching

For the conversational agent to respond to input text, the first step is to identify the most relevant section of the knowledge base. To do this, the preprocessed input text is used in combination with the Universal Sentence Encoder (Cer et al., 2018) to find the most relevant, or more specifically, semantically similar section of the knowledge base. Semantic similarity refers to identifying the degree to which two texts have the same meaning. As discussed in the data treatment section, the knowledge base section is split into smaller sections that are a more optimized size for the semantic similarity tool used: the Universal Sentence Encoder. This process is depicted in Figure 3.

The Universal Sentence Encoder is optimized for short phrases or paragraphs and outputs a 512-dimensional vector. Semantic similarity computation is accomplished by computing the inner product between the input and knowledge base text. The semantic similarity between generated embeddings was computed using normalized cosine similarity of the embeddings. Semantic similarity computation at the sentence level is more accurate than the aggregate of word-level similarities and is therefore preferred in this application. Models trained to understand words in context are often better suited for identifying semantic similarities of phrases and sentences. In application, we may take input such as "What is scale factor?" By finding the most semantically similar section in the knowledge base, we can use this section to input the response generation.

If the text's semantic similarity and the knowledge base sections do not achieve a pre-defined threshold, the system responds from the unknown category. For this demonstration the threshold was set to 0.80 after empirical evaluation of semantic coherence. This threshold value will be further tested and empirically evaluated in future iterations of this system.

In the unknown category, one of the six random responses (pre-defined) is selected to convey to the pre-service teacher that the system does not understand the user input. This pre-defined selection represents a hand-crafted dialogue policy that was determined by domain experts.

If the semantic similarity is greater than or equal to the threshold for a given knowledge base section, the system then selects this knowledge section. The initial input text along with the selected knowledge base section are used as the inputs to a question-answering module. The question-answering module is a pre-trained BERT model that is fine-tuned on the Stanford Question Answering Dataset (SQuaD). This module is then used to generate a response in the user interface for the subsequent turn of the conversation. The dialogue manager retains the dialogue states of the conversation for record and reference within the conversation.

4.3 Dialogue Manager

4.3.1 Dialogue State Tracking

Dialogue State Tracking is a core component of the dialogue system. The goal of the dialogue state tracking system is to estimate the goal at each turn of the conversation. There are multiple formulations of dialogue state tracking systems like hand-crafted rules (Wang and Lemon, 2013) and web-style ranking (Williams, 2014). In our approach we use the most recent question-answering paradigm for dialogue state tracking (Gao et al., 2019). Unlike Gao et al. (2019) we do not train our reading comprehension based model, but instead use the question-answering paradigm to understand the dialogue states. We append each of the pre-service teacher utterances along with the student responses. Since conversational agent responses can either be mathematical (evaluating an expression) or responding to a pre-service teacher utterance, we evaluate each stage as a question-answer task. So at the end an utterance questions prompted include: "Did the teacher ask a probing and exploratory question?", "Did the conversational agent answer the question correctly?", "Did the pre-service teacher acknowledge the answer". This iterative framework of question answering helps keep track of the dialogue state. Since this is a task-specific dialogue system being evaluated for a specific mathematical scenario, we are already aware of the dialogue states of the conversation. At each turn in the conversation, we use all the previous pre-service teacher utterances to determine the current dialogue state of the conversation.

4.3.2 Dialogue Policy

In our task-specific dialogue system, our dialogue policy is rule-based. Depending on the dialogue state accomplished up to turn n, our utterance at $n + 1$ depends on the dialogue states accomplished up to that point. The hand-crafted rules for our dialogue policy also enable the use of direct evaluation based on simple metrics such as the number of questions in each adapted IQA category or development of metrics like Initiate Response Evaluate (IRE) (Mehan, 1979).

4.4 Response Generation

The response generation component extracts relevant sections of the knowledge base as a question-answering task. A question-answering task, also referred to as a reading comprehension task, is a supervised learning problem, where given a segment of text of i tokens, a question of j tokens, it returns an answer segment of k tokens. The answer in question-answering tasks can be cloze-style as in CNN/Daily Mail (Hermann et al., 2015), span prediction (like SQuaD (Rajpurkar et al., 2016)), or be similar to NarrativeQA (Kočiský et al., 2018). We retrieved our knowledge from semantic matching of web-text categories and thus our response generation pipeline matched closely to span prediction tasks. We implemented the response generation pipeline using the transformers library (Wolf et al., 2020), where a BERT model (Devlin et al., 2018) was fine-tuned on the SQuaD dataset. We did not fine-tune our question-answering system for the response generation module, rather relying on semantically-matched unstructured data sections to be used as inputs in generating answers to questions.

4.5 Session Feedback

All text input by the pre-service teacher is retained as well as the associated adapted IQA category classification. The compilation of classifications of the pre-service teachers' input texts are provided in an assessment report which is used as feedback for the pre-service teacher at the end of the session.

5 Results

This section will discuss the step by step interaction with the developed interface that is developed. Only one scenario currently exists and is defined as a 4th-5th grade average understanding of the mathematics topic scale factor.

5.1 IQA Classifier

To train the IQA classifier, we used BERT (Devlin et al., 2018) and DistillBERT (Sanh et al., 2019) for classification based on the open source Transformers (Wolf et al., 2020) implementation. We trained the classifiers on 80% of the data and sectioned the remaining data as a 10% validation set and 10% for the test set. The validation set accuracy for the BERT and DistillBert models were 75.8 and 74.3 respectively. Since, the performance increase with Bert was minimal we used Distillbert for faster inference.

5.2 Walk Through

This platform is currently hosted on Python Anywhere. Pre-generated credentials for instructors are generated for a given user ID. Each user uses the unique ID to create an associated password. Following the prompts the user is able to read through the IRB consent form and sign in to access the conversational interface. Figure 4 shows the first conversational agent interaction screen as well as an example inputs where the pre-service teacher may ask several questions to assess the conversational agents current level of understanding.

The pre-service teacher, or user, can then interact with the conversational agent by typing questions or statements. The Appendix contains additional screen captures of the developed interface. Currently the system only supports text-based conversation.

An example of a text snippet that does not meet the set semantic matching threshold with the generated conversational agent response is demonstrated in Figure 4. There are instances when the conversation breaks despite the teacher re-framing their questions or input differently. This is intended to reflect how a student may sometimes fail to answer a properly framed question or statement appropriately.

Once the session is completed, the pre-service teacher receives a session report which incorporates the adapted IQA rubric and the number of their interactions that would be classified within each of the sections. They are also provided a report of the entire conversation that is shared with expert teachers as well in an effort to identify how the conversational agent stages can be designed better.

6 Conclusion and Future Work

Our goal in this paper is to demonstrate the implementation of a conversational agent with very little training data that relied on foundational and well-studied metrics like IQA. By leveraging state of the art modules for natural language processing and deep learning we could build a functional prototype that is now going to be used as a pilot for training for a specific mathematical scenario of "scale factor". By integrating pre-trained models such as SQuAD, BERT, and the Universal Sentence Encoder as well as using weak supervision approaches in data treatment we have leveraged minimal amounts of domain-expert-labeled data and knowledge base data in order to create a usable interface. Approaches like this help evaluate pre-service teachers in a scalable fashion and can also be deployed across the web for large scale participation. There are several areas we are pursuing to improve this interface in order to provide a more robust interface as well as a more useful assessment tool. Some of the current features that we are working on are as follows:

- **Improved IQA model:** We plan to continue collecting domain-expert labeled data that can then be used to improve the trained classification model. The improved classification model will better reflect a realistic assessment of pre-service teacher sessions using the IQA-developed categories as a rubric.

- **Increased Knowledge Base:** This first scenario is limited to a specific knowledge base on the topic "Scale Factor". We plan to incorporate a wider variety of data related to expected knowledge on this topic (from 4th grade to 10th grade) as well as associated topics such as perimeter, volume, and ratio. With these knowledge bases compiled we will be able to test techniques that can assist in generating responses that are representative of a limited understanding of the desired topic to a

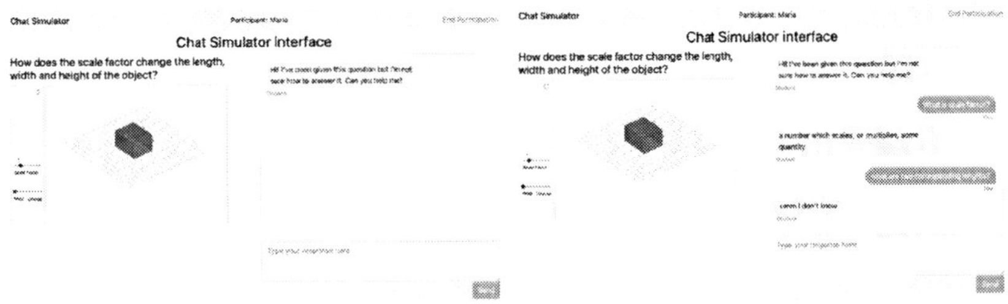

Figure 4: Conversational Agent Interface Screen. Left image shows initial screen. Right image shows interaction example where conversational agent has identified a statement that does not meet semantic matching threshold within the knowledge base.

more advanced level of understanding on the topic.

- **Response Generation:** Currently there are some features within the response that appear to represent the way a student is more likely to respond. We would like to further develop these features by incorporating more student-like speech features. This would allow for more realistic conversational agent interaction and result in less formal or textbook-like responses. Additionally, current responses generated are most coherent when responding to a question which is not necessarily reflective of all student-teacher interactions. Future developments are planned to improve the robustness of responses to better account for the different forms of inputs.

Finally, we plan to be deploy this tool with a group of pre-service teachers under the direction of expert teachers in order to test the qualitative aspects and realism of this system.

Acknowledgments

This work was funded in part by the Robertson Foundation. The authors wish to acknowledge the use of de-identified classroom dialogue from NSF 1535024.

References

Jo Boaler and Karin Brodie. 2004. The importance, nature and impact of teacher questions. In *Proceedings of the twenty-sixth annual meeting of the North American Chapter of the International Group for the Psychology of Mathematics Education*, volume 2, pages 774–782.

Melissa Boston. 2012. Assessing instructional quality in mathematics. *The Elementary School Journal*, 113(1):76–104.

Melissa Boston, Jonathan Bostic, Kristin Lesseig, and Milan Sherman. 2015. A comparison of mathematics classroom observation protocols. *Mathematics Teacher Educator*, 3(2):154–175.

Melissa D Boston and Amber G Candela. 2018. The instructional quality assessment as a tool for reflecting on instructional practice. *ZDM*, 50(3):427–444.

Samuel R Bowman, Gabor Angeli, Christopher Potts, and Christopher D Manning. 2015. A large annotated corpus for learning natural language inference. *arXiv preprint arXiv:1508.05326*.

Daniel Cer, Yinfei Yang, Sheng yi Kong, Nan Hua, Nicole Limtiaco, Rhomni St. John, Noah Constant, Mario Guajardo-Cespedes, Steve Yuan, Chris Tar, Yun-Hsuan Sung, Brian Strope, and Ray Kurzweil. 2018. Universal sentence encoder.

Nalin Chhibber and Edith Law. 2019. Using conversational agents to support learning by teaching. *arXiv preprint arXiv:1909.13443*.

Debajyoti Datta, Valentina Brashers, John Owen, Casey White, and Laura E Barnes. 2016. A deep learning methodology for semantic utterance classification in virtual human dialogue systems. In *International Conference on Intelligent Virtual Agents*, pages 451–455. Springer.

Jacob Devlin, Ming-Wei Chang, Kenton Lee, and Kristina Toutanova. 2018. Bert: Pre-training of deep bidirectional transformers for language understanding. *arXiv preprint arXiv:1810.04805*.

Shuyang Gao, Abhishek Sethi, Sanchit Agarwal, Tagyoung Chung, and Dilek Hakkani-Tur. 2019. Dialog state tracking: A neural reading comprehension approach. In *Proceedings of the 20th Annual SIGdial Meeting on Discourse and Dialogue*, pages 264–273.

Melody Guan, Varun Gulshan, Andrew Dai, and Geoffrey Hinton. 2018. Who said what: Modeling individual labelers improves classification. In *Proceedings of the AAAI Conference on Artificial Intelligence*, volume 32.

Karl Moritz Hermann, Tomas Kocisky, Edward Grefenstette, Lasse Espeholt, Will Kay, Mustafa Suleyman, and Phil Blunsom. 2015. Teaching machines to read and comprehend. *Advances in neural information processing systems*, 28:1693–1701.

Brian William Junker, Yanna Weisberg, Lindsay Clare Matsumura, Amy Crosson, Mikyung Wolf, Allison Levison, and Lauren Resnick. 2005. *Overview of the instructional quality assessment*. Regents of the University of California.

Yoon Kim. 2014. Convolutional neural networks for sentence classification. In *EMNLP*.

Tomáš Kočiský, Jonathan Schwarz, Phil Blunsom, Chris Dyer, Karl Moritz Hermann, Gábor Melis, and Edward Grefenstette. 2018. The narrativeqa reading comprehension challenge. *Transactions of the Association for Computational Linguistics*, 6:317–328.

Labelbox. 2020. Labelbox: Training data platform.

Pengfei Liu, Xipeng Qiu, and Xuanjing Huang. 2016. Recurrent neural network for text classification with multi-task learning. *arXiv preprint arXiv:1605.05101*.

Yinhan Liu, Myle Ott, Naman Goyal, Jingfei Du, Mandar Joshi, Danqi Chen, Omer Levy, Mike Lewis, Luke Zettlemoyer, and Veselin Stoyanov. 2019. Roberta: A robustly optimized bert pretraining approach.

Lindsay Clare Matsumura, Brian Junker, Yanna Weisberg, and Amy Crosson. 2006. Overview of the instructional quality assessment.

Hugh Mehan. 1979. 'what time is it, denise?": Asking known information questions in classroom discourse. *Theory into practice*, 18(4):285–294.

Nikola Mrkšić, Diarmuid O Séaghdha, Blaise Thomson, Milica Gašić, Pei-Hao Su, David Vandyke, Tsung-Hsien Wen, and Steve Young. 2015. Multi-domain dialog state tracking using recurrent neural networks. *arXiv preprint arXiv:1506.07190*.

Robert C Pianta and Bridget K Hamre. 2009. Conceptualization, measurement, and improvement of classroom processes: Standardized observation can leverage capacity. *Educational researcher*, 38(2):109–119.

Pranav Rajpurkar, Jian Zhang, Konstantin Lopyrev, and Percy Liang. 2016. Squad: 100,000+ questions for machine comprehension of text. *arXiv preprint arXiv:1606.05250*.

Alexander J Ratner, Christopher M De Sa, Sen Wu, Daniel Selsam, and Christopher Ré. 2016. Data programming: Creating large training sets, quickly. In *Advances in neural information processing systems*, pages 3567–3575.

Victor Sanh, Lysandre Debut, Julien Chaumond, and Thomas Wolf. 2019. Distilbert, a distilled version of bert: smaller, faster, cheaper and lighter. *arXiv preprint arXiv:1910.01108*.

Pavel Smutny and Petra Schreiberova. 2020. Chatbots for learning: A review of educational chatbots for the facebook messenger. *Computers & Education*, page 103862.

Maxim Tkachenko, Mikhail Malyuk, Nikita Shevchenko, Andrey Holmanyuk, and Nikolai Liubimov. 2020. Label Studio: Data labeling software. Open source software available from https://github.com/heartexlabs/label-studio.

Zhuoran Wang and Oliver Lemon. 2013. A simple and generic belief tracking mechanism for the dialog state tracking challenge: On the believability of observed information. In *Proceedings of the SIGDIAL 2013 Conference*, pages 423–432.

Jason D Williams. 2014. Web-style ranking and slu combination for dialog state tracking. In *Proceedings of the 15th Annual Meeting of the Special Interest Group on Discourse and Dialogue (SIGDIAL)*, pages 282–291.

Thomas Wolf, Lysandre Debut, Victor Sanh, Julien Chaumond, Clement Delangue, Anthony Moi, Pierric Cistac, Tim Rault, Rémi Louf, Morgan Funtowicz, Joe Davison, Sam Shleifer, Patrick von Platen, Clara Ma, Yacine Jernite, Julien Plu, Canwen Xu, Teven Le Scao, Sylvain Gugger, Mariama Drame, Quentin Lhoest, and Alexander M. Rush. 2020. Transformers: State-of-the-art natural language processing. In *Proceedings of the 2020 Conference on Empirical Methods in Natural Language Processing: System Demonstrations*, pages 38–45, Online. Association for Computational Linguistics.

Zhao Yan, Nan Duan, Peng Chen, Ming Zhou, Jianshe Zhou, and Zhoujun Li. 2017. Building task-oriented dialogue systems for online shopping. In *Proceedings of the AAAI Conference on Artificial Intelligence*, volume 31.

Appendix

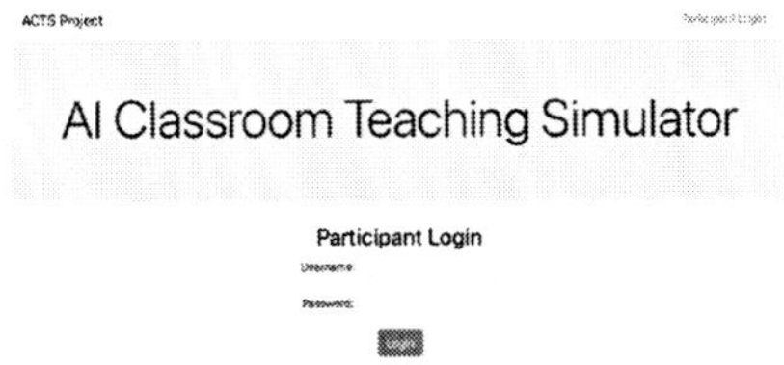

Figure 5: Conversational Agent Session Example: Login

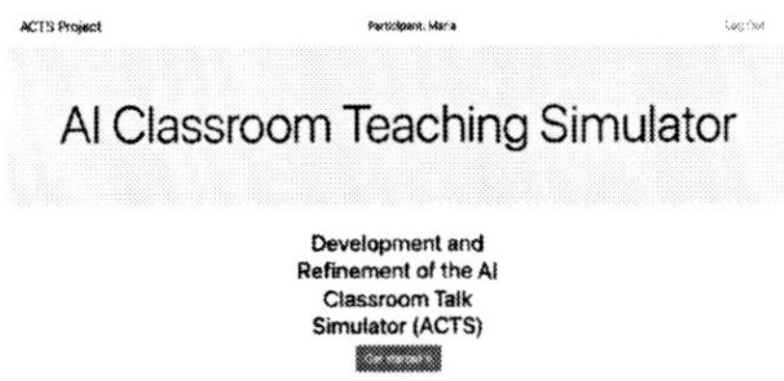

Figure 6: Conversational Agent Session Example: Acknowledgement

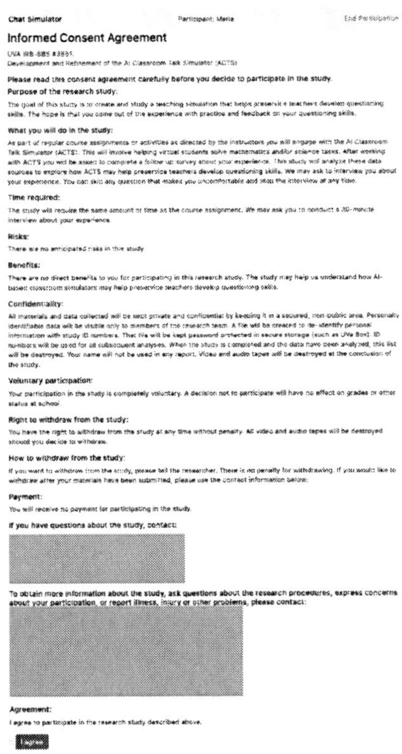

Figure 7: Conversational Agent Session Example: Institutional Review Board consent

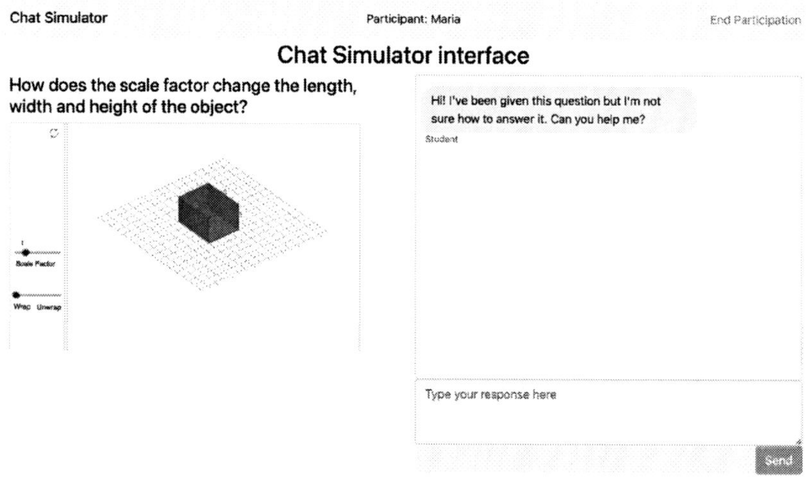

Figure 8: Conversational Agent Session Example: Initial Session Screen

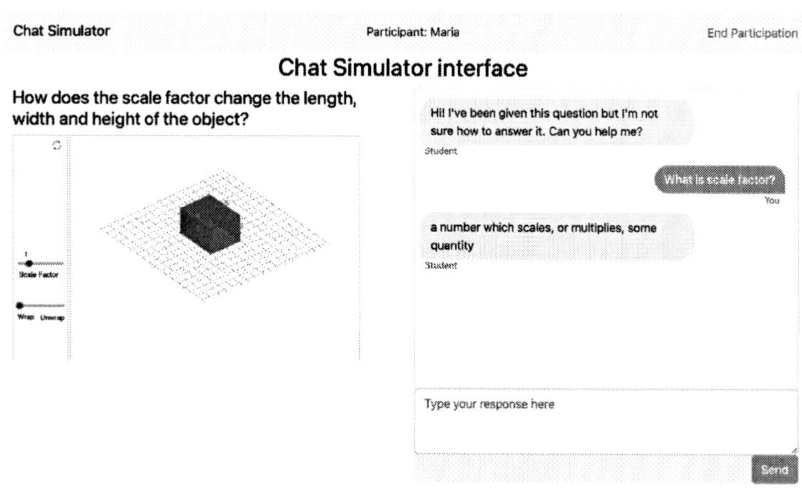

Figure 9: Conversational Agent Session Example: Testing Scale Factor Knowledge

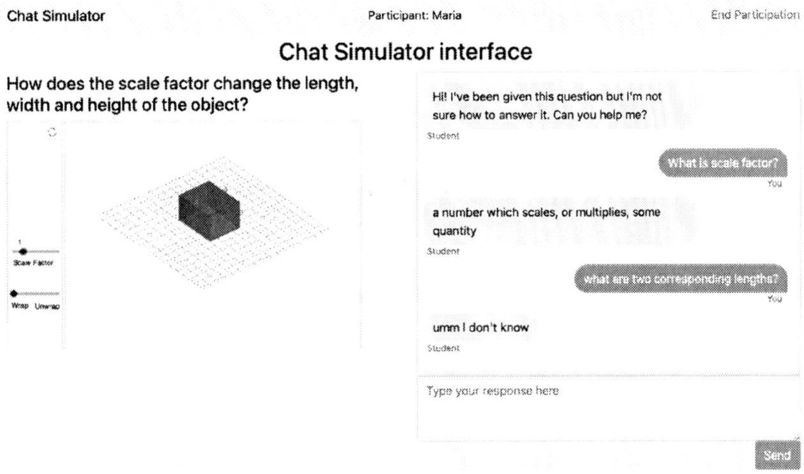

Figure 10: Conversational Agent Session Example: Improperly Phrased Question

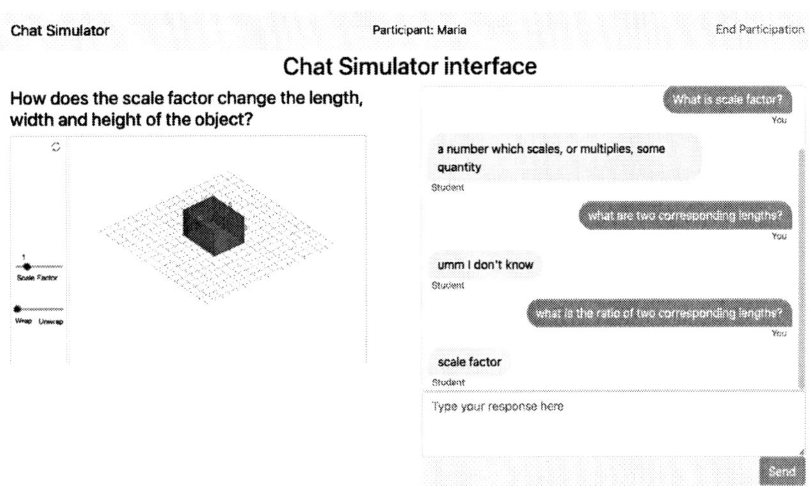

Figure 11: Conversational Agent Session Example: Properly Phrased Question

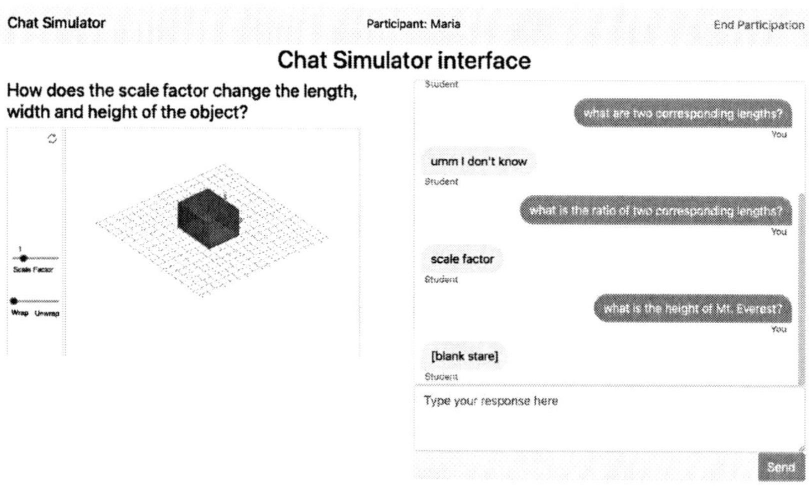

Figure 12: Conversational Agent Session Example: Irrelevant Question

Automated Classification of Written Proficiency Levels on the CEFR-Scale through Complexity Contours and RNNs

Elma Kerz[1] **Daniel Wiechmann**[2] **Yu Qiao**[1] **Emma Tseng**[3] **Marcus Ströbel**[1]
[1]RWTH Aachen University, [2]University of Amsterdam, [3]University of Washington
elma.kerz@ifaar.rwth-aachen.de, d.wiechmann@uva.nl
yu.qiao@rwth-aachen.de, eftseng@uw.edu
marcus.stroebel@rwth-aachen.de

Abstract

Automatically predicting the level of second language (L2) learner proficiency is an emerging topic of interest and research based on machine learning approaches to language learning and development. The key to the present paper is the combined use of what we refer to as 'complexity contours', a series of measurements of indices of L2 proficiency obtained by a computational tool that implements a sliding window technique, and recurrent neural network (RNN) classifiers that adequately capture the sequential information in those contours. We used the EF-Cambridge Open Language Database (Geertzen et al., 2014) with its labelled Common European Framework of Reference (CEFR) levels (Council of Europe, 2018) to predict six classes of L2 proficiency levels (A1, A2, B1, B2, C1, C2) in the assessment of writing skills. Our experiments demonstrate that an RNN classifier trained on complexity contours achieves higher classification accuracy than one trained on text-average complexity scores. In a secondary experiment, we determined the relative importance of features from four distinct categories through a sensitivity-based pruning technique. Our approach makes an important contribution to the field of automated identification of language proficiency levels, more specifically, to the increasing efforts towards the empirical validation of CEFR levels.

1 Introduction

The Common European Framework of Reference (CEFR) is an internationally recognized standard for describing language proficiency based on six reference levels – A1, A2, B1, B2, C1 and C2 – the same letter pairs corresponding to a three level distinction between beginner, intermediate and advanced (Council of Europe, 2018). Each proficiency level is related to specific linguistic features and skills, establishing a progression from rudimentary language to varied and sophisticated language. The CEFR descriptors, available for all four fundamental language skills (receptive skills: reading & listening and productive skills: writing & speaking), describe the expected competencies in terms of functional *can-do* statements. For example, a learner at a vantage or upper intermediate B2 level in the domain of writing is expected to have "a sufficient range of language to be able to give clear descriptions, express viewpoints and develop arguments without much conspicuous searching for words, using some complex sentence forms to do so" (Council of Europe, 2018: 131). The *can-do* descriptors formulated for each of the six CEFR proficiency levels are typically vague and subjective and are only useful for orientation purposes. Thus, there is an urgent need for research on empirical validation of CEFR levels at the interface between areas of language learning, testing and assessment, and natural language processing and machine learning (Wisniewski, 2017).

A closely related line of research has been directed toward automated essay scoring (AES) (for overviews see (Higgins et al., 2015; Ke and Ng, 2019; Klebanov and Madnani, 2020)). This line of research has benefited from the increasing availability of publicly accessible learner corpora of L2 writing, such as CLC-FCE (Yannakoudakis et al., 2011), TOEFL11 (Blanchard et al., 2013), MERLIN (Boyd et al., 2014) and EFCAMDAT (Geertzen et al., 2014). Supervised approaches to AES have recast the task as (1) a regression task aimed at predicting the score of an essay (Yannakoudakis et al., 2011; Klebanov and Flor, 2013), (2) a classification task aimed at classifying a text as belonging to one of a specified number of classes, e.g. the three score levels (low, medium or high) in the TOEFLL11 corpus or the six CEFR levels (A1-C2) in the MERLIN corpus (Hancke and Meurers, 2013; Pilán et al., 2016; Vajjala and Rama,

Proceedings of the 16th Workshop on Innovative Use of NLP for Building Educational Applications, pages 199–209
April 20, 2021 ©2021 Association for Computational Linguistics

2018; Weiß and Meurers, 2018; Caines and Buttery, 2020)[1] or (3) a ranking task aimed at ranking two or more texts based on their quality (Yannakoudakis and Briscoe, 2012; Taghipour and Ng, 2016). Previous work on AES has taken both feature-based approaches and neural approaches (see (Ke and Ng, 2019) for a discussion of (dis)advantages of these two approaches). The features employed are diverse, ranging from the use of descriptive metrics of the text related to word or sentence length to more abstract features related to proficiency development in the area of (second) language learning ((Vajjala, 2018) for a recent overview). The existing studies that have used a feature-based approach have typically relied on text averages of a given feature. However, the use of such aggregate scores may obscure the considerable degree of variation in distribution of feature values within the text.

In this paper, we present experiments geared towards the automated assessment of written language proficiency of non-native learners (L2) of English. For the experiments, we take advantage of the EF-Cambridge Open Language Database (EF-CAMDAT, (Geertzen et al., 2014)), a large-scale learner corpus consisting of 1.8 million texts labeled with the six CEFR proficiency levels (A1-C2). The aim of the paper is twofold: (1) to apply a sliding window technique in a feature-based modeling approach to automated proficiency classification and (2) to determine what features contribute the most to the classification accuracy. The features employed in this paper are derived from numerous studies in the field of L2 acquisition centering around the notion of 'complexity'[2] (see e.g. (Lu, 2010a, 2012; Bulté and Housen, 2012)). The inclusion of such features is further motivated by the fact that, according to the CEFR descriptors, learners are expected to acquire the ability to produce increasingly varied and sophisticated written language, as they progress through the six proficiency levels. Such diverse and sophisticated language use should be evident not only in vocabulary growth, but also in the choice of individual words and multi-word phrases, and in the complexity of sentence, clause, and phrase structures. Through the sliding window technique we obtain a series of measurements for a given feature tracking the progression of complexity within a text in a sentence-by-sentence fashion. We refer to such series of measurements as 'complexity contours'. These contours are then fed into recurrent neural network (RNN) classifiers – adequate to take into account the sequential information in the contours – to perform grade-level classification tasks. We demonstrate the utility of the approach by comparing the performance of 'contour-based' RNN models against those of 'means-based' RNN models trained on text-average performance scores.

In a second step, we determine what features drive classification accuracy through a Sensitivity-Based Pruning (SBP) technique. The approach taken in this paper was already successfully applied in the area of first language (L1) writing development. Kerz et al. (2020) showed that RNN classifiers trained on complexity contours achieve higher classification accuracy in predicting secondary school children's grade levels in both English and German (second-, sixth-, ninth- and eleventh-grade in English schools and fifth- and ninth-grade in German). Here we set out to extend the approach to automated proficiency classification in L2 English. The remainder of the paper is organized as follows: In Section 2, we provide a concise overview of related work. Section 3 presents the dataset and Section 4 the features used in the experiments. Section 5 describes the sliding-window approach to generating complexity contours. Sections 6 presents the architecture of the RNNs and the training procedure. Sections 7 introduces the SBP method used to determine the relative feature importance. Section 8 reports the results before conclusions are drawn in Section 9 along with indications of future research directions.

2 Related work

In this section, we present two types of previous work: L2 studies that have investigated the relationship between certain linguistic features and proficiency levels, and those that have used supervised machine learning approaches to predict learner proficiency on the CEFR scale.

Numerous studies reveal that syntactic complexity can be considered as one of the key skills that strongly influence L2 proficiency (see e.g. (Ortega, 2003) for a synthesis of twenty-five studies, see

[1]The latter paper has been published in the context of a recent shared task on Language Proficiency Scoring at the LREC 2020 – REPROLANG Task D.2 https://lrec2020.lrec-conf.org/en/reprolang2020/selected-tasks/

[2]Complexity – commonly defined as "the range of forms that surface in language production and the degree of sophistication of such forms" (Ortega 2003:492) – is one of the three dimensions of the 'Complexity–Accuracy–Fluency' triad that has emerged as a prominent conceptual framework for L2 assessment (see e.g. (Wolfe-Quintero et al., 1998; Larsen-Freeman, 2006)

also (Kuiken et al., 2019) for a recent special issue). These studies have measured this multidimensional construct along both global features, such as length measures and subordination ratios, as well as more specific features pertaining to the usage of particular structures. For example, Lu (2011) conducted an evaluation of 14 features of syntactic complexity in a corpus of English essays written by Chinese L1 students and found that the complexity measures that best discriminated between proficiency levels were the number of complex nominals per sentence and the mean sentence length. Another series of studies indicate the importance of lexical complexity (aka lexical richness) subsuming its three sub-dimensions (lexical density, sophistication and variation) in the assessment of L2 proficiency (see (Lu, 2012)). For example, Kyle and Crossley (2014) showed 47.5% of the variance in holistic scores of lexical proficiency and 48.7% of the variance in holistic scores of speaking proficiency can be explained using a range of lexical sophistication indices. This study also introduced the use of multi-word sequences (MWS) as an indicator of language proficiency, operationalized in terms of register-specific n-gram measures (bigrams and trigrams). The inclusion of such features reflects the growing interest of MWS in language learning and development. This interest stems from an extensive body of evidence demonstrating that both child and adult populations, including adult second-language learner populations, can develop the sensitivity to the statistics of MWS and rely on knowledge of such statistics to facilitate their language processing and boost their acquisition (for overviews see e.g. (Shaoul and Westbury, 2011; Christiansen and Arnon, 2017)). Garner et al. (2020), for instance, investigated the relationship of the usage of MWS and human judgments of writing proficiency based on the CEFR-graded Yonsei English Learner Corpus (Rhee and Jung, 2014) and found that essays from higher CEFR levels include a greater proportion of frequent academic trigrams and more strongly associated spoken trigrams. Finally, in recent years the L2 literature has introduced information-theoretic features based on Kolmogorov complexity (Ehret, 2016; Ehret and Szmrecsanyi, 2019). Ehret and Szmrecsanyi (2019) investigated essays written by advanced learners of English from International Corpus of Learner English (Granger et al., 2002) and showed that more advanced learners use considerably more complex texts than beginner learners, although this tendency is not always reflected in a clear, linear relationship between proficiency and complexity.

Studies that have employed supervised machine learning approaches to predict proficiency on the CEFR scale for different L2s have used numerous linguistic features in combination with a host of classifiers (Hancke and Meurers, 2013; Volodina et al., 2016; Vajjala and Rama, 2018; Vajjala and Lõo, 2014; Ballier et al., 2019; Caines and Buttery, 2020). The classification accuracy reported in these studies ranged between 62.7% and 83.8%. Hancke and Meurers (2013) reached a classification accuracy of 62.7% in predicting five (out of six) CEFR levels of professionally rated free text essays from the MERLIN database comprising CEFR exams taken by second language learners of German based on a total of 3821 lexical, morphological, and syntactic features using the Sequential Minimal Optimization (SMQ) algorithm implemented in WEKA. Using the same SMQ algorithm, Volodina et al. (2016) achieved an accuracy of 67% in correctly identifying the CEFR level of L2 Swedish learner essays on the basis of 61 count-based, lexical, syntactic, morphological, and semantic features extracted from the linguistic annotation available in the SweLL corpus[3]. Ballier and Gaillat (2019) achieved 70% accuracy in predicting CEFR-levels of L1 French and Spanish L2 English users on the basis of manually annotated errors in the L1 French and Spanish subsets of the EFCAMDAT corpus. Vajjala and Lõo (2014) reported a classification accuracy of 79% in an experiment on the Estonian Interlanguage Corpus[4].

In another study, Vajjala and Rama (2018) performed experiments with cross-lingual and multilingual classifiers on individual language classification. The data used in their study included 2,286 manually graded texts (five levels, A1 to C1) from the MERLIN learner corpus (German, 1,029 texts; Italian, 803 texts, and Czech, 434 texts). Trained on a wide range of feature, such as word and POS n-grams, task-specific word and character embeddings, dependency n-grams, features pertaining to lexical richness and error features, their classification models obtained an accuracy of 0.68 for German, 0.84 for Italian and 0.73 for Czech for monolingual classification. For multilingual classification, their models reached classification accuracy up to 0.73. The data set and findings ob-

[3]https://spraakbanken.gu.se/eng/research/icall/swellcorpus

[4]http://evkk.tlu.ee/?language=en

tained in this study have served as the baseline for the REPROLANG 2020 shared task on 'Language proficiency scoring'[5]. In the context of this task, Caines and Buttery (2020) reproduce and extend the finding described in (Vajjala and Rama, 2018) reaching a classification accuracy of up to 83.8% for the Italian component. Their results indicate that feature-based approaches perform better than neural network classifiers for text datasets of the given size.

3 Data

The data come from the EFCAMDAT, an open access corpus compiled at Cambridge University in collaboration with EF Education First, an international school of English as a second/foreign language (Geertzen et al., 2014). The corpus consists of writing assignments submitted to the Englishtown, the online school of EF Education First, summing up to a total of 1,180,309 individual writing samples by 174,743 L2 learners. The curriculum of Englishtown covers all six proficiency levels, from CEFR A1 to C2 organized along 16 EF teaching levels with each level subsuming 8 teaching units and ending with an open-ended writing task (128 distinct writing assignments). The length of the writing samples in the corpus increases monotonically with Englishtown levels, ranging from an average of 30.1 words at the lowest level (1) to an average of 170 words at the highest level (16). Since one of our main aims is to demonstrate the usefulness of the sliding window technique and the inclusion of a set of measurements per individual feature (complexity contours), we filtered the original dataset to obtain texts containing at least 100 words. This resulted in a total of 163,657 writing samples. In addition, we removed texts that had received exceptionally low scores on writing performance, since their inclusion would add bias and variance and may skew the results (Bøvelstad et al., 2017). Specifically, texts whose writing score fell more than 1.5 times the interquartile range below the first quartile, corresponding to a threshold score of 75%, were removed, which resulted in a loss of 7% of the data. The final dataset comprised a total of 152,314 individual learner texts. whose distributions across CEFR levels along with associated text length statistics are shown in Table 1.

[5]http://www.lrec-conf.org/proceedings/lrec2020/index.html

Table 1: Distribution of texts by CEFR proficiency level and text length statistics (in words)

CEFR	N texts	Mean length	SD
A1	8313	132.24	42.62
A2	19587	119.70	27.22
B1	61396	118.86	24.94
B2	48535	142.89	35.03
C1	12831	174.08	37.36
C2	1652	180.79	63.49

4 Features

The 57 features used in this paper fall into four distinct groups: (1) measures of syntactic complexity, (2) measures of lexical richness, (3) measures pertaining to the usage of multi-word sequences (MWS) and (4) information-theoretic measures. The first group consists of 16 features used in the past to measure syntactic complexity in writing and its relation to writing proficiency reviewed in Section 2. These features are implemented based on descriptions in Lu (2010b) and using the Tregex tree pattern matching tool (Levy and Andrew, 2006) with syntactic parse trees for extracting specific patterns. The second group subsumes 13 features pertaining to lexical richness: five measures of lexical variation, one measure of lexical density, seven measures of lexical sophistication. The operationalizations of these measures follow those described in Lu (2012) and (Ströbel, 2014). The third group includes 25 n-gram frequency features that are derived from the five register sub-components of the Contemporary Corpus of American English (COCA, (Davies, 2008)): spoken, magazine, fiction, news and academic language[6]. Our frequency n-gram measures differ from those used in the earlier studies reviewed in Section 2. Instead of using only bigrams and trigrams, we extend them to include longer word combinations (four- and five-grams) and use a more nuanced definition to operationalize the usage of such combinations given in equation (1):

$$\text{Norm}_{n,s,r} = \frac{|C_{n,s,r}| \cdot \log \left[\prod_{c \in |C_{n,s,r}|} freq_{n,r}(c) \right]}{|U_{n,s}|} \quad (1)$$

Let $A_{n,s}$ be the list of n-grams ($n \in [1,5]$) appearing within a sentence s, $B_{n,r}$ the list of n-

[6]The Contemporary Corpus of American English is the largest genre-balanced corpus of American English, which at the time the measures were derived comprised of 560 million words.

gram appearing in the n-gram frequency list of register r ($r \in \{\text{acad, fic, mag, news, spok}\}$) and $C_{n,s,r} = A_{n,s} \cap B_{n,r}$ the list of n-grams appearing both in s and the n-gram frequency list of register r. $U_{n,s}$ is defined as the list of unique n-gram in s, and $freq_{n,r}(a)$ the frequency of n-gram a according to the n-gram frequency list of register r.

A total of 25 measures results from the combination of (a) a 'reference list' containing the top 100,000 most frequent n-grams and their frequencies from one of five register subcomponents of the COCA corpus and (b) the size of the n-gram ($n \in [1, 5]$). The fourth group includes three information-theoretic measures that are based on Kolmogorov complexity. These measures use the Deflate algorithm (Deutsch, 1996) to compress a text and obtain complexity scores by relating the size of the compressed file to the size of the original file (for the operationalization and implementation of these measures see (Ströbel, 2014)).

5 A Sliding-Window Approach

Text complexity of the writing samples was automatically assessed using the CoCoGen, a computational tool that implements a sliding-window technique to generate a series of measurements for a given complexity measure (CM) (Ströbel 2014). In contrast to the standard approach that represents text complexity as a single score, providing a 'global assessment' of the complexity of a text, the use of a sliding-window technique enables a 'local' (sentence-level) assessment of complexity within a text. A sliding window can be conceived of as a window of size ws, which is defined by the number of sentences it contains. The window is moved across a text sentence-by-sentence, computing one value per window for a given CM. The series of measurements generated by CoCoGen captures the progression of linguistic complexity within a text for a given CM and is referred here to as a 'complexity contour' (see Figure 1). To compute the complexity score of a given window, a measurement function is applied to each sentence in the window. The size of the window (ws) is user-defined parameter whose optimal value depends on the goals of the analysis: When complexity is measured for each sentence, i.e. $ws = 1$, the resulting complexity contour will typically exhibit many sharp turns. By increasing the window size, i.e. the number of sentences in a window, the complexity contour can be smoothened akin to a moving average technique.[7] In this paper, the window size parameter was set to one sentence, meaning that no smoothing of the curve was performed. Figure 1 illustrates complexity contours on three randomly selected texts across three CEFR levels (A2, B2 and C2) for eight selected complexity measures. CoCoGen uses the Stanford CoreNLP suite (Manning et al., 2014) for performing tokenization, sentence splitting, part-of-speech tagging, lemmatization and syntactic parsing (Probabilistic Context Free Grammar Parser (Klein and Manning, 2003)).

6 Classification Models

We used a Recurrent Neural Network (RNN) classifier, specifically a dynamic RNN model with Gated Recurrent Unit (GRU) cells (Cho et al., 2014). A dynamic RNN was chosen as it can handle sequences of variable length[8]. As shown in Figure 2, the input of the contour-based model is a sequence $X = (x_1, x_2, \ldots, x_l, x_{l+1}, \ldots, x_n)$, where x_i, the output of CoCoGen for the ith window of a document, is a 57 dimensional vector, l is the length of the sequence, $n \in \mathbb{Z}$ is a number, which is greater or equal to the length of the longest sequence in the data and $x_{l+1}, \cdots, x_n$ are padded 0-vectors. The input of the contour-based model was fed into a RNN that consists of two layers of GRU cells with 200 hidden units for each. To predict the class of a sequence, the last output of the RNN, i.e. the output of the RNN right after the feeding of x_l, is transformed through a feed-forward neural network. The feed-forward neural-network consists of three fully connected layers, whose output dimensions are 512, 256, and 6 respectively. The Rectifier Linear Unit (ReLU) was used as an activation function. Before the final output, a softmax layer was applied. For the mean-based model, we used the same neural network as in the contour-based model, except that the network was trained with vectors of text-average complexity scores. The models were implemented using PyTorch (Pytorch, 2019).

We evenly split our data into 10 folds and applied a 10-fold cross validation, i.e. each time a fold (10% of data) is taken out as test set and the rest (90% of data) are used as the training set. In both

[7]When the window size is specified to be greater than 1, CoCoGen returns complexity scores for a given measures as fractions (wn_m/wd_m). In this case, the denominators and numerators of the fractions from the first to the last sentence in the window are added up to form the denominator and numerator of the resulting complexity score of a given window.

[8]The lengths of the feature vector sequences depends on the number of sentences of the texts in our corpus.

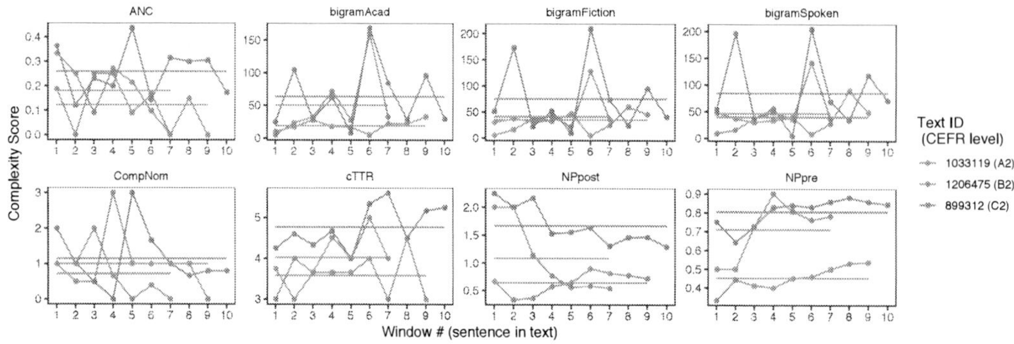

Figure 1: Complexity contours (window size = 1 sentence) for eight selected measures of complexity for three random texts from CEFR levels A2, B2 and C2.

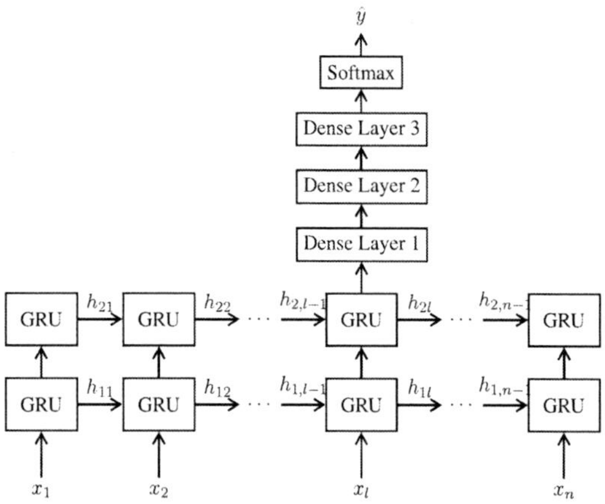

Figure 2: Roll-out of the contour-based RNN model based on complexity contours

datasets, the distributions of classes were identical. As the loss function for training cross entropy was used:

$$\mathcal{L}(\hat{Y}, c) = -\sum_{i=1}^{C} p(y_i)\log(p(\hat{y}_i))$$

in which c is the true class label of the current observation, C is the number of classes, $(p(y_1), \ldots, p(y_C))$ is a one-hot vector with

$$p(y_i) = \begin{cases} 1 & i = c \\ 0 & \text{otherwise} \end{cases}$$

and $\hat{Y} = (p(\hat{y}_1), p(\hat{y}_2), \ldots, p(\hat{y}_C))$ is the output vector of the softmax layer, which can be viewed as the predicted probabilities of the observed instance falling into to each of the classes. Since the EFCamDat dataset is hightly imbalanced, we additionally assigned weights to the classes for the cross entropy function, such that a_k is weight for class k:

$$a_k = \frac{N}{100N_k}$$

where N is the total number of instance in the dataset and N_k is the number of instance in the dataset with label k. For optimization, we used Stochastic Gradient Descent (SGD) with a learning rate $\eta = 0.01$ $momentum = 0.9$ and a learning rate decay factor of 0.1. The minibatch size is 32, which was shown as a reasonable value for modern GPU (Masters and Luschi, 2018).

7 Feature Ablation

To determine the relative importance of the individual features, we conducted feature ablation experiments for the contour-based RNN. Classical forward or backward sequential selection algorithms that proceed by sequentially adding or discarding features require a quadratic number of model training and evaluation in order to obtain a feature ranking (Langley, 1994). In the context of neural network model training a quadratic number of models can become prohibitive. To alleviate this problem, we used an adapted version of the iterative sensitivity-based pruning algorithm proposed by Díaz-Villanueva et al. (2010). This algorithm ranks the features based on a 'sensitivity measure' (Moody, 1994; Utans and Moody, 1991) and removes the least relevant variables one at a time. The classifier is then retrained on the resulting subset and a new ranking is calculated over the remaining features. This process is repeated until all features are removed (see Algorithm 1). In this fashion, rather than training $\frac{n(n+1)}{2}$ required for sequential algorithms, the number of models trained is reduced to $\frac{n}{m}$, where m is the number of features that can be removed at each step. We report the results obtained with m = 1, i.e. the removal of a single feature at each step. The procedure of finding the rank order of feature importance is described as following. To increase the robustness of the feature importance rank order, k-fold cross-validation is applied. At step t, neural network models $M_{t,n}, n \in \{1, \ldots, k\}$ are trained on the training sets of a k-fold cross-validation, where n is the fold ID. The training sets at step t consist of instances with feature set $F_t = \{f_1, f_2, \ldots, f_{D_t}\}$ where $f_1, \ldots f_{D_t}$ are the remaining features at the current step, whose importance rank is to be determined. We define $X_{t,n}$ as the test set of the nth fold with feature set F_t and $X^i_{t,n}$ as the same dataset as $X_{t,n}$ except we set the ith feature f_i of each instance within the dataset to its average. Furthermore, we define $g(X)$ as the classification accuracy of $M_{t,n}$ for a dataset X. The sensitivity of feature f_i on the nth fold at step t is obtained from:

$$S_{i,t,n} = g(X_{t,n}) - g(X^i_{t,n})$$

The final sensitivity for a feature f_i at step t is:

$$S_{i,t} = \frac{1}{k} \sum_{n=1}^{k} S_{i,t,n}$$

The most important feature at step t can be found by:

$$f_{\hat{i}} : \hat{i} = \underset{i: f_i \in F_t}{\arg\max}(S_{i,t})$$

Then we set the rank for feature $f_{\hat{i}}$:

$$Rank_{\hat{i}} = t$$

In the end, feature $f_{\hat{i}}$ is dropped from F_t and the corresponding columns in training and test dataset are also dropped simultaneously:

$$F_{t+1} = F_t - \{f_{\hat{i}}\}$$

This procedure is repeated, until $|F_{t'}| = 1$.

8 Results and Discussion

An overview of the performance statistics of the models in terms of precision, recall and F1 scores is presented in Table 2. The classification accuracy results indicated that the inclusion of complexity contours led to an increase in overall classification accuracy of 9.3% from 66.1% for the means-based RNN model to 75.4% for the contour-based RNN model. Classification performance of the contour-based RNN model was consistently higher than those of the means-based RNN model across all six CEFR proficiency levels. Its performance was higher for the beginner and intermediate CEFR proficiency levels (A1 to B2) with F1 scores ranging between 0.73 and 0.81 compared to the advanced levels (C1 and C2) with F1 scores dropping to 0.61 for the C1 level and 0.42 for the C2 level. The confusion matrix of the contour-based RNN model is presented in Table 3. As is evident in this table, most classification errors appeared in adjacent categories, with few classification errors occurring between distant categories.

Algorithm 1: Feature ablation algorithm

Input: N training instances with feature set $F = \{f_1, \ldots, f_D\}$
Input: m features to remove at each step
Result: $list$ containing the feature importance rank order

begin
  $t \leftarrow 0$
  $list \leftarrow []$
  while $|F| > 0$ **do**
    Train a classifier with $|F|$ input features;
    Compute $S_{i,t}, i \in F$;
    Find $f_{i_1}, \ldots, f_{i_m}$, where $S_{i_1,t}, \ldots, S_{i_m,t}$ are m largest among all $S_{i,t} (i \in F)$ in descending order;
    $list \leftarrow list.append([f_{i_1}, \ldots, f_{i_m}])$;
    $F \leftarrow F - \{f_{i_1}, \ldots, f_{i_m}\}$;
    $t \leftarrow t + 1$;
  return $list$

The top 20 features that contributed most to the classification accuracy of the contour-based RNN model are shown in Table 2 (see the column 'Acc after Del'). The results of the feature ablation experiments revealed that classification accuracy was mainly driven by frequency n-grams measures pertaining to the usage of multiword sequences (MWS). The twelve of the top 20 features are uni-, bi-, and trigram frequency measures from all five register sub-components of the COCA corpus. Writing samples from higher CEFR levels exhibit higher scores for all five unigram measures. A similar pattern can be observed for bigram scores from the academic register. A more differentiated pattern is apparent in trigram measures: For example, trigram scores from the fiction register show a U-shaped progression, such that they first increase up to the B2 level and then decrease (see Table 5 and Figure 3 in the Appendix for an overview). Overall, these findings indicate the importance of including n-gram frequency measures for the task of automated language performance classification. Moreover, they are consistent with results reported

Table 2: Performance statistics of RNN classifiers (left) and results of feature ablation (right). Values in '()' indicate standard deviations. 'Base Mod Acc'= Accuracy of baseline model; 'Acc after Del' = Accuracy of model after deletion of feature (only top-20 features are shown).

Performance statistics	**Means-based** RNN Model	**Contour-based** RNN Model
Accuracy train	0.938 (0.012)	0.976 (0.012)
Accuracy test	0.661 (0.004)	**0.754** (0.004)
Precision_{A1}	0.677 (0.021)	0.784 (0.016)
Precision_{A2}	0.640 (0.013)	0.745 (0.007)
Precision_{B1}	0.710 (0.005)	0.795 (0.005)
Precision_{B2}	0.657 (0.007)	0.739 (0.004)
Precision_{C1}	0.479 (0.008)	0.632 (0.014)
Precision_{C2}	0.436 (0.050)	0.505 (0.043)
Recall_{A1}	0.677 (0.021)	0.784 (0.016)
Recall_{A2}	0.640 (0.013)	0.745 (0.007)
Recall_{B1}	0.710 (0.005)	0.795 (0.005)
Recall_{B2}	0.657 (0.007)	0.739 (0.004)
Recall_{C1}	0.479 (0.008)	0.632 (0.014)
Recall_{C2}	0.436 (0.050)	0.505 (0.043)
F1_{A1}	0.634 (0.010)	0.744 (0.010)
F1_{A2}	0.626 (0.009)	0.725 (0.007)
F1_{B1}	0.713 (0.004)	0.803 (0.002)
F1_{B2}	0.671 (0.006)	0.751 (0.003)
F1_{C1}	0.467 (0.007)	0.614 (0.008)
F1_{C2}	0.374 (0.044)	0.419 (0.038)

Feature importance CM	Base Mod Acc	Acc after Del
Bigram fic	0.754 (0.004)	0.684 (0.005)
Bigram acad	0.748 (0.003)	0.686 (0.005)
ANC	0.744 (0.006)	0.691 (0.006)
MLWs	0.732 (0.003)	0.689 (0.002)
MLWc	0.728 (0.004)	0.675 (0.005)
Bigram spok	0.720 (0.002)	0.664 (0.004)
Unigram acad	0.712 (0.005)	0.659 (0.004)
Trigram fic	0.712 (0.004)	0.665 (0.005)
BNC	0.706 (0.004)	0.669 (0.004)
Bigram news	0.695 (0.004)	0.661 (0.004)
Unigram fic	0.691 (0.004)	0.660 (0.006)
NGSL	0.687 (0.005)	0.655 (0.005)
LD	0.681 (0.004)	0.646 (0.003)
Unigram spok	0.667 (0.004)	0.631 (0.006)
Trigram news	0.670 (0.005)	0.634 (0.006)
Unigram mag	0.666 (0.005)	0.634 (0.006)
Unigram news	0.667 (0.004)	0.604 (0.005)
Bigram mag	0.661 (0.004)	0.613 (0.005)
KolDef	0.655 (0.003)	0.626 (0.004)
KolDefMor	0.653 (0.003)	0.622 (0.005)

Table 3: Confusion matrix of the contour-based RNN model (sum across 10-fold cross validation). The $C_{i;j}$ value is the number of predictions known to be in group i and predicted to be in group j.

	A1	A2	B1	B2	C1	C2
A1	5885	460	935	683	327	23
A2	428	13849	3754	1317	212	27
B1	526	2923	49842	7125	899	81
B2	428	1097	6951	37078	2715	266
C1	226	207	1115	3443	7652	188
C2	20	57	131	552	298	594

in numerous studies indicating that the knowledge of MWS is a key component of both L1 and L2 writing and speaking skills (see e.g. (Christiansen and Arnon, 2017; Garner et al., 2020; Saito, 2020). Another group of features that figures prominently in the top 20 list are five measures of lexical sophistication: Higher CEFR levels are characterized by higher proportions of unusual/advanced words and words of greater surface length (compare *same* vs. *equal* vs. *identical* vs. *tantamount*). These results replicate and extend the findings reported in Durrant and Brenchley (2019) and (Kerz et al., 2020). Both studies found that measures of lexical sophistication are good predictors of children's L1 writing development. And finally, the top-20 list includes two of the three information-theoretic measures, indicating that more advanced learners produce considerably more complex (i.e. informationally denser) texts than beginner learners. The fact that two measures from the smallest subset of CMs were ranked among the top-20 most important features is an indication of their usefulness in research on automated proficiency classification. As discussed in detail in Ehret (2016) and Ehret and Szmrecsanyi (2019), CMs based on Kolmogorov complexity have the potential to avoid some of the known problems of traditional metrics that are based on different measures of unit length and that involve frequencies of various types of forms, which gives rise to 'concept reductionism' (Ortega, 2012, 128).

9 Conclusion and Outlook

In this paper, we applied a sliding window technique in a feature-based modeling approach to automated classification of written proficiency levels on the CEFR-scale (A1-C2 levels). We made use of 'complexity contours' obtained through this technique to represent the distribution of scores per linguistic feature within a text in combination with RNN classifiers that exploit the sequential information in those contours. We demonstrated that an RNN classifier trained on complexity contours achieved higher classification accuracy across all six CEFR proficiency levels compared to one trained on text-average scores with an increase in performance of up to 14% in terms of precision and 15% in terms of recall. We also showed that iterative sensitivity-based pruning approach is a viable way of assessing relative feature importance in text classification tasks performed with neural network models. This approach taken in our paper has the potential to provide a valuable contribution to increasing efforts to identify 'criterial features', i.e. features that are characteristic and indicative of language proficiency at each level (Hawkins and Filipović, 2012). In our future work, we intend to include additional sets of features of language use based on crowd-sourced language metrics entitled word prevalence (Johns et al., 2020) as well as LIWC-style features that relate language use with behavioral and self-reported measures of personality, social behavior, and cognitive styles (Tausczik and Pennebaker, 2010). We also intend to take into account the effects of task type on the features of language use investigated in this paper (Alexopoulou et al., 2017).

References

Theodora Alexopoulou, Marije Michel, Akira Murakami, and Detmar Meurers. 2017. Task effects on linguistic complexity and accuracy: A large-scale learner corpus analysis employing natural language processing techniques. *Language Learning*, 67(S1):180–208.

Nicolas Ballier and Thomas Gaillat. 2019. Investigating the scope of textual metrics for learner level discrimination and learner analytics. In *Learner Corpus Research Conference*.

Nicolas Ballier, Thomas Gaillat, Andrew Simpkin, Bernardo Stearns, Manon Bouyé, and Manel Zarrouk. 2019. A supervised learning model for the automatic assessment of language levels based on learner errors. In *European Conference on Technology Enhanced Learning*, pages 308–320. Springer.

Daniel Blanchard, Joel Tetreault, Derrick Higgins, Aoife Cahill, and Martin Chodorow. 2013. Toefl11: A corpus of non-native english. *ETS Research Report Series*, 2013(2):i–15.

Hege Marie Bøvelstad, Einar Holsbø, Lars Ailo Bongo, and Eiliv Lund. 2017. A standard operating procedure for outlier removal in large-sample epidemiological transcriptomics datasets. *BioRxiv*, page 144519.

Adriane Boyd, Jirka Hana, Lionel Nicolas, Detmar Meurers, Katrin Wisniewski, Andrea Abel, Karin Schöne, Barbora Stindlová, and Chiara Vettori. 2014. The MERLIN corpus: Learner language and the CEFR. In *LREC*, pages 1281–1288. Reykjavik, Iceland.

Bram Bulté and Alex Housen. 2012. Defining and operationalising l2 complexity. *Dimensions of L2 performance and proficiency: Complexity, accuracy and fluency in SLA*, pages 23–46.

Andrew Caines and Paula Buttery. 2020. Reprolang 2020: Automatic proficiency scoring of czech, english, german, italian, and spanish learner essays. In *Proceedings of The 12th Language Resources and Evaluation Conference*, pages 5614–5623.

KyungHyun Cho, Bart van Merrienboer, Dzmitry Bahdanau, and Yoshua Bengio. 2014. On the properties of neural machine translation: Encoder-decoder approaches. *CoRR*, abs/1409.1259.

Morten H Christiansen and Inbal Arnon. 2017. More than words: The role of multiword sequences in language learning and use. *Topics in Cognitive Science*, 9(3):542–551.

Mark Davies. 2008. The corpus of contemporary american english (coca): 560 million words, 1990-present.

Peter Deutsch. 1996. Deflate compressed data format specification version 1.3. *IETF RFC 1951*.

Wladimiro Díaz-Villanueva, Francesc J Ferri, and Vicente Cerverón. 2010. Learning improved feature rankings through decremental input pruning for support vector based drug activity prediction. In *International Conference on Industrial, Engineering and Other Applications of Applied Intelligent Systems*, pages 653–661. Springer.

Philip Durrant and Mark Brenchley. 2019. Development of vocabulary sophistication across genres in English children's writing. *Reading and Writing*, 32(8):1927–1953.

Council of Europe. Council for Cultural Co-operation. Education Committee. Modern Languages Division. 2018. *Common European Framework of Reference for Languages: learning, teaching, assessment*. Cambridge University Press.

Katharina Ehret. 2016. *An information-theoretic approach to language complexity: variation in naturalistic corpora*. Ph.D. thesis, Universität.

Katharina Ehret and Benedikt Szmrecsanyi. 2019. Compressing learner language: An information-theoretic measure of complexity in sla production data. *Second Language Research*, 35(1):23–45.

James Garner, Scott Crossley, and Kristopher Kyle. 2020. Beginning and intermediate l2 writer's use of n-grams: an association measures study. *International Review of Applied Linguistics in Language Teaching*, 58(1):51–74.

Jeroen Geertzen, Theodora Alexopoulou, and Anna Korhonen. 2014. Automatic linguistic annotation of large scale L2 databases: The EF-Cambridge Open Language Database(EFCamDat).

Sylviane Granger, Estelle Dagneaux, and Fanny Meunier. 2002. The international corpus of learner english. handbook and cd-rom.

Julia Hancke and Detmar Meurers. 2013. Exploring CEFR classification for German based on rich linguistic modeling. *Learner Corpus Research*, pages 54–56.

John A Hawkins and Luna Filipović. 2012. *Criterial features in L2 English: Specifying the reference levels of the Common European Framework*, volume 1. Cambridge University Press.

Derrick Higgins, Chaitanya Ramineni, and Klaus Zechner. 2015. Learner corpora and automated scoring. In Sylviane Granger, Gaetanelle Gilquin, and Fanny Meunier, editors, *The Cambridge Handbook of Learner Corpus Research*, pages 587–604. Cambridge University Press.

Brendan T Johns, Melody Dye, and Michael N Jones. 2020. Estimating the prevalence and diversity of words in written language. *Quarterly Journal of Experimental Psychology*, 73(6):841–855.

Zixuan Ke and Vincent Ng. 2019. Automated essay scoring: A survey of the state of the art. In *IJCAI*, pages 6300–6308.

Elma Kerz, Yu Qiao, Daniel Wiechmann, and Marcus Ströbel. 2020. Becoming linguistically mature: Modeling english and german children's writing development across school grades. In *Proceedings of the Fifteenth Workshop on Innovative Use of NLP for Building Educational Applications*, pages 65–74.

Beata Beigman Klebanov and Michael Flor. 2013. Word association profiles and their use for automated scoring of essays. In *Proceedings of the 51st Annual Meeting of the Association for Computational Linguistics (Volume 1: Long Papers)*, pages 1148–1158.

Beata Beigman Klebanov and Nitin Madnani. 2020. Automated evaluation of writing–50 years and counting. In *Proceedings of the 58th Annual Meeting of the Association for Computational Linguistics*, pages 7796–7810.

Dan Klein and Christopher D Manning. 2003. Accurate unlexicalized parsing. In *Proceedings of the 41st Annual Meeting on Association for Computational Linguistics-Volume 1*, pages 423–430. Association for Computational Linguistics.

Folkert Kuiken, Ineke Vedder, Alex Housen, and Bastien De Clercq. 2019. Variation in syntactic complexity: Introduction. *International Journal of Applied Linguistics*, 29(2):161–170.

Kristopher Kyle and Scott A Crossley. 2014. Automatically assessing lexical sophistication: Indices, tools, findings, and application. *Tesol Quarterly*, 49(4):757–786.

Pat Langley. 1994. Selection of relevant features in machine learning. In *Proceedings of the AAAI Fall symposium on relevance*, pages 1–5.

Diane Larsen-Freeman. 2006. The emergence of complexity, fluency, and accuracy in the oral and written production of five chinese learners of english. *Applied linguistics*, 27(4):590–619.

Roger Levy and Galen Andrew. 2006. Tregex and tsurgeon: tools for querying and manipulating tree data structures. In *LREC*, pages 2231–2234. Citeseer.

Xiaofei Lu. 2010a. Automatic analysis of syntactic complexity in second language writing. *International Journal of Corpus Linguistics*, 15(4):474–496.

Xiaofei Lu. 2010b. Automatic analysis of syntactic complexity in second language writing. *International journal of corpus linguistics*, 15(4):474–496.

Xiaofei Lu. 2011. A corpus-based evaluation of syntactic complexity measures as indices of college-level esl writers' language development. *Tesol Quarterly*, 45(1):36–62.

Xiaofei Lu. 2012. The relationship of lexical richness to the quality of esl learners' oral narratives. *The Modern Language Journal*, 96(2):190–208.

Christopher Manning, Mihai Surdeanu, John Bauer, Jenny Finkel, Steven Bethard, and David McClosky. 2014. The stanford corenlp natural language processing toolkit. In *Proceedings of 52nd annual meeting of the association for computational linguistics: system demonstrations*, pages 55–60.

Dominic Masters and Carlo Luschi. 2018. Revisiting small batch training for deep neural networks. *arXiv preprint arXiv:1804.07612*.

John Moody. 1994. Prediction risk and architecture selection for neural networks. In *From statistics to neural networks*, pages 147–165. Springer.

Lourdes Ortega. 2003. Syntactic complexity measures and their relationship to l2 proficiency: A research synthesis of college-level l2 writing. *Applied linguistics*, 24(4):492–518.

Lourdes Ortega. 2012. Interlanguage complexity. *Linguistic complexity: Second language acquisition, indigenization, contact*, 13:127.

Ildikó Pilán, Elena Volodina, and Torsten Zesch. 2016. Predicting proficiency levels in learner writings by transferring a linguistic complexity model from expert-written coursebooks. In *Proceedings of COLING 2016, the 26th International Conference on Computational Linguistics: Technical Papers*, pages 2101–2111.

Pytorch. 2019. Pytorch: Tensors and dynamic neural networks in Python with strong GPU acceleration. https://github.com/pytorch/pytorch.

Seok-Chae Rhee and Chae Kwan Jung. 2014. Compilation of the yonsei english learner corpus (yelc) 2011 and its use for understanding current usage of english by korean pre-university students. *The Journal of the Korea Contents Association*, 14(11):1019–1029.

Kazuya Saito. 2020. Multi-or single-word units? the role of collocation use in comprehensible and contextually appropriate second language speech. *Language Learning*, 70(2):548–588.

Cyrus Shaoul and Chris Westbury. 2011. Formulaic sequences: Do they exist and do they matter? *The mental lexicon*, 6(1):171–196.

Marcus Ströbel. 2014. *Tracking complexity of l2 academic texts: A sliding-window approach.* Master thesis. RWTH Aachen University.

Kaveh Taghipour and Hwee Tou Ng. 2016. A neural approach to automated essay scoring. In *Proceedings of the 2016 conference on empirical methods in natural language processing*, pages 1882–1891.

Yla R Tausczik and James W Pennebaker. 2010. The psychological meaning of words: LIWC and computerized text analysis methods. *Journal of Language and Social Psychology*, 29(1):24–54.

Joachim Utans and John Moody. 1991. Selecting neural network architectures via the prediction risk: Application to corporate bond rating prediction. In *Proceedings First International Conference on Artificial Intelligence Applications on Wall Street*, pages 35–41. IEEE.

Sowmya Vajjala. 2018. Automated assessment of non-native learner essays: Investigating the role of linguistic features. *International Journal of Artificial Intelligence in Education*, 28(1):79–105.

Sowmya Vajjala and Kaidi Lõo. 2014. Automatic CEFR level prediction for Estonian learner text. In *Proceedings of the third workshop on NLP for computer-assisted language learning*, pages 113–127, Uppsala, Sweden. LiU Electronic Press.

Sowmya Vajjala and Taraka Rama. 2018. Experiments with universal CEFR classification. In *Proceedings of the Thirteenth Workshop on Innovative Use of NLP for Building Educational Applications*, pages 147–153, New Orleans, Louisiana. Association for Computational Linguistics.

Elena Volodina, Ildikó Pilán, and David Alfter. 2016. Classification of Swedish learner essays by CEFR levels. *CALL communities and culture–short papers from EUROCALL*, 2016:456–461.

Zarah Weiß and Detmar Meurers. 2018. Modeling the readability of German targeting adults and children: An empirically broad analysis and its cross-corpus validation. In *Proceedings of the 27th International Conference on Computational Linguistics*, pages 303–317, Santa Fe, New Mexico, USA. Association for Computational Linguistics.

Katrin Wisniewski. 2017. Empirical learner language and the levels of the common european framework of reference. *Language Learning*, 67(S1):232–253.

Kate Wolfe-Quintero, Shunji Inagaki, and Hae-Young Kim. 1998. *Second language development in writing: Measures of fluency, accuracy, & complexity.* 17. University of Hawaii Press.

Helen Yannakoudakis and Ted Briscoe. 2012. Modeling coherence in esol learner texts. In *Proceedings of the Seventh Workshop on Building Educational Applications Using NLP*, pages 33–43.

Helen Yannakoudakis, Ted Briscoe, and Ben Medlock. 2011. A new dataset and method for automatically grading ESOL texts. In *Proceedings of the 49th Annual Meeting of the Association for Computational Linguistics: Human Language Technologies*, pages 180–189, Portland, Oregon, USA. Association for Computational Linguistics.

“Sharks are not the threat humans are”: Argument Component Segmentation in School Student Essays

Tariq Alhindi *
Department of Computer Science
Columbia University
tariq@cs.columbia.edu

Debanjan Ghosh
Educational Testing Service
dghosh@ets.org

Abstract

Argument mining is often addressed by a pipeline method where segmentation of text into argumentative units is conducted first and proceeded by an argument component identification task. In this research, we apply a token-level classification to identify claim and premise tokens from a new corpus of argumentative essays written by middle school students. To this end, we compare a variety of state-of-the-art models such as discrete features and deep learning architectures (e.g., BiLSTM networks and BERT-based architectures) to identify the argument components. We demonstrate that a BERT-based multi-task learning architecture (i.e., token and sentence level classification) adaptively pretrained on a relevant unlabeled dataset obtains the best results.

1 Introduction

Computational argument mining focuses on subtasks such as identifying the Argumentative Discourse Units (ADUs) (Peldszus and Stede, 2013), their nature (i.e., claim or premise), and the relation (i.e., support/attack) between them (Ghosh et al., 2014; Wacholder et al., 2014; Stab and Gurevych, 2014, 2017; Stede and Schneider, 2018; Nguyen and Litman, 2018; Lawrence and Reed, 2020). Argumentation is essential in academic writing as it enhances the logical reasoning, as well as, critical thinking capacities of students (Ghosh et al., 2020). Thus, in recent times, argument mining has been used to assess students' writing skills in essay scoring and provide feedback on the writing (Song et al., 2014; Somasundaran et al., 2016; Wachsmuth et al., 2016; Zhang and Litman, 2020).

Should Artificial Sweeteners be Banned in America?

Diet soda , sugar - free gum, and low - calorie sweeteners are what most people see as a way to sweeten up a day without the calories.

Despite the lack of calories, artificial sweeteners have multiple negative health effects.

Over the past century, science has made it possible to replicate food with fabricated alternatives that simplify weight loss.

Although many thought these new replacements would benefit overall health, there are more negative effects on manufactured food than the food they replaced.

Artificial sweeteners have a huge impact on current day society.

Legends: B-Claim I-Claim B-Premise I-Premise O-Arg

Figure 1: Excerpt from an annotated essay with Claim Premise segments in BIO notation

While argument mining literature has addressed students writing in the educational context, so far, it has primarily addressed college level writing (Blanchard et al., 2013; Persing and Ng, 2015; Beigman Klebanov et al., 2017; Eger et al., 2017) except for a very few ones (Attali and Burstein, 2006; Lugini et al., 2018; Correnti et al., 2020). Instead, in this paper, we concentrate on identifying arguments from essays written by *middle school students*. To this end, we perused a new corpus of 145 argumentative essays written by middle school students to identify the argument components. These essays are obtained from an Educational app - *Writing Mentor* - that operates as a Google-docs Add-on.[1]

Normally, research that investigates college

*Work performed during internship at ETS

[1] https://mentormywriting.org

Proceedings of the 16th Workshop on Innovative Use of NLP for Building Educational Applications, pages 210–222
April 20, 2021 ©2021 Association for Computational Linguistics

students writing in the context of argument mining apply a pipeline of subtasks to first detect arguments at the token-level text units and subsequently classify the text units to argument components (Stab and Gurevych, 2017). However, middle school student essays are vastly different from college students' writing (detailed in Section 3). We argue they are more difficult to analyze through the pipeline approach due to run-on sentences, unsupported claims, and the presence of several claims in a sentence. Thus, instead of segmenting the text into argumentative/non-argumentative units first, we conduct a token-level classification task to identify the type of the argument component (e.g., B/I tokens from claims and premises) directly by joining the first and the second subtask in a single task. Figure 1 presents an excerpt from an annotated essay with their corresponding gold annotations of claims (e.g., "Diet soda ... the calories") and premises (e.g., "there are ... replaced"). The legends represent the tokens by the standard BIO notations.

We propose a detailed experimental setup to identify the argument components using both feature-based machine learning techniques and deep learning models. For the former, we used several structural, lexical, and syntactic features in a sequence classification framework using the Conditional Random Field (CRF) classifier (Lafferty et al., 2001). For the latter, we employ a BiLSTM network and, finally, a transformer architecture - BERT (Devlin et al., 2019) with its pretrained and task-specific fine-tuned models. We achieve the best result from a particular BERT architecture (7.5% accuracy improvement over the discrete features) that employs a joint multitask learning objective with an uncertainty-based weighting of two task-specific losses: (a) the *main task* of token-level sequence classification, and (b) the *auxiliary task* of sentence classification (i.e., whether a sentence contains argument or not). We make the dataset (student essays) from our research publicly available.[2]

2 Related Work

The majority of the prior work on argument mining addressed the problems of argument segmentation, component, and relation identification modeled in a pipeline of subtasks (Peldszus and Stede, 2015; Stab and Gurevych, 2017; Potash et al., 2017; Niculae et al., 2017) except a few research (Schulz et al., 2019). However, most of the research assumes the availability of segmented argumentative units and do the subsequent tasks such as the classification of argumentative component types (Biran and Rambow, 2011; Stab and Gurevych, 2014; Park and Cardie, 2014), argument relations (Ghosh et al., 2016; Nguyen and Litman, 2016), and argument schemes (Hou and Jochim, 2017; Feng and Hirst, 2011).

Previous work on argument segmentation includes approaches that model the task as a sentence classification to argumentative or non-argumentative sentences (Moens et al., 2007; Palau and Moens, 2009; Mochales and Moens, 2011; Rooney et al., 2012; Lippi and Torroni, 2015; Ajjour et al., 2017; Chakrabarty et al., 2019), or by defining heuristics to identify argumentative segment boundaries (Madnani et al., 2012; Persing and Ng, 2015; Al-Khatib et al., 2016). Although we conduct segmentation, we focus on the token-level classification to directly identify the argument component's type. This setup is related to Schulz et al. (2018) where authors analyzed students' diagnostic reasoning skills via token level identification. Our joint model using BERT is similar to (Eger et al., 2017). However, we set the main task as the token-level classification where the auxiliary task of argumentative sentence identification assists the main task to attain a better performance.

As stated earlier, most of the research on argumentative writing in an educational context focuses on identifying argument structures (i.e., argument components and their relations) (Persing and Ng, 2016; Nguyen and Litman, 2016) as well as to predict essays scores from features derived from the essays (e.g., number of claims and premises, number of supported claims, number of dangling claims) (Ghosh et al., 2016). Related investigations have also examined the challenge of scoring a certain dimension of essay quality, such as relevance to the prompt (Persing and Ng, 2014), opinions and their targets (Farra et al., 2015), argument strength (Persing and Ng, 2015) among others.

[2]https://github.com/EducationalTestingService/argument-component-essays

Majority of the above research are conducted in the context of college-level writing. For instance, Nguyen and Litman (2018) investigated argument structures in TOEFL11 corpus (Blanchard et al., 2013) which was also the main focus of (Ghosh et al., 2016). Beigman Klebanov et al. (2017) and Persing and Ng (2015) analyzed writing of university students and Stab and Gurevych (2017) used data from "essayforum.com", where college entrance examination is the largest forum. Although, writing quality in essays by young writers has been addressed (Attali and Burstein, 2006; Attali and Powers, 2008; Deane, 2014), identification of arguments was not part of these studies. Computational analysis of arguments from school students is in infancy except for a few research (Lugini et al., 2018; Afrin et al., 2020; Ghosh et al., 2020). We believe our dataset (Section 3) will be useful for researchers working at the intersection of argument mining and education.

3 Data

We obtained a large number of English essays (over 10K) through the *Writing Mentor* Educational App. This App is a Google Docs add-on designed to provide instructional writing support, especially for academic writing. The add-on provides students to write argumentative or narrative essays and receive feedback on their writings. We selected a subset of 145 argumentative essays for the annotation purpose. Essays were either self-labeled as "argumentative" or annotators identified their argumentative nature from the titles (e.g., "Should Artificial Sweeteners be Banned in America ?").[3] Essays covered various social issues related to climate change, veteran care, effects of wars, whether sharks are dangerous or not, etc. We denote this corpus as *ARG*2020 in the remaining sections of the paper. We employed three expert annotators (with academic and professional background in Linguistics and Education) to identify the argument components. The annotators were instructed to read sentences from the essays and identify the *claims* (defined as, "a potentially arguable statement that indicates a person is arguing for or arguing against something. Claims are not clarification or elaboration statements.") that the argument is in reference to. Next, once the claims are identified, the annotators annotated the *premises* (defined as, "reasons given by either for supporting or attacking the claims making those claims more than mere assertions").[4] Earlier research has addressed college level writing, and even such resources are scarce except for a few corpora (Stab and Gurevych, 2017) (denoted as *SG*2017 in this paper). On the contrary, *ARG*2020 is based on middle school students writing, which differs from college level writing *SG*2017 in several aspects briefly discussed in the next paragraph.

First, we notice that essays in *SG*2017 maintain distinct paragraphs such as the introduction (initiates the major claim in the essay), the conclusion (summarizes the arguments), and a few paragraphs in between that express many claims and their premises. However, essays written by middle school students do not always comply with such writing conventions to keep a concrete introduction and conclusion paragraph, rather, they write many short paragraphs (7-8 paragraphs on average) per essay while each paragraph contains multiple claims. Second, in general, claims in college essays in *SG*2017 are justified by one or multiple premises, whereas *ARG*2020 has many unsupported claims. For instance, the excerpt from the annotated essay in Figure 1 contains two unsupported claims (e.g., "Diet soda, sugar ... without the calories" and "artificial sweeteners ... health effects"). Third, middle school students often put opinions (e.g., "Sugar substitutes produce sweet food without feeling guilty consequences") or matter-of-fact statements (e.g., "Even canned food and dairy products can be artificially sweetened") that are not argumentative claims but structurally they are identical to claims. Fourth, multiple claims frequently appear in a single sentence that are separated by discourse markers or commas. Fifth, many essays contain run-on sentences (e.g., "this is hard on the family, they have a hard time adjusting") that make the task of parsing even tricky. We argue these reasons

[3]Other metadata reveal that middle school students write these essays. However, we did not use any such information while annotating the essays.

[4]Definitions are from (Stab and Gurevych, 2017) and Argument: Claims, Reasons, Evidence - Department of Communication, University of Pittsburgh (https://bit.ly/396Ap3H)

Corpora	Split	Essays	B-Claim	I-Claim	B-Premise	I-Premise	O-Arg	Total
*ARG*2020	*training*	100	1,780	21,966	317	3,552	51,478	79,093
	dev	10	171	1,823	32	371	4,008	6,405
	test	35	662	8,207	92	1,018	14,987	24,966

Table 1: Token counts of each category in the *training*, *dev*, and *test* sets of *ARG2020*

make identifying argument claims and premises from *ARG*2020 more challenging.

The annotators were presented with specific guidelines and examples for annotation. We conducted a pilot task first where all the three annotators annotated ten essays and exchanged their notes for calibration. Following that, we continued pair-wise annotation tasks (30 essays for each pair of annotators), and finally, individual annotators annotated the remaining essays. Since the annotation task involves identifying each argumentative component's words, we have to account for fuzzy boundaries (e.g., in-claim vs. not-in-claim tokens) to measure the IAA. We considered the Krippendorff's α (Krippendorff, 2004) metric to compute the IAA. We measure the α between each pair of annotators and report the average. For *claim* we have a modest agreement of 0.71 that is comparable to (Stab and Gurevych, 2014) and for *premise*, we have a high agreement of 0.90.

Out of the 145 essays from *ARG*2020 we randomly assign 100 essays for *training*, 10 essays for *dev*, and the remaining 35 essays for *test*. Table 1 represents the data statistics in the standard BIO format. We find the number of claims is almost six times the number of premises showing that the middle school students often fail to justify their proposed claims. We keep identifying opinions and argumentative relations (support/attack) as future work.

4 Experimental Setup

Majority of the argumentation research first segment the text in argumentative and non-argumentative segments and then identify the structures such as components and relations (Stab and Gurevych, 2017). Petasis (2019) mentioned that the granularity of computational approaches addressing the second task of argument component identification is diverse because some approaches consider detecting components at the clause level (e.g., approaches focused on the *SG*2017 corpus (Stab and Gurevych, 2014, 2017; Ajjour et al., 2017; Eger et al., 2017)) and others at the sentence levels (Chakrabarty et al., 2019; Daxenberger et al., 2017). We avoided both approaches for the following two reasons. First, middle school student essays often contain run-on sentences, and it is unclear how to handle clause level annotations because parsing might be inaccurate. Second, around 62% of the premises in the *training* set appears to be in the same sentence as their claims. This makes sentence classification to either claim or premise impractical (Figure 1 contains one such example). Thus, instead of relying on the pipeline approach, we tackle the problem by identifying argument components from the token-level classification akin to Schulz et al. (2019). Our unit of sequence tagging is a sentence, unlike a passage (Eger et al., 2017). We apply a five-way token-classification (or sequence tagging) task while using the standard BIO notation for the claim and premise tokens (See Table 1). Any token that is not "B-Claim", "I-Claim", "B-Premise", or "I-Premise" is denoted as "O-Arg". As expected, the number of "O-Arg" tokens is much larger than the other categories (see Table 1).

We explore three separate machine learning approaches well-established for studying token-based classification. First, we experiment with the sequence classifier Conditional Random Field (CRF) that exploits state-of-the-art discrete features. Second, we implement a BiLSTM network (with and without CRF) based on the BERT embeddings. Finally, we experiment with the fine-tuned BERT models with/without multitask learning setting.

4.1 Feature-based Models

Akin to (Stab and Gurevych, 2017) we experiment with three groups of discrete features: *structural*, *syntactic* and *lexico-syntactic* with some modifications. In addition, we experiment with embedding features extracted from the contextualized pre-trained language model of BERT.

Discrete Features For each token in a given essay, we extract structural features that include token position (e.g., the relative and absolute position of the token in the sentence, paragraph and, essay from the beginning of the essay) and punctuation features (e.g., whether the token is, preceded, or succeeded by punctuation). Such position features have shown to be useful in identifying claims and premises against sentences that do not contain any argument (Stab and Gurevych, 2017). We also extract syntactic features for each token that include part-of-speech tag of the token and normalized length to the lowest common ancestor (LCA) of the token and its preceding (and succeeding) token in the parse tree. In contrast with (Stab and Gurevych, 2017), we use dependency parsing as the base for the syntactic features rather than constituency parsing. Finally, we extract lexico-syntactic features (denoted as *lexSyn* in Table 2) that include the dependency relation governing the token in the dependency parse tree and the token itself, plus its governing dependency relation as another feature. This is also different than (Stab and Gurevych, 2017) where the authors used lexicalized-parse tree (Collins, 2003) to generate their lexico-syntactic features. These features are effective in identifying the argumentative discourse units. We also observed that using dependency parse trees as a basis for the lexico-syntactic features yields better results than constituency parse trees in our pilot experiments.

Embedding Features from BERT BERT (Devlin et al., 2019), a bidirectional transformer model, has achieved state-of-the-art performance in many NLP tasks. BERT is initially trained on the tasks of masked language modeling (MLM) and next sentence prediction (NSP) over very large corpora of English Wikipedia and BooksCorpus. During its training, a special token "[CLS]" is added to the beginning of each training instance, and the "[SEP]" tokens are added to indicate the end of utterance(s) and separate, in case of two utterances.

Pretrained BERT ("bert-base-uncased") can be used directly by extracting the token representations' embeddings. We use the average embeddings of the top four layers as suggested in Devlin et al. (2019). For tokens with more than one word-piece when running BERT's tokenizer, their final embeddings feature is the average vector of all of their word-pieces. This feature yields a 768D-long vector that we use individually as well as in combination with the other discrete features in our experiments. We utilize the sklearn-crfsuite tool for our CRF experiments.[5]

4.2 BiLSTM-CRF Models

To compare our models with standard sequence tagging models for argument segmentation (Petasis, 2019; Ajjour et al., 2019; Hua et al., 2019), we experiment with the BiLSTM-CRF sequence tagging model introduced by Ma and Hovy (2016) using the flair library (Akbik et al., 2019). We use the standard BERT ("bert-base-uncased") embeddings (768D) in the embedding layer and projected to a single-layer BiLSTM of 256D. BiLSTMs provide the context to the token's left and right, which proved to be useful for sequence tagging tasks. We train this model with and without a CRF decoder to see its effect on this task. The CRF layer considers both the output of the BiLSTM layer and the other neighboring tokens' labels, which improves the accuracy of the modeling desired transitions between labels (Ma and Hovy, 2016).

4.3 Transformers Fine-tuned Models

Pre-trained BERT can also be used for transfer learning by fine-tuning on a downstream task, i.e., claim and premise token identification task where training instances are from the labeled dataset *ARG*2020. We denote this model as $BERT_{bl}$. Besides fine-tuning with the labeled data, we also experiment with a *multitask learning* setting as well as conducted *adaptive pretraining* (Gururangan et al., 2020), that is continued pretraining on unlabeled corpora that can be task and domain relevant. We discuss the settings below.

Transformers Multitask Learning Multitask learning aims to leverage useful information in multiple related tasks to improve the performance of each task (Caruana, 1997). We treat the *sequence labeling* task of five-way token-level argument classification as the *main* task while we adopt the binary task

[5]https://sklearn-crfsuite.readthedocs.io

of *sentence-level argument* identification (i.e., whether the candidate sentence contains an argument (Ghosh et al., 2020) as the *auxiliary* task. Here, if any sentence in the candidate essay contains claim or premise token(s), the sentence is labeled as the positive category (i.e., argumentative), otherwise non-argumentative. We hypothesize that this auxiliary task of identifying argumentative sentences in a multitask setting could be useful for the main task of token-level classification.

We deploy two classification heads - one for each task - and the relevant gold labels are passed to them. For the auxiliary task, the learned representation for the "[CLS]" token is passed to the classification head. The two losses from these individual heads are added and propagated back through the model. This allows BERT to model the nuances of both tasks and their interdependence simultaneously. However, instead of simply adding the losses from the two tasks, we employ *dynamic weighting* of task-specific losses during the training process, based on the homoscedastic uncertainty of tasks, as proposed in Kendall et al. (2018):

$$L = \sum_t \frac{1}{2\sigma_t^2} L_t + \log \sigma_t^2 \qquad (1)$$

where L_t and σ_t depict the task-specific loss and its variance (updated through backpropagation), respectively, over the training instances. We denote this model as $BERT_{mt}$.

Adaptive Pre-training Learning We adaptively pretrained BERT over two unlabeled corpora. First, we train on a *task relevant* Reddit corpus of 5.5 million opinionated claims that was released by Chakrabarty et al. (2019). These claims are self-labeled by the acronym: IMO/IMHO (in my (humble) opinion), which is commonly used in Reddit. We denote this model as $BERT_{IMHO}$. Next, we train on a *task and domain relevant* corpus of around 10K essays that we obtained originally (See section 3) from the *Writing Mentor* App, excluding the annotated set of *ARG*2020 essays. We denote this model as $BERT_{essay}$. Figure 2 displays the use of the *adaptive pretraining* step (in orange block) and the two classification heads (in green blocks) employed for the multitask variation.

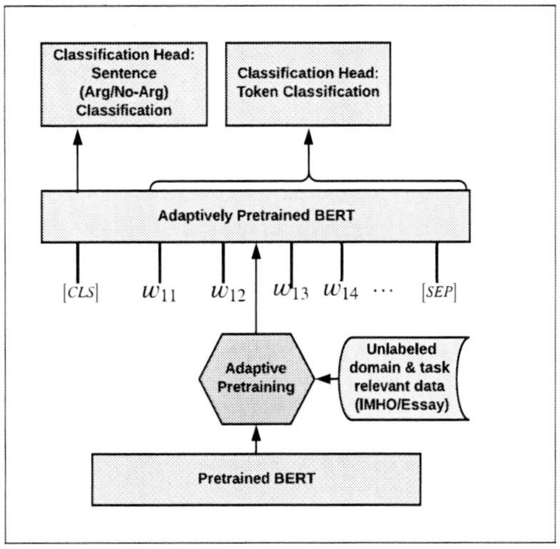

Figure 2: BERT fine-tuning with adaptive pretraining on unlabeled data from a relevant domain followed by fine-tuning on the labeled dataset with the multitask variation.

For brevity, the parameter tuning description for all the models and experiments - discrete feature-based and deep-learning ones (e.g., CRF, BiLSTM, BERT) is in the supplemental material.

5 Results and Discussion

We present our experiments' results using the CRF, BiLSTM, and BERT models under different settings. We report the individual F1, Accuracy, and Macro-F1 (abbrev. as "Acc." and "F1") scores for all the categories in Table 2 and Table 3.

We apply the discrete features (structural, syntactic, lexico-syntactic ("lexSyn")) together and individually to the CRF model. We observe the structural and syntactic features do not perform well individually, especially in the case of premise tokens (See Table 5 in Appendix A.3) and therefore, we only report the results of all discrete features (Discrete* in Table 2) and individually only the performance of the lexSyn features. Stab and Gurevych (2017) noticed that structural features are effective to identify argument components, especially from the introduction and conclusion sections of the college level essays because they contain few argumentatively relevant content. On the contrary, as stated earlier, school student es-

	CRF						
Features	B-Claim	I-Claim	B-Premise	I-Premise	O-Arg	Acc.	F1
lexSyn	.395	.530	.114	.176	.768	.673	.397
Discrete*	.269	.504	0	.013	.695	.595	.296
Embeddings	.401	.560	.048	.139	.769	.676	.384
Embeddings+lexSyn	.482	.610	.134	.180	.764	<u>.682</u>	<u>.434</u>
Embeddings+Discrete*	.434	.593	.055	.152	.762	.676	.399
	BiLSTM						
Setup	B-Claim	I-Claim	B-Premise	I-Premise	O-Arg	Acc.	F1
BiLSTM	.556	.680	.239	.438	.797	<u>.735</u>	<u>.542</u>
BiLSTM-CRF	.558	.676	.199	.378	.789	.727	.520
	BERT						
Setup	B-Claim	I-Claim	B-Premise	I-Premise	O-Arg	Acc.	F1
BERT_{bl}	.563	.674	.274	.425	.795	.728	.546
$\text{BERT}_{bl_{IMHO}}$	.571	.681	.304	.410	.795	.730	.540
$\text{BERT}_{bl_{essay}}$	.564	.676	.261	.406	.792	<u>**.747**</u>	<u>.561</u>
BERT_{mt}	.567	.685	.242	.439	.805	.741	.548
$\text{BERT}_{mt_{IMHO}}$	.562	.684	.221	.413	.794	.731	.534
$\text{BERT}_{mt_{essay}}$	.580	.702	.254	.427	.810	<u>**.752**</u>	<u>**.574**</u>

Table 2: F1 scores for Claim and Premise Token Detection on the test set. <u>Underlined</u>: highest Accuracy/F1 in group. **Bold**: highest Accuracy/F1 overall. *Discrete: includes structural, syntactic, and lexSyn features.

says do not always comply with such writing conventions. Table 2 displays that the lexSyn feature independently performs better by almost 8% accuracy than the combination of the other discourse features. This correlates to the findings from prior work on *SG*2017 (Stab and Gurevych, 2017) where the lexSyn features reached the highest F1 on a similar corpus. Next, we augment the embedding features from the BERT pre-trained model with the discrete features and notice a marginal improvement in the accuracy score (less than 1%) over the performance of lexSyn features. This improvement is achieved from the higher accuracy in detecting the claim terms (e.g., Embedding+Discrete* achieves around 17% and 10%, an improvement over Discrete* features in the case of B-Claim and I-Claim, respectively). However, the accuracy of detecting the premise tokens is still significantly low. We assume that this could be due to the low frequency of premises in the *training* set, which seems to be more challenging for the CRF model to learn useful patterns from the pre-trained embeddings. On the contrary, the O-Arg token is the most frequent in the essays and that is reflected in the overall high accuracy scores for the O-Arg tokens (i.e., over 76% on average).

The overall performance(s) improve when we apply the BiLSTM networks on the *test* data. Accuracy improves by 5.3% in the case of BiLSTM against the Embeddings+lexSyn features. However, results do not improve when we augment the CRF classifier on top of the LSTM networks (BiLSTM-CRF). Instead, the performance drops by 0.8% accuracy (See Table 2). On related research, Petasis (2019) have conducted extensive experiments with the BiLSTM-CRF architecture with various types of embeddings and demonstrated that only the specific combination of embeddings (e.g., GloVe+Flair+BERT) achieves higher performance than BiLSTM-only architecture, but we leave such experiments for future work.

In the case of BERT based experiments, we observe BERT_{bl}, obtains an accuracy of 73% that is comparable to the BiLSTM performance. In terms of the individual categories, we observe BERT_{bl} achieves around 7.5% improvement over the BiLSTM-CRF classifier for the B-Premise tokens. We also observe that the two adaptive-pretrained models (e.g., BERT_{IMHO} and BERT_{essay}) perform better than the BERT_{bl} where BERT_{essay} achieves the best accuracy of 74.7%, a 2% improvement over BERT_{bl}. Although BERT_{IMHO} was trained on a much larger corpus than BERT_{essay}, we assume since BERT_{essay} was trained on a *domain relevant* corpus it achieves the highest F1. Likewise, in the case of multitask models, we observe BERT_{mt} performs better than BERT_{bl} by 1.3%. This shows that using argumentative sentence identification as an auxiliary task is beneficial for token-level classification. With regards to the adaptive-pretrained models, akin to the BERT_{bl} based experiments, we observe $\text{BERT}_{mt_{essay}}$ perform best by achieving the highest accuracy over 75%.

Argument Segmentation We choose the five-way token-level classification of argument component over the standard pipeline approach because the standard level of granularity (sentence or clause-based) is not applicable to our *training* data. In order to test the benefit of the five-way token-level classification, we also compare it against the traditional approach of segmentation of argumentative units into argumentative and non-argumentative tokens. We again follow the standard BIO notation for a three-way token classification setup (B-Arg, I-Arg, and O-Arg) for argument segmentation. In this setup, the B-Claim and B-Premise classes are merged into B-Arg, and I-Claim and I-Premise are merged into I-Arg, while the O-Arg class remains unchanged. The results of all of our models on this task are shown in Table 3. We notice similar patterns (except for $\text{BERT}_{mt_{IMHO}}$ that performs better than BERT_{mt} this time) in this three-way classification task as we saw in the five-way classification. The best model remains to be the $\text{BERT}_{mt_{essay}}$ with 77.3% accuracy, which is an improvement of 2-3% over the BiLSTM and other BERT-based architecture.

In summary, we have two main observations from Table 2 and Table 3. First, the best model in Table 3 reports only about 3% improvement over the result from Table 2 which shows that the five-way token-level classification is comparable against the standard task of argument segmentation. Second, the accuracy of the argument segmentation task is much lower than the accuracy of college-level essay corpus *SG*2017 (Stab and Gurevych, 2017) reported accuracy of 89.5%). This supports the challenges of analyzing middle school student essays.

5.1 Qualitative Analysis

Since we have explored three separate machine learning approaches with a variety of experiments, we analyze the results obtained from the $\text{BERT}_{mt_{essay}}$ model that has performed the best (Table 2). According to the confusion matrix, there are three major sources of errors: (a) around 2500 "O-Arg" tokens are wrongly classified as "I-Claim" (b) 2162 "I-Claim" tokens are wrongly classified as "O-Arg", and (c) 273 "I-Premise" tokens are erroneously classified as "I-Claim". Here, (a) and (b) are not surprising given these are the two categories with the largest number of tokens. For (c) we looked at a couple of examples, such as "because of [Walmart 's goal of saving money]$_{premise}$, [customers see value in Walmart that is absent from other retailers]$_{claim}$". Here, the premise tokens are wrongly classified as O-Arg tokens. This is probably because the premise appears before the claim, which is uncommon in our *training* set. We notice some of the other sources of errors, and we discuss them as follows:

	CRF				
Features	B-Arg	I-Arg	O-Arg	Acc.	F1
lexSyn	.385	.518	.768	.683	.557
Discrete	.288	.493	.710	.625	.497
Embeddings	.379	.596	.767	.699	.581
Emb+lexSyn	.468	.622	.768	<u>.708</u>	<u>.619</u>
Emb+Discrete	.381	.599	.767	.699	.582
	BiLSTM				
Setup	B-Arg	I-Arg	O-Arg	Acc.	F1
BiLSTM	.546	.730	.792	<u>.759</u>	<u>.689</u>
BiLSTM-CRF	.553	.707	.793	.752	.684
	BERT				
Setup	B-Arg	I-Arg	O-Arg	Acc.	F1
BERT_{bl}	.567	.698	.795	.750	.687
$\text{BERT}_{bl_{IMHO}}$	.558	.717	.778	.744	.684
$\text{BERT}_{bl_{essay}}$	.567	.707	.795	<u>.754</u>	<u>.690</u>
BERT_{mt}	.555	.702	.803	.758	.688
$\text{BERT}_{mt_{IMHO}}$	.568	.719	.804	.764	.700
$\text{BERT}_{mt_{essay}}$	.563	.735	.811	<u>**.773**</u>	<u>**.710**</u>

Table 3: F1 scores for Argument Token Detection on the test set. <u>Underlined</u>: highest Accuracy/F1 in group. **Bold**: highest Accuracy/F1 overall.

non-arguments classified as arguments: This error occurs often, but it is more challenging for *opinions* or *hypothetical examples* that resemble arguments but are not necessarily arguments. For instance, the opinion "that actually makes me feel good afterward ..." and the hypothetical example "Next , you will not be eating due to your lack of money" are similar to an argument, and the classifier erroneously classifies them as claim. In the future, we plan to include the labeled *opinions* during training to investigate how the model(s) handle opinions vs. arguments during the classification.

missing multiple-claims from a sentence: In many examples, we observe multiple claims appear in a single sentence, such as: "[Some coral can recover from this]$_{claim}$ though [for most it is the final straw .]$_{claim}$". During prediction, the model predicts the first claim correctly but then starts the second claim with an "I-Claim" label, which is an impossible transition from "Arg-O" (i.e., does not enforce well-formed spans). Besides, the model starts the second claim wrongly at the word "most" rather than "for". This indicates the model's inability to distinguish discourse markers such as "though" as potential separators between argument components. This could be explained by the fact that markers such as "though" or "because" are frequently part of an argument claim. Such as, in "[those games do not seem as violent even though they are at the same level]$_{claim}$", "though" is labeled as "I-Claim'.

investigating run-on sentences: Some sentences contain multiple claims, which are written as one sentence via a comma-splice run-on such as "[Humans in today 's world do not care about the consequences]$_{claim}$, [only the money they may gain .]$_{claim}$" which has two claims in the gold annotations but it was predicted as one long claim by our best model. Another example is "[The oceans are also another dire need in today's environment]$_{claim}$, each day becoming more filled with trash and plastics.", in which the claim is predicted correctly in addition to another predicted claim starting at the word *"each"*. The model tends to over predicts claims when a comma comes in the middle of the sentence followed by a noun. However, in the former example, the adverb "only" that has a "B-Claim" label follows the comma rather than the more frequent nouns. Such instances add more complexity to understand and model argument structures in middle school student writing.

effect of the multitask learning: We examined the impact of multitask learning and notice two characteristics. First, as expected, the multitask model can identify claims and premises that are missed by the single task model(s), such as: "[many more negative effects that come with social media ..."]$_{claim}$" that was correctly identified by the multitask model. Second, the clever handling of the back-propagation helps the multitask model to reduce false positives to be more precise. Many non-argumentative sentences, such as: "internet's social networks help teens find communities ..." and opinions, such as: "take $1.3 billion off $11.3 billion the NCAA makes and give it to players" are wrongly classified as claims by the single task models but are correctly classified as non-argumentative by the multitask model.

6 Conclusion

We conduct a token-level classification task to identify the type of the argument component tokens (e.g., claims and premises) by combining the argument segmentation and component identification in one single task. We perused a new corpus collected from essays written by middle school students. W Our findings show that a multitask BERT performs the best with an absolute gain of 7.5% accuracy over the discrete features. We also conducted an in-depth comparison against the standard segmentation step (i.e., classifying the argumentative vs. non-argumentative units) and proposed a thorough qualitative analysis.

Middle school student essays often contain run-on sentences or unsupported claims that make the task of identifying argument components much harder. We achieve the best performance using a multitask framework with an adaptive pretrained model, and we plan to continue to augment other tasks (e.g., opinion and stance identification) under a similar multitask framework (Eger et al., 2017). We plan to generate personalized feedback for the students (e.g., which are the supported claims in the essay?) that is useful in automated writing assistance.

Acknowledgments

The authors would like to thank Tuhin Chakrabarty, Elsbeth Turcan, Smaranda Muresan and Jill Burstein for their helpful comments and suggestions.

References

Tazin Afrin, Elaine Lin Wang, Diane Litman, Lindsay Clare Matsumura, and Richard Correnti. 2020. Annotation and classification of evidence and reasoning revisions in argumentative writing. In *Proceedings of the Fifteenth Workshop on Innovative Use of NLP for Building Educational Applications*, pages 75–84, Seattle, WA, USA → Online. Association for Computational Linguistics.

Yamen Ajjour, Milad Alshomary, Henning Wachsmuth, and Benno Stein. 2019. Modeling frames in argumentation. In *Proceedings of the 2019 Conference on Empirical Methods in Natural Language Processing and the 9th International Joint Conference on Natural Language Processing (EMNLP-IJCNLP)*, pages 2922–2932, Hong Kong, China. Association for Computational Linguistics.

Yamen Ajjour, Wei-Fan Chen, Johannes Kiesel, Henning Wachsmuth, and Benno Stein. 2017. Unit segmentation of argumentative texts. In *Proceedings of the 4th Workshop on Argument Mining*, pages 118–128.

Alan Akbik, Tanja Bergmann, Duncan Blythe, Kashif Rasul, Stefan Schweter, and Roland Vollgraf. 2019. FLAIR: An easy-to-use framework for state-of-the-art NLP. In *Proceedings of the 2019 Conference of the North American Chapter of the Association for Computational Linguistics (Demonstrations)*, pages 54–59, Minneapolis, Minnesota. Association for Computational Linguistics.

Khalid Al-Khatib, Henning Wachsmuth, Johannes Kiesel, Matthias Hagen, and Benno Stein. 2016. A news editorial corpus for mining argumentation strategies. In *Proceedings of COLING 2016, the 26th International Conference on Computational Linguistics: Technical Papers*, pages 3433–3443, Osaka, Japan. The COLING 2016 Organizing Committee.

Yigal Attali and Jill Burstein. 2006. Automated essay scoring with e-rater v.2. *The Journal of Technology, Learning and Assessment*, 4(3).

Yigal Attali and Don Powers. 2008. A developmental writing scale. *ETS Research Report Series*, 2008(1):i–59.

Beata Beigman Klebanov, Binod Gyawali, and Yi Song. 2017. Detecting Good Arguments in a Non-Topic-Specific Way: An Oxymoron? In *Proceedings of the 55th Annual Meeting of the Association for Computational Linguistics (Volume 2: Short Papers)*, pages 244–249, Vancouver, Canada. Association for Computational Linguistics.

Or Biran and Owen Rambow. 2011. Identifying justifications in written dialogs. In *2011 IEEE Fifth International Conference on Semantic Computing*, pages 162–168. IEEE.

Daniel Blanchard, Joel Tetreault, Derrick Higgins, Aoife Cahill, and Martin Chodorow. 2013. Toefl11: A corpus of non-native english. *ETS Research Report Series*, 2013(2):i–15.

Rich Caruana. 1997. Multitask learning. *Machine learning*, 28(1):41–75.

Tuhin Chakrabarty, Christopher Hidey, and Kathy McKeown. 2019. IMHO fine-tuning improves claim detection. In *Proceedings of the 2019 Conference of the North American Chapter of the Association for Computational Linguistics: Human Language Technologies, Volume 1 (Long and Short Papers)*, pages 558–563, Minneapolis, Minnesota. Association for Computational Linguistics.

Michael Collins. 2003. Head-driven statistical models for natural language parsing. *Computational linguistics*, 29(4):589–637.

Richard Correnti, Lindsay Clare Matsumura, Elaine Wang, Diane Litman, Zahra Rahimi, and Zahid Kisa. 2020. Automated scoring of students' use of text evidence in writing. *Reading Research Quarterly*, 55(3):493–520.

Johannes Daxenberger, Steffen Eger, Ivan Habernal, Christian Stab, and Iryna Gurevych. 2017. What is the essence of a claim? cross-domain claim identification. In *Proceedings of the 2017 Conference on Empirical Methods in Natural Language Processing*, pages 2055–2066.

Paul Deane. 2014. Using writing process and product features to assess writing quality and explore how those features relate to other literacy tasks. *ETS Research Report Series*, (1):1–23.

Jacob Devlin, Ming-Wei Chang, Kenton Lee, and Kristina Toutanova. 2019. BERT: Pre-training of deep bidirectional transformers for language understanding. In *Proceedings of the 2019 Conference of the North American Chapter of the Association for Computational Linguistics: Human Language Technologies, Volume 1 (Long and Short Papers)*, pages 4171–4186, Minneapolis, Minnesota. Association for Computational Linguistics.

Steffen Eger, Johannes Daxenberger, and Iryna Gurevych. 2017. Neural end-to-end learning for computational argumentation mining. In *Proceedings of the 55th Annual Meeting of the Association for Computational Linguistics (Volume 1: Long Papers)*, pages 11–22.

Noura Farra, Swapna Somasundaran, and Jill Burstein. 2015. Scoring persuasive essays using opinions and their targets. In *Proceedings of the Workshop on Innovative Use of NLP for Building Educational Applications*, pages 64–74.

Vanessa Wei Feng and Graeme Hirst. 2011. Classifying arguments by scheme. In *Proceedings of the 49th Annual Meeting of the Association for Computational Linguistics: Human Language Technologies*, pages 987–996, Portland, Oregon, USA. Association for Computational Linguistics.

Debanjan Ghosh, Beata Beigman Klebanov, and Yi Song. 2020. An exploratory study of argumentative writing by young students: A transformer-based approach. In *Proceedings of the Fifteenth Workshop on Innovative Use of NLP for Building Educational Applications*, pages 145–150, Seattle, WA, USA. Association for Computational Linguistics.

Debanjan Ghosh, Aquila Khanam, Yubo Han, and Smaranda Muresan. 2016. Coarse-grained argumentation features for scoring persuasive essays. In *Proceedings of the 54th Annual Meeting of the Association for Computational Linguistics (Volume 2: Short Papers)*, pages 549–554, Berlin, Germany. Association for Computational Linguistics.

Debanjan Ghosh, Smaranda Muresan, Nina Wacholder, Mark Aakhus, and Matthew Mitsui. 2014. Analyzing argumentative discourse units in online interactions. In *Proceedings of the first workshop on argumentation mining*, pages 39–48.

Suchin Gururangan, Ana Marasović, Swabha Swayamdipta, Kyle Lo, Iz Beltagy, Doug Downey, and Noah A. Smith. 2020. Don't stop pretraining: Adapt language models to domains and tasks. In *Proceedings of the 58th Annual Meeting of the Association for Computational Linguistics*, pages 8342–8360. Association for Computational Linguistics.

Yufang Hou and Charles Jochim. 2017. Argument relation classification using a joint inference model. In *Proceedings of the 4th Workshop on Argument Mining*, pages 60–66, Copenhagen, Denmark. Association for Computational Linguistics.

Xinyu Hua, Zhe Hu, and Lu Wang. 2019. Argument generation with retrieval, planning, and realization. In *Proceedings of the 57th Annual Meeting of the Association for Computational Linguistics*, pages 2661–2672, Florence, Italy. Association for Computational Linguistics.

Alex Kendall, Yarin Gal, and Roberto Cipolla. 2018. Multi-task learning using uncertainty to weigh losses for scene geometry and semantics. In *Proceedings of the IEEE conference on computer vision and pattern recognition*, pages 7482–7491.

Klaus Krippendorff. 2004. Measuring the reliability of qualitative text analysis data. *Quality and quantity*, 38:787–800.

John Lafferty, Andrew McCallum, and Fernando CN Pereira. 2001. Conditional random fields: Probabilistic models for segmenting and labeling sequence data.

John Lawrence and Chris Reed. 2020. Argument mining: A survey. *Computational Linguistics*, 45(4):765–818.

Marco Lippi and Paolo Torroni. 2015. Context-independent claim detection for argument mining. In *Twenty-Fourth International Joint Conference on Artificial Intelligence*.

Luca Lugini, Diane Litman, Amanda Godley, and Christopher Olshefski. 2018. Annotating student talk in text-based classroom discussions. In *Proceedings of the Thirteenth Workshop on Innovative Use of NLP for Building Educational Applications*, pages 110–116.

Xuezhe Ma and Eduard Hovy. 2016. End-to-end sequence labeling via bi-directional LSTM-CNNs-CRF. In *Proceedings of the 54th Annual Meeting of the Association for Computational Linguistics (Volume 1: Long Papers)*, pages 1064–1074, Berlin, Germany. Association for Computational Linguistics.

Nitin Madnani, Michael Heilman, Joel Tetreault, and Martin Chodorow. 2012. Identifying high-level organizational elements in argumentative discourse. In *Proceedings of the 2012 Conference of the North American Chapter of the Association for Computational Linguistics: Human Language Technologies*, pages 20–28, Montréal, Canada. Association for Computational Linguistics.

Raquel Mochales and Marie-Francine Moens. 2011. Argumentation mining. *Artificial Intelligence and Law*, 19(1):1–22.

Marie-Francine Moens, Erik Boiy, Raquel Mochales Palau, and Chris Reed. 2007. Automatic detection of arguments in legal texts. In *Proceedings of the 11th international conference on Artificial intelligence and law*, pages 225–230.

Huy Nguyen and Diane Litman. 2016. Context-aware argumentative relation mining. In *Proceedings of the 54th Annual Meeting of the Association for Computational Linguistics (Volume 1: Long Papers)*, pages 1127–1137.

Huy V Nguyen and Diane J Litman. 2018. Argument mining for improving the automated scoring of persuasive essays. In *Thirty-Second AAAI Conference on Artificial Intelligence*.

Vlad Niculae, Joonsuk Park, and Claire Cardie. 2017. Argument mining with structured SVMs and RNNs. In *Proceedings of the 55th Annual Meeting of the Association for Computational*

Linguistics (Volume 1: Long Papers), pages 985–995, Vancouver, Canada. Association for Computational Linguistics.

Raquel Mochales Palau and Marie-Francine Moens. 2009. Argumentation mining: The detection, classification and structure of arguments in text. In *Proceedings of the 12th International Conference on Artificial Intelligence and Law*, ICAIL '09, page 98–107, New York, NY, USA. Association for Computing Machinery.

Joonsuk Park and Claire Cardie. 2014. Identifying appropriate support for propositions in online user comments. In *Proceedings of the First Workshop on Argumentation Mining*, pages 29–38, Baltimore, Maryland. Association for Computational Linguistics.

Andreas Peldszus and Manfred Stede. 2013. From argument diagrams to argumentation mining in texts: A survey. *International Journal of Cognitive Informatics and Natural Intelligence (IJCINI)*, 7(1):1–31.

Andreas Peldszus and Manfred Stede. 2015. Joint prediction in MST-style discourse parsing for argumentation mining. In *Proceedings of the 2015 Conference on Empirical Methods in Natural Language Processing*, pages 938–948, Lisbon, Portugal. Association for Computational Linguistics.

Isaac Persing and Vincent Ng. 2014. Modeling prompt adherence in student essays. In *Proceedings of the 52nd Annual Meeting of the Association for Computational Linguistics (Volume 1: Long Papers)*, pages 1534–1543.

Isaac Persing and Vincent Ng. 2015. Modeling argument strength in student essays. In *Proceedings of the 53rd Annual Meeting of the Association for Computational Linguistics and the 7th International Joint Conference on Natural Language Processing (Volume 1: Long Papers)*, pages 543–552.

Isaac Persing and Vincent Ng. 2016. End-to-end argumentation mining in student essays. In *Proceedings of the 2016 Conference of the North American Chapter of the Association for Computational Linguistics: Human Language Technologies*, pages 1384–1394.

Georgios Petasis. 2019. Segmentation of argumentative texts with contextualised word representations. In *Proceedings of the 6th Workshop on Argument Mining*, pages 1–10, Florence, Italy. Association for Computational Linguistics.

Peter Potash, Alexey Romanov, and Anna Rumshisky. 2017. Here's my point: Joint pointer architecture for argument mining. In *Proceedings of the 2017 Conference on Empirical Methods in Natural Language Processing*, pages 1364–1373.

Niall Rooney, Hui Wang, and Fiona Browne. 2012. Applying kernel methods to argumentation mining. In *FLAIRS Conference*, volume 172.

Claudia Schulz, Steffen Eger, Johannes Daxenberger, Tobias Kahse, and Iryna Gurevych. 2018. Multi-task learning for argumentation mining in low-resource settings. In *Proceedings of the 2018 Conference of the North American Chapter of the Association for Computational Linguistics: Human Language Technologies, Volume 2 (Short Papers)*, pages 35–41, New Orleans, Louisiana. Association for Computational Linguistics.

Claudia Schulz, Christian M Meyer, and Iryna Gurevych. 2019. Challenges in the automatic analysis of students' diagnostic reasoning. In *Proceedings of the AAAI Conference on Artificial Intelligence*, volume 33, pages 6974–6981.

Swapna Somasundaran, Brian Riordan, Binod Gyawali, and Su-Youn Yoon. 2016. Evaluating argumentative and narrative essays using graphs. In *Proceedings of COLING 2016, the 26th International Conference on Computational Linguistics: Technical Papers*, pages 1568–1578.

Yi Song, Michael Heilman, Beata Beigman Klebanov, and Paul Deane. 2014. Applying argumentation schemes for essay scoring. In *Proceedings of the First Workshop on Argumentation Mining*, pages 69–78.

Christian Stab and Iryna Gurevych. 2014. Identifying argumentative discourse structures in persuasive essays. In *Proceedings of the 2014 Conference on Empirical Methods in Natural Language Processing (EMNLP)*, pages 46–56.

Christian Stab and Iryna Gurevych. 2017. Parsing argumentation structures in persuasive essays. *Computational Linguistics*, 43(3):619–659.

Manfred Stede and Jodi Schneider. 2018. Argumentation mining. *Synthesis Lectures on Human Language Technologies*, 11(2):1–191.

Nina Wacholder, Smaranda Muresan, Debanjan Ghosh, and Mark Aakhus. 2014. Annotating multiparty discourse: Challenges for agreement metrics. In *Proceedings of LAW VIII-The 8th Linguistic Annotation Workshop*, pages 120–128.

Henning Wachsmuth, Khalid Al-Khatib, and Benno Stein. 2016. Using argument mining to assess the argumentation quality of essays. In *Proceedings of COLING 2016, the 26th International Conference on Computational Linguistics: Technical Papers*, pages 1680–1691, Osaka, Japan. The COLING 2016 Organizing Committee.

Haoran Zhang and Diane Litman. 2020. Automated topical component extraction using neural network attention scores from source-based essay scoring. In *Proceedings of the 58th Annual Meeting of the Association for Computational Linguistics*, pages 8569–8584, Online. Association for Computational Linguistics.

A Appendix

A.1 Parameter Tuning

CRF experiment: For the CRF model, we search over the two regularization parameters c1 and c2 by sampling from exponential distributions with 0.5 scale for c1 and 0.05 scale for c2 using a 3 cross-validation over 50 iterations, which takes about 20 minutes of run-time. The final values are 0.8 for c1 and 0.05 for c2 for the best CRF model that uses LexSyn and BERT embeddings features.

BiLSTM experiment: For BiLSTM networks based experiments we searched the hyper parameters over the *dev* set. Particularly we experimented with different mini-batch size (e.g., 16, 32), dropout value (e.g., 0.1, 0.3, 0.5, 0.7), number of epochs (e.g., 40, 50, 100 with early stopping), hidden state of sized-vectors (256). Embeddings were generated using BERT ("bert-base-uncased") (768 dimensions). After tuning we use the following hyper-parameters for the *test* set: mini-batch size of 32, number of epochs = 100 (stop between 30-40 epochs), and dropout value of 0.1. The model has one BiLSTM layer with size 256 of the hidden layer.

BERT based models: We use the *dev* partition for hyperparameter tuning (batch size of 8, 16, 32, 48), run for 3,5,6 epochs, learning rate of 3e-5) and optimized networks with the Adam optimizer. The training partitions were fine-tuned for 5 epochs with batch size = 16. Each training epoch took between 08:46 $\sim$ 9 minutes over a K-80 GPU with 48GB vRAM.

A.2 Results of Discourse Feature Groups

We show below the results of using each of the three feature groups individually: structural, syntactic and lexical-syntactic. As mentioned in the results section of the paper, we can see below that the structural and syntactic features do not do well when used individually. Therefore, they were excluded from further experimentation with BERT embeddings. Only the LexSyn features were tested individually with the embeddings.

Features	Structural	Syntactic	LexSyn	All Discrete
B-claim	.294	.218	.395	.269
I-claim	.461	.390	.530	.504
B-premise	0	0	.114	0
I-premise	.018	.009	.176	.013
O-Arg	.655	.745	.768	.695
Accuracy	.560	.625	.673	.595
Macro F1	.285	.272	.397	.296

Table 4: Accuracy and F1 scores for Claim and Premise Token Detection on the test set for each group of the discrete features in the CRF model.

Using Linguistic Features to Predict the Response Process Complexity Associated with Answering Clinical MCQs

Victoria Yaneva[1] **Daniel Jurich**[1] **Le An Ha**[2] **Peter Baldwin**[1]

[1]National Board of Medical Examiners, Philadelphia, USA
{vyaneva, djurich, pbaldwin}@nbme.org
[2]University of Wolverhamton, UK
ha.l.a@wlv.ac.uk

Abstract

This study examines the relationship between the linguistic characteristics of a test item and the complexity of the response process required to answer it correctly. Using data from a large-scale medical licensing exam, clustering methods identified items that were similar with respect to their relative difficulty and relative response-time intensiveness to create *low response process complexity* and *high response process complexity* item classes. Interpretable models were used to investigate the linguistic features that best differentiated between these classes from a descriptive and predictive framework. Results suggest that nuanced features such as the number of ambiguous medical terms help explain response process complexity beyond superficial item characteristics such as word count. Yet, although linguistic features carry signal relevant to response process complexity, the classification of individual items remains challenging.

1 Introduction

The success of high-stakes exams, such as those used in licensing, certification, and college admission, depends on the use of items (test questions) that meet stringent quality criteria. To provide useful information about examinee ability, good items must be neither too difficult, nor too easy for the intended test-takers. Furthermore, the timing demands of items should be such that different exam forms seen by different test-takers should entail similar times to complete. Nevertheless, while an extreme difficulty or mean response time can indicate that an item is not functioning correctly, within these extremes variability in difficulty and item response time is expected. For good items, it is hoped that this variability simply reflects the breadth and depth of the relevant exam content.

The interaction between item *difficulty* (as measured by the proportion of examinees who respond correctly) and *time intensiveness* (as measured by the average time examinees spend answering) can help quantify the complexity of the response process associated with an item. This is valuable, since the more we know about the way examinees think about the problem presented in an item, the better we can evaluate exam validity. Although easier items usually require less time than difficult items, the interaction between these two item properties is not strictly linear – examinees may spend very little time responding to certain difficult items and, likewise, examinees may spend a great deal of time on items that are relatively easy. The idea of response process complexity is best illustrated with items that have similar difficulty but different mean response times. In such cases, one item may require the formation of a complex cognitive model of the problem and thus take a long time, while another item with a similar level of difficulty may require factual knowledge that few examinees recall (or that many recall incorrectly) and thus take a short time on average. The interaction between item difficulty and time intensity can therefore provide valuable information about the complexity of the response process demanded by an item, which, we argue, can be further explained by examining the linguistic properties of the item.

In this paper, we use a data-driven approach to capture the interaction between item difficulty and response time within a pool of 18,961 multiple-choice items from a high-stakes medical exam, where each item was answered by 335 examinees on average. For our data, this resulted in the definition of two clusters, one of which consisted of items that are relatively easy and less time-intensive, and another one which consisted of items that are relatively difficult and/or time-intensive. For the purposes of this study, we name these two clusters *low-complexity* class and *high-complexity* class, respectively. The use of the term *response process*

Proceedings of the 16th Workshop on Innovative Use of NLP for Building Educational Applications, pages 223–232
April 20, 2021 ©2021 Association for Computational Linguistics

A 16-year-old boy is brought to the emergency department because of a 2-day history of fever, nausea, vomiting, headache, chills, and fatigue. He has not had any sick contacts. He underwent splenectomy for traumatic injury at the age of 13 years. He has no other history of serious illness and takes no medications. He appears ill. His temperature is 39.2°C (102.5°F), pulse is 130/min, respirations are 14/min, and blood pressure is 110/60 mm Hg. On pulmonary examination, scattered crackles are heard bilaterally. Abdominal shows a well-healed midline scar and mild, diffuse tenderness to palpation. Which of the following is the most appropriate next step in management?
(A) Antibiotic therapy (B) Antiemetic therapy
(C) CT scan of the chest (D) X-ray of the abdomen
(E) Reassurance

Table 1: An example of a practice item

complexity here is not based on an operational definition of this construct, which would require extensive research on its own, but rather, as a succinct label that summarises the differences between the two classes along the interaction of empirical item difficulty and item time intensiveness.

Studying the linguistic characteristics of these two categories may help test developers gain a more nuanced understanding of how cognitively complex items differ from those with a straightforward solution. Provided that strong relationships are found, such insight can also be used to guide item writers or inform innovative automated item generation algorithms when seeking to create high- or low-complexity items. For this reason, our goal is not to train a black-box model to predict item complexity; instead, our goal is to isolate interpretable relationships between item text and item complexity that can inform our understanding of the response process and provide better item-writing strategies.

In addition to its utility for improving high-stakes exams, the problem of modeling response process complexity is interesting from an NLP perspective because it requires the modeling of cognitive processes beyond reading comprehension. This is especially relevant for the data used here because, as we explain in Section 3 below, the items in our bank assess expert-level clinical knowledge and are written to a common reading level using standardized language.

Contributions: i) We use unsupervised clustering to define classes of high and low response-process complexity from a large sample of items and test-takers in a high-stakes medical exam; ii) the study provides empirical evidence that linguistic characteristics carry signal relevant to an item's response process complexity; iii) the most predictive features are identified through several feature selection methods and their potential relationship to response process complexity is discussed; iv) the errors made by the model and their implications for predicting response process complexity are analysed.

2 Related Work

This section discusses related work on the topics of modeling item difficulty and response time.

Most NLP studies modeling the difficulty of test questions for humans have been conducted in the domain of reading comprehension, where the readability of reading passages is associated with the difficulty of their corresponding comprehension questions (Huang et al., 2017; Beinborn et al., 2015; Loukina et al., 2016). For other exams, taxonomies representing knowledge dimensions and cognitive processes involved in the completion of a test task have been used to predict the difficulty of short-answer questions (Padó, 2017) and identify skills required to answer school science questions (Nadeem and Ostendorf, 2017). Difficulty prediction has also been explored in the context of evaluating automatically generated questions (Alsubait et al., 2013; Ha and Yaneva, 2018; Kurdi, 2020; Kurdi et al., 2020) through measures such as question-answer similarity.

Response time prediction has mainly been explored in the field of educational testing using predictors such as item presentation position (Parshall et al., 1994), item content category (Parshall et al., 1994; Smith, 2000), the presence of a figure (Smith, 2000; Swanson et al., 2001), and item difficulty and discrimination (Halkitis et al., 1996; Smith, 2000). The only text-related feature explored in these studies was *word count*, and it was shown to have a very limited predictive power in most domains.

Several studies have explored the prediction of item difficulty and response time in the context of clinical multiple choice questions (MCQs). Ha et al. (2019) propose a large number of linguistic features and embeddings for modeling item difficulty. The results show that the full model outperforms several baselines with a statistically significant improvement, however, its practical significance for successfully predicting item difficulty remains limited, confirming the challenging nature of the problem. Continuations of this study include the use of transfer learning to predict difficulty and response time (Xue et al., 2020), as well as using predicted difficulty for filtering out items that are too easy or too difficult for the intended examinee population (Yaneva et al., 2020). Baldwin et al. (2020) used a broad range of linguistic features and embeddings (similar to those in Ha et al. (2019)) to predict item response time, showing that a wide range of linguistic predictors at various levels of linguistic processing were all relevant to response-time prediction. The predicted response times were then used in a subsequent experiment to improve fairness by reducing the time intensity variance of exam forms.

3 Data

The data[1] used in this study comprises 18,961 Step 2 Clinical Knowledge items from the United States Medical Licensing Examination (USMLE®), a large-scale high-stakes medical assessment. All items were MCQs. An example practice item[2] is given in Table 1. The exam comprises several one-hour testing blocks with 40 items per block. All items test medical knowledge and are written by experienced item-writers following guidelines intended to produce items that vary in their difficulty and response times only due to differences in the medical content they assess. These guidelines stipulate that item writers adhere to a standard structure and avoid excessive verbosity, extraneous material not needed to answer the item, information designed to mislead the test-taker, and grammatical cues (e.g., correct answers that are more specific than the other options). All items were administered between 2010 and 2015 as pretest items and presented alongside scored items on operational exams. Examinees were medical students from accredited US and Canadian medical schools taking the exam for the first time and had no way of knowing which items were pretest items and which were scored. On average, each item was attempted by 335 examinees (SD = 156.8).

3.1 Identifying items with high and low response process complexity

We base our definition of the two classes of items on empirical *item difficulty* and *time intensity*. Item difficulty is measured by the proportion of examinees who answered the item correctly, a metric commonly referred to by the educational testing community as *p-value* and calculated as follows:

$$P_i = \frac{\sum_{n=1}^{N} U_n}{N},$$

where P_i is the p-value for item i, U_n is the 0-1 score (incorrect-correct) on item i earned by examinee n, and N is the total number of examinees in the sample. Thus, difficulty measured in this way ranges from 0 to 1 and higher values correspond to easier items.

Time intensity is found by taking the arithmetic mean response time, measured in seconds, across all examinees who attempted a given item. This includes all time spent on the item from the moment it is presented on the screen until the examinee moves to the next item, as well as any revisits.

To assign items to classes, p-value and mean response time are rescaled such that each variable has a mean of 0 and a standard deviation of 1. Moreover, we use two quantitative methods to categorize items and retain only those items where there was agreement between the two methods.

Method 1: Items were classified by applying a K-means clustering algorithm via the `kmeans` function in Python's `Scikit-learn` (Pedregosa et al., 2011). K-means is an unsupervised data classification technique that discovers patterns in the data by assigning instances to a pre-defined number of classes (Wagstaff et al., 2001). This approach also allows us to evaluate the plausibility of categorizing items into more than two complexity classes, or whether the items fail to show any meaningful separation along the interaction of p-value and duration (one class). Results suggest that two classes best fit these data and identified 11,067 items as low complexity and 7,894 items as high complexity[3].

[1] The data cannot be made available due to exam security considerations.

[2] Source: https://www.usmle.org/pdfs/step-2-ck/2020_Step2CK_SampleItems.pdf

[3] We also experimented with hierarchical clustering, which led to similar results. The hierarchical clustering dendrogram suggested that there are meaningful distances between two clusters in the data, and much smaller distances between a higher number of more fine-grained clusters.

Method 2: Any item with a rescaled p-value greater than its rescaled mean response time – indicating that the item is relatively easier than it is time-consuming – is classified as low-complexity (11,682 items). Likewise, the remaining items, which had rescaled p-values less than their rescaled mean response times, were assigned to the high-complexity class (7,279 items). Put another way, if an item takes less time than we would expect given its difficulty, the item is classified as *low response process complexity* and if it takes more time than we would expect, it is classified as *high response process complexity*.

The two methods achieved strong agreement, with only 673 (3.5%) items being assigned to different classes across methods. These discrepant items are excluded, leaving a total of 18,288 items for further analysis: 11,038 low-complexity items and 7,250 high-complexity ones. Figure 1 shows the class assignment, p-value, and mean response time for each item.

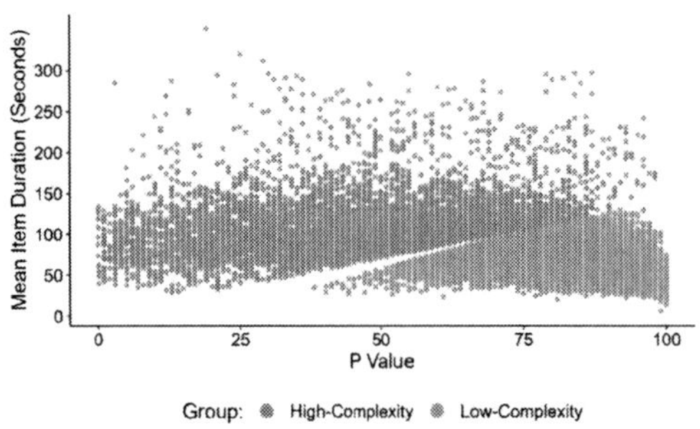

Figure 1: Class assignment by p-value and response time for each item. Note that discrepant items were excluded, as illustrated by the gap between the two class distributions.

As can be seen from the figure, the class of *low-complexity* items was dense and homogenous compared to the *high-complexity class*, meaning that it contained a large number of easy items whose response times were always below 125 seconds. The high-complexity class on the other hand was highly heterogeneous, with items whose response times and p-values spanned almost the entire scale.

4 Features

We use a set of interpretable linguistic features, many of which were previously used for predicting item difficulty (Ha et al., 2019) and response time (Baldwin et al., 2020) in the domain of clinical MCQs. These features were extracted using code made available by Ha et al. (2019) and to these, we add several predictors specifically related to the medical content of the items, as well as standard item metadata.

4.1 Linguistic features

As noted, this study replicates the feature extraction procedure described and made available by Ha et al. (2019). Approximately 90 linguistic features were extracted from each item's text (the full item including answer options) and are summarized in Table 2. They span several levels of linguistic processing including surface lexical and syntactic features, semantic features that account for ambiguity, and cognitively motivated features that capture properties such as imageability and familiarity. Common readability formulae are used to account for surface reading difficulty. The organization of ideas in the text is captured through text cohesion features that measure the number and types of connective words within an item. Finally, word frequency features (including threshold frequencies) measure the extent to which items utilize frequent vocabulary.

Combinations of these features have the potential to capture different aspects of item content that are relevant to response complexity. For example, medical terms can be expected to have lower absolute frequencies and familiarity ratings, among other characteristics, and combinations of these features may suggest a higher density of medical terms and specialized language in some items compared to others. Another example is the temporal organization of the information about the patient history and symptoms described in the item and captured by temporal connectives, where it is reasonable to expect that more temporally intricate cases would require higher response process complexity to solve. Similarly, a high number of causal connectives would indicate a higher complexity of causal relationships among the events that led to the patient seeing a doctor, which may also be associated with higher cognitive demands.

4.2 Clinical content features

This group of features relates to the *medical content of the items* by mapping terms and phrases in the text to medical concepts contained in the Unified Medical Language System (UMLS) Metathesaurus (Schuyler et al., 1993) using Metamap (Aronson, 2001). The number of UMLS terms that appear in an item may indicate the amount of medical content

Group	N	Summary of features	Resources
Lexical	5	Word Count, Content word count, Content word count without stop-words, Average word length in syllables, Complex word count	
Syntactic	29	POS count, Phrase count (for each POS), Type count, Comma count, Average phrase length, Negation, Type-token ratio, Average sentence length, Average depth of tree, Clause count (relative, conditional), Average number of words before the main verb, Passive-active ratio, Proportion active VPs, Proportion passive VPs, Agentless passive count	Stanford NLP Parser (Manning et al., 2014)
Semantic	11	Polysemic word count, Average senses for: content words, nouns, verbs, adjectives, auxiliary verbs, adverbs; Average noun/verb distance to WordNet root, Average noun-and-verb distance to WordNet root, Answer words in WordNet ratio	WordNet (Miller, 1995)
Readability	7	Flesch Reading Ease, Flesch-Kincaid grade level, Automated Readability Index, Gunning Fog, Coleman Liau, SMOG, SMOG Index	See Dubay (2004) for definitions
Cognitive	14	Absolute values, ratios, and ratings for Concreteness, Imageability, Familiarity, Age of acquisition, Meaningfulness (Colorado norms), Meaningfulness (Paivio norms)	MRC Psycholinguistic Database (Coltheart, 1981)
Frequency	10	Average frequency (relative, absolute and rank) for all words and for content words; Threshold frequencies for words not in the first 2,000/3,000/4,000/5,000 most common words	British National Corpus (Leech et al., 2014)
Cohesion	5	Counts of Temporal, Causal, Additive connectives and All connectives; Referential pronoun count	

Table 2: Linguistic features extracted for each item following Ha et al. (2019)

the item contains (note that a given term found in the items can refer to multiple UMLS concepts).

First, we ask: *how many of the words and phrases in the items are medical terms?* This information is captured by *UMLS Terms Count*, indicating the number of terms in an item that appear in the UMLS wherein each instance of a given term contributes to the total count, as well as *UMLS Distinct Terms Count:* the number of terms in an item that appear in the UMLS wherein multiple instances of a given term contribute only once to the total count. The same kinds of counts are done for medical phrases – *UMLS Phrases Count* refers to the number of phrases in an item. For example, Metamap maps *'ocular complications of myasthenia gravis'* to two phrases: the noun phrase *'ocular complications'* and the prepositional phrase *'of myasthenia gravis'* (Aronson, 2001).

Next, we introduce features that measure the ambiguity of medical terms within the items. These include *Average Number of Competing UMLS Concepts Per Term Count*, which captures the average number of UMLS concepts that a term could be referring to, averaged for all terms in an item, and weighted by the number of times Metamap returns the term. A similar version of this feature but without weighting by the number of times Metamap returns the term is *Average Number of UMLS Concepts Per Term Count*. This metric is then computed at the level of sentences and items, resulting in: *Average Number of UMLS Concepts per Sentence*, which measures the medical ambiguity of sentences and *UMLS Concept Count*, which measures item medical ambiguity through the total number of UMLS concepts all terms in an item could refer to. Finally, *UMLS concept incidence* refers to the number of UMLS concepts per 1000 words.

4.3 Standard Item Features

This group of features refers to metadata describing item content. *Presence of an image* is a binary categorical variable indicating whether the item includes an image such an X-ray or an MRI that needs to be examined. Another variable is *Content category*, which describes 18 generic topic categories such as "Cardiovascular", "Gastrointestinal", "Behavioral Health", 'Immune System", and so on. Another variable, *Physician Task* describes tasks required by the item, e.g., determine a diagnosis, choose the correct medicine, apply foundational science concepts, and others. Finally, we also include the *Year* the item was administered as a predictor (2010 - 2015) to account for potential changes in response process complexity and examinee samples over time.

4.4 Classification

This section describes three baseline models (Section 4.5), the training of classifiers using the full feature set (Section 4.6), and the feature selection procedures (Section 4.7).

	Logistic regression			Random forests		
	Precision	**Recall**	**Weighted F1**	**Precision**	**Recall**	**Weighted F1**
Majority class	0.37	0.6	0.46	0.37	0.6	0.46
Word count	0.57	0.6	0.48	0.56	0.6	0.54
Standard item features	0.62	0.63	0.59	0.59	0.59	0.59
Full feature set	0.64	0.65	0.63	0.68	0.68	**0.67**
Selected linguistic features	0.63	0.65	0.63	0.67	0.68	**0.66**

Table 3: Weighted F1 scores for different models on the test set

4.5 Baseline Models

Three classification baselines were computed to benchmark the predictive benefit given by linguistics features over standard item characteristics:

Majority Class Baseline: Since the low-complexity class contains a higher number of items, it is more likely that an item would be correctly predicted as belonging to this class.

Word Count: This baseline examines the possibility that response process complexity is simply a function of item length.

Standard Item Features: This baseline comprises *Word count, Presence of an image, Content category, Physician task* and *Year*. This model reflects the standard item characteristics that most testing organizations would routinely store.

4.6 Full feature models

After scaling the features, two models were fit using Python's `scikit-learn` library and the full set of features: a logistic regression model and a random forests one (400 trees). Twenty percent of the data (3,658 items) were used as a test set.

4.7 Feature selection

Feature selection was undertaken to better understand which features were most strongly associated with class differences. The selection process utilized three distinct strategies, where the final set of selected features comprises only those features retained by all three methods. After applying feature selection to the training set, the predictive performance of the selected features is evaluated on the test set and compared to the performance of the full feature set and the baseline models outlined above.

Embedded methods: The first method is LASSO regularized regression wherein the coefficients of variables that have low contributions towards the classification performance are shrunk to zero by forcing the sum of the absolute value of the regression coefficients to be less than a fixed value. We use the LassoCV algorithm with 100-fold cross validation and maximum iterations set to 5,000.

Wrapper methods: We next apply recursive feature elimination, performed using two different classification algorithms: random forests classifier (400 trees, step = 5) and gradient boosting classifier (Friedman, 2002) (default parameters, step = 5).

The final set of selected linguistic features comprised 57 features that were retained by all three strategies. These features and their evaluation are discussed in sections 5 and 7.

5 Results

Table 3 presents the classification results for the baselines, the full feature set, and the selected features for both logistic regression and random forests. Results are reported using a weighted F1 score, which is a classification accuracy measure based on the mean between the precision and recall after adjusting for class imbalance.

The linguistic and clinical content features improve predictive accuracy above the baselines, yielding a higher F1 score than the strongest baseline (.67 compared to .59). The reduced feature set does not lead to a meaningful performance drop compared to the full feature set, suggesting that no signal was lost due to feature elimination.

Figure 2 reports the eight best-performing features: *UMLS phrases count, Unique word count, Polysemic word count, Average noun phrase length, Automated readability index, Prepositional phrases, UMLS distinct terms count,* and *Concreteness ratio*.

6 Error analysis

The output of the selected-features prediction model was analyzed further in order to get insight into this model's performance. As could be expected, the majority class of low-complexity items was predicted more accurately than the high-complexity class, as shown by the confusion matrix in Table 4. An interesting observation was made during a follow-up classification experiment, which showed that this effect remained when using

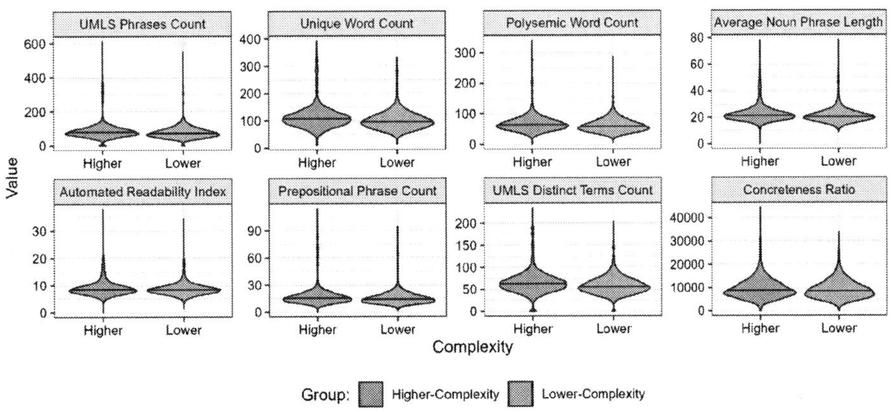

Figure 2: Distributions and median values for the top eight features by group.

balanced classes[4]. This shows that the success in predicting this class cannot be attributed solely to its prevalence but potentially also to its high homogeneity compared to the high-complexity class.

	High Complexity	Low Complexity
High Complexity	617	828
Low Complexity	332	1881

Table 4: Confusion matrix for the results from the selected features model using random forests (F1 = 0.66)

Next, we plot the model errors across the two classes of low-complexity and high-complexity items, as shown in Figure 3. Notably, items with average response times below 150 seconds were predicted as low-complexity most of the time, with minimal consideration of their p-value. This shows that what the model effectively learned was to distinguish between items with long and short mean response times, which overpowered its ability to predict the p-value parameter. This finding is consistent with previous work, where response times in Baldwin et al. (2020) were predicted more successfully than p-value using a similar set of linguistic features in Ha et al. (2019). Finally, analysis of the feature distributions across these four classes revealed no unexpected patterns.

7 Discussion

The results presented in the previous section lead to three main findings: i) the linguistic characteristics of the items carry signal relevant to response process complexity; ii) no individual features stand out as strong predictors, and iii) the most important features were those related to syntax and semantics.

The first of these findings relates to the fact that the linguistic characteristics of the items carry signal that is predictive of response process complexity, revealing that the problems posed by low-complexity and high-complexity items are described using slightly different language. While this signal outperformed several baselines, the overall low predictive utility of the models suggests that there are other factors, yet to be captured, that have a significant effect on response process complexity.

The retention of 56 features indicates that individual linguistic predictors provide a weak classification signal but, taken together, they complement each other in a way that ultimately provides a higher accuracy. The fact that there are many predictive features with none standing out is also a positive evaluation outcome for item writing quality, as it shows that the response process complexity associated with an item is not distributed along a small number of linguistic parameters.

The most important features that helped with classification were those related to syntax and semantics (Figure 2). The poor performance of the *Word Count* baseline suggests that differences in response process complexity cannot be explained solely by item length and that more complex linguistic features capture some of the nuance in the response process. As can be seen in Figure 2, high-complexity items contain a slightly higher number of UMLS phrases and (distinct) medical terms, as well as a higher number of unique words. These features suggest high-complexity items re-

[4]Classes were balanced using the `balanced_subsample` setting of the `class_weight` parameter in Scikit-learn's `RandomForrestClassifier`

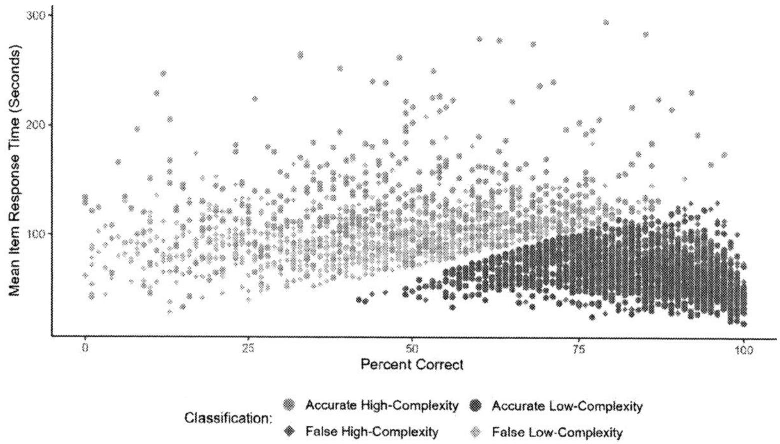

Figure 3: Error distribution for the two classes

peat words less frequently and may contain a higher concentration of new information and specialized terminology than low-complexity items. The individual phrases in high-complexity items are also slightly longer, which naturally influences readability metrics that are based on word and sentence length, such as the *Automated Readability Index* (higher values are indicative of a more complex text). Prepositional phrases were also identified as more important than other phrase types in distinguishing between response process complexity. Prepositional phrases often serve as modifiers of the primary noun phrase and the higher number of prepositional phrases in the high-complexity items suggests the use of more specific descriptions (e.g., "small cell carcinoma of the ovary" instead of just "small cell carcinoma"). The words contained in the high-complexity items also have slightly higher concreteness levels, providing another indication that they may contain more terms, as terms tend to be more concrete than common words. Finally, the words contained in the high-complexity items also tend to have more possible meanings, as indicated by the polysemous word count variable, which results in higher complexity owing to disambiguation efforts. Overall, these features indicate that the language used in the low-complexity items is less ambiguous and descriptive, and potentially contains fewer medical terms.

One limitation of the study is the fact that it treats item difficulty and time intensiveness as independent variables. This may not always be the case, as examinees do employ strategies to optimize their time. Given finite time limits, examinees may ignore time intensive items if they believe the time needed for such items can be better utilized attempting other, less time intensive items. Therefore, the relationship between difficulty and response time and their association with item text would differ for exams that do not impose strict time limits.

When using data-driven approaches to defining item classes, our data did not lend itself to a categorization that would allow investigating high difficulty/low response time items and vice-versa. While the approach taken in this paper has a higher ecological validity, studying such cases in the future may lead to a greater understanding of various aspects of response process complexity and their relationship to item text. Other future work includes exploration of potential item position effects.

8 Conclusion

The experiments presented in this paper are, to the best of our knowledge, the first investigation of the relationship between item text and response process complexity. The results showed that such a relationship exists. To the extent that items were written as clearly and as concisely as possible, the findings suggest that high-complexity medical items generally include longer phrases, more medical terms, and more specific descriptions.

While the models outperformed several baselines, they required a large number of features to do so and the predictive utility remained low. Ultimately, this shows the challenging nature of modeling response process complexity using interpretable models and the lack of a straightforward way to manipulate this item property.

References

Tahani Alsubait, Bijan Parsia, and Ulrike Sattler. 2013. A similarity-based theory of controlling mcq difficulty. In *e-Learning and e-Technologies in Education (ICEEE), 2013 Second International Conference on*, pages 283–288. IEEE.

Alan R Aronson. 2001. Effective mapping of biomedical text to the umls metathesaurus: the metamap program. In *Proceedings of the AMIA Symposium*, page 17. American Medical Informatics Association.

Peter Baldwin, Victoria Yaneva, Janet Mee, Brian E Clauser, and Le An Ha. 2020. Using natural language processing to predict item response times and improve test construction. *Journal of Educational Measurement*.

Lisa Beinborn, Torsten Zesch, and Iryna Gurevych. 2015. Candidate evaluation strategies for improved difficulty prediction of language tests. In *Proceedings of the Tenth Workshop on Innovative Use of NLP for Building Educational Applications*, pages 1–11.

Max Coltheart. 1981. The mrc psycholinguistic database. *The Quarterly Journal of Experimental Psychology Section A*, 33(4):497–505.

William H. Dubay. 2004. *The Principles of Readability*. Impact Information.

Jerome H Friedman. 2002. Stochastic gradient boosting. *Computational statistics & data analysis*, 38(4):367–378.

Le An Ha and Victoria Yaneva. 2018. Automatic distractor suggestion for multiple-choice tests using concept embeddings and information retrieval. In *Proceedings of the Thirteenth Workshop on Innovative Use of NLP for Building Educational Applications*, pages 389–398.

Le An Ha, Victoria Yaneva, Peter Balwin, and Janet Mee. 2019. Predicting the difficulty of multiple choice questions in a high-stakes medical exam. In *Proceedings of the Fourteenth Workshop on Innovative Use of NLP for Building Educational Applications*.

Perry N Halkitis et al. 1996. Estimating testing time: The effects of item characteristics on response latency.

Zhenya Huang, Qi Liu, Enhong Chen, Hongke Zhao, Mingyong Gao, Si Wei, Yu Su, and Guoping Hu. 2017. Question difficulty prediction for reading problems in standard tests. In *AAAI*, pages 1352–1359.

Ghader Kurdi. 2020. *Generation and mining of medical, case-based multiple choice questions*. Ph.D. thesis, PhD thesis, University of Manchester.

Ghader Kurdi, Jared Leo, Bijan Parsia, Uli Sattler, and Salam Al-Emari. 2020. A systematic review of automatic question generation for educational purposes. *International Journal of Artificial Intelligence in Education*, 30(1):121–204.

Geoffrey Leech, Paul Rayson, et al. 2014. *Word frequencies in written and spoken English: Based on the British National Corpus*. Routledge.

Anastassia Loukina, Su-Youn Yoon, Jennifer Sakano, Youhua Wei, and Kathy Sheehan. 2016. Textual complexity as a predictor of difficulty of listening items in language proficiency tests. In *Proceedings of COLING 2016, the 26th International Conference on Computational Linguistics: Technical Papers*, pages 3245–3253.

Christopher D Manning, Mihai Surdeanu, John Bauer, Jenny Rose Finkel, Steven Bethard, and David McClosky. 2014. The stanford corenlp natural language processing toolkit. In *ACL (System Demonstrations)*, pages 55–60.

George A Miller. 1995. Wordnet: a lexical database for english. *Communications of the ACM*, 38(11):39–41.

Farah Nadeem and Mari Ostendorf. 2017. Language based mapping of science assessment items to skills. In *Proceedings of the 12th Workshop on Innovative Use of NLP for Building Educational Applications*, pages 319–326.

Ulrike Padó. 2017. Question difficulty–how to estimate without norming, how to use for automated grading. In *Proceedings of the 12th Workshop on Innovative Use of NLP for Building Educational Applications*, pages 1–10.

Cynthia G Parshall et al. 1994. Response latency: An investigation into determinants of item-level timing.

Fabian Pedregosa, Gaël Varoquaux, Alexandre Gramfort, Vincent Michel, Bertrand Thirion, Olivier Grisel, Mathieu Blondel, Peter Prettenhofer, Ron Weiss, Vincent Dubourg, et al. 2011. Scikit-learn: Machine learning in python. *the Journal of machine Learning research*, 12:2825–2830.

Peri L Schuyler, William T Hole, Mark S Tuttle, and David D Sherertz. 1993. The umls metathesaurus: representing different views of biomedical concepts. *Bulletin of the Medical Library Association*, 81(2):217.

Russell Winsor Smith. 2000. An exploratory analysis of item parameters and characteristics that influence item level response time.

David B Swanson, Susan M Case, Douglas R Ripkey, Brian E Clauser, and Matthew C Holtman. 2001. Relationships among item characteristics, examine characteristics, and response times on usmle step 1. *Academic Medicine*, 76(10):S114–S116.

Kiri Wagstaff, Claire Cardie, Seth Rogers, Stefan Schrödl, et al. 2001. Constrained k-means clustering with background knowledge. In *Icml*, volume 1, pages 577–584.

Kang Xue, Victoria Yaneva, Christopher Runyon, and Peter Baldwin. 2020. Predicting the difficulty and response time of multiple choice questions using transfer learning. In *Proceedings of the Fifteenth Workshop on Innovative Use of NLP for Building Educational Applications*, pages 193–197.

Victoria Yaneva, Le An Ha, Peter Baldwin, and Janet Mee. 2020. Predicting item survival for multiple choice questions in a high-stakes medical exam. In *Proceedings of The 12th Language Resources and Evaluation Conference*, pages 6812–6818.

Association for Computational Linguistics
209 N. Eighth Street
Stroudsburg, Pennsylvania 18360

ISBN 978-1-7138-2957-7

CURRAN ASSOCIATES INC.
proceedings
.com